THE DORSEY FAMILY

Descendants

of

Edward Darcy-Dorsey of Virginia and Maryland
For Five Generations

and

ALLIED FAMILIES

By

MAXWELL J. DORSEY and JEAN MUIR DORSEY
Urbana, Illinois

And

NANNIE BALL NIMMO
Baltimore, Maryland

CLEARFIELD

Originally published
Baltimore, Maryland, 1947

Reprinted for
Clearfield Company, Inc. by
Genealogical Publishing Co., Inc.
Baltimore, Maryland
1997, 2000, 2006

International Standard Book Number: 0-8063-4749-X

Made in the United States of America

HOME OF MAXWELL AND JEAN MUIR DORSEY - BUILT 1926 - URBANA, ILLINOIS

CONTENTS

ILLUSTRATIONS

INTRODUCTION

The authors of this family history have attempted to trace the descendants of Edward Darcy-Dorsey, the immigrant, through both male and female lines as far as the fifth generation. This information should enable the living descendants, who are interested, to trace their own lines without great difficulty.

The material contained in this book is based almost entirely on the research of the authors. The examination of many original records has brought to light new and valuable data, as well as the signatures and seals of a number of the early men and women of the family. In presenting abstracts of original records, the exact spelling of words and names has been followed, even when incorrect or different from that used elsewhere.

The records, which are arranged in chronological order, prove the family relationship in each line of descent. They also show the activities, interests, and achievements of many members of the family. To increase the usefulness of this material, the authors have given the references to all records used in the book. The number which appears before the name of each descendant indicates the order of birth in the family, while the one which follows the name designates the generation.

The maps which show the locations of the plantations of the early members of the family are based on information found in land records. It is hoped that these maps may be helpful to those who are interested in visiting the old homes and ancestral acres in Maryland.

In the compilation of such a large amount of data, errors in copying may have been overlooked. For all of these the authors ask consideration.

The authors wish to express their gratitude for the courtesy and cooperation shown them at the Hall of Records, Annapolis, the Maryland Historical Society, Baltimore, and the County Court Houses, while the research was being done. They are also deeply grateful to those members of the family who so graciously contributed their lines of descent which are included in the book, and to those who have helped in other ways.

Maxwell Jay Dorsey
Jean Muir Dorsey
Nannie Ball Nimmo

Urbana, Illinois
Baltimore, Maryland

ABBREVIATIONS AND EXPLANATIONS

A.A. Co. . . . . Anne Arundel County
Balt. Co.. . . . . Baltimore County
Chas. Co.. . . . . Charles County
Fred. Co.. . . . . Frederick County
Harf. Co.. . . . . Harford County
Mont. Co.. . . . . Montgomery County
Pr. Geo. Co. . . . . . . Prince George's County
Arch. of Md. . . . . . . Archives of Maryland
Accts. . . . . Accounts
Admr.. . . . . Administrator
Admrx. . . . . Administratrix
Exr. . . . . Executor
Exrx.. . . . . Executrix
Bal. Bk. . . . . Balance Book
Chanc. Rec.. . . . . . . Chancery Record
Ct. Rec. . . . . Court Record
Invts. . . . . Inventories
Prov. Ct. Rec. . . . . . Provincial Court Record
Prov. Ct. Judg.. . . . . Provincial Court Judgment
Test. Proc.. . . . . . . Testamentary Proceedings
Test. Papers . . . . . . Testamentary Papers

Parish Registers:

A.H. . . . . All Hallow's
St.A.. . . . . St. Anne's
St. Mrgts. . . . . . . St. Margaret's
St. Thos.. . . . . . . St. Thomas
St. Jn. and St. Geo. St. John's and St. George's

The testamentary materials, Provincial Court Judgments, Provincial Court Records, Patents, Warrants, Chancery Records, Rent Rolls, Debt Books, and Deeds of the State of Maryland prior to 1777, referred to in this family history, are found in the Hall of Records, Annapolis, Maryland. Later records are found in the County Court Houses.

Parish Registers, Tax Lists, and many interesting documents from which data have been taken are in the Maryland Historical Society in Baltimore.

EDWARD DARCY-DORSEY THE IMMIGRANT

The founder of this family in Maryland was Edward Darcy-Dorsey, who had lived several years in Virginia before he came to Anne Arundel County in 1650. Various spellings of his name appear in the deeds and land patents of Lower Norfolk County, Virginia, between the years 1642 and 1648.

At a County Court held on November 3, 1645, at the house of William Shipp, it was recorded that John Browne of Elizabeth River in the County of Lower Norff^{e}, planter, had on the 11th of February, 1642, sold unto *Edward Darsey* of the county aforesaid planter three head of Cattle (Vizt) one Cowe aged about seaven yeares of a brinded Coulor and marked with a Cropp on the right Eare and the left Eare whole, and a steare of a Coulor as aforesaid aged about one yeare and a halfe and marked with a Cropp on the left eare and the right Eare slitt allsoe one heifar Calfe brinded as aforesaid aged about three quarters of a yeare and marked with a Cropp on both eares and a slitt in one and doe by these presents give graunt bargaine and sell unto the said *Edward Darsey* his heirs execut^{rs} administrators and assignes for ever for a Valuable consideration pt in hand paid. Dated the 11th of February, 1642. (*Minute Book A*, f. 293, Lower Norfolk Co., Portsmouth, Va.)

On December 15, 1642, Cornelius Lloyd received a grant of land for bringing 60 persons into the colony. Among the list of names was that of *Edw: -orsey*, the first letter of the last name being obliterated. (*Ibid.*, f. 160) (*New Eng. Hist. Gen. Reg.* Vol. 47, f. 63) On October 7, 1646, Thomas Brown was given 240 acres in Lower Norfolk County due by assignment of the rights of 5 persons transported by Cornelius Lloyd - among them *Edward Dorsey*. (*Patents 2, State of Va.*, f. 113)

The County Court held at the house of William Shipp on December 15, 1645, ordered Thomas Todd to pay *Edward Darcy* and Thomas Hall forty pownds of tobacco a piece for theire tyme and charge in attendance of the Court for two days, and on December 10, 1649, when Edward Dorsey witnessed a quit-claim deed executed by Thomas Tod, his signature was Edward *E D:* Dorsy (*Minute Book A*, f. 299; *Minute Book B*, f. 133a, Lower Norfolk Co., Portsmouth, Va.)

On October 31, 1649, William Julian of Lower Norfolk County, Virginia, sold to Robert Taylor of Elizabeth River 200 Acres of land being a neck of land upon the south turning of the said river, east upon a creek, and south upon a creek, and north into the woods. This deed was endorsed on the back as follows:

> "Mem. I Robert Tayler doe make sale of a neck of Land Cont. about 200 acres wthin mentioned unto *Edward Dorcey* for him & his heires to Injoy wth all Rights and previledges As Wittnes my hand this 20th of Octob A° 1648." (*Ibid.*, f. 126a)

Various spellings of the name - Dorsey - continue to appear on the records in Maryland, but the original signatures of the sons of the immigrant show the family spelled the name - Dorsey. (See page 6)

More than twenty times, the name with its different spellings is listed in Burke's and other Heraldries as Darsey, Darsy, Darcey, Darcie, D'Arcy, D'Arcey, but never as Dorsey. Numerous coats of arms and crests are given as belonging to this family, though nothing reveals the one to be used by the Virginia - Maryland settlers.

The original wills and other papers at the Hall of Records, Annapolis, Maryland, show the names of various members of the Dorsey family affixed with seals of many different types. (See pages 6,63,122A,137,143,163,169)

DORSEY FAMILY

By the year 1648, freedom of worship in Virginia had been prohibited and life there became less attractive. As a result, many settlers turned to the newly erected county of Anne Arundel in Maryland, where alluring inducements to obtain land were being offered, and where freedom of worship was said to be guaranteed. Among those who went, were Edward Dorsey, John Norwood, Matthew Howard, Thomas Todd, and Nicholas Wyatt. (See pages 190,192,197,203)

Most of these men, however, maintained a close association with Virginia, and on November 15, 1652, Edward Dorsey and four others who had gone to Maryland, returned to Virginia, where Francis Fleetwood received a grant of land for their transportation. (*Patents 3, State of Va.*, f. 179)

In November 1650, Edward Dorsey of the County of Ann Arundell was granted a warrant for 200 acres of land in Maryland, and in 1651, for 200 acres more, half of a warrant for 400 acres granted John Norwood and the said Dorsey. The omission of the descriptions of these surveys makes it impossible to determine the location of these tracts of land. (*Patents 11*, f. 98) (See pages 8 and 10)

A tract of land called Norwood, containing 200 acres, was laid out in Calvert County, on October 27, 1651, for John Norwood of Ann Arundell County, planter, on the west side of Chesapeake Bay adjoining the land of Thomas Mears. (*Patents A.B. & H*, f. 264)

On July 3, 1650, a tract of 350 acres of land called Howard was laid out for Matthew Howard of the County of Ann Arundell, planter, lying on the south side of the Severn River near a creek called Marshes Creek beginning at a Hollow in the said creek called Howard's Hollow and extending south of the creek and a swamp called Howard's Swamp. There was also laid out for him a parcell of land of 45 acres adjoining the above tract on the east, and also 255 acres south of Howard's Swamp lying on the west, all containing 650 acres. (*Ibid.*, f. 254)

On July 8, 1651, a tract of 100 acres of land called Todd was laid out for Thomas Todd of the County of Ann Arundell, Shipwright. The land lay on the west side of Chesapeake Bay upon the Severn River and on the south side of the said river, beginning at a marked white oak standing upon Oyster Shells point running up the river to Deep Cove Creek, bounded on the north with the said creek to a marked pine tree, and on the west and south by Richard Acton's and Thomas Hall's lands, and on the east with the said river and Todd's Creek. This tract was a portion of the present city of Annapolis. (*Ibid.*, f. 258) (See page 5)

A parcell of land called Wyat, containing 90 acres, was laid out for Nicholas Wyatt of the County of Ann Arundell, planter, on November 22, 1651, lying on the south side of the Severn River upon a creek running betwixt Underwood's Neck and the Mountainy Neck on the south bound of Matthew Howard's land. (*Ibid.*, f. 265) (See page 5)

Sometime before 1655, Edward Darcy in partnership with Thomas Manning bought from Thomas Marsh of the County of Ann Arundell, Merchant, a tract of 600 acres lying on the west side of Chesapeake Bay, bounded on the north by the land of John Norwood and on the west by the said bay, for which no patent was issued until 1661. (*Ibid.*, f. 261) (*Patents 4*, f. 541) (*Patents 10*, f. 19) (See pages 10 and 202)

On August 3, 1658, there was laid out for John Norwood of Ann Arundell County, 200 acres of land called Norwood, on the west side of the bay and adjoining the land of Thomas Mears that had been granted him for having transported himself and wife Ann into the Province; and on February 8th of the same year, there was granted the said John Norwood, 230 acres, also called Norwood, for having transported his sons John and Andrew into the Province in the year 1650, and his servant Elizabeth Fletcher in the year 1657. This land lay on the west side of Chesapeake Bay and on the south side of the Severn River, beginning at Norwood's Cove running northwest up the river to a creek called Norwood's Creek, Bounding on the north by the said creek running south west by west to a marked Pine by the creek side, on the west by a line drawn south and by east from said Pine to a marked oak, on the south by a line drawn northeast and by east from said oak unto *land formerly laid out unto Nicholas Wyatt* of the said county, planter, and by the said land unto Norwood's Cove and on the east by said Cove and River. (*Patents Q,* folios 78, 396) (See page 5)

At a Court held on August 3, 1659, Thomas Miles petitioned the Court against John Freeman showing that he had bought a parcell of land of Freeman *containing 10 acres lying on the south side of the Severn River between the land belonging to Edward Dorcy and John Norwood* yet had no assurance that he may peaceably enjoy the same. The bill of sale shows that *Nicholas Wyatt first took up the land* and sold same to John Freeman, having no right thereto, in not complying with the condicons of Plantaon... (*Arch. of Md.* XLI, 320) (See page 5)

Sometime before 1658, Edward Dorsey took up another tract of land, containing 400 acres, lying in Ann Arundell County on the south side of the Severn River and or a branch of Broad Creek. This tract was later patented by his three sons and called Hockley in the Hole. (*Patents 7, f.* 378) (See pages 5,9,10,11)

On February 27, 1658, Ensign Thomas Gates, who transported himself into the Province in 1649, was granted a Parcell of Land called Gatenby lying on the west side of Chesapeake Bay, on the south side of the Severn River and on the north side of *Darcy's Creek.* Beginning at a Pine Tree by the Creekside the said Pine being the *Bound of Ten acres formerly laid out to the said Gates,* running north by west unto the land lately laid out unto John Norwood of same county, and west south west by said land unto a marked oak, bounding on the west by a line drawn south from said oak to a marked oak by the Head of a Branch, on the south by a line drawn west from the said oak to a marked oak by the said creek, on the east by the said creek, and on the north by the first west line and Norwood's land, containing 100 acres. (*Patents Q, f.* 392) (See page 5)

The will of Thomas Gates made May 2, 1659, indicates that the Dorsey family was then living on a nearby tract of land, as Thomas Gates left his plantation to Michael Bellott and John Hollowday with *the desire and will that they shall give to Edward Dorceys children a free outlet to the woods and also to the spring an Inlett, for their cattle as formerly they had had in my time.* (*Wills 1, f. 105*) (See page 5)

The failure of refusal on the part of some of the early settlers to have their grants of land patented, as well as loss of the early records at Annapolis through carelessness of clerks and destruction by fire, makes it impossible to locate all of the tracts of land owned by these five men, and especially those of Edward Dorsey. (*Arch. of Md.* III, f. 290)

The descriptions of the above surveys, which were recorded after the fire of 1706, however, show that Thomas Todd was located on the south side of the Severn River between Todd's Creek (now Spa Creek) and Deep Cove Creek, which was called Darcy's Creek in the 1658 surveys. The name was later changed to Sprigg's Creek, then to Graveyard Creek, and finally to the present name of College Creek.*

To the west and north across Darcy's Creek, which no doubt bears the name of the immigrant, were the tracts taken up by Edward Dorsey and Capt. John Norwood, with the land of Nicholas Wyatt lying between.

On Darcy's Creek was Gatenby and a tract of ten acres taken up earlier by Thomas Gates and where he was living when he died in 1659.

Farther up the Severn River near Marshes Creek, later called Hockley Creek, was the land taken up by Matthew Howard. Adjoining this land on the south was the tract called Wyatt, laid out for Nicholas Wyatt. Nearby these two tracts was Hockley in the Hole, taken up by Edward Dorsey and later patented by his three sons, Edward, Joshua, and John Dorsey.*

* Information regarding the different names given to the creeks along the Severn River was furnished by Mr. Arthur Trader of the Land Commissioner's Office, Annapolis.

The map on page 5, showing the location of the tracts of land owned or taken up by Edward Dorsey and his neighbors, is based on the descriptions given in the previous records. It will be seen that the land on which Edward Dorsey's children were living in 1659 is in the same locality as the tract called Dorsey, which was assigned to Edward Dorsey, son of the immigrant, in 1668. (See pages 10 and 18)

In 1658 the Quakers came into Maryland spreading their religion among the settlers, claiming as their converts Thomas Mears, Nicholas Wyatt, Edward Dorsey and Ann, his wife, and many others. That the Dorseys did embrace this faith is shown by a letter written by Robert Clarkson, a Quaker convert, to Elizabeth Harris, then in England, in which he said that Ann Dorsey had abundant grace, but he seemed doubtful that her husband would stick to the faith. (*Md. Hist. Mag.* XXXII, 47)

Edward Darcy was drowned before August 2, 1659 off the Isle of Kent. This incident which is recorded in a Court Record reads:

"Att a Court holden in Anarundel County on twesday August 2d 1659
Whereas Thomas Hinson hath petitioned this Court, Showing that hee hauing taken up the Boate wherein Edward Darcy & some others were drowned, neare the Isle of Kent, being desyred by the sd Darcys Ouesser to take up the same, wch he did, delivering the same Boate to the chiefe in Authority taking a discharge upon the delivery of the same under his hand att Anarundell & now by his Petn crauing for his paynes taking therein, as the Court now sitting shall adjudge him.
It is ordered that the sd Thomas Hinson have one hundd pownds of Tob. payd him for his sd paynes & Care, by those (Woeuer they bee) that possesse & enjoy the sd Boate." (*Prov. Ct. Rec. S.I.*, f. 282)

Ann Dorsey, wife of Edward is thought to have outlived her husband, and to have returned to their former home in Virginia, for no further record is found of her in Maryland. It seems reasonable to suppose that their children were born in Virginia.

Children of Edward and Ann Dorsey:
(Known by land patents, deeds, and wills)

I. Edward[2] Dorsey, d. 1705 m. (1) Sarah Wyatt
m. (2(Margaret Lacon, who m. (2) John Israel
II. Joshua Dorsey, d. 1688, m. Sarah Richardson, who m. (2) Thomas Blackwell
III. John Dorsey, d. 1714, m. Pleasance ________ who m. (2) Thomas Wainwright
IV. Sarah Dorsey, d bef. 1691, m. Matthew Howard Jr.

MAP SHOWING THE
APPROXIMATE LOCATIONS OF LAND TAKEN UP BY
EDWARD DORSEY AND SOME OF HIS NEIGHBORS IN
ANNE ARUNDEL COUNTY, MARYLAND

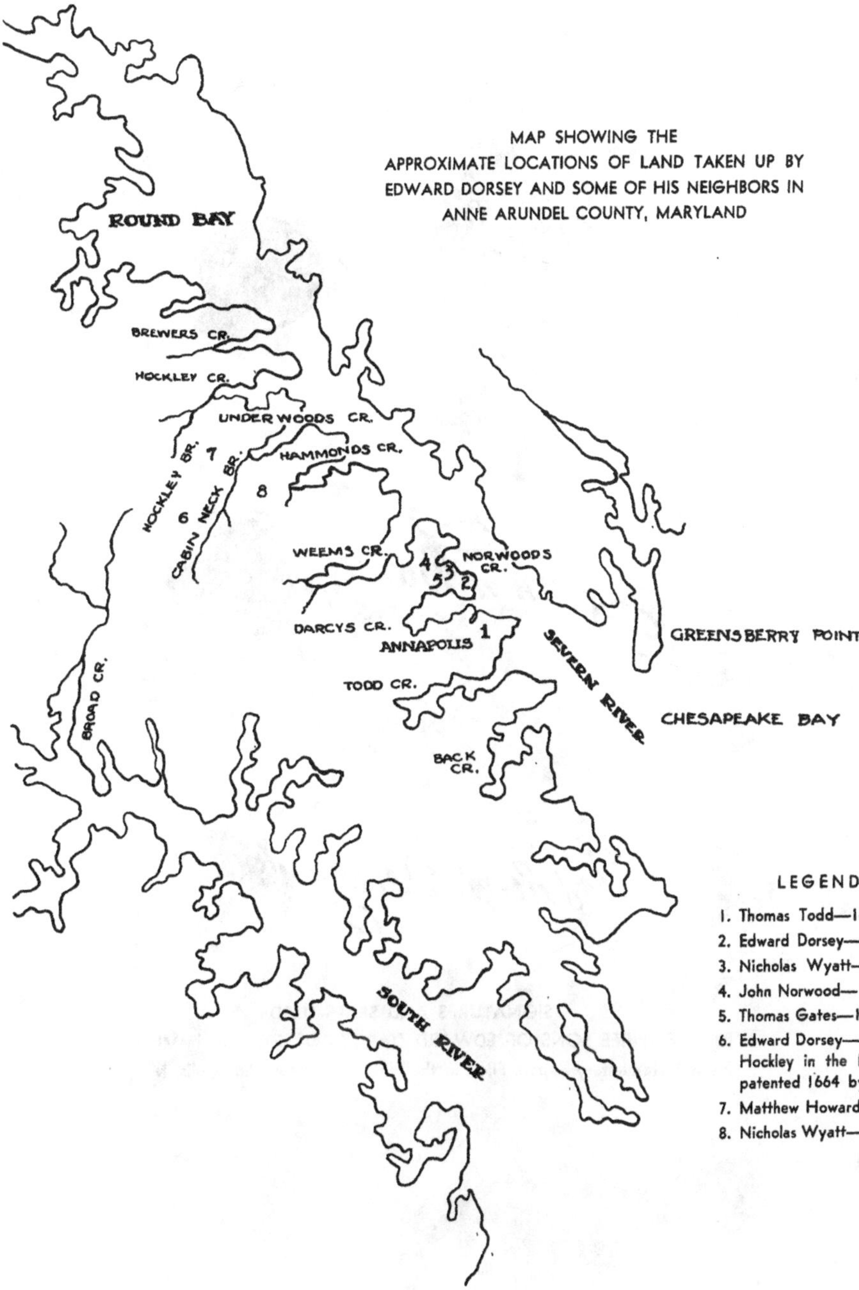

LEGEND

1. Thomas Todd—1651
2. Edward Dorsey—1651
3. Nicholas Wyatt—1651
4. John Norwood—1658
5. Thomas Gates—1651
6. Edward Dorsey—
   Hockley in the Hole
   patented 1664 by sons
7. Matthew Howard—1650
8. Nicholas Wyatt—1651

SIGNATURES AND SEALS USED
BY THE THREE SONS OF EDWARD DARCY-DORSEY, THE IMMIGRANT
From Testamentary Papers Filed in the Hall of Records, Annapolis, Maryland

EDWARD DARCY-DORSEY THE IMMIGRANT

THREE GENERATIONS OF THE DORSEY FAMILY

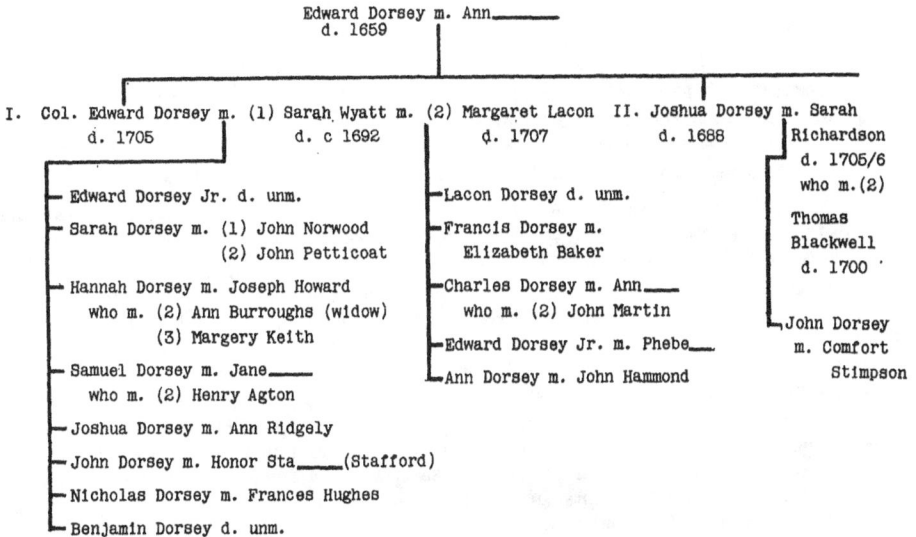

Edward Dorsey m. Ann_____
d. 1659

I. Col. Edward Dorsey m. (1) Sarah Wyatt m. (2) Margaret Lacon
d. 1705 — d. c 1692 — d. 1707

Children of (1):

- Edward Dorsey Jr. d. unm.
- Sarah Dorsey m. (1) John Norwood
  (2) John Petticoat
- Hannah Dorsey m. Joseph Howard
  who m. (2) Ann Burroughs (widow)
  (3) Margery Keith
- Samuel Dorsey m. Jane_____
  who m. (2) Henry Agton
- Joshua Dorsey m. Ann Ridgely
- John Dorsey m. Honor Sta_____(Stafford)
- Nicholas Dorsey m. Frances Hughes
- Benjamin Dorsey d. unm.

Children of (2):

- Lacon Dorsey d. unm.
- Francis Dorsey m.
  Elizabeth Baker
- Charles Dorsey m. Ann_____
  who m. (2) John Martin
- Edward Dorsey Jr. m. Phebe_____
- Ann Dorsey m. John Hammond

II. Joshua Dorsey m. Sarah Richardson
d. 1688 — d. 1705/6
who m. (2) Thomas Blackwell
d. 1700

- John Dorsey
  m. Comfort
  Stimpson

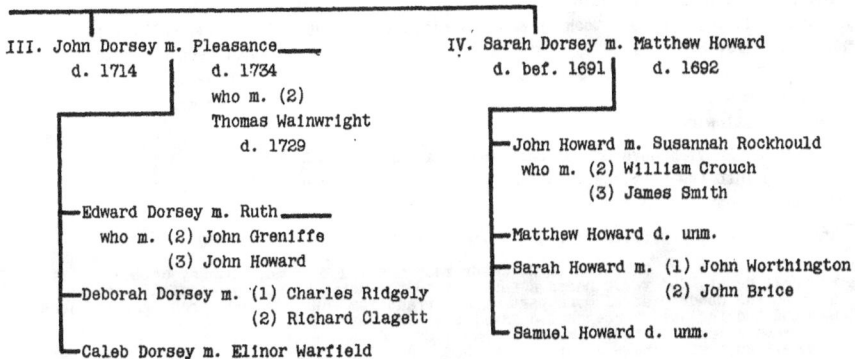

III. John Dorsey m. Pleasance_____
d. 1714 — d. 1734
who m. (2)
Thomas Wainwright
d. 1729

- Edward Dorsey m. Ruth_____
  who m. (2) John Greniffe
  (3) John Howard
- Deborah Dorsey m. (1) Charles Ridgely
  (2) Richard Clagett
- Caleb Dorsey m. Elinor Warfield

IV. Sarah Dorsey m. Matthew Howard
d. bef. 1691 — d. 1692

- John Howard m. Susannah Rockhould
  who m. (2) William Crouch
  (3) James Smith
- Matthew Howard d. unm.
- Sarah Howard m. (1) John Worthington
  (2) John Brice
- Samuel Howard d. unm.

COLONEL EDWARD DORSEY

I. COLONEL EDWARD[2] DORSEY (Edward[1])

d. 1705 at Major's Choice, Baltimore County, Maryland

m. (1) c 1670 Sarah Wyatt, d. c 1692

m. (2) c 1693 Margaret Lacon, d. 1707, who m. (2) John Israel, d. 1723.

The birth date of Edward Dorsey, eldest son of the immigrant, is unknown, but he was over 16 years of age, when having left the province, he was again transported into it by Robert Bullen on March 25, 1661. (*Patents 4, f.* 88)

Edward Dorsey first comes on the records as a planter in 1664, when he and his brothers were living on one of their father's surveys, as seen in a land patent of that date. He next appears as a boatwright, and so signs himself in 1667. After this he is found as a builder of houses and other buildings in the port of Annapolis, and in 1675 is recognized as a successful young lawyer. From then on he quickly rose to prominence in both state and military affairs.

He was Justice of Anne Arundel County in 1679 and 1685; Captain of Militia in 1686; Major, 1687; Field Officer of Calvert County, 1694; and Colonel in 1702. He was Judge of the High Court of Chancery and Keeper of the Great Seal, 1695 and 1696; a member of the House of Burgesses from Anne Arundel County, 1694 to 1697, and from Baltimore County, 1701 to 1705. He also served upon many important committees. (*Arch. of Md.* XV,V,XIII,XXIV,XX,XIX,XXVI)

He acquired large tracts of land in both Anne Arundel and Baltimore Counties, which he divided among his ten sons and three daughters.

The first land known to have been owned by Edward Dorsey was one of his father's surveys, which he and his two brothers took up and had patented on August 25, 1664, calling it Hockley in the Hole. (*Patents 7, f.* 378) This land adjoined tracts which had been surveyed for Cornelius and Samuel Howard at the head of Hockley Creek in 1662. A copy of the original patent, which was in possession of the owners of Hockley in the Hole for many years, is reproduced on the following page.

On May 11, 1667, Edward Dorsey received a warrant for 350 acres of land for transporting seven persons into the province. As Edward Dorsey of Ann Arundell County, boatwright, he assigned the said warrant unto Cornelius Howard. (*Patents 10, f.* 498)

In 1667 he sold a portion of the land taken up by his father in 1650.

"A Warrant was the XIth of November 1650 Granted to Edward Dorsey of Ann Arundell County for two hundred acres of land the which he assigns as followeth, as also two hundred acres more part of a warrant for four hundred acres, granted John Norwood and the said Dorsey dated XXVII of February, 1651.

Know all men by these presents that I Edward Dorsey of the County of Ann Arundell Boatwright have granted bargained and Sold, for a valuable consideration all ready received, all my right title interest clame and demand, of and in a warrant for two hundred acres of land, bearing date one thousand six hundred and fifty and also two hundred acres more, being the one half of a warrant for four hundred acres the one half belonging to Capt. John Norwood bearing date one thousand and six hundred fifty one, unto George Yate of the said county his heirs or assigns forever from me the said Dorsey my heirs or assigns forever Witness my hand and seal forever the XXIII day of April.

Signed Sealed and delivered in the presence of us, Cornelius Howard
John Howard

Edward Dorsey (Seale)

Came George Yate of Ann Arundell County and demanded Land by virtue of the aforesaid assignment

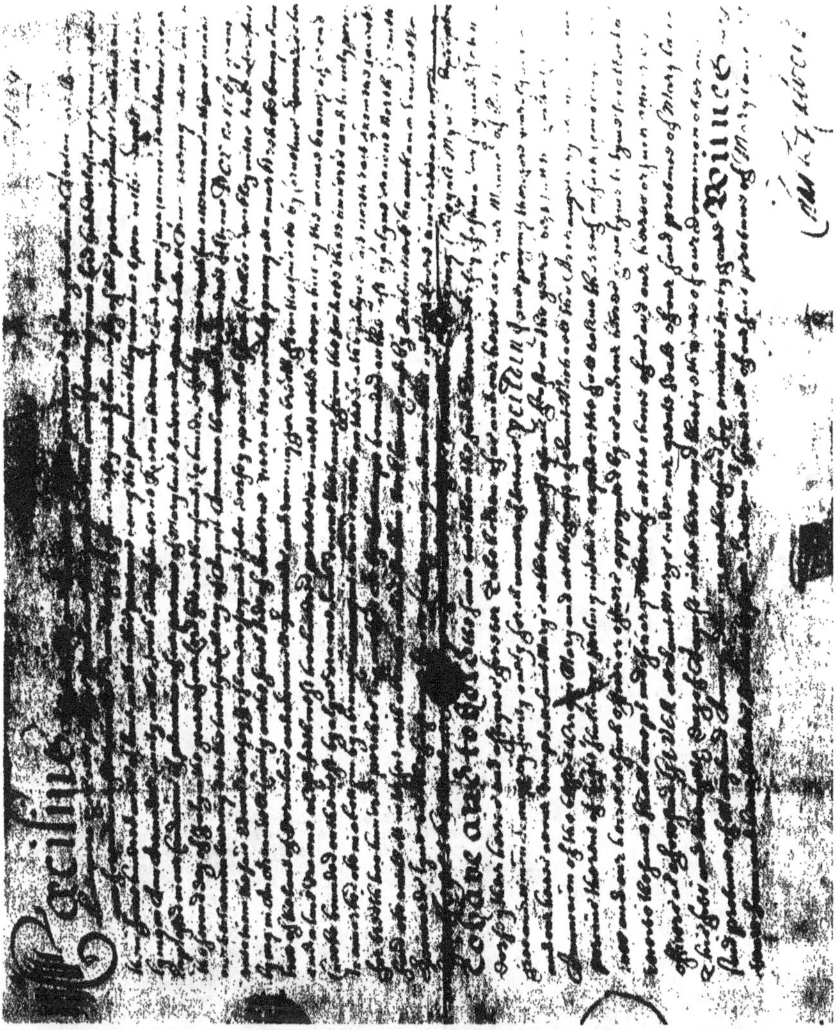

FACSIMILE OF THE ORIGINAL PATENT OF HOCKLEY IN THE HOLE, ANNE ARUNDEL COUNTY, MARYLAND

We are indebted to Dr. Henry Ridgely Evans for a copy of the original patent of HOCKLEY IN THE HOLE, which was published in his book, *Founders of the Colonial Families of Ridgely, Dorsey and Greenberry of Maryland*, facing page 32.

Dr. Evans states, "When I visited 'Hockley' in 1898 Miss Anne Elizabeth Dorsey, a descendant of Hon. John Dorsey, resided there, but not in the original mansion that formerly graced the plantation. With her lived her niece Miss Anne E.D. Sellman, who now resides in Baltimore. Miss Dorsey opened the drawer of an old escritoire, took out a roll of parchment, and handed it to me remarking, 'Here is the original patent for "Hockley in the Hole" to Col. Edward, Hon. John, and Joshua Dorsey, dated August 25, 1664.'"

Miss Dorsey permitted Dr. Evans to have a photograph made of the Hockley patent, which unfortunately was lost in the mail some time before her death. Dr. Evans' realization of the significance of this original record, and his forethought in having a copy made, has preserved this highly valuable and historic document for the members of the Dorsey family.

Warrant then issued in the name of George Yate for five hundred acres of land one hundred thereof due to him by assignment from Ann Covill being a warrant for the same quantity to her formerly granted, two hundred acres more by assignment from Edward Dorsey, being a warrant for the same quantity to him likewise formerly granted, and two hundred acres more by assignment from the said Dorsey, part of a warrant formerly granted him and Capt. John Norwood, for four hundred acres. Cert. returnable XIIth January next." (*Patents 11, f.* 98)

In August 1668, Edward Dorsey was assigned 60 acres of land called Dorsey by George Yate Deputy Surveyor lying on the south side of Ann Arundell River (Severn) and on a creek called Dorsey's Creek. Beginning at a bounded pine upon a point and running up the said River for the length of one hundred and twenty perches to a coave called freemans coave there up the said coave to the line of the land of Capt. John Norwood then by the said Norwoods line south west for the length of two hundred and four perches to a bounded red oake in the said Norwoods line then bounding on the line of a parcell of land formerly laid out for Thomas|Gates to the said Creek then bounding on the said creek to the first bounded tree. (*Patents 11, f.* 488)

The first Edward Dorsey and his family had lived upon this creek, which before 1659 had been named for him. From the description of the adjoining surveys, it seems probable that this tract was a part of the original Dorsey grant of land. (See pages 4,5,18,23)

On November 30, 1670, he appointed his friend Capt. Thomas Stockett High Sheriff of Ann Arundell County to acknowledge a Bill of Sale of 300 acres of land sold to Capt. Thomas Manning of Calvert County. This sale of land signed, sealed, and delivered in the presence of *Sarah Dorsey* and Thomas Wainwright is here recorded.

"This indenture made the *26th of November 1670 between Edward Dorsey son and heir of Edward Dorsey late of Ann Arundell County Planter of the one part, and Thomas Manning of the Cliffs in Calvert County, Gent on the other part witnesseth That whereas Thomas Marsh late of Ann Arundell County Merchant (d. 1656) Did Bargaine & sell unto my father Edward Dorsey of Ann Arundell County Planter three hundred acres of land* being a part of a Dividend of six hundred acres of land the one halfe whereof the said Marsh Sould the said Thomas Manning as by bill of sale and the said Marshes hands bearing date the seventh day of May 1655... Now this indenture Witnesseth that the said Edward Dorsey for and in consideration of 6,000 pounds of tobacco... to him and in hand and paid by the said Thomas Manning hath hereby sould the above 300 acres of land..." (*Prov. Ct. Rec. J.J, f.* 133) (See page 2)

A description of this tract which was patented as Theobush Manning on April 6, 1661, in the name of Thomas Manning and Edward Darcy is here given.

"Cecelius - To all persons to whom these presents shall come Greetings in our Lord God Everlasting Know Yee that we for and in consideration that Thomas Marsh transporteth Six persons into this our Province, here to inhabit as appeareth upon Entryes made in our County of Ann Arundell and Upon such conditions and terms of our sd Province of Maryland as under our great Seal at Arms bearing date at London on the second day of July in the yeare of our Lord God one thousand six hundred and forty nine & remaining upon record in our said Province of Maryland Do hereby grant unto *Thomas Manning and Edward Dorsey assignes of the said Thomas Marsh all that tract or parcell of land called Theobush Manning* lying on the west side of Chesapeake Bay next to the land of John Norwoods beginning at a marked tree the said tree being the Southermost bound of said Norwoods land and running South East and by South down the bay for the length of three hundred perches to a marked Locust tree then to the South with a Line Drawne West from the said Locust tree to the length of Three hundred and twenty perches on the west with a line Drawne North and West and by Nor E from the End of the line unto the land of the said Norwood, on the North side and the East with the said bay containing and laid out for six hundred acres more or less... To have and to hould the same unto them the said Thomas Manning and Edward Darcy and their heirs..." (*Patents A.B.& H. f.* 261; *Patents 4, f.* 541; *Patents 10, f.* 1)

In 1664 Capt. Thomas Manning purchased Edward Darcy's share of Theobush Manning and had the entire tract patented in his name, but the Bill of Sale was not recorded by Edward Dorsey until 1670. (*Patents 7, f.* 98) (*Arch. of Md.* XLIX, 126, 248)

In 1681 Edward and Joshua Dorsey sold their right to Hockley in the Hole to their brother John Dorsey. This tract, which was one of their deceased father's surveys, had been taken up and patented by the three brothers in 1664. (See pages 8,9,173)

COLONEL EDWARD DORSEY

Fortunately, Caleb Dorsey son of Hon. John Dorsey had the original deed, from which another record was made in 1707. At that time he also had other deeds recorded.

"Mr. Caleb Dorsey comes into Court and prays that the following Deeds and pattents may be recorded for his relief with Cornelius Howards Deed to Jno Dorsey for one hundred and fifty acres of land called Howard's Heirship, Joshua Dorseys Deed of release to John Dorsey for four hundred acres of land called Hockley in the Hole, Edward Dorseys release to Jno Dorsey for D° Robert and Lawrence Gudgeons pattent for eighty five acres called Orphans Addicon, John Dorseys Pattent for confirmation for Eight hundred Forty two acres called Hockley in the Hole all which deeds and Pattents on Perusal of the Court are adjudged and Decreed to be recorded and follow Viz:

To all Christian People to whom this present wrighting shall come be heard or read or seen *Edward Dorsey of the County of Ann Arundell Gent son and heir of Edward Dorsey late of the County of Ann Arundell in the Province of Maryland Deceased sendeth greetings in our Lord God Everlasting Whereas the Honorable Cecilius Lord Barron of Baltimore did by his pattent bearing date the twentieth day of August One thousand six hundred and sixty four for the consideration herein mentioned Grant unto the said Edward Dorsey Joshua Dorsey and John Dorsey my brothers a parcell of land called Hockley in ye Hole lying in Ann Arundell County* aforesaid on ye south side Severne River in ye woods beginning at a marked oake being a bounded tree of the land of Cornelius and Sam[l] Howard and running for breadth from ye said oake by Cornelius Howards land and a line drawn west Southwest two hundred perches to a marked white oake upon a Hill by ye main branch of Broad Creek bounded on ye west side by a line drawn down the branch from ye said oake three hundred and twenty perches to a marked oake in a bottom by a branch running in Broad Creek on ye south by a line drawn east northeast from the said oake for breadth two hundred perches to a marked oake by a swamp bounded on ye east by a line drawn north from the said oake until it intersect with a branch called Cabbin Neck Branch and by Cabbin Neck Branch and Samuel Howards line into ye first marked oake containing and now layed out for four hundred acres of land unto us the said Edward Dorsey John Dorsey and Joshua Dorsey and our heirs and assignes forever as by the said pattent more at large it doth appear Now know ye that I the said Edward Dorsey for and in consideration of Twenty four Thousand pounds of good merchantable leafe tobacco to me in hand paid by my said brother John Dorsey... Whereof I do hereby acknowledge and thereof and of every part and parcell thereof acquitt and discharge the said John Dorsey and for other good causes and considerations thereunto Mooving have... and do forever quitt claim unto my said brother John Dorsey now in possession of the said four hundred acres of land and to his heirs and assignes forever all my right title interest claim property and demand which land my heirs now have to the said four hundred acres of land or to any part or parcell thereof or to any dwelling house tob° house fences orchards woods underwoods lumber and lumber trees now growing lying or standing upon the said four hundred acres of land or any other profitt commodity or appurtenances whatsoever to the land belonging or any right title or interest which I & my heirs may have or claim thereafter by virtue of ye aforesaid pattent or grant of ye said Lord Baltimore to me the said Edward Joshua and John Dorsey in joint tenancy as aforesaid or *by order of any title claim or demand that may or might descend or accrue from my said father Edward Dorsey Deceased for or by reason of any right due to him in his life time or for or by reason of any survey by him made or warrants returned* or by reason of any peticon or exchange lines of ye said patent aforesaid Granted for or by reason of any other matters cause or thing whatsoever And the said Edward Dorsey doth for himself his heirs Exc & Adm Covenant promise and agree to and with the said John Dorsey his heirs & assigns that he the said Edward Dorsey and his heirs shall upon request and at the cost and charges in ye law of him the said John Dorsey and his heirs within ye space of seven years from ye date hereof do make and Execute or cause to be made done & Executed any other or further Act or Acts thing or things appurtenance or appurtenances in ye law or shall by the said John Dorsey his heirs or assigns or his or their Councill bound in ye law be reasonably bound or required for ye further and better assurance surety and lawmaking the said land and promises to the said John Dorsey his heirs & Assigns for ever in Witness whereof I the said Edward Dorsey have hereunto sett my hand and seale this sixth day of December in ye Yeare of our Lord One thousand Six hundred Eighty and one.
Sealed and Delivered in ye Presence
Rich[d] Hill Nicho Greenberry — Edward Dorsey (Seal)"

After his signature fully attested, follows a deed from Joshua Dorsey for his right in Hockley in the Hole for a consideration of eight thousand pounds of tobacco to his brother John Dorsey, after which John asks for a resurvey of the tract. This resurvey subsequently increased the tract to 842 acres. (*A.A. Co. Deeds I.H. No. 3,* folios 62-65)

Some time before 1680, Edward Dorsey, in partnership with Cornelius Howard, purchased a 500-acre tract of land in Talbot County, on which one or the other must have lived long enough to seat. On December 7, 1701, he renounced all claim to his land declaring that:

"Whereas Capt. Cornelius Howard late of Ann Arundell County deceased did purchase a parcel of land of William Parrot in Talbot County containing five hundred acres joyntly with Mr. Edward Dorsey w[ch] land we did joyntly purchase seat and possess several years before the death of the said Howard (1680) and never any partition or division made of the said land and premises so that as I am the survivor where may be a claim hereafter of my heirs to the whole five hundred acres. Now whereas I faithfully promised the said Deceased Howard on his death bed that I nor my heirs should never lett hinder nor molest his heirs from the peacable enjoyment of our moyety of the said land and premises Know ye that I the sd Dorsey for myself my heirs excs and administrators do forever renounce and quitt all claims to the other or our moyety of the said five hundred acres of land lying and being on the north side of Great Choptank River up in the Freshes on the north side of a creek called Tuckahoe Creek bought by the aforesaid Howard and Dorsey from Wm Parrot my moyety I formerly sold to John Edmondson of Talbott County, the other moyety is and right forever to be in possession of the heirs assigns of the said Howard from me and my heirs and assigns forever as witness my hand and seal this 17th day of December anno 1701.
Signed sealed and delivered in presence of Edward Dorsey
David Catsaw, Mary Dorsey, John Twell." (*A.A. Co. Deeds W.T. No. 2, f.* 52).

On June 12, 1688, Edward Dorsey was granted a tract of land in the western part of Ann Arundell County (now Howard County) called Major's Choice, to which he and his family moved before the year 1700.

"To all persons to whom these presents shall come Greeting in our Lord God Everlasting. Know yee that for and in consideration that Maj[r] Edward Dorsey of Ann Arundell County in our said Province of Maryland hath due unto him ffive hundred and Ninety and nine acres of land within our said province by assignment of part of two several warrants (viz[t]) ffour hundred and fifty acres from John Edwards of the said county part of a warrant for six hundred acres granted him the said Edwards the thirteenth day of October one thousand six hundred eighty six, and one hundred forty and nine acres more from Madam Ursula Burgess of the same county, widow Admx of all and singular the goods and Chattels of Coll. William Burgess late of the said county decd and being part of a warrant for three hundred acres of land Renewed to him the said Burgess the Thirtieth day of October one thousand six hundred eighty six as appears upon our record and upon such condicons and forms as are expressed in the condicons of plantacon of this our province bearing date the fifth day of April one thousand six hundred eighty ffour.... We doe therefore hereby grant unto him the said Maj[r] Edward Dorsey all that tract or parcell of land called Major's Choice lyeing between the ffalls of Patapsco River and Patuxent River on a Ridge called Elk Ridge Beginning at a bounded Poplar standing in a branch of Patuxent River and running north east one hundred and sixteen perches to a bounded white oake then north half a point west one hundred eighty three perches to a bound Red oak then northwest and by north one hundred fforty eight perches to a bounded Red oak then south two hundred and twelve perches to a bounded Red Oake then by a straight line to that first bounded poplar containing and now laid our for ffive hundred ninety and nine acres of land more or less... the twelfth day of June , 1688." (*Patents N.S. No. 2, f.* 717)

Through generations Major's Choice remained in possession of some of the descendants of Col. Edward Dorsey. His grandson, Charles Hammond, son of his daughter Ann and her husband John Hammond, on August 23, 1794, sold for five shillings one acre of this land situated near Bellow's Spring in Ann Arundell County to Charles White, Elizabeth Dorsey, and Achsah Howard for the purpose of erecting a meeting house thereon for the society of Methodists. (*A.A. Co, Deeds N.H. No. 7, f.* 293) (See pages 74 and 175A)

A deed in Howard County dated June 30, 1854 states that William B. Dorsey's land goes to Charles Hammond's gate, it being a boundary to Major's Choice, Phelps Luck, and New Year's Gift from a Rock marked C.H.... 1795, the beginning of Hammond's Elk Ridge, and going to a hickory stump of the Bellow's Spring Meeting House Lot. (*Howard Co. Deeds 14, f.* 324)

In 1693 Edward Dorsey had surveyed 50 acres of Cypruss Swamp, back of Magothy River on Round Bay, and another tract containing 85 acres south of the Severn River.

(*Warrants A, No. 13, f.* 34)

Major's Fancy, containing 180 acres, was surveyed for him March 12, 1694, between the South and the Severn Rivers, and by virtue of a warrant, Long Reach was granted unto him at Elk Ridge, Beginning at a bound white oak of Samuel Chews and running with the said Chew's line southwest Six hundred and forty perches to a bound white Oak, and now laid out for four hundred and forty eight acres.. (*Patents B, No. 23, f.* 303)

Before 1700, Edward Dorsey bought a tract of land containing 100 acres called Hockley on the south side of Patapsco River and on the northeast side of Forster's Fancy. (*A.A. Co. Rent Rolls*)

As Edward Dorsey of Baltimore County, he bought from John and Thomas Larkin of Ann Arundell County, June 25, 1702, one half of a tract called United Friendship, in Baltimore County, on the north side of the Patapsco River, containing 350 acres. There seems to have been no other conveyance of land between Edward Dorsey and John Larkin, nor anything to show that Margaret Lacon, wife of Col. Edward Dorsey, was the daughter of John Larkin. (*Prov. Ct. Rec. T.L. No. 2, f.* 611) (See page 25)

In 1704 he purchased from Richard Owens 225 acres of land called Owen's Adventure, (*Balto. Co. Deeds H.W. No. 2, f.* 354) also 100 acres of Barnes Folly, and the following year from Thomas Taylor he bought Tailor's Forest containing 900 acres, on the north side of the Patapsco River.

Edward Dorsey also bought lots in the town of Annapolis and build houses upon a number of them. In 1695 he made over to his brother Hon. John Dorsey, in trust for his children, ten lotts of ground commonly called by the name of Bloomsberry Square with several houses thereon built and part of a lot adjoining Mr. Proctors Remainder of that lot whereon the Hon[1], the then Governour lived together with all the buildings thereon. These lots were to cause much controversy at a later date. (*Chanc. Rec. P.C, f.* 779) (See pages 17,18,19,24)

While Edward Dorsey bought and sold land, he was not neglectful to his personal obligations or the affairs of the county.

In 1675 his interest centered in a suit brought to contest the will of his wife's father Nicholas Wyatt, made in 1671, for Sarah's brother Samuel Wyatt had died in 1673, and Sarah was heir at law. Among other claims brought to the court was that of Thomas Bland and Damaris, his wife, former wife of Nicholas Wyatt, citing that Edward and Sarah while on a visit to the Quarter, where he and Damaris lived, had taken property not belonging to them, further claiming that they had maintained *Edward and Sarah, their two children and four servants, from June 1677 until the following January.* These charges Edward and Sarah refuted. They won the suit. (*Arch. of Md.* LI,155,165,197,544-550) (See page 191)

Edward Dorsey, as a lawyer and man of affairs, was called upon to make wills, witness them, go surety on bonds, and appraise estates. On May 31, 1676, he and Richard Hill appraised the estate of Edward Gardiner. A copy of Edward Dorsey's original signature and the seal used appears on page 6.

On September 13, 1687, Edward and Sarah Dorsey witnessed the administration bond of Michael Cussack. Their original signatures are reproduced on page 26.

As one of the Justices of the Peace for the County of Ann Arundell, Edward Dorsey brought the news to Robert Proctor on September 1, 1681, late at night that the Indians had robbed John Marriot, beaten him and turned him and his wife out of doors. (*Arch. of Md.* XVII, 19)

In 1683 he was appointed one of the commissioners to manage and build the Court House, to survey and lay out the Port Towns and Places in Ann Arundell County, and erect a building for the Courts and Assembly of the Province for the keeping of records of the secretary's office. (*Arch. of Md.* VII,515,611)

On November 28, 1689, he signed an address to the King, as one of the Freeholders of Baltimore County, but by 1691, he was again living in Ann Arundell County, and a letter written by Micajah Perry to John Povey Esquire, London, October 17, 1691 records that he Micajah Perry had that day met a gentleman newly come from Maryland, one Mr. John Hammond, who presented him with a list of Gentlemen in Maryland, who were good honest Substantial Protesants, who are well affected. Among this list of persons recommended to be of their Majesty's Council, were Major Dascey and Sir Thomas Lawrence. Major Dascey was endorsed by his Lord's party, and by the Merchants. (*Arch. of Md.* VIII, 283-285)

It is possible that Edward Dorsey was over-shrewd in the practice of law and the transaction of business, for he did not escape the acrimony of Sir Thomas Lawrence, who wrote, "Edward Dorsey lives near Annapolis and builds houses there, those who have dealings with him say his honesty more often fails him than his wit."

This did not prevent Edward Dorsey from being elected a member of his Majesty's Council, and on September 21, 1694, he was appointed a member of the House of Burgesses. (*Arch. of Md.* XIX, 30)

On October 18, 1693, an act was passed making Ann Arundell Town in Ann Arundell County the seat of Justice within the Province, and on February 28th the Assembly was held at the house of Major Edward Dorsey. On March 1st the Assembly voted that the Records of the Commissioner's office be kept in Maj. Dorsey's house where they are lodged at the present until the next session of the Assembly. (*Arch. of Md.* XXVIII, 24; XIX, 122)

This same year, Edward Dorsey was appointed a commissioner to lay out Lotts for the Town and Porte of Ann Arundell in Ann Arundell County, and it was ordered that the land where the town was formerly shall from hence forth be Town, Port, and Place of Trade where all ships may come to for Entering and Clearing.

The committee was authorized to survey and lay out the said town into lots, streets and lanes, with open space to be left on which to erect a church, market house, and other public charge. (*Arch. of Md.* XIX, 111.)

On February 28, 1694, it was voted to keep a public Ferry upon the South River in Ann Arundell County for Carrying all persons that have business in the Provincial Court. Capt. John Hammond and Major Edward Dorsey were to agree with persons to keep the rate cheap. (*Ibid.*, 134)

When the Chancery Judges were appointed on October 17, 1694, it was ordered that Mr. Kenelm Cheseldyn & Maj. Edward Dorsey be added to the Hono^{ble} Coll Henry Jowles Keeper of the Great Seale, for the hearing and determining all Matters in Chancery. (*Arch. of Md.* XX, 137)

On May 14, 1695, the Hono^{ble} Henry Jowles Chancelor, Kenelm Chesldyn Esq. & Maj. Edward Dorsey joynt in the said Commission, had administered unto them the Oathes Appointed by Act of Parliament to be taken instead of the Oathes of Allegiance & Supremacy and Subscribed to the Test. Also Severally tooke the oath of Commissioners appointed for keeping the Great Seale. (*Ibid.*, 327)

On October 15, 1695, Coll. Henry Jowles Keeper of the Broad Seal of the province do for the future, lodge said seal with Maj. Edward Dorsey one of the Commissioners in Chancery, by him to be kept in the absence of Coll. Jowles. On May 16, 1696, Came the hono^{ble} Maj. Edward Dorsey one of the Commissioners in Chancery & delivered at the Board the Broad Seal of the province, which was by order surrendered to the Hon. Coll. Henry Jowles Chancellor for keeping during his residence in Town. (*Ibid.*, 327, 426)

Maj. Edward Dorsey was paid 4,000 pounds of tobacco for his House under the Hill, October 12, 1695. (*Arch. of Md.* XIX, 266)

The Assembly, on May 1, 1696, appointed His Excellency Sir Francis Nicholson, Sir Thomas Lawrence, Hon. Nicholas Greenberry, Hon. Thomas Tench, Major John Hammond, Major Edward Dorsey, Mr. James Sanders, and Capt. Richard Hill a commission for keeping good rules and order making them a body corporate for the Porte and Town of Annapolis. Mr. Richard Beard, surveyor, made a map of the place. This body was authorized to erect a market house and hold a fair yearly; a new State House was ordered to be built. It was voted that a handsome pair of Gates be made at the coming in of the town and two Triangular Houses built for the Ranger, to have the way from the Gates to go directly to the top of the Hill, without the Town to be ditched on each side for Public Builders and if in case the same happen to come within the said Major Dorsey's Lotts Proposed that land be given him elsewhere for it. (*Ibid.*, 292, 498)

On July 8, 1696, Edward Dorsey served on a committee to inspect and peruse the Laws of the Province and make a report to the next session of the Assembly, and on September 29, 1696, he came from the House of Burgesses, with Mr. Hatch and Mr. Blay to acquaint his Excellency that they were appointed a Committee to Inspect what Tobacco is collected towards building a church at Annapolis, and to make some report thereof, and to desire that his Excellency would be pleased to appoint two of his Majesty's honourable Council to joyn with them therein. Sir Thomas Lawrence Baronet Secretary and Esq[r] Brooks were the two appointed. (*Ibid.*, 412, 450)

It was ageed on September 17, 1696 that the arms sent from England should be stored in Major Dorsey's House for the present, and the following day an account was made of said arms brought in and in good condition and lodged at the house of Major Dorsey within the port of Annapolis. (*Ibid.*, 435) On September 30th, it was ordered that arms be sent away by the opportunity of several boats now in Harbour and that Maj[r] Dorsey deliver them. At the Port of Annapolis on the 3rd of October was reported, Received from Major Dorsey these following arms together with an order of Council directing that none of the said things should be made use of unless in case of invasion or insurrection. (*Arch. of Md.* XXIII, 12, 15)

A committee was appointed May 2, 1700 by the House to talk with Major Edward Dorsey about buying a house for securing public arms and ammunition. The committee reported that said Dorsey will rent three houses for twelve years space and cover the great house for 100 pounds Sterling, but can make no title to the land further than for this aforesaid time. (He had entailed the land and houses to his children.) (*Arch. of Md.* XXIV, 52, 65, 66)

On May 15th, the Assembly having taken into consideration a convenient place for the council to sett in and a handsome place to lodge the public arms in, answers they have purchased a house from Maj. Dorsey for the later purpose. (*Ibid.*, 185) This same year Edward Dorsey received rent for the storage of the King's Powder in one of his houses. (*Ibid.*, 119)

Edward Dorsey was appointed one of the trustees of the free school in the Port of Annapolis called King William's School (now St. John's College), in 1696. He was one of the first subscribers and contributed 2,000 pounds of tobacco to the fund for founding the school. He was also one of the trustees appointed for the erecting and endowing Grammar Scholes within the Province. (*Arch. of Md.* XIX, 421; XXVIII, 27; XXIII, 77)

When asked in 1696 for a report from the committee appointed to inspect the proposals about building the church & free schole, he Reported that there is in Banck for building the church at Annapolis 458 pounds sterl: We have Discoursed Workeman and the Carpenter demands for his work 250 pounds. The bricklayer having all Stuffe upon the place 220 pounds. The Brickmaker 90 pounds. We find no other means to raise money therefore without the assistance of some charitable disposed persons, we also find that the charge of building the said church will not amount to less than 1,200 pounds Sterling. (*Arch. of Md.* XIX, 490)

When proposals in relation to building the church and school were made by Maj. Edward Dorsey the Board said they would leave it to his own management to make what Bargain he thinks fit with his Workmen. (*Arch. of Md.* XXIII, 78, 397)

On April 30, 1696, he was a member of a committee to consider proposals and agreement with Col. Herman for building the Court House, and on May 1st, the committee met to consider plans for the State House. In December he was appointed one of two members of the House of Burgesses to view the new Stadt House Building and make a report on what remains to be done. (*Arch. of Md.* XIX, 332, 293, 547)

The following year the state house was finished and Major Dorsey and Major Hammond were appointed to view the ditch, supervise the building of the two triangular houses and draws, and see that the gate house be built with a gate and good lock and key. For their services the Western shore was to pay these men eight thousand pounds of tobacco. (*Ibid.*, 517)

When on April 3, 1698, an act was passed for ascertaining the bounds and limits of Ann Arundel and Baltimore Counties, Major John Hammond and Major Dorsey were appointed to see about a better division. (*Arch. of Md.* XXII, 147)

On May 31st of this year, Major Edward Dorsey presented a petition to the Assembly craveing longer time for building the Church and Schoole. (*Arch. of Md.* XIX, 518)

A fine of 200 pounds Sterling was imposed upon Edward Dorsey on June 9, 1699 by the General Assembly for failing to build a church at the port of Annapolis before November 30, 1698. He was called before the House of Delegates and after examination it being put to his choice whether he would stand Tryall in an Action that should be commenced against him for not keeping his Covenant or that he would Submitt to such fine as the General Assembly would impose upon him. Answered That he would and did Submitt to such fine Provided he might for ever be discharged from building and finishing the said Church thereupon the House of Delegates did fine the said Edward Dorsey two hundred pounds Sterling. (*Arch. of Md.* XXII, 556)

On May 4, 1700, his friend, Rev. Thomas Bray, Lord Bishops of London Commissary within this province, interceded for him, and prayed that the fine be lessened as *Major Edward Dorsey had a great charge of a wife and twelve children the most of them being small.*

(*Arch. of Md.* XXIV, 19, 61, 62)

The House then ordered that if Maj Edward Dorsey at or before the next Provincial Court shall convey and make over to his son Dorsey a reall Estate Equivalent to the Lott and houses which his said son hath at Annapolis and shall at his proper Cost and Charge sufficiently new cover and repair the said houses and at the same County Convey the said Houses and Lott to his Majesty for a Publick store or Magazine then his fyne of two hundred pounds shall not be levyed. (*Ibid.*, 29, 30)

The State House, which was finished about 1697, was destroyed by fire in 1704. Until it was rebuilt, the Assembly held its meetings in a house rented from Col. Edward Dorsey. On December 7, 1704, the said Dorsey agreed to rent his Greate House at twenty pounds Sterling per annum for the Assembly and Courts to Sitt in, to which the Board assented provided the public be not obliged to make any repairs of said house. (*Arch. of Md.* XXVI, 377, 398)

The same month it was ordered that the Speaker and Delegates of Assembly meet at the House of Col. Edward Dorsey in Annapolis every Day during this session at Eight in the morning & sit till Twelve in the Afternoon and from two till four. And ordered that Notice be given by Beat of Drum twice in the Morning and once in the Afternoon and Likewise that Mr. Wooten the Minister be desired to attend for Prayers at Eight o'clock in the morning and at tolling the Bell in the afternoon. (*Ibid.*, f. 391)

The house built by Col. Edward Dorsey in 1694, and which was occupied by Governor Nicholson during the years 1694 to 1699, and later rented for the Assembly and Courts to sit in, is now referred to as the Dorsey-Nicholson House or Gross Tavern.

On February 1, 1715/6, the land on which this house stood was sold by Samuel Dorsey to Thomas Jones of the city of Annapolis for 10 pounds Sterling... all that part of land situated in Annapolis which my deceased father took up and hereafter built a Dwelling according to the Act of Assembly... and within which house Mrs. Hester Warman lately called Hester Gross lately dwelt and Inhabited as a Tenant to my said Father until ye same was burnt and destroyed by fire. (*A.A. Co. Deeds I.B. No. 2*, f. 25)

Charles Kilburne, later called to give evidence of the location of this house, declared that within fifty foot from the northeast end of the house now built by Mr. John Carpenter in the said city stood a house built for Maj. Edward Dorsey and rented to a certain Hester Gross now Hester Warman who kept ordinary for some time and Accomodated Governor Nicholson, and after burnt out, lived in the house where William Brynor now lives and followed the same employ for some time. (*Chanc. Rec. P.L.*, f. 266)

For the location of this house, see page 18.

On January 4, 1700, Edward Dorsey, as always anxious about his children's future, and foreseeing that all might not go well between the children by his wife, Sarah, and his second wife, Margaret, when he would no longer be living to manage the affairs of his family, made a deed of gift.

"I Edward Dorsey of Baltimore County and Margaret my wife, namely for the settling and dispersing of such goods and chattels as God hath bestowed upon us with all for the advancement and profit of our children after my death to avoid controversy... that might arise between my wife and children after I bequeath the same by will. To beloved friends Maj. John Hammond, Capt. Charles Hammond and my son Edward Dorsey five small plantations in Baltimore County, four of which adjoins the *plantation I now live on at Elkridge* (Major's Choice), the other on the south side of the Patapsco River a little below falls of Patapsco, With what men and women negroes there is now upon the said plantations and 100 acres of land adjoining of the said plantation, 3 cows, 3 sows, 2 Iron potts, bed and furniture, two plates, dishes, 6 alcemy spoons, eleven barrels of Indian corn to each plantation to said Maj. Hammond Capt. Charles Hammond and Edward Dorsey Jr., to the use and behoof of 5 of my sons hereafter named Samuel, Joshua, John, Nicholas, and Benjamin Dorsey.

First to my son Samuel Dorsey that plantation of mine near the falls of the Patapsco River, 3 negroes belonging to it namely Chang, Jenny, and Ellick with cows, sows, furniture and corn.

Secondly to my son Joshua Dorsey that plantation where Black Dick lives, and to the southward of said plantation, 2 negroes, now upon said plantation, namely Dick and Mariah his wife with cows and barrels of corn at his brother Samuels above.

Thirdly to my son John Dorsey that plantation that Bacon now lives on with one hundred acres of land next adjoining and 2 negroes now upon it B___and Beck his wife and their increase if any, with cows, sows and corn.

Fourthly to son Nicholas Dorsey, plantation on which negro Tom now lives with 100 acres of land next adjoining, 2 negroes, Tom and Hagar his wife and their increase, cows, sows, and corn.

Fifthly to son Benjamin Dorsey, piece of land lying betwixt Dick and Bacon with that piece of cleared ground cleared this year and where a Quarter built at ye falls with 100 acres next adjoining, 2 negroes Robin and Nell with their increase if any, and cows, sows, corn etc., as his brothers have.

In case of death of any son his land and portion to be equally divided among his brothers. Sons to be placed on their plantations and receive negroes and other things at age of 16 years, and to be at work for a living, not to dispose of any thing of his labour and estate without the consent and approbation of his eldest brother and my friends... after my death when my son Edward shall have the trouble of Looking after his brothers and their estates providing them playne and decent apparrell and holdsome diet out of the produce of their several crops being shipped to England and having cloathed their servants out of the remainder he shall take to himself a twelveth part for his trouble until they come of age of twenty one years and shall every May Day render his account of his proceedings therein to my other two friends mentioned with himself above *at the house where I now live at Elk Ridge* where there Shall be a collation of three pounds Sterling provided every May Day and Every respective son that comes of age of twenty one years shall pay to my said two friends each of them a guiney in Gold and if any one of my sons prove refractory and will not be ruled by my said two friends and their brother bind them or send them out to some handy Craff trade until he or they arrive at the age of 21 years as witness our hands and seals the day and Yeare above written, January 4, 1700.

In presence of John Hammond
Phillip Hammond

Edward Dorsey (Seal)
Margaret Dorsey (Seal)"
(*Prov. Ct. Rec. T.L. No. 2*, f. 169)

On September 18, 1704, Edward Dorsey presented a bill to the Assembly to enable him to sell some entailed lands and houses in the Port of Annapolis. On the third of October he represented to the General Assembly that he has built in the Town and Port of Annapolis several houses which he afterwards entailed upon his children and that the said houses are now and have been for a considerable time untenanted whereby they are in Ruinous Condition and will in a little time be quite decayed and totally lost to the said children with whose Convenciency it does not consist to reside in the same themselves but could in case the said Intaile were cut out dispose of the same to some advantage whereof it was prayed that an Act might be passed in favour of the said children that the said Entaile may be cut off and the said Edward

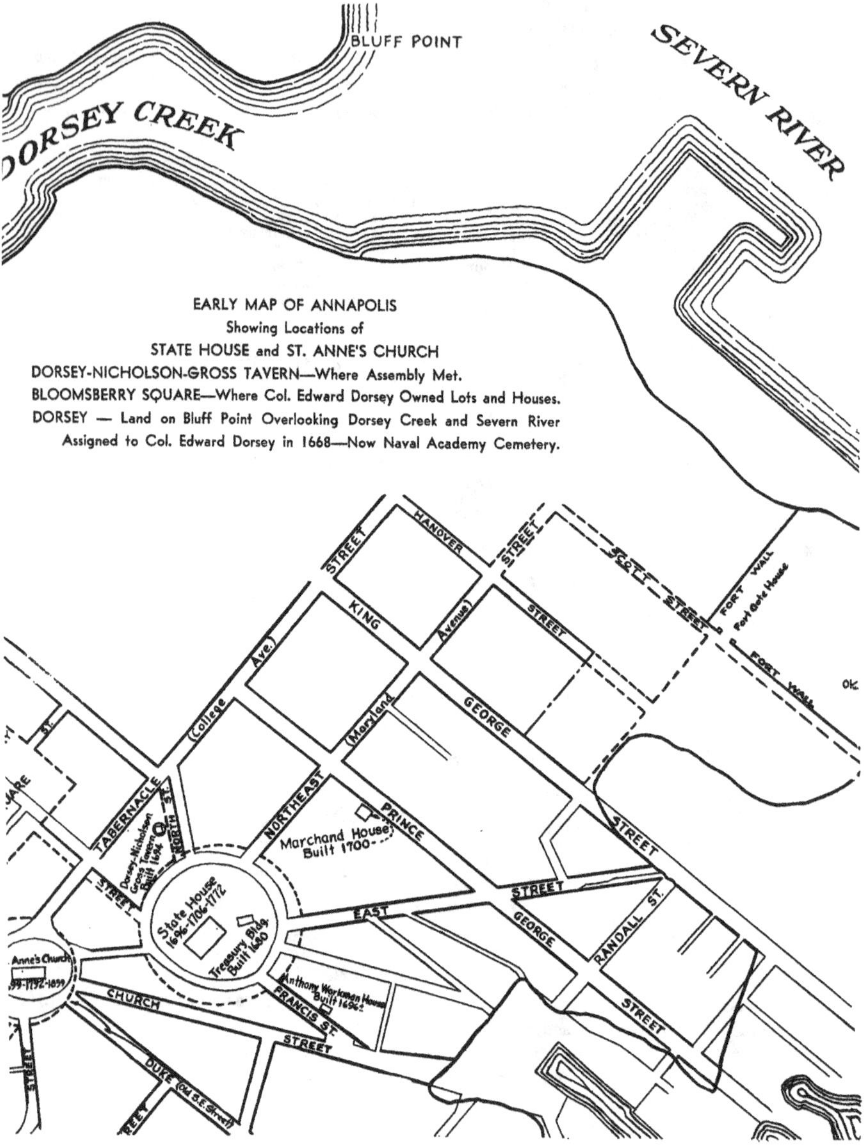

EARLY MAP OF ANNAPOLIS
Showing Locations of
STATE HOUSE and ST. ANNE'S CHURCH
DORSEY-NICHOLSON-GROSS TAVERN—Where Assembly Met.
BLOOMSBERRY SQUARE—Where Col. Edward Dorsey Owned Lots and Houses.
DORSEY — Land on Bluff Point Overlooking Dorsey Creek and Severn River
Assigned to Col. Edward Dorsey in 1668—Now Naval Academy Cemetery.

empowered to make sale of the said houses for the benefit and advantage of his said children. (*Arch. of Md.* XXVI, 57, 135, 365)

Samuel Dorsey, the eldest son of Edward, was sent for to appear at Court in reference to above said lands. When asked if he had anything to say why a bill should not pass for the sale of land, he answered that forasmuch as it is entailed and he is a party concerned Could not Consent to it unless the money that shall be raized by sale thereof or so much thereof as he is concerned with will be paid and delivered to him.

It was declared by Coll. Dorsey that it was always so intended upon which terms the said Sam[ll] Dorsey is willing the bill should pass. The Act was passed that same day and the Entaile cut off forever. (*Ibid.*, 149, 366)

On May 22, 1705, Edward Dorsey sold Tenn Lotts of ground commonly called by the name Bloomsberry Square with several houses built thereon to William Bladen and Charles Carrol of Anne Arundel County. Consideration 150 pounds Sterling. The same day he sold to Charles Carrol one Lott and the houses thereon erected in occupation of George Jackson lying close upon Shipping Creek and next adjoining a parcel of ground laid out for a Ship Yard, for want of tenants & repair in ruinous condition... for 30 pounds Sterling. (*A.A. Co. Deeds W.T. No. 2,* folios 213, 215)

In the year 1706, William Bladen showeth to the Court by his petition That when the Town and Port of Annapolis was first laid out according to Act of Assembly Col. Edward Dorsey residing there and undertaker of the Public Buildings took up two lots next adjoining the public Place where the Court House was designed to be built but the said Dorsey failing in his undertaking turned a Brick Kilne and other materials upon the Country as also a forty foot House built upon the said Lots which the Country offered your petitioner for 3,000 pounds of tobacco... (*Arch. of Md.* XXVI, 589)

Col. Edward Dorsey was appointed a member of the House of Burgesses from Baltimore County, May 22, 1705, and on the 25th was chosen a member of a committee to lay, assess and apportion public levy. (*Ibid.*, 476)

On April 2, 1706, Col. Edward Dorsey was listed as dead at a meeting of the Assembly, and an order was issued for the election of a member from Baltimore County in room of Col. Edward Dorsey deceased. (*Ibid.*, 561, 562)

His will made October 26, 1704 was proved December 31, 1705. A copy of the original will is reproduced on pages 20 and 21. (*Balt. Co. Original Wills*, Hall of Records, Annapolis) (*Wills* 3, f. 725)

The will was exhibited in Court and letters of administration on the estate of Col. Edward Dorsey, gentleman, were granted to his widow Margaret Dorsey on February 28, 1705. Bonds were given by Joseph Howard, Andrew Wellplay, John Petticoat, and William Taylor, all of Anne Arundel County. (*Test. Proc. 19b*, f. 118)

The estate of Col. Edward Dorsey was appraised April 1, 1706 by Thomas Hammond and William Talbot. (*Invts. & Accts. 26*, f. 100)

Margaret Dorsey, executrix of Col. Edward Dorsey deceased, petitioned the Court on April 10, 1706 for rent of the house in which the Courts were held, Samuel Dorsey contending that it was rightfully his as heir at law.

Upon hearing the petition of Samuel Dorsey, it appeared by a former contract that the same rent is the right of the said Samuel Dorsey, and it was resolved that he be paid the Rent of the House for the year past by the Treasurer of the Western Shore being 20 pounds.

(*Arch. of Md.* XXVI, 586, 587)

Margaret Dorsey, widow of Col. Edward, m. (2) in 1706 John Israel, d. 1723
On February 15, 1706, an administration account was given on the estate of Col. Edward

In the name of God amen I Edward Dorsey of Baltemore County In the Province of Maryland
Being weake of Body butt of sound and perfect minde and Memory (thankes to almighty God)
butt Calling to Minde the Mortallity of my Body & knowing the Uncertainty of this present life doe make
and ordaine this My Last Will & Testam^t. In Maner and forme following

First and principally I Comitt My soule into the hands of Allmighty God who gave itt me and My body
to the Earth from whence itt came to be buried In decent and Christian maner as my Executrix hereafter
named shall thinke fitt nothing doubting butt att the Generall Resurrection I shall receive the same againe by
the allmighty power of God And as touching such Worldly Estate wherew^th itt hath pleased almighty God
to bless me wth In this life I give devise bequith and dispose the same In maner & forme followinge

Item — I give & Bequith unto My son Lacon Dorsey and his heirs for Ever a tract or parcell of land lyinge
neere the Maine falls of Patapsco knowne by the name of Stockly Con^t — one hundred acres and also
one negro Boy named [illegible] one white boy named Wm Bacson one feather bead and furniture three
Cows and three sowes two putter dishes and six alchmy spoones two Iron potts and ten barrills of
Indian Corne and My Will is that my s^d son Lacon Receive the s^d land Servants and stock att
the age of ~~[illegible]~~ twenty one yeares

Item — I give unto My Wellbeloved wife Margrett Dorsey My Chest of drawers wth one large seale skin
trunck and one horse named Ekes over and above her third part of My personall Estate that I have
not already by deed of gift and otherwayes freely given before the date of this my Last Will to my
severall Children

Item — I give & bequith unto my sons Charles Dorsey Lacon Dorsey Frances Dorsey and Edward Dorsey and to
there heirs for Ever all My land on the north side of Patapsco River to be Equally devided
betweene them assone as either of them shall come of age and whereas I am contracting for part
of a parcell of land called Tailors fforrest if I have any title to itt befor my death or to any
other land on the s^d North side of Patapsco I give and bequith all such lands to my
s^d sons Charles Lacon Francis and Edward and there heirs for Ever to be Equally devided as
afores^d — and In case either of them die befor they come of age My Will is that all My afores^d
lands be Equally devided amongst the rest of my s^d fower sons

Item — I give unto My son Charles Dorsey three Cowes [illegible] dishes six alchmy spoons
two Iron potts one feather bead and furniture ten [illegible] Indian Corne and one negro boy
Named Dick to be delivered to him when he comes of age

Item — I give unto my son Francis three Cows three Sowes two putter dishes six alchmy spoones two
Iron potts one feather bead and furniture ten Barrills of Indian Corne and one negro boy
named Harry to be delivered to him when he comes of age

Item — I give unto My son Edward Dorsey three Cows three sowes two putter dishes six alchmy spoones
two Iron potts one feather bead and furniture ten barrills of Indian Corne the value
of all My wearinge Cloths and the value of a horse named Sparke My best Gun my Case of
silver tanckett My silver tobacco box My seale Gold Ring and one of My Seale skin trunks
Marked ED to be delivered him when he comes of age

Item — I give and bequith unto My daughter Ann Dorsey one negro girle named little Jenny wth one
feather Bead and furniture and fifty pounds Star. one silver Cup of a Quart two silver
spoones to be delivered her att the age of Sixteen or day of Mariage

Item — I give unto My son Joshua Dorsey and his heirs for Ever that Plantation knowne by the
name of Barnes folly wth one hundred acres of land to the s^d Plantation adjoyning and
one hundred acres of land out of the land called Long Reach to be delivered Into his possession
att My decease and also one troopers sadell holsters and pistolls

Item — I give unto My son Sam^ll one silver hilted sord wth all the rem^d part of the land called
Majors Choyce & what he hath already received by deed of Gift &c^t is to be In full of
Childs part

Item — I give & bequith unto My son Nicholas Dorsey and his heirs for Ever one hundred acres of
land out of a tract of land called Long Reach lying att Elke Ridge wth two silver spoones
one new Gun and My horse named Dick to be delivered him att the age of sixteen yeares

Item — I give unto My son Benj^a Dorsey and his heirs for Ever one hundred acres of land called
Long Reach being p^t of s^d tract contains fower hundred forty eighte acres wth two silver
spoones the little Gun to be delivered him att the age of Sixteen yeares

Item — I give unto My son John Dorsey one hundred forty eighte acres of land beinge the rem^d part of the
land called Long Reach to him & his heirs for Ever one new gun two silver spoones to be deli^d him att the age
of sixteen

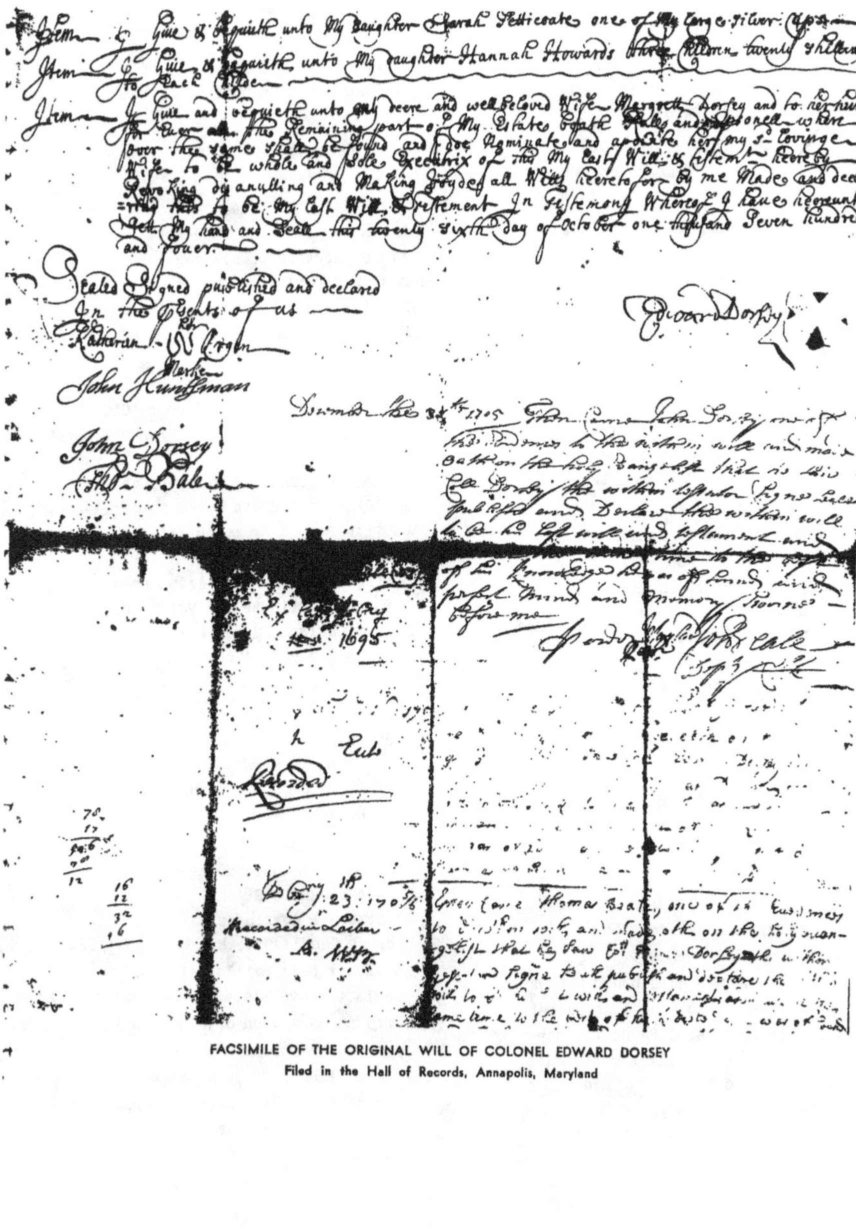

Item I Give & bequieth unto My daughter Sarah Petticoate one of My Large Silver Cups
Item I Give & bequieth unto My daughter Hannah Howards three pounds twenty shillings to Buy a Ring
Item I Give and bequieth unto my deere and well beloved Wife Margrett Dorsey and to her heirs for Ever all the Remaining part of My Estates both Reales and personell where ever the same shall be found and I doe Nominate and appoint her my s^d Loving Wife to be whole and sole Executrix of this My Last Will & Testament hereby Revoking disanulling and Making Voyde of all Wills heretofore By me Made and declare this to be My Last Will & Testement In Testemony Whereof I have hereunto Sett My hand and Seale this twenty sixth day of October one thousand Seven hundred and Fower.

Sealed Signed published and declared In the presents of us
Katherine K Organ (her marke)
John Hunfman
John Dorsey
Tho Bale

Edward Dorsey

FACSIMILE OF THE ORIGINAL WILL OF COLONEL EDWARD DORSEY
Filed in the Hall of Records, Annapolis, Maryland

Dorsey by John Israel, who had married Margaret Dorsey, the widow and administratrix of Col. Dorsey, and on August 7, 1707, an additional account rendered by John Israel shows the deceased's estate amounted to £688/10/11. Funeral charges allowed this accountant by His Honor ye Cmy General for special consideration 3,000 pounds of tobacco, equal to 12 pounds 10 shillings. (*Invts. & Accts. 26*, f. 147; *27*, f. 59)

The copy of the original will of Col. Edward Dorsey and the inventory of his estate which follow bear evidence of the family's manner of life and the extent of their holdings in Anne Arundel and Baltimore County.

The inventory of the goods of Col. Edward Dorsey deceased was taken and appraised April 1, 1706 by Thomas Hammond and William Talbot.

Wearing apparel
12 new silver spoons
5 old ones
2 Qt Silver Tankard
1 Qt Silver Tankard
2 Silver Cordial cups
2 small dram cups
Parcel broken Silver
Silver Salt and Pepper Box
Silver Hilted Sword
1 Gould Seal ring 1 pr gould shirt buttons
1 Silver Seale 4 pr Silver buttons
Ivory headed cane 1 Silver tob° box

In the new house
1 feather bed and furniture
Chest Drawers Old Seal Skin trunk
1 small table 7 old chairs
1 pr tongs 2 pr andirons
1 small trunk 1 Spice box
2 spring locks 3 brushes 1 comb
5 old chairs 1 troopers sadle houlsters and pistols

In ye nursery house
2 feather beds and furniture
Couch bed and covering
1 pr andirons tongs and Chaffin dish
1 box Iron and heater Candle box and Iron Candle Stick
1 warming pan 1 pr Taylor Sheers
5 Chairs table chest deal box
Pins needles and thread
3 childrens trunks hand brush 2 baskets
1½ yd Checkered Lin tape 1 pr pockett Stilliards Ink Case 1 Razor 2 old pen knives
A pcell earthenware flint glass ware
1 old chest old trunk 1 Iron Ladle 2 cow bells
1 pr tongs 1 scrubbing brush
1 pcell old books 1 survey chaine
2 earthen potts 1 oyle jar

In ye little house
2 feather beds and furniture
17 pr sheets 6 pr pillows 3 boulster cases
3 diaper table cloathes 12 napkins
12 old diaper huckaback napkins
2 flaxen table cloths and napkins 8 pillow beers
5 white lin^n towels 4 coarse pillow beers and table cloths 4 Calico Cubbard Cloths 1 good quilt & 1 ordinary one 3 trunks 1 chest Deal Box
1 looking glass 3 fowling pieces
3 old gunns 2 deare skins powder & shot
Castile soap 1 pr men's falls 20 Candles 1 broome
3 Ells bro: lin^n 1 pr Irish hose
2 Suites Curtinnes and Vallines
Lincey woolsey 24 pds printed paper
1 chest 2 old deal boxes

In ye milk house
11 Tin panns 1 Tin cullender
3 Stone Juggs 2 earthen butter pots
1 old jar and stew pan
3 pr Stilliards 4 reap hooks
4 casks & Lumber

In ye Kitchen
33 pewter dishes and basons
3 pewter Candle Sticks
30 plates 1 porringer
3 brass Candle Sticks 1 brass skillett 9 brass kettles 1 bell mettle Skillet 1 mortar & pestle 1 brass ladle 4 bread Greaters 12 tin patty panns 1 Iron driping pan 1 Iron Spitt 4 Iron potts & hooks 2 frying panns
1 Great Iron 3 pr pott hangers
1 pr Handirons 1 fender 1 chopping knife 3 payles 2 wooden trays
2 tin funnels

In the Store
Carpenters and smiths tools 3 whips
1 speaking trumpet 1 hammock scales
1 copper cauldron grnadstone

In a little flatt house
1 bed furniture & chest

In a little flatt house
1 flock bed furniture 1 pr tongs and a chest

At ye home Quarter
3 Iron potts 2 pr potthooks
1 frying pan and some lumber
1 pr andirons and 2 beds

Att the falls quarter
1 pott 2 payles lumber bedding
pigs Indian Corn

Att Elk Ridge Quarter
30 barrills Corne 1 steel mill pigs
Coopers tooles 4 old tin panns 1 payle
2 old chests 1 pr sheep sheers
3 Iron potts & pott hooks 1 bed 2 frying
panns 1 hand mill

White Serv^{ts}
1 Servt man named Jam: Tibbett
1 Servt man named Jackson

Slaves

1 negroe man named Bacon	Val	28/0/0
1 negroe man named Tom		28/0/0
1 negroe Punch		28/0/0
1 negroe Robin		28/0/0
1 negroe woman Beck		25/0/0
1 negroe woman Hager		25/0/0
1 negroe woman Nell		25/0/0
1 negroe Isabele		25/0/0
1 negroe boy Dick		18/0/0
1 negroe boy Charles		16/0/0
1 negroe boy Harry		10/0/0
1 negroe girl Jeney		15/0/0
1 negroe girl Hager		5/0/0

Cattle steers heiffers yearling calves hoggs
Timber
1 horse Gilding Sparke
1 horse Gilding frollick

Tobacco Total value £525/10/11
(*Invts. & Accts. 26,* f. 100)

On November 29, 1706, John Israel of Baltimore County and Margaret, his wife, lately called Margaret Dorsey Relict and Devisee of Coll Edwd Dorsey late of Anne Arundel and Baltimore Counties, deceased, sold to William Bladen Sixty acres of land called Dorsey lying on Dorseys Creeke near ye Towne and Port of Annapolis in Anne Arundel County and two Lotts of land lying on ye northeast side of ye High Street in ye said Towne and Porte some tyme heretofore in ye tenour and occupation of ye sd Coll Dorsey. (*A.A. Co. Deeds W.T. No. 2,* f. 471) (See pages 10,18)

A number of suits were filed against John Israel and his wife Margaret, administrators of the estate of Col. Edward Dorsey.

John Dorsey Jr., son of Joshua, brother of Col. Edward Dorsey, on May 16, 1706 petitioned the Court for part of his father's estate not yet turned over to him by Col. Edward Dorsey. (*Test Proc. 19c,* f. 180) (See page 124)

In 1706 Samuel Dorsey on behalf of his brother Benjamin Dorsey complained that John Israel and Margaret his wife Executrix of Col. Edward Dorsey late of Baltimore County deceased, had failed to give Benjamin his share of his father's estate. (*Ibid.,* f. 111)

In 1708 John Israel, administrator of Col. Edward Dorsey, deceased, who was administrator of Edward Dorsey Jr., deceased, complained to the Court that although the said Col. Edward Dorsey in his life time as administrator aforesaid, had paid large sums of money out of the said Edward's estate to the relations of sd deceased as their portions of said Edward's estate, yet nevertheless there appears nothing thereof upon the records of this Court whereby to Exonerate the estate of Col. Edward Dorsey from being yet liable to answer ye whole inventory or amount of the said estate (as if there had been nothing paid thereout to said Edward's relations) whereupon citation having been issued against the said relations Vizt: John Petticoat who married one of the sisters of said deceased Edward Dorsey Jr., acknowledged himself to have received from the sd Col. Edward Dorsey, his portion of the sd deceased Edward Dorsey Jr's estate £37/0/10, and also as guardian to John Dorsey Jr., the brother of the sd Edward Dorsey Jr., the portion £37/50/0. Mr. Samuel Dorsey, brother, acknowledged receiving

£88/14/10, also Mr. Joseph Howard, who had married a sister, £44/5/0. Mr. Joshua Dorsey, another brother, received £64/13/2, and also as guardian of his brother Nicholas Dorsey, 30 pounds. In all, ye relations received of Col. Edward Dorsey as administrator of Edward Dorsey Jr., £301/18/10½. (*Test. Proc. 21*, f. 3) (See page 27)

Benjamin Dorsey, on March 2, 1715, petitioned the Court, stating that he had received no part of his brother Edward's estate, though he was entitled to one seventh part.

(*Test Proc. 29*, f. 408)

In 1711 Samuel Dorsey brought suit against John Israel and William Bladen in connection with the settlement of his father's estate, stating:

That Edward Dorsey late of Anne Arundel County Gent. father of the said Samuel Dorsey was seized and possessed of several houses and Lotts in the Towne and port of Annapolis and that in consideration of the fatherly love which said Edward bore to his children and for their better advancement together with Margaret his wife the said Samuel's (step) mother by Indenture the 6th of November 1695 granted and conveyed to a certain John Dorsey of Baltimore County Brother of the said Edward Dorsey and to his assigns all the severall Lotts lying in the Towne and port aforesaid, number 69, 66, 65, 76, 77, 68, 71, 72, 73, 74, and part of a Lott adjoining to Mr. Proctors Remainder of that Lot whereon the Hon. and the then Governor lived together with all the buildings on them or any of them Erected and that the said John Dorsey his heirs and assigns should stand and be thereof seized to the use in the said Indenture expressed that is to say lots 66 & 69 and houses thereon to the use of *Edward Dorsey Eldest son* of the said Edward Dorsey his heirs and assigns forever and that part of the Lott adjoining to Proctors and houses thereon where the Governor dwelt to the use of *Samuel Dorsey second son* of the said Edward Dorsey the father his heirs and assigns forever, and the other lotts and houses for the use of the other children. Soon after Edward Dorsey the eldest son Died without issue whereby your orator or his next brother and heir became Lawfully entitled to same Lotts 66 & 69 with houses thereon and your orator further sets forth that in the year 1704 his said father Edward Dorsey having a great necessity for money petitioned the Assembly that a Bill might be past to permit him to sell all the said Lotts and houses for use and benefit of his children without ye consent of ye Complt then of full age. Samuel stated that he would not consent to the breaking of the entail until assured that his portion of the money from the sale would be given him after which assurance the Act was passed. He added that his father had conveyed said houses and Lotts to Charles Carrol and Wm Bladen and their heirs for 150 pounds Sterling.

John Israel, answering this complaint, declared that he did not know that Col. Edward Dorsey had such a necessity for money in 1704, but he did know that he asked the Court to permit the breaking of the entail of certain lots in Bloomsberry Square, reserving a moiety of these lots to William Bladen and Charles Carrol and that William Bladen had given Col. Edward Dorsey a note for 150 pounds Sterling payable in 3 installments, no payment to be made until the London Fleets next sailing. He further said that soon after selling the Lotts Col. Edward Dorsey died having previously made over to his brother John Dorsey much of his property in trust for his children, and that neither he John Israel, nor Margaret his wife had received one farthering from William Bladen, nor had he been asked to give them one, for no payment was to be made by William Bladen until the fleet sailed.

William Bladen then declared that though he was not bound to pay until the sailing of the fleet, he had been willing to pay part of the debt to Samuel, but that he had met Col. John Hammond and Col. John Freeman, who had told him not to pay until due, that Samuel was an idle young Ladd, who had over reached his father. (*Chanc. Rec. P.C*, f. 779) (See page 35)

Sarah Wyatt, the first wife of Col. Edward Dorsey, was the daughter of Nicholas Wyatt and probably of his wife Damaris, who had been previously married. Sarah signed her name with that of her husband on an administration bond in 1687, showing that she was a woman of education. (See page 26) She inherited a number of tracts of land from her father, which upon her death descended to her eldest son Edward Dorsey Jr., and when he died to his next brother Samuel. The tracts which she inherited were Wyatt's Neck, Wyatt's Hills, Wyatt's Ridge, and Bear Ridge. (*A.A. Co. Deeds* W.T. No. 2, folios 517, 574) Sarah and Edward were married by 1670 (See page 10) and she died about 1692, leaving two daughters and six sons.

The parentage of Margaret Lacon, second wife of Col. Edward Dorsey, is unknown. There were several immigrants who came to America by this name and settled in Barbados and Virginia. Francis Lacon witnessed the will of Thomas Pierce in 1707, Cecil County, Maryland, and a Francis Lacon died in Prince William County, Virginia, leaving a will dated 1744.

Just why the name Lacon was confused with Larkin had not been discovered. Col. Edward Dorsey and his wife Margaret named one of their sons Lacon, and his name always appeared as Lacon on the land deeds. Furthermore, Edward Dorsey Jr. and Francis Dorsey, sons of Col. Edward and Margaret Dorsey, each named a son Lacon, and John Israel, who married Margaret Dorsey, widow of Col. Edward Dorsey, called his eldest son, John Lacon Israel. He was always known by his full name. (See pages 69,71,239)

The name Larkin came into the Dorsey family through Rebecca, daughter of John Larkin, who as widow of Thomas Lightfoot, married Thomas Hammond, son of Maj. Genl John Hammond. Their descendants married into the family.

Margaret signed her name with that of Edward Dorsey on a deed in 1700, which shows that she was a woman of education. (See page 17) She died in 1707.

Children of Col. Edward and Sarah (Wyatt) Dorsey:
(Named in father's will and in deeds)

1. Edward[3] Dorsey Jr., b. bef. 1677; d. unm.
2. Sarah Dorsey, b. bef. 1677, m. (1) John Norwood
   m. (2) John Petticoat
3. Hannah Dorsey, b. c 1679, m. Joseph Howard
4. Samuel Dorsey, b. c 1682, m. Jane ______
5. Joshua Dorsey, b. 1686, m. Ann Ridgely
6. John Dorsey, b. 1688, m. Honor Sta ____ (Stafford)
7. Nicholas Dorsey, b. c 1690, m. Frances Hughes
8. Benjamin Dorsey, b. c 1692; d. unm.

Children of Col. Edward and Margaret (Lacon) Dorsey:
(Named in father's will)

9. Lacon Dorsey, b. c 1694; d. underage
10. Francis Dorsey, b. c 1696, m. Elizabeth Baker
11. Charles Dorsey, b. c 1698, m. Ann ______
12. Edward Dorsey Jr., b. c 1700, m. Phebe ______
13. Ann Dorsey, b. c 1702, m. John Hammond

EDWARD DORSEY JR.

1. EDWARD[3] DORSEY JR. (Col. Edward,[2] Edward[1])
   b. bef. 1677; d. 1703 Anne Arundel County

Edward Dorsey Jr. was the eldest son of Col. Edward and Sarah Dorsey, and one of the children mentioned in connection with the settlement of the estate of Nicholas Wyatt in 1677. (See page 13)

On January 4, 1700, Edward Dorsey Jr., Major John Hammond, and Capt. Charles Hammond were

SIGNATURES OF COL. EDWARD DORSEY AND HIS WIFE SARAH
AND FOUR OF THEIR CHILDREN
AND THREE OF THE CHILDREN OF EDWARD DORSEY AND HIS WIFE MARGARET
From Testamentary Papers Filed in the Hall of Records, Annapolis, Maryland

appointed by Col. Edward Dorsey as trustees to look after five of his younger sons and the plantations which were to be theirs at the age of 16 years. (*Prov. Ct. Rec. T.L. No. 2,* f. 164) (See page 17)

Upon the death of his mother Sarah Dorsey, Edward Dorsey Jr., as the eldest son of Edward and Sarah Dorsey, inherited his mother's part of the estate of her father Nicholas Wyatt.

He was possessed of this land about six years when he died intestate, whereupon the said land became the right of his brother Samuel Dorsey as heir at law. (*A.A. Co. Deeds* W.T. No. 2, Folios 316, 430, 517, 574)

The right to administer upon the estate of his brother Edward Dorsey Jr. was turned over by Samuel Dorsey to his father Col. Edward Dorsey on December 3, 1703. (*Test. Proc. 20,* f. 15) (See page 23)

The inventory of the estate of Edward Dorsey Jr. was taken by Silvester Welsh and Joseph Howard on April 8, 1704. It included a horse called Sparke, 2 gold rings, a silver headed cane, Testament, and bible, parcel of books, furniture etc., and 7 servants at his own house, and furniture and stock at the upper Plantation and at the Round Bay Plantation. (*Wills 3,* f. 530)

SARAH DORSEY

2. SARAH[3] DORSEY (Col. Edward[2], Edward[1])
   b. bef. 1677; d. after 1727 Baltimore County
   m. (1) c 1695 John Norwood; d. bef. 1700 Anne Arundel County

Sarah Dorsey was probably the eldest daughter of Col. Edward and Sarah Dorsey, and one of the children mentioned in connection with the settlement of the estate of Nicholas Wyatt in 1677. (See page 13) She was left by the will of her uncle Joshua Dorsey in 1687, twenty shillings to buy her a ring, and from her father she inherited a large silver cup in 1704.

John Norwood, the husband of Sarah, was the son of John Norwood, who died in Calvert County in 1673, and Elizabeth, his wife. He was the grandson of Capt. John Norwood, who died in Anne Arundel County in 1672. (See page 206)

He is named in the will of Robert Taylor of Calvert County in 1681, which reads,

> "I give unto John Norwood and Mary Norwood 1 cow and one yearling, for each of them and ye same to be delivered unto them at ye appraisement of my estate, and ye same to runne upon the plantation and they to enjoy and have all ye increase when they come att age and if either of them should die before they come att age the survivor to enjoy the same." (*Wills 4,*f. 73)

Sarah and John Norwood were living in Annapolis in 1695, where he had built a house upon land reserved for Publick builders in opposition to the Act of Assembly of this Province. (*Arch. of Md.* XIX, 230)

He died before 1700, for on December 10, 1700, Sarah Norwood, widow of John Norwood late of Anne Arundel County deceased, asked for letters of administration on his estate. (*Test. Proc. 18B,* f. 24) The inventory of his goods was taken December 16, 1700. (*Invts. & Accts. 20,* f. 157) Sarah Norwood appeared as administratrix of John Norwood deceased, on April 10, 1702. (*Test. Proc. 19A,* f. 95)

In the settlement of the estate of Richard Beard of Anne Arundel County, who died in 1703, the names of John and Andrew Norwood are found among the list of those owing tobacco to the estate. (*Prov. Ct. Judg. P.L. No. 1,*f. 21)

Children of John and Sarah (Dorsey) Norwood:

1. John Norwood, b. c 1692, m. Rachel Lawrence, widow of Benjamin
2. Phillip Norwood, bapt. Feb. 5, 1706 (*St. A.*) m. Comfort ________
3. Samuel Norwood, bapt. Feb. 5, 1706 (*St. A.*) m. Mary Mulikan

Sarah Norwood, widow of John, m. (2) bef. 1702 John Petticoat (*A.A. Co. Judg. G, f.* 163) b. 1699 (*A.A. Co. Deeds R.D. No. 2, f.* 120)

On October 1, 1702, Mrs. Sarah Petticoat, lately called Sarah Norwood the executrix of John Norwood late of Anne Arundel County deceased, filed an account of his estate. (*Invts. & Accts. 22, f.* 40) The final account was given by John Petticoat administrator of John Norwood deceased and Sarah, his wife, on February 25, 1703/4. (*Wills 3, f.* 131)

John Petticoat is thought to have been the son of William Petticoat transported into Maryland by Cornelius Howard before 1667, for whom a tract of land called Petticoat's Rest was laid out on the south side of the Severn River. This tract he sold to Thomas Freeborne of the Severn, cooper, June 13, 1684/5. Edward Dorsey was a witness to the deed. (*A.A. Co. Deeds I.H. No. 3, f.* 16)

In a deposition given by John Petticoat in June 1729 regarding the boundary line of Crouchfield owned by Caleb Dorsey, he asserted that he was about 60 years old, and that about 27 years past when he was at work in the woods for one Edward Dorsey near the place he now is at, that one John Howard told him his bound tree stood near that place, but he saw no bound tree, but thought it stood near the place where Richard Warfield declares. He signed with his mark, John I.P. Petticoat. (*A.A. Co. Deeds R.D. No. 2, f.* 120)

According to this deposition, it appears that the Dorseys and Petticoats were close neighbors and that John Petticoat was working for Col. Edward Dorsey around the time he married his daughter Sarah, then a widow.

After the death of Sarah's eldest brother, Edward Dorsey Jr., she and John Petticoat received their share of his estate. (*Test. Proc. 21, f.* 3) On October 6, 1704, John Petticoat of Baltimore County purchased 70 acres of Wyatt's Ridge from Samuel Dorsey, and on January 22, 1707, John Petticoat and Sarah, his wife, of Baltimore County and Samuel Dorsey of Anne Arundel County sold the entire tract of Wyatt's Ridge, 225 acres, to Amos Garret. The deed was signed with the marks of John and Sarah. (*A.A. Co. Deeds W.T. No. 2,* folios 316, 574)

On June 10, 1717, a warrant was granted John Pettycoat, Baltimore County, for 300 acres of land, 150 acres of which he laid out in Pettycourt's Addition and 150 acres in Pettycourt's Benefit on the north side of the main falls of Patapsco River on a draught of Ben's Run. (*Patents, I.L. No. A, f.* 276)

On April 25, 1718, a tract called Poplar Spring Garden was patented to John Petticoat, (*Patents C.E. No. 1, f.* 252) which tract John and Sarah Petticoat sold to Pleasance Dorsey, November 29, 1720. The same day, they sold to the said Pleasance Dorsey sundry goods for 15 pounds. John Petticoat signed with his mark, I.P. (*Balt. Co. Deeds T.R. No. DS, f.* 185)

On November 1, 1725, a warrant for 200 acres was granted to John Petticoat Jr., Baltimore County, 100 acres of which he assigned to his father John Petticoat Sr., November 4, 1726. He signed as John Petticoat Jr. (*Warrants C.C, f.* 202)

Following this, John Petticoat and Sarah had difficult times, for the records state that on October 13, 1726, John Petticoat was a languishing prisoner in the goal, for debt, and a petition was filed for his relief. This petition was put off from time to time until at last one interceding for John Petticoat and others bearing the same fate, stated that imprisonment was doing no good to the creditors or families, the later being fit objects for charity, and the prisoners would gladly make over to their creditors, all their estate for their freedom.

They were later commanded by the court to make over everything excepting the wearing apparel of wife and children to their creditors. John Petticoat was still in prison in 1727. (*Arch. of Md.* XXVI, 11, 55, 62, 63, 95)

On July 7, 1737, John Peddicord, Baltimore County, planter mortgaged to Richard Gist, Baltimore merchant, 3 mares, 4 cows, a heifer, 3 steers, and three good hogsheads of Tobacco to be shipped by the said Gist to any merchant in London and to continue to do this until the proceeds shall be sufficient to discharge the debt of £36/8/4. John Petticoat signed with his mark, I.P. (*Balt. Co. Deeds I.S. No. IK, f.* 470)

Children of John and Sarah (Dorsey) Petticoat:

1. John[4] Petticoat, bapt. Feb. 5, 1706 (*St. A.*), b. c 1702
2. William Petticoat, b. c 1703
3. Keturah Petticoat, bapt. Feb. 5, 1706 (*St. A.*)
4. Nathan Petticoat, b. c 1710, m. Sarah ______
5. Nicholas Petticoat, b. c 1712, m. Ann Jacks
6. Dorsey Petticoat, b. c 1714, m. Sarah ______

1. JOHN[4] NORWOOD (Sarah[3] (Dorsey) Norwood, Col. Edward,[2] Edward[1])
b. c 1692; d. 1737 Anne Arundel County
m. c 1726 Rachel (Marriarte) Lawrence, widow of Benjamin

On January 4, 1713, John Norwood and John Israel were witnesses to the will of Henry Knowles of Baltimore County. (*Wills 13, f.* 705)

John Norwood also witnessed the Deed of Conveyance, when Pleasance Dorsey bought Poplar Spring Garden, March 29, 1720, from John Petticoat. (*Balt. Co. Deeds T.R. No. DS, f.* 185)

With Rachel, his wife, administratrix of the estate of her late husband, Benjamin Lawrence, he filed an account of said estate, September 13, 1726. (*Accts. 7, f.* 522)

Being in debt to Phillip Hammond, John Norwood made a deed February 2, 1730/1, making over to his brother Samuel Norwood, who at his insistence and request, had paid to Phillip Hammond 30 shillings and 11 pence, 947 pounds of tobacco and other personal estate. (*A.A. Co. Deeds I.H. T.I. No. 1, f.* 120)

The paying of this debt did not keep him out of prison, for on September 3, 1731, a petition was filed for the release of John Norwood of Anne Arundel County, seconded by the approval of the sheriffs of Anne Arundel and Prince George's Counties. (*Arch. of Md.* XXXVII, 262)

He made another deed the 9th of December 1734 -

> "I John Norwood am Indebted to Phillip Hammond & Company, Merchant for 17 pounds, 2 sh, 5 pence Sterling, and Whereas Phillip Hammond hath promised and contracted to supply me with coarse goods and common necessities such as I may have occasion for towards the support of myself and family to the value of 12 pounds, 17 sh, 7 pence Sterling upon condition that I said John Norwood make safe that amount. Now know that I John Norwood in consideration of whole sum sold to Phillip Hammond 30 bushels of corn also other crops upon the plantation where I at present reside..."
> Wit: John Howard, Mary Israel (*A.A. Co. Deeds R.D. No. 2, f.* 180)

John Norwood died in 1737 intestate. His administration bond was exhibited by Rachel Norwood, with Thomas Todd and John Dorsey Jr., of Anne Arundel County his securities, on April 12, 1737. (*Test. Proc. 30, f.* 262) His inventory was signed by Samuel Norwood and Benjamin Lawrence as nearest of kin. Rachel Norwood, administratrix of John Norwood late of Anne Arundel County, being of the people called Quakers, affirmed the inventory, which included his servants William and Margaret Middleton. (*Invts. 22, f.* 256)

Rachel Norwood, widow of John, was the daughter of Edward and Honor Marriarte and was left real estate in the will of her mother in 1701. (*Wills 11, f.* 21)

By her husband Benjamin Lawrence to whom she was married in 1701, she had:
(Births from Thomas Book - taken from Quaker Records)

1. Elizabeth Lawrence, b. Dec. 8, 1702
2. Benjamin Lawrence, b. Jan. 27, 1704/5, m. Ruth Dorsey (See page 53)
3. Sophia Lawrence, b. June 2, 1707
4. Levin Lawrence, b. Mar. 6, 1711/2, m. Susannah Dorsey (See page 55)
5. Margaret Lawrence, b. June or Jan. 11, 1716/7
6. Dorsey Lawrence, b. Dec. 12, 1717; d. 1756

Children of John and Rachel, if any, are unknown.

2. PHILLIP^4 NORWOOD (Sarah^3 (Dorsey) Norwood, Col. Edward,^{2} Edward^1)
b. c 1694, d. 1733 Anne Arundel County
m. Comfort ________

Phillip Norwood moved with his mother, step-father, John Petticoat, brothers, and half brothers from Anne Arundel County to Baltimore County, and is found on records in both counties.

On July 21, 1724, he bought from John Dorsey 148 acres of a tract called Desart, which lay on the west side of the north branch of the Patuxent River beginning at a bounded white oak of Thomas Brown's land. This tract had been granted to Thomas Blackwell, Innholder, late of Anne Arundel County, on June 12, 1696, and bequeathed unto said John Dorsey by the last will of Thomas Blackwell. (*Balt. Co. Deeds I.S. No. H,* f. 179)

In 1726 Phillip Norwood of Anne Arundel County mortgaged part of this land to Phillip Hammond, also 25 head of cattle, one old steer with the mark of Nicholas Dorsey and Phillip Norwood and other personal estate. (*A.A. Co. Deeds S.Y. No. 1,* f. 335)

On March 3, 1727, Phillip Norwood of Baltimore County mortgaged the above land to Richard Bennet of Queen Anne County, (*Prov. Ct. Rec. P.L. No. 6,* f. 187) and on November 26, 1732, Phillip Norwood of Anne Arundel County states that the mortgage made to Phillip Hammond November 10, 1727 for 180 acres of Desart had been paid. (*A.A. Co. Deeds I.H.T.I.* No. 1, f. 519)

Phillip Norwood died in 1733 intestate. His inventory was appraised by John Dorsey Jr. and Richard Gassaway, May 22, 1733. Samuel Norwood signed as a relation. Phillip Hammond declared the inventory was true, February 2, 1746. (*Invts. 36,* f. 36)

3. SAMUEL^4 NORWOOD (Sarah^3 (Dorsey) Norwood, Col. Edward,^{2} Edward^1)
b. c 1692; d. after 1756
m. April 21, 1730 Mary Mulikan (A.H.)

With his mother, step-father and brothers, Samuel Norwood moved from Anne Arundel County to Baltimore County. On July 10, 1725, he was granted 100 acres of land called Norwood's Delight, by virtue of a warrant dated March 13, 1722. (*Patents P.L. No. 6,* f. 318) This land was laid out for him on the north side of the main falls of the Patapsco River at the head of Brice's Great Run by John Dorsey Depty Surveyor. (*Patents I.L. No. A,* f. 557)

On June 30, 1725, he was living in Anne Arundel County, and as Samuel Norwood of Anne Arundel County, sold the above tract to (his half brother) William Petticoat.
(*Balt. Co. Deeds I.S. No. H,* f. 244)

At the request of his brother John Norwood, who was indebted to Phillip Hammond, he paid a debt of 30 pounds, 11 sh, and on February 2, 1730/1, received by deed from his brother John Norwood, his white woman Eleanor Barry, 947 pounds of tobacco, and other personalty.
(*A.A. Co. Deeds I.H.T.I. No. 1,* f. 120)

He signed, as next of kin, the inventories of his brother John in 1737, and his brother Phillip in 1733. (*Invts. 22,* f. 256; *Invts. 36,* f. 36)

On May 10, 1743, he sold cattle to John Dorsey, and on August 20, 1751 he sold to Richard Snowden for 200 pounds of tobacco, the crops on his plantation. (*A.A. Co. Deeds R.B. No. 1,* f. 281; *A.A. Co. Deeds R.B. No.3,* f. 411)

On September 22, 1753, Samuel Norwood for 13 pounds, 18 sh, sold to his son James Norwood his right and title in his dwelling plantation, as his son had paid that amount to Richard Snowden, to whom his father was indebted. (*A.A. Co. Deeds B.B. No. 1,* f. 232)

On March 6, 1756, he sold his crops to Robert Davis. The witnesses were Henry Howard and Lancelot Todd. (*A.A. Co. Deeds B.B. No. 1,* f. 154) His name is not found upon the records after this time.

Mary Norwood, wife of Samuel, was the daughter of James and Charity (Belt) Mullikin, and grandaughter of John Belt and his wife, Elizabeth. She is named in the will of her father James Mullikin of Prince George's County, March 4, 1739. (*Wills 22*, f. 179)

Children of Samuel and Mary (Mullikin) Norwood:
(Named in deed)

1. James[5] Norwood, m. Elizabeth ______
   James Norwood sold Charity's Purchase and James' Lott on the Patuxent River, October 30, 1771. Elizabeth, his wife, signed. (*A.A. Co. Deeds I.B. No. 3*, f. 222)
   Perhaps others

1. JOHN[4] PETTICOAT JR. (Sarah[3] (Dorsey) Petticoat. Col. Edward,[2] Edward[1])
   b. c 1702

John Petticoat Jr. was granted a warrant for 200 acres of land November 1, 1725, 100 acres of which he assigned to his father John Petticoat Sr., November 4, 1726. (*Warrants C.C.* f. 202)

In 1720 Petticoat's Addition containing 150 acres was granted John Petticoat Jr., and in 1724, Petticoat's Wish containing 180 acres. (*Patents P.L. No. 5*, f. 403)

On June 29, 1725, he paid a bond which he had given to Zebediah Baker, for which he had given the tract called Petticoat's Wish as security. (*Balt. Co. Deeds I.S.* No. H, f. 246) On February 2, 1726, John Petticoat Jr. sold to William Petticoat, Petticoat's Wish for 20 pounds silver, and states that there is no mortgage on it and that he hath full power to sell. (*Ibid.*, f. 334)

In 1745 one John Petticoat and several others petitioned to have an order of court for a road to be cleared from the main road against Robinson's Plantation the most convenient way to the church which is accordingly granted. (*Balt. Co. Ct. Proc.* November)

No further record.

2. WILLIAM[4] PETTICOAT (Sarah[3] (Dorsey) Petticoat, Col. Edward,[2] Edward[1])
   b. c 1703; d. 1776 Baltimore County
   m. Sarah ______

On January 30, 1725, William Petticoat bought from Samuel Norwood a tract of 100 acres called Norwood's Delight lying on the north side of the Patapsco River on Ben's Run. (*Balt. Co. Deeds I.S. No. H*, f. 244)

On February 2, 1726, William Petticoat purchased Petticoat's Wish of 100 acres from his brother John Petticoat Jr. (*Ibid.*, 234)

Petticoat's Banter, originally known as Petticoat's Wish, was resurveyed for William Petticoat on September 1, 1741, and patented Aug. 16, 1744. He mortgaged this tract to Stewart and Campbell, October 31, 1765. (*Balt. Co. Deeds B. No. P*, f. 203)

In 1733 William Petticoat was appointed overseer of the upper half of Soldier's Delight Hundred, and in 1734, he was appointed overseer of all roads in Soldier's Delight Hundred lying between the main falls and Gwinn Falls of the Patapsco River. (*Md. Hist. Mag.* XVI. 229)

The will of William Peddicoart made May 30, 1770 and proved July 26, 1776 left:

To six sons, Nathan, William, Jasper, Humphrey, and Caleb Peddicoart, all lands equally
To wife Sarah Peddicoart, all personal estate during life, at her decease to be sold and money equally divided among 6 children, Jasper, Humphrey, Nicholas, Altheia, Esther, and Caleb Peddicoart
To daughter Altheia Peddicoart, personalty
To sons Nicholas and Caleb Peddicoart, stock
To eldest son (unnamed), personalty
To daughter Cassandra Johnson, 25 pounds
Exrs: sons Jasper and Nicholas Peddicoart (*Wills 41*, f. 266)

Children of William and Sarah Peddicoart (Petticoat):
(Named in father's will)

1. Nathan[5] Petticoard (Petticoat), Washington Co., Md.
2. Jasper Petticoat, m. Oct. 8, 1785 Amelia Hobbs, dau. of Thomas, To Mont. Co.
3. Humphrey, m. Apr. 1, 1809 Elizabeth Hooker, Balt. Co.
4. Nicholas Petticoat
5. Altheia Petticoat
6. Esther Petticoat
7. Caleb Petticoat
8. Cassandra Petticoat, m. ______ Johnson
9. William Petticoat, d. 1779 (*Balt. Co. Wills 3, f.* 374)
   m. Sophia Barnes, who m. (2) Sept. 3, 1782 Thomas Greenwood (See page 53)

4. NATHAN[4] PETTICOAT (Sarah[3] (Dorsey) Petticoat, Col. Edward,[2] Edward[1])
b. c 1710; d. 1763 Frederick County
m. c 1738 Sarah ______

Nathan Pedycourt was in the French and Indian Wars under Capt. George Beall, Troop of Horse, 1748.

He died in 1762 intestate. (*Accts. 49, f.* 374)

Children of Nathan and Sarah Pettycoart - Petticoat:
(Births recorded in Rock Creek Church Register, Fred. Co., Md.)

1. William[5] Petticoat, b. Apr. 5, 1739
2. Basil Petticoat, b. July 2, 1740; d. 1767 (*Accts. 56, f.* 220)
3. Eleanor Petticoat, b. Apr. 2, 1744
4. Thomas Petticoat, b. Feb. 4, 1745

5. NICHOLAS[4] PETTICOAT (Sarah[3] (Dorsey) Petticoat, Col. Edward,[2] Edward[1])
b. c 1712, living in 1778
m. Dec. 23, 1735 Ann Jacks (*St. Paul's*)

On June 30, 1741, Nicholas Peddicoart, Anne Arundel County, conveyed to Charles Ridgely of Baltimore County, negro Tom and all tobacco on dwelling plantation. (*A.A. Co. Deeds R.B. No. 1, f.* 69)

Petticoat's Hope of 60 acres was surveyed for Nicholas Petticoat, Baltimore County, on the 20th of July, 1745. On November 5, 1755, he sold this tract to William Chamier and William Lux. (*Balt. Co. Deeds B.B. No. 1,f.* 178)

In 1768 he signed the petition for pardon of Abraham Becraft, Frederick County. (*Arch. of Md.* XXXII, 233)

Children, if any, are unknown

6. DORSEY[4] PETTICOAT (Sarah[3] (Dorsey) Petticoat, Col. Edward,[2] Edward[1])
b. c 1714
m. Sarah ______

In 1735 Dorsey Petticoat was appointed overseer of roads in room of John Hamilton. (*Balt. Ct. Rec. T.B. No. T.R, f.* 159)

On September 10, 1744, Pedicoard, originally called Friendly Purchase, was resurveyed for Dorsey Pedicoard. In 1749 he sold this tract to John Randall. Sarah, his wife, signed. (*Balt. Co. Deeds T.R. No. D,f.* 132)

This same year Dorsey Petticoat witnessed the will of Francis Dorsey.

Petticoat's Hole of 50 acres was surveyed for Dorsey Petticoat on August 20, 1760. The following year he sold Petticoat's Loose, originally called Petticoat's Hole to Frederick Shaclor. (*Balt. Co. Deeds B, No. 1,* f. 399)

In 1761 Petticoat's Meadows was surveyed for Dorsey Petticoat. In 1784 he sold this tract to John Foster. Sarah, his wife, signed. (*Balt. Co. Deeds W.G. No. S,* f. 589) In 1762 Dorsey Petticoat bought from Jeremiah Boring 518 acres, part of Boring's Range.
(*Balt. Co. Deeds B. No. K,* f. 435)

Children of Dorsey and Sarah Petticoat:

1. Dorsey^{5} Petticoat, m. Oct. 21, 1801 Ann Banks
   Perhaps others

HANNAH DORSEY

3. HANNAH^{3} DORSEY (Col. Edward,^{2} Edward^{1}.)
   b. c 1679; d. 1703/4 Anne Arundel County
   m. Joseph Howard, b. 1676; d. 1736 at Howard's Inheritance, Anne Arundel County

Hannah and Joseph Howard lived on Howard's Inheritance adjoining Hockley in the Hole, which he had inherited from his father, Cornelius Howard. (*Wills 2,* f. 207) Hannah died before October 1704, leaving three children, who were bequeathed 20 shillings each, in the will of her father, Col. Edward Dorsey. In 1703/4 Joseph Howard received Hannah's share of her brother Edward Dorsey's estate. (*Test. Proc. 21,* f. 3) He took up other tracts of land on both sides of Doughoregan Manor, which he gave to his sons.

Children of Joseph and Hannah (Dorsey) Howard:

1. Joseph^{4} Howard Jr., bur. Feb. 1, 1717 (*A.H.*)
2. Hannah Howard, b. c 1701, m. Richard Jacobs
3. Henry Howard, b. Jan. 14, 1703 (*A.H.*) m. Sarah Dorsey (See page 54)

Joseph Howard m. (2) Oct. 12, 1706 Ann Burrass (Burroughs) (*A.H.*); buried Oct. 24, 1707 (*A.H.*), widow of William (*Test. Proc.* 19, f. 266, part C)
m. (3) Sept. 28, 1708 Margery Keith (*St. A.*), d. 1739

In his will made June 6, 1736 and probated July 23, 1736 Joseph Howard left:

To son Henry Howard and heirs, 100 acres Kilhenny at Elkridge, 100 acres Howard's Package, 310 acres Second Discovery and personalty
To son Ephriam Howard, 500 acres of Discovery and personalty
To son Joseph Howard, 200 acres out of Discovery being a part of tract which Phillip Hammond claims as his, dwelling plantation Howard's Inheritance, south side Severn River, 30 acres Sarah's Inheritance and personalty
To son Cornelius Howard Jr. and heirs, residue of Discovery, 400 acres Howard's Purchase and personalty
To grandson Joseph Hitchings, 100 acres Second Discovery
To wife Margery Howard, daughters Sarah, Ruth Duvall, and Hannah Jacobs, personalty, after wife's thirds are deducted. Dr. Richard Hill to have care of son Joseph until 21 years of age.
Exrs: Wife and sons Henry, Ephriam, and Cornelius Howard. (*Wills 21,* f. 623)

Children of Joseph and Margery (Keith) Howard:
(Named in father's will)

1. Ruth^{4} Howard, bapt. Mar. 20, 1708 (*St. A.*), m. Oct. 1, 1724 Mareen Duvall Jr.
2. Margery Howard, m. _______ Hitchings
3. Ephriam Howard, b. Feb. 26, 1714 (*A.H.*), m. Martha _______
4. Cornelius Howard Jr., bapt. Feb. 1, 1717 (*A.H.*), m. Rachel Worthington
5. Sarah Howard, bapt. June 20, 17-- (*A.H.*), m. Edward Gaither
6. Joseph Howard Jr., d. 1783, m. Margaret Gaither

DORSEY FAMILY

2. HANNAH[4] HOWARD (Hannah[3] (Dorsey) Howard, Col. Edward,[2] Edward[1])
b. c 1701; d. bef. 1777 Anne Arundel County
m. June 1, 1718/9 Richard Jacobs (*St. A.*); d. 1779 Anne Arundel County

On November 20, 1725, Jacob's Improved Purchase containing 1,017 acres was resurveyed for Richard Jacobs on the west side of Curtis Creek. It was composed of three tracts, Coxes Range, Coxes Enlarged, and Jacob's Resurvey Contrived. (*Patents 6*, f. 166)

The will of Richard Jacobs made November 28, 1777 and proved June 25, 1779 left:

To maiden daughter Ann Jacobs, use of dwelling plantation during her natural life or until marriage, and 3 slaves
To Zachariah Jacobs, dwelling plantation, 592 acres with the condition he allow sister Ann to use same, also negroes
To sons John and Samuel Jacobs, and heirs of deceased son Joseph, each 1 shilling
To Dorsey Jacobs, 1 negro
To daughters Sarah Robinson, Hannah Hall, Rachel Fish, personalty
To daughter Susannah Pumphrey, 1 negro and increase to her son Richard Boone
To granddaughter Ann of Samuel, 1 negro
Residue of estate to be divided between Ann and Zachariah Jacobs
Exr: Zachariah Jacobs (*A.A. Co. Wills E.V. No. 1*, f. 95)

Children of Richard and Hannah (Howard) Jacobs:
(Named in father's will and parish registers)

1. Joseph[5] Jacobs, bapt. June 29, 1720 (*A.H.*); d. 1773 (*Wills 39*, f. 243)
m. Hannah Wright
2. Sarah Jacobs, b. June 12, 1722 (*A.H.*) m.____ Robinson
3. Hannah Jacobs, m.____ Hall
4. Richard Jacobs, b. Aug. 22, 1730 (*St. Mrgts.*); d. 1782 (*A.A. Co. Wills T.G. No. 1*, f. 94) m. Patience Stansbury
5. Samuel Jacobs, b. Apr. 11, 1734 (*St. Mrgts.*)
m. July 25, 1780 Elizabeth Gray
6. Susannah Jacobs, b. Dec. 23, 1736 (*St. Mrgts.*); d. 1823 (*A.A. Co. Wills J.G.E.V. No. 1*, f. 163)
m. (1) Nicholas Boone
(2) Samuel Fowler, d. 1789 intestate
(3) William Pumphrey, d. 1797 (*A.A. Co. Wills J.G. No. 1*, f. 630)
7. Ann Jacobs, b. Dec. 2, 1738 (*St. Mrgts.*) d. unm.
8. Rachel Jacobs, b. Oct. 18, 1740 (*St. Mrgts.*)
m. Benjamin Fish, d. 1790 (*A.A. Co. Wills J.G. No. 1*, f. 174)
9. John Jacobs, b. Nov. 29, 1742 (*St. Mrgts.*)
10. Zachariah Jacobs, twin, d. 1798 (*A.A. Co. Wills J.G. No. 2*, f. 19)
m. Feb. 7, 1793 Margaret Gambrill, who m. (2) Apr. 1, 1800 Joshua Powell
11. Elizabeth Jacobs, b. Apr. 11, 1745 (*St. Mrgts.*); d. bef. 1777
12. Dorsey Jacobs, b. May 19, 1746 (*St. Mrgts.*); d. 1804 (*A.A. Co. Wills J.G. No. 2*, f. 275)
m. Aug. 29, 1773 Ruth Merriken (*St. Mrgts.*)

SAMUEL DORSEY

4. SAMUEL[3] DORSEY (Col. Edward,[2] Edward[1])
b. c 1682 (of age 1703); d. 1724 Anne Arundel County
m. bef. 1715 Jane ____ d. bef. 1762

During his early years, Samuel Dorsey, with his brother Joshua and cousin Edward, served on a merchant ship under Capt. Richard Hill. (*Arch. of Md.* XXV, 596) Before Samuel came of age, his father gave him a plantation near the falls of the Patapsco River in Baltimore County, and by the will of his father in 1704, he inherited one silver hilted sword and all the remaining part of Major's Choice (200 acres), which on March 15, 1705/6 he conveyed to Samuel Norwood. (*Prov. Ct. Rec. T.L. No. 2, f.* 901)

He also, upon the death of his brother Edward Dorsey Jr., in 1703, came into possession of much of the estate left by his grandfather Nicholas Wyatt. (*Test. Proc. 20, f.* 15) (See page 27)

He exchanged with his brother Joshua Dorsey, on August 29, 1706, a tract called Bear Ridge formerly laid out for Nicholas Wyatt, for 180 acres of Major's Fancy, Anne Arundel County. On November 8, 1706, he sold the tracts, Wyatt's Neck and Wyatt's Hills to John Brice. The next year an indenture was made between Samuel Dorsey of Anne Arundel County planter and John Petticoate and Sarah, his wife, and Amos Garret, showing that 225 acres of the tract called Wyatt's Ridge, by the will of Nicholas Wyatt, or otherwise, became the right of Sarah Wyatt who married Edward Dorsey of the same county. After Sarah died the land became the right of her eldest son Edward Dorsey Jr., who being possessed thereof about 6 years died intestate, whereupon said 225 acres became the right of Samuel Dorsey his next brother (and grandson of said Nicholas Wyatt), who conveyed 70 acres of the tract to John Petticoat. The present indenture witnesses that Samuel Dorsey, John Petticoat and Sarah, his wife, for 80 pounds Sterling sell to Amos Garret 155 acres and 70 acres being 225 acres of Wyatt's Ridge. (*A.A. Co. Deeds W.T. No. 2,* folios 464, 430, 517, 316, 574)

The will of Amos Garret, merchant, dated September 4, 1714, mentions other tracts of land bought from Samuel Dorsey and John Petticoat in Anne Arundel County. (*Wills 19, f.* 353)

In 1706 Samuel Dorsey received 20 pounds rent for the house in which the courts were held. (*Arch. of Md.* XXVI, 586) (See page 19) On February 1, 1715/6, he sold the land on which this house stood, before it was burned, to Thomas Jones. (*A.A. Co. Deeds I.B. No. 2, f.* 25) (See page 16)

In 1711 he filed a claim against John Israel in connection with the settlement of his father, Col. Edward Dorsey's, estate. (*Chanc. Rec. P.C, f.* 779) (See page 24)

Samuel Dorsey was constable for Middle Neck Hundred, and on August 9, 1707, his petition to the Court for leave to be horse ranger for Anne Arundel County was granted. (*A.A. Co. Judg. T.B. No. 2, f.* 73) On March 26, 1714, he witnessed the will of his uncle John Dorsey of Baltimore County.

On March 23, 1718, Samuel Dorsey as heir at law to Sarah Dorsey, who was the only surviving daughter of Nicholas Wyatt, Anne Arundel County deceased, for 10 pounds money of Maryland sold to Mrs. Anne Bladen land called Gatenby surveyed for Thomas Gates and afterwards by conveyances descended to the said Samuel, the said tract of land lying on the south side of the Severn River on Dorsey's Creek containing 100 acres. Jane, wife of Samuel, signed.

(*A.A. Co. Deeds C.W. No. 1, f.* 24)

On July 2, 1719, as elder brother and heir at law to Benjamin Dorsey of Baltimore County deceased, Samuel Dorsey of the same county confirmed the conveyance of 200 acres of Long Reach by said Benjamin, on May 30, 1715, to Thomas Worthington. Jane, wife of Samuel, signed.

(*Balt. Co. Deeds T.R. No. DS, f.* 3)

On July 13, 1722, Samuel and Joshua Dorsey, planters, Baltimore County, for 4 pounds current money sold their right to one pew in the church of St. Anne's to Thomas Worthington and Nicholas Ridgely. (*St. Anne's Vestry Proc. f.* 70)

Samuel Dorsey died at the house of Richard Warfield where he made a nuncupative will on February 4, 1724. Richard Warfield and John Meek the testators testified that Samuel Dorsey declared that if he died in that sickness he appointed Mr. Edmund Benson his executor and they further declared that the said Samuel departed this life about two o'clock that morning.

(*Wills 18, f.* 342)

The inventory of his estate taken on May 20, 1725, was signed by John Dorsey son of Edward, and Jane Dorsey as kin. (*Invts. 10, f.* 360) The account of Edmund Benson administrator shows the value of the estate to be £93/10/11. (*Accts. 22, f.* 102)

Children of Samuel and Jane Dorsey:

1. Jane[4] Dorsey, m. Richard Ayton
2. Sarah Dorsey, b. May 16, 1716; d. Mar. 7, 1717 (*St. A.*)
3. Ann Dorsey, b. Aug. 21, 1718, bur. same day (*St. A.*)

Jane Dorsey, widow of Samuel, whose maiden name is unknown, m. (2) July 9, 1726 as second wife Henry Agton (*St. A.*), d. 1762

On March 15, 1727, Henry Ridgely Depty Surveyor of Anne Arundel County, resurveyed in the name of Henry Ayton and Jane, his wife, and *Jane Dorsey, the daughter and only child of Samuel Dorsey,* all that tract called Forster's Fancy taken up by Edward Dorsey as escheat land in 1700. This parcel of land containing 93 acres lying in Anne Arundel County on the south side of the Patapsco River near the head thereof, was to fall to Jane Dorsey at the death of Henry and Jane Ayton. (*Patents E.I. No. 1, f.* 28)

The will of Henry Ayton made May 5, 1762 and proved October 2, 1762 named his daughter Ann Regan, wife of Cornelius Regan, daughter-in-law Jane Dorsey, granddaughters Jane Shipley, wife of Richard Shipley, Elizabeth Ayton, and grandson Henry Ayton. Jane Ayton, daughter-in-law, and Richard Shipley to serve as executors. (*Wills 31, Pt. 2,* f. 731)

1. JANE[4] DORSEY (Samuel,[3] Col. Edward,[2] Edward[1])
   d. after 1673
   m. Richard Ayton, son of Henry; d. bef. 1762 Anne Arundel County

Jane Ayton came into possession of Foster's Fancy at the death of her mother and step-father. On June 19, 1763, Jane Ayton of Anne Arundel County, widow, formerly Jane Dorsey daughter of Samuel Dorsey deceased, sold to Charles Carrol, Foster's Fancy laid out for 98 acres, and whereas the said Jane party hereto, afterwards intermarried with Richard Ayton son of the aforesaid Henry Ayton, and the said Richard Ayton, Henry Ayton, and Jane his wife, are all dead and the said Jane Ayton party hereto is possessed of the tract of land...

(*Prov. Ct. Rec, D.D. No. 3,* f. 162)

Children of Richard and Jane (Dorsey) Ayton:
(Named in Henry Ayton's will)

1. Jane[5] Ayton, m. Richard Shipley
2. Elizabeth Ayton
3. Henry Ayton

CAPTAIN JOSHUA DORSEY

5. CAPTAIN JOSHUA[3] DORSEY (Col. Edward,[2] Edward[1])
   b. 1686 (*A.A. Co. Land Commissions I.B. No. 1,* f. 36)
   d. Nov. 8, 1747 (Q. Car.) at Major's Choice, Anne Arundel County
   m. May 16, 1711 Ann Ridgely (Q. Car.); d. Dec. 11, 1771

When a young boy, Joshua Dorsey, with his older brother Samuel, was apprenticed on merchant ships which went out from the port of Annapolis. (*Arch. of Md.* XXV, 596) Before he became of age in 1700, his father gave him 100 acres of Major's Choice in Baltimore County, and at the death of his father in 1705, he received the plantation known as Barnes Folly and 100 acres out of land called Long Reach, and also one horse's saddle, holster and pistol.

In 1703 Joshua Dorsey was willed by Capt. John Howard,

> "my silver-hilted Sword that is at John Greeniffe's house, that his father Dorsey gave me,"

and the same year he also received his share of his brother Edward Dorsey's estate. (*Wills 11,* f.405)

He took an active part in the affairs of the state. On October 30, 1711, he was commissioned Justice of Baltimore County, and again in 1714 and 1715. (*Balt. Co. Ct. Rec. I.S.B. II,* 446, 474, 625) In 1732 he was appointed one of the commissioners to buy the land and lay out the town of Elk Ridge Landing near the head of Patapsco River, and in 1742 he served as Captain of the Elk Ridge Militia. (*Arch. of Md.* XXXIX, 125, 42)

On August 29, 1706, he exchanged with his brother Samuel Dorsey a tract called Major's Fancy containing 180 acres, for 175 acres of Bear Ridge, which he later sold to Amos Garret. (*A.A. Co. Deeds P.K.* f. 311) On May 8, 1715, he bought for 40 pounds Sterling from his brother Benjamin Dorsey, 100 acres of Major's Choice, which was by deed of gift on April 9, 1700 given by Col. Edward Dorsey to his son Benjamin. This same year Joshua Dorsey and his wife, Ann, also sold 100 acres of the tract called Long Reach to Benjamin Dorsey. (*Balt. Co. Deeds T.R. No. A,* folios 338, 340)

On October 7, 1720, Brother's Partnership was patented to Joshua and John Dorsey on the west side of Good Range, Anne Arundel County, (*Patents E.I. No. 4, f.* 221) and on February 21, 1722, they were granted by patent a tract called Gore containing 135 acres, which they sold on April 26, 1725 to Caleb Dorsey. Oner, wife of John, and Ann, wife of Joshua, consented to the sale. (*Balt. Co. Deeds I.S. No. H,* f. 41)

In 1722 Joshua Dorsey and his brother Samuel sold their right to one pew in St. Anne's Church, and Joshua became a communicant of Queen Caroline Parish and occupied pew No. 1, in Christ Church with his brother-in-law Henry Ridgely. On June 15, 1751, after it had been decided to build a Chapel of Ease for the inhabitants of the upper part of the parish, Joshua Dorsey and Henry Ridgely, churchwardens of Christ Church, were appointed to let out the building. (*Vestry Proc.*)

Toward the end of his career Joshua Dorsey became very much indisposed, suffering from what he termed fits, which may have been vertigo. However, he no longer felt able to hold public office and asked to be relived from his duties. (*Balt. Co. Ct. Rec. I.S.B.*II,f. 625)

The will of Joshua Dorsey made November 14, 1747 and proved June 2, 1747 left:

To his wife Ann, 250 acres, my dwelling plantation called Major's Choice
To son Henry Dorsey, 2 tracts, one called Anglia containg 20 acres, the other Dorsey's Hills containing 200 acres both lying in the county
To son Philemon Dorsey one-half tract called Brother's Partnership taken up jointly between my brother John Dorsey and myself, 632 acres
To son Joshua Dorsey, 250 acres bequeathed unto my son Joshua Dorsey
To son Nicholas Dorsey, tract Huntington Quarter, 256 acres, original tract was some years ago resurveyed by my brother-in-law Henry Ridgely
To daughters Rachel Warfield and Elizabeth Dorsey, 20 pounds Sterling each
To daughter Ann Dorsey, slaves
To son Charles Dorsey, my dwelling plantation and 250 acres
Names his youngest children, Nicholas and Charles Dorsey to be supported with their provisions at their own stock
Exrs: Two eldest sons and wife Ann (*Wills 25,* f. 315)

Ann Dorsey, wife of Joshua, was the granddaughter of Col. Henry Ridgely, d. 1710, Justice of Anne Arundel County, Capt. of Foot, Major and Colonel, and daughter of Henry Ridgely Jr., who died 1700 and Katherine Greenberry, daughter of Col. Nicholas Greenberry, Keeper of the Great Seal, and acting governor of the Province of Maryland. Ann survived her husband some twenty years. She inherited one-half of the tract called Huntington Quarter, which was taken up by her father and grandfather. (*Wills 6,* f. 371)

In her will made October 17, 1771 and proved December 11, 1771 Ann Dorsey left:

To daughter Sarah Dorsey, 80 pounds, negro Lucy and 4 children, horse and saddle
To son Joshua, 35 pounds
To son Nicholas Dorsey, right and title to land he now lives on, Huntington Quarter
To granddaughter Sarah Ridgely, 12 pounds
Remainder of estate to be divided into 8 equal parts and given to each of children vizt: Philemon, Joshua, Nicholas, Elizabeth Dorsey, Rachel Warfield, Sarah Dorsey,

and 1/8 to 4 grandchildren, children of son Henry, Charles, Vachel, Henry, Ariana, the remaining 1/8th part to be divided among children of my deceased daughter Ann Ridgely. (*Wills 38*, f. 444)

Children of Joshua and Ann (Ridgely) Dorsey:
(Births recorded in Queen Caroline Parish Register)

1. Henry[4] Dorsey, b. Nov. 8, 1712, m. Elizabeth Worthington
2. Capt. Philemon Dorsey, b. Jan. 20, 1714/5, m. (1) Catherine Ridgely
   (2) Rachel Lawrence
3. Rachel Dorsey b. July 6, 1717, m. John Warfield
4. Elizabeth Dorsey, b. Mar. 6, 1719/20, m. John Dorsey (See page 158)
5. Joshua Dorsey, b. Mar. 6, 1722/3; d. 1790 unm. (*A.A. Co. Wills J.G. No. 1*, f. 142) The settlement of his estate names the children of his sister Ann Ridgely (See page 47)
6. Nicholas Dorsey, b. June 2, 1725, m. Elizabeth Worthington
7. Catherine Dorsey, b. Dec. 21, 1727; d. Apr. 20, 1746 unm.
8. Ann Dorsey, b. Oct. 15, 1730, m. Henry Ridgely
9. Sarah Dorsey, b. May 27, 1733, living in 1771
10. Charles Dorsey, b. Nov. 11, 1736; d. bef. 1770 unm.

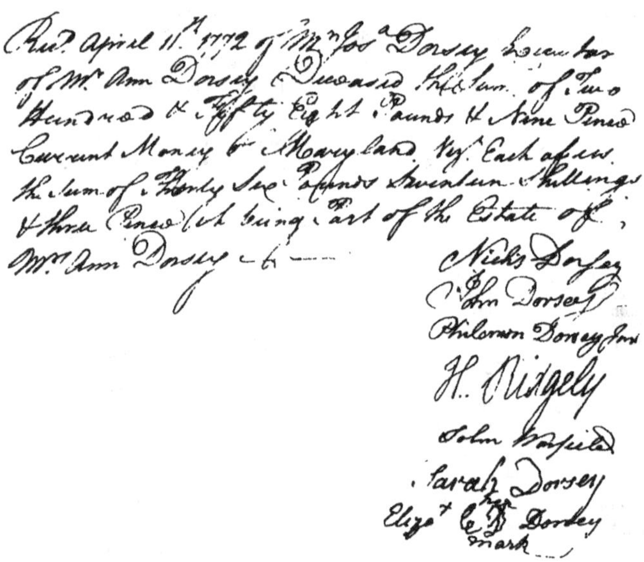

SIGNATURES OF SONS, DAUGHTERS, AND SONS-IN-LAW OF MRS. ANN DORSEY, WIFE OF JOSHUA
Testamentary Papers Filed in the Hall of Records, Annapolis, Maryland

1. HENRY[4] DORSEY (Joshua,[3] Col. Edward,[2] Edward[1])
b. Nov. 8, 1712; d. Feb. 1770 at Dorsey's Hills, Anne Arundel County
m. July 31, 1735 (*Q. Car.*) Elizabeth Worthington, b. 1717; d. 1776

Henry Dorsey inherited from his father Joshua Dorsey in 1747 two tracts, one called Anglia of 20 acres, the other Dorsey's Hills containing 200 acres.

He was a communicant of Christ Church and occupied pew No. 2 with Basil Dorsey.

The will of Henry Dorsey made February 12, 1770 and probated June 14, 1770 left:

To son Joshua Dorsey, 300 acres of land with plantation included where mother now lives to be laid out above my lower meadow, and 2 negroes
To son Thomas Dorsey, 60 acres, Dorsey's Addition and two negroes
To son Nicholas Dorsey, ½ of my land with plantation purchased from Samuel Mansel and if he die without heirs land to go to son Charles. Also 2 negroes, stock and furniture
To son Charles Dorsey, remaining ½ land purchased from Samuel Mansel
To son Vachel Dorsey, all lands where son Joshua now keeps his quarter containing 518 acres, negroes and furniture
To son Henry Dorsey, remainder of land where I now live
To daughters Ann Warfield, Elizabeth Dorsey, and Arranah Dorsey, negroes and furniture
To wife Elizabeth, remainder of estate, to receive full part of brother Charles estate at my mother's death
Wit: Henry Griffith
Nicholas Dorsey
Caleb Dorsey (*Wills 38,* f. 4)

Elizabeth, widow of Henry Dorsey, was the daughter of Thomas and Elizabeth (Ridgely) Worthington. In 1753 she inherited from her father 368 acres of Worthington's Range.
(*Wills 28,* f. 445) (See page 183)

In her will made October 2, 1775 and proved February 19, 1776, she left the plantation and personalty to sons Joshua, Thomas, Nicholas, Vachel, Henry, and Charles Dorsey, and daughters Ann Warfield, wife of Davidge Warfield, Elizabeth Warfield, wife of Elisha, Sarah Dorsey, wife of Benjamin, and Ariana Dorsey.
Exr: Nicholas Dorsey (*Wills 40,* f. 699)

Children of Henry and Elizabeth (Worthington) Dorsey:
(Births recorded in Queen Caroline Parish Register)

1. Joshua[5] Dorsey, b. July 8, 1736; d. 1799, m. Feb. 6, 1759 Elizabeth Hall
2. Thomas Dorsey, b. Mar. 15, 1737/8, m. Mary Warfield, dau. of Benjamin (See page 227)
3. Henry Dorsey, b. Feb. 22, 1739/40; d. Mar. 3, 1761 unm.
4. Anne (Nancy) Dorsey, b. Feb. 7, 1741/2, m. Davidge Warfield
5. Elizabeth Dorsey, b. Feb. 15, 1743/4, m. Elisha Warfield
6. Sarah Dorsey, b. Apr. 22, 1746, m. Benjamin Dorsey (See page 143)
7. Nicholas Dorsey, b. Jan. 8, 1750; d. Oct. 7, 1788, m. Lucy Sprigg (See below)
8. Charles Dorsey, b. Oct. 20, 1752; d. 1776 unm. (*Wills 40,* f. 705)
9. Ariana Dorsey, b. Feb. 24, 1755, m. Benjamin Warfield
10. Vachel Dorsey, b. Mar. 15, 1758; d. 1805 (*A.A. Co. Test. Papers,* Box 68, Folder 75), m. Feb. 24, 1778 Elizabeth Battee
11. Henry Dorsey.

7. NICHOLAS[5] DORSEY (Henry,[4] Joshua,[3] Col. Edward,[2] Edward[1])
b. Jan. 8, 1750; d. Oct. 7, 1788 Anne Arundel County
m. 1773/4 Lucy Belt Sprigg, b. 1752; d. Dec. 1, 1825 (posthumus daughter of Col. Edward Sprigg, Prince George's County) (*Chanc. Rec.* 25, f. 212)

Nicholas Dorsey inherited from his father Henry Dorsey in 1770 one half of his father's land with the plantation purchased from Samuel Mansel, 2 negroes, stock and furniture.

DORSEY FAMILY

Nicholas Dorsey son of Henry took the Oath of Fidelity and Support to the State of Maryland in 1778. He was killed in a fall from his horse the 9th of October in 1788. The inventory of his estate was taken in 1788 (*A.A. Co. Test. Papers*, Box 19, Folder 34)

Children of Nicholas and Lucy (Sprigg) Dorsey:
(Family Records and *Chanc. Rec.* 41, folios 30-57)

1. Francis[6] Dorsey, b. Mar. 27, 1774
   m. (1) Nov. 18, 1805 Sarah Forbes, b. Aug. 25, 1782
   Francis and his brother John went to Georgia about 1800

   Children:

   1. John[7] Dorsey, b. Aug. 16, 1806
   2. Eliza Dorsey, b. June 2, 1808
   3. Edgar Dorsey, b. May 3, 1811
   4. Lucyan Dorsey, b. Dec. 25, 1812
   5. Margaretha Dorsey, b. Feb. 25, 1813; d. Jan. 31, 1914, m._____ Newson
   6. Nelson Dorsey, b. Apr. 5, 1816

   m. (2) Eliza Crowe, Maryland
2. Dr. Frederick[6] Dorsey, b. May 4, 1776; d. Oct. 26, 1858 Washington County, Md.
   m. Sarah (Sally) Clagett (J. Thomas Scharf, *History of Western Maryland* Vol. II, 1134-1137)
   Children:
   1. Richard[7] Dorsey, d.y.
   2. Freeland Dorsey, d.y.
   3. Lucy Dorsey
   4. John Clagett Dorsey, b. 1805, m. 1828 Louisa Hughes
3. John[6] Dorsey, b. Aug. 3, 1780, m. Mary Phillips (See page 41)
4. Roderick[6] Dorsey, b. Jan. 1, 1784; d. 1858 Frederick Co.
   m. Apr. 11, 1821 Rachel Hobbs, b. Oct. 26, 1791; d. June 23, 1830, dau. of William and Henrietta

   Children:

   1. Henrietta Sprigg[7] Dorsey
   2. Katherine Hobbs Dorsey
   3. William Roderick Dorsey

5. Samuel[6] Dorsey, d. unm.
6. Dennis[6] Dorsey, m. Jan. 5, 1811 Maria Owings Frederick County

   Children:

   1. Samuel Owings[7] Dorsey, m. Mary Riggs Griffith
   2. Gustavus Dorsey, m. Sophia Buzzard
   3. Roderick Dorsey, m. Mary Davis
   4. Nicholas Dorsey, d. unm.
   5. Mary Ann Dorsey

7. Mary[6] Dorsey

Lucy Belt Sprigg Dorsey, widow of Nicholas, m. (2) May 4, 1794 Thomas Sprigg

Children:

1. Harriet Sprigg, b. 1795, m._____Bentley
2. Mary Sprigg, b. 1800, d.y.

3. JOHN[6] DORSEY (Nicholas,[5] Henry,[4] Joshua,[3] Col. Edward,[2] Edward[1])
b. Aug. 3, 1780; d. Jan. 18, 1870 Henry County, Georgia (now Clayton County)
m. (1) Sept. 17, 1808 Mary Phillips, b. Mar. 4, 1791; d. July 27, 1851, dau. of Isham and Mary Phillips, Henry County, Ga.

John Dorsey left Maryland about 1800 and settled in Georgia, where he became a successful planter.

Children of John and Mary (Phillips) Dorsey:
(Records from Family Bible of John Dorsey)

1. Henry[7] Dorsey, b. July 10, 1809
2. Isham Dorsey, b. July 1, 1811
3. Sary Dorsey, b. Feb. 25, 1814; d. Aug. 25, 1827
4. Althea Dorsey, b. Sept. 13, 1816
5. John Madison Dorsey, b. May 25, 1820
6. Stephen Green Dorsey, b. Aug. 22, 1822; d. Apr. 13, 1915
7. Solomon Dawson Dorsey, b. Aug. 22, 1825, m. Sarah Glass (See below)
8. Maryan Elizabeth Dorsey, b. Nov. 6, 1827; d. Nov. 12, 1827

John Dorsey m. (2) Everline ______ d. Jan. 18, 1870

7. SOLOMON DAWSON[7] DORSEY (John,[6] Nicholas,[5] Henry,[4] Joshua,[3] Col. Edward,[2] Edward[1])
b. Aug. 22, 1825 Jones County, Georgia; d. June 6, 1901 Fayetteville, Georgia
m. Dec. 15, 1842 Sarah Glass, b. Aug. 27, 1824, Henry County, now Clayton County, Georgia; d. July 30, 1886, dau. of Manson Glass

Children of Solomon D. and Sarah (Glass) Dorsey:
(Records from Family Bible of Solomon Dorsey)

1. John Manson[8] Dorsey, b. Apr. 22, 1846
2. Rufus Thomas Dorsey, b. Oct. 2, 1848, m. Sarah Matilda Bennett (See below)
3. Mary Panola Dorsey, b. May 22, 1854
4. Benn Hill Dorsey, b. May 4, 1854
5. Emily Hester Dorsey, b. Oct. 28, 1856
6. Edgar Favor Dorsey, b. Mar. 10, 1859
7. Elvy Olitipa Dorsey, b. Nov. 11, 1861

2. RUFUS THOMAS[8] DORSEY (Solomon,[7] John,[6] Nicholas,[5] Henry,[4] Joshua,[3] Col. Edward,[2] Edward[1])
b. Oct. 2, 1848; d. Feb. 3, 1909 Fayette County, Georgia
m. May 12, 1870 Sarah Matilda Bennett, b. Sept. 9, 1848; d. 1925, dau. of Cammelius E. and Emily Strickland Bennett, Fayette County, Ga.

Rufus Dorsey, too young for active military service at the outbreak of the war between the states, volunteered and joined an organization composed of old men, disabled soldiers and boys, formed and equipped for guard duty only. He was captured at Macon, Georgia, just before the surrender when that city capitulated, but he shortly after effected his escape. He studied law and was admitted to the bar in his home town of Fayetteville in 1869.

He was the first democratic member of the Legislature from his county after the Civil War. In 1879 he moved to Atlanta, Georgia, and later became one of the distinguished jurists of Georgia.

Children of Rufus T. and Sarah (Bennett) Dorsey:
(Records from Family Bible of Rufus Dorsey)

1. Judge Hugh Manson[9] Dorsey, b. July 10, 1871 Fayetteville, Ga.
m. June 29, 1911 Mary Adair Wilkinson, dau. of James M. and Carolyn Howell Wilkinson (See page 225)

Hugh Manson Dorsey studied law. He served as Governor of Georgia for two terms, 1917-19, 1919-21. He has served as Judge of Superior Court, Atlanta Jud. Circuit since 1935. (See Who's Who)

Children:

1. Hugh Manson[10] Dorsey Jr.
2. James Wilkinson Dorsey

2. Dr. Rufus Thomas[9] Dorsey Jr., b. Sept. 4, 1873; d. Nov. 10, 1934
m. Oct. 18, 1906 Laura Witham, dau. of William Stuart and Jean Cochran Witham
3. Mary Faith[9] Dorsey, b. Nov. 15, 1875; d. Nov. 1934
m. Nov. 9, 1898 Samuel B. Yow, son of Morris Yow, Franklin Co., Ga.
4. Cammelius (Cam) Dawson[9] Dorsey, b. Feb. 1, 1882 Atlanta, Ga. (See page 225)
m. Dec. 4, 1909 Minnie Wynn Adams, dau. of Judge Samuel Bernard Adams, Chatham, Ga.

He studied law and was admitted to the bar in 1904, and has practiced law in Atlanta, Ga. since 1907. He was counsel United States Shipping Board Emergency Fleet Corporation in 1918, and District Counsel United States Emergency Fleet Corporation, Southern Territory, 1919 to 1921; Standing Master in Chancery, Federal Court, Northern District of Georgia about nine years. (See Who's Who)

Children:

1. Samuel Adams[10] Dorsey, b. Nov. 30, 1910
2. Rufus Thomas Dorsey, b. Sept. 25, 1915; d. Feb. 27, 1922
3. Cam Dawson Dorsey, b. Oct. 18, 1918
4. Roy Adams Dorsey, b. May 17, 1922

5. Erastus Roy[9] Dorsey, b. Nov. 10, 1885; d. Jan. 11, 1935
m. Jan. 9, 1915 Margaret Swift Northen, dau. of Charles S. and Nora Earnest Northen
6. Sarah Emily[9] Dorsey, b. July 16, 1890
m. Nov. 22, 1911 Luther Zeigler Rosser Jr., son of Luther Z. Rosser, Fulton County, Ga.

2. CAPTAIN PHILEMON[4] DORSEY (Joshua,[3] Col. Edward,[2] Edward[1])
b. Jan. 20, 1714/5; d. 1771 at Brother's Partnership, Anne Arundel County
m. (1) Feb. 19, 1738/9 Catherine Ridgely, b. Nov. 14, 1723; d.c 1749

Philemon Dorsey lived on the tract called Brother's Partnership, which he had inherited from his father. He was a vestryman of Christ Church, and one of the builders of the Chapel of Ease upon Poplar Spring Branch in 1750. During the year 1757 and again in 1762, he served as a commissioner from Anne Arundel County.

Children of Philemon and Catherine (Ridgely) Dorsey:
(Births recorded in Queen Caroline Parish Register)

1. Ann[5] Dorsey, b. Oct. 2, 1740, m. John Dorsey (See page 83)
2. Elizabeth Dorsey, b. May 13, 1742, m. William Ridgely (see page 149)
3. Philemon Dorsey, b. Feb. 7, 1743/4; d. 1806, m. Aug. 16, 1770 Ann Dorsey (See page 159)
4. Catherine Dorsey, b. Nov. 30, 1745; d. 1769, m. Benjamin Warfield
5. Sarah Dorsey, b. Sept. 9, 1747, m. Vachel Warfield
6. Amelia Dorsey, b. Aug. 23, 1749, m. 1767 Samuel Riggs, d. 1814

Philemon Dorsey, m. (2) Dec. 13, 1759 Rachel Lawrence, who m. (2) Jan. 19, 1775 Nathan Harris (See page 56)

In his will made December 1, 1771 and probated 1772 Philemon Dorsey bequeathed:

To wife Rachel, during her life the dwelling plantation called Brother's Partnership and Pillage Resurveyed
To son Philemon Dorsey, tract called Friendship where he was then living near Frederick Town, and Sapling Range
To son Joshua Dorsey, tracts, Beyond Far Enough, and 60 acres, Barnes Purchase Tracts, Silence, Peace, Second Thought, Disappointment and Defiance Resurveyed to 5 sons-in-law and their wives, Viz: John Dorsey son of Michael and wife Ann, Wm Ridgely son of Wm and wife Elizabeth, Benjamin Warfield and wife Katherine, Vachel Warfield and wife Sarah, Samuel Riggs and wife Amelia, 400 acres.
Exrs: wife Rachel and son Philemon (*Wills 38*, f. 605)

On December 19, 1772, Charles Griffith and wife Sarah, Frederick County, transferred to Ann Dorsey, Elizabeth Ridgely, Catherine Warfield, Sarah Warfield, and Amelia Riggs, daughters and coheirs of the estate of Philemon Dorsey deceased, one part of the tract called Silence formerly taken up between Mrs. Elizabeth Ridgely and Philemon Dorsey. (*A.A. Co. Deeds I.B. No. 4*, f. 86)

Children of Philemon and Rachel (Lawrence) Dorsey:
(Births recorded in Queen Caroline Parish Register)

1. Joshua[5] Dorsey, b. Jan. 30, 1762, m. Apr. 15, 1795 Janet Kennedy, Fred. Co.
2. Henrietta Dorsey, b. Feb. 20, 1766, m. Dec. 13, 1786 William Hobbs
3. Ariana Dorsey, b. Mar. 24, 1769, m. May 15, 1788 Samuel Owings

3. RACHEL[4] DORSEY (Joshua,[3] Col. Edward,[2] Edward[1])
b. July 6, 1717; d. Dec. 14, 1775 (*Q. Car.*) Anne Arundel County
m. John Warfield, d. Jan. 30, 1776 (*Q. Car.*)

John Warfield, son of John and grandson of Capt. Richard Warfield, was granted part of Warfield's Range and 180 acres of Warfield's Forest in the division of his father's estate.

In his will made February 8, 1773 and probated March 13, 1776 John Warfield left:

To wife Rachel, executrix, dwelling plantation and lands adjoining (except 50 acres and 7 negroes) also stock and furniture and 1/3 of all other lands, if she marry only her thirds
To son Charles Warfield, 500 acres of land in the Barrens to include the plantation where he now lives, 1 negro, 25 pounds, also 10 pounds to pay for land bought of John Cook and Charles Grayham lying in his plantation
To son Joshua Warfield, 350 acres of land in the Barrens adjoining Benny Warfield's land and 50 acres of land adjoining dwelling plantation and also my dwelling plantation and all lands adjoining after his mother's decease, if he die without issue, land in the Barrens to go to my son Charles and other lands divided between all his sisters and 25 pounds to son Joshua
To son John Warfield, executor, lands called The New Design and remainder of lands in the Barrens, if he die without issue all lands to go to son Joshua
To daughters Ann Wyman and Sarah Griffith, a negro each
To daughters Amelia and Rachel Warfield, 2 negroes each and £27/10/0 pounds each
To six children, Ann, Sarah, Amelia, Rachel, Charles, and Joshua Warfield, residue of my estate equally divided
Exrs: Henry Ridgely and Henry Griffith (*Wills 40*, f. 702)

Rachel Warfield, wife of John, died before the will of her husband was probated.

Children of John and Rachel (Dorsey) Warfield:
(Births recorded in Queen Caroline Parish Register)

1. Ann[5] Warfield, b. Dec. 6, 1741, m. John Wyman
2. John Warfield, b. Apr. 29, 1744, d. 1776 unm. (*Wills 40*, f. 704)
3. Sarah Warfield, b. Nov. 12, 1746, m. Henry Griffith
4. Henry Warfield, b. Jan. 13, 1748/9
5. Charles Warfield, b. Feb. 1, 1750, m. Catherine Dorsey

6. Amelia Warfield, b. Apr. 3, 1755, d. unm. (*A.A. Co. Invts. J.G. No. 7 (57) f.* 36)
7. Rachel Warfield, b. Oct. 1, 1757, m. Capt. Samuel Griffith
8. Joshua Warfield, b. Apr. 27, 1761, m. Oct. 8, 1781 Elizabeth Dorsey

6. NICHOLAS[4] DORSEY (Joshua,[3] Col. Edward,[2] Edward[1])

b. June 2, 1725; d. Sept. 27, 1792 at Huntington Quarter, Anne Arundel County
m. Elizabeth Worthington, b. 1722; d. 1804

Nicholas Dorsey inherited from his father 256 acres of Huntington Quarter, and in 1749 his uncle Col. Henry Ridgely willed him the other half of this tract, where he was then living. (*Wills 27,* f. 45)

Other tracts of land owned by Nicholas Dorsey are mentioned in his will made March 6, 1789 and proved September 30, 1792. He bequeathed:

To son Nicholas Dorsey, 3 negroes and what else he has in his possession of my estate
To daughter Elizabeth Warfield, 2 negroes
To granddaughters Eliza and Juliet Warfield
To son Lloyd Dorsey, tracts, part of Huntington Quarter and 2 resurveys on same, 120 acres of escheated land called Harrison's Beginning after his mother's decease or marriage and after he pays his brother Nicholas W. Dorsey 250 pounds, part of Rich Neck and Riggs Hills containing 329 acres, also 3 negroes
To daughter Ann Worthington, 50 acres called Pinkstone's Thicket and 3 negroes
To daughter Mary Dorsey, 50 acres Benson's Lott, Mongomery County
To son Joshua Dorsey, part of a tract in Montgomery County, William's Range
To daughter Sarah Ball, 3 negroes
To daughters Achsah, Henrietta, and Lydia Dorsey, 3 negroes each, furniture and stock
To wife Elizabeth, home plantation and after her death or marriage to be equally divided among Nicholas, Elizabeth, Lloyd, Ann, Mary, Joshua, Sarah, Achsah, Henrietta, Lydia or heirs. (*A.A. Co. Wills J.G. No. 1,* f. 310)

Elizabeth, wife of Nicholas, was the daughter of John Worthington. She inherited from her father Todd's Risque and part of Andover, and all negroes which her husband has now in his possession. (*Wills 34,* f. 30) (See pages 181-182)

In her will made October 2, 1803 and probated April 19, 1804 she left:

To daughter Elizabeth Warfield, wife of Joseph Warfield, 120 pounds
To son Lloyd Dorsey, tract called Andover, 100 acres
To daughter Henrietta Dorsey, one-third of tract called Todd's Risque, and personalty
To daughter Achsah Owings one-third of Todd's Risque. Should she die without heirs land to be sold by Orphan's Court and money divided between children Nicholas, Elizabeth, Lloyd, Ann, Mary, Joshua, Sarah, and Henrietta.
To daughter Lydia Dorsey, one-third of Todd's Risque and personalty
Land bought in Baltimore County from son-in law Owen Dorsey to be rented to pay debts, after which land is devised to Lydia Dorsey
Exrs: son Lloyd Dorsey and daughter Henrietta Dorsey
(*A.A. Co. Wills J.G. No. 2,* f. 273)

Children of Nicholas and Elizabeth (Worthington) Dorsey:
(Named in parent's wills)

1. Nicholas[5] W. Dorsey, b. Nov. 1, 1759; d. Oct. 16, 1821 Mont. Co.
   m. Dec. 14, 1779 Rachel Warfield, d. Dec. 25, 1839 (See page 228)
2. Elizabeth Dorsey, m. June 26, 1776 Joseph Warfield
3. Lloyd Dorsey, b. 1762; d. 1812 (*A.A. Co. Wills J.G. No. 2,* f. 567)
   m. Catherine Thompson, d. Nov. 9, 1809 (See page 215)
4. Ann Dorsey, m. Sept. 14, 1792 John Worthington
5. Mary Dorsey, m. May 8, 1784 Amos Dorsey
6. Joshua Dorsey, d. 1815 (*Mont. Co. Wills Y,* f. 257)
   m. Feb. 16, 1789 Henrietta Hammond
7. Sarah Dorsey, b. 1771; d. Oct. 23, 1828 (See page 46)
   m. Feb. 16, 1788 William Ball, b. 1768; d. July 17, 1841
8. Achsah Dorsey, m. Mar. 18, 1794 Isaac Owings (*St. Thos.*) d. 1805

HOUSE BUILT BY NICHOLAS DORSEY ON HUNTINGTON QUARTER

Said to be the house where Sarah Dorsey, daughter of Nicholas, climbed from a second-story window when she eloped with William Ball in 1788.

ONE OF THE HANDMADE MANTLES IN THE NICHOLAS DORSEY HOUSE

Shown Through The Courtesy of Noah Ernest Dorsey
Annapolis Junction, Maryland

9. Henrietta Dorsey, m. Oct. 14, 1794 Owen Dorsey (See page 100)
10. Lydia Dorsey, d. 1807 unm. (*Balt. Co. Wills 8, f.* 258)

7. SARAH[5] DORSEY (Nicholas,[4] Joshua,[3] Col. Edward,[2] Edward[1])
b. 1771; d. Oct. 23, 1828, Baltimore County
m. Feb. 16, 1788 William Ball, b. 1768; d. July 17, 1841 Baltimore

William Ball, the son of William Ball of Virginia, was born in Maryland, but lived in Virginia until 19 years of age, when he came to Anne Arundel County, Maryland, and shortly after eloped with Sarah, the auburn-haired 16-year-old daughter of Nicholas and Elizabeth (Worthington) Dorsey of Huntington Quarter. In her climb from the second-story window of her home to join her lover, she lost her white satin slipper in the snow. (See page 45)

Provoked at this elopment, Nicholas Dorsey predicted that the pair would not get far without financial aid, but his displeasure soon vanished, and on the 15th of October, 1792, Sarah Ball was given 100 acres of Andover, lying in Huntington Hundred Anne Arundel County, by her father Nicholas Dorsey and her mother Elizabeth.

This same year Nicholas Dorsey died leaving to Sarah Ball, 3 slaves, Nell, George, and Charles. (*A.A. Co. Deeds N.H. No. 6, f.* 411)

On April 1, 1793, William Ball made over to Elizabeth Dorsey (his mother-in-law) in trust for his two children, William and Achsah Ball, the tract called Andover, 3 negroes, 1 bay horse, 5 head of cattle, 18 hogs, 3 feather beds and furniture.

(*A.A. Co. Deeds N.H. No. 7, f.* 666)

This tract and articles, Elizabeth released before 1797.

William and Sarah Ball moved to Baltimore, where he became Sheriff of Baltimore City and County. He was a Lieutenant in Capt. Abner Linthicum's Detachment in the War of 1814.

Sarah Ball in her will made February 25, 1828 and probated January 28, 1829, named her children William, Walter, Lloyd, Elizabeth Worthington, Louisa King, Achsah Robb, Sarah, and Henrietta Ball. (*Balt. Co. Wills 13, f.* 168)

William Ball died in 1841 intestate.

Children of William and Sarah (Dorsey) Ball:
(Family records)

1. William[6] Ball, b. 1760
   m. (1) 1809 Hannah Jones - one son William Ball, d. unm.
   m. (2) Elizabeth Dorsey (See page 104)
2. Achsah Ball, b. 1793; d. Jan. 31, 1860, m. Rev. John Robb
3. Elizabeth Ball, m. (1) Enoch Betz (2) Lloyd Worthington
4. Louisa Ball, d. Oct. 3, 1882, m. Charles King
5. Henrietta Ball, m. Lieut. Levin Handy
6. Lloyd Ball, b. 1803; d. 1857 unm.
7. Sarah Ball, m. John D. Wilson
8. John Ball, d. unm.
9. Walter Ball, b. Sept. 26, 1795; d. Sept. 25, 1863
   m. Sept. 13, 1815, Mary Ball b. 1794; d. 1865
   Children:
   1. Elizabeth[7] Ball, b. 1818; d. 1838 unm.
   2. Eleanor Ball, b. Mar. 18, 1821; d. Dec. 1909
      m. June 27, 1837 James A. Garrettson (See page 220)
   3. Mary Louisa Ball, m. John R. Ridgely
   4. Walter Ball, m. Eleanor Ford
   5. Joshua Ball, m. Emily Ann Cole
   6. James McCabe Ball, m. Fannie Walker

8. ANN[4] DORSEY (Joshua,[3] Col. Edward,[2] Edward[1])
b. Oct. 15, 1730; d. Sept. 15, 1767 (*Q. Car.*) Anne Arundel County
m. Nov. 11, 1750 Maj. Henry Ridgely (*Q. Car.*), b. 1728 (*A.A. Co. Deeds N.H. No. 4*, f. 268); d. 1791

Ann Ridgely died at the age of 47 years, leaving a family of eight children. She was remembered in her father's will and her children were named in her mother's will.

Henry Ridgely, the fourth, was son of Col. Henry Ridgely and Elizabeth, only daughter of Benjamin Warfield. He inherited the tracts Broken Land, Sapling Range, and Cooper's Lott from his father in 1749.

Capt. Henry Ridgely paid taxes on Broken Land, Poplar Bottom, Curry Galls, and Cooper's Lott from 1756 to 1768. As Major Henry Ridgely, he paid taxes from 1769 to 1774 on Broken Land, Poplar Bottom, Cooper's Lott, Jone's Luck, Bite the Skinner, Ridgely's Range, Ridgely's Choice, Curry's Galls, Ridgely's Lott and other tracts. (*A.A. Co. Debt Books*)

On May 26, 1776, a memorial was lodged with the Convention of the Province of Maryland, which explains the services he performed for his country.

The memorial of Henry Ridgely of Elk Ridge, Anne Arundel County, sheweth that your Memorialist did early in life quite a Domestick Happiness to commence soldier, and had the honor of Commanding a Company of Rangers on the western Frontiers of this Province soon after the defeat of General Braddock in 1755, and that your memorialist was promoted to the Command of the Elk Ridge Troop of Horse, which station he filled many years, to the entire Satisfaction of his field officers: Whereupon the late Governor Sharp promoted him to be a Major of the County afore-said, in the year 1761, & he was continued as such until the year 1773 when the present Governor Eden raised your Memorialist to the office of Lieut Coll in said County. Further that your memorialist was one of the first men in the Elkridge District, that requested a meeting of the people, to form themselves into a Company of Militia... Asks to be relieved from being a Militia man May 20, 1776, in which he enrolled as a private.

(*Arch. of Md.* XI, 432)

Children of Henry and Ann (Dorsey) Ridgely:
(Births recorded in Queen Caroline Parish Register)

1. Henry[5] Ridgely, b. Sept. 5, 1751; d. 1751
2. Elizabeth Ridgely; b. Sept. 25, 1752; d. Sept. 8, 1808
   m. Nov. 21, 1771 Dr. Charles Alexander Warfield, d. Jan. 29, 1813 (See page 222)
3. Ann Ridgely, b. Oct. 2, 1754; d. 1834, m. Maj. Thomas Snowden
4. Polly Ridgely, b. July 2, 1756, m. Thomas Sappington Jr., d. 1783
5. Henry Ridgely Jr., b. July 9, 1758, living in 1800
6. Henrietta Ridgely, b. May 19, 1760; d. 1760
7. Henrietta Ridgely, b. Aug. 24, 1761
8. Joshua Ridgely, b. Aug. 26, 1763; d. Sept. 6, 1767
9. Sarah Ridgely, b. Jan 30, 1766; d. 1804 (*A.A. Co. Wills J.G. No. 2*, f. 271)
   m. after 1790 ______ Dorsey

In 1790 a dispute arose between Philemon Dorsey and Benjamin Dorsey executors of Joshua Dorsey, brother of Ann (Dorsey) Ridgely of the one part and Henry Ridgely Jr., and Dr. Charles Alexander Warfield for himself and as agent for Thomas Snowden, Polly Sappington and Sally Ridgely of the one part. It was agreed to pay the above named heirs, the legal representatives of their mother the sum of £61/7/2. (*A.A. Co. Test. Papers*, Box 21, Folder 103) (See page 38)

Henry Ridgely, m. (2) 1773 Rachel (Dorsey) Hall, d. 1792 (*A.A. Co. Wills J.G. No. 1*, f. 301), widow of William Hall, d. 1770. (See page 142)

Their intended marriage is revealed in a deed in which it was mutually agreed that each should have absolute power of dispensing of their respective estates.

(*A.A. Co. Deeds I.B. No. 4*, f. 79)

On April 12, 1773, Major Henry Ridgely sold to John Dorsey of Michael, planter a 209 acre tract called Bite the Skinner. (*A.A. Co. Deeds I.B. No. 4*, f. 83)

On May 19, 1778, Henry Ridgely was commissioned Justice of the Peace of Anne Arundel County, and on January 17, 1779, Money, Books, Paper of the Continental Loan Office were taken to the home of Henry Ridgely of Elkridge for safety, since the office had to be moved.

(*Arch. of Md.* XXI, 241, 398)

In 1789 Henry Ridgely being indebted to Thomas Snowden and Dr. Charles Alexander Warfield mortgaged lands: Ridgely's Great Park, 300 acres, Ridgely's First Little Park, Second and Third Little Park, 80 acres, Poplar Bottom, 387 acres, Jones' Luck, 50 acres, Williams Contrivance, 320 acres, Patuxent Mill Seat, 34 acres, Victory, 2,800 acres, Part of Broken Land, 330 acres, part of Holland Adventure, 130 acres, Cooper's Lott, 100 acres, part of second Addition to Snowden Manor, 240 acres, Planter's Pleasure, 125 acres, and the land the said Henry Ridgely exchanged for with John Burgess being part of the Addition to Snowden Manor, 380 acres, Lewis Lot, 260 acres, part of Gremits Chance, 40 acres, also tracts in Montgomery County, part of Prospect Hill, 1,800 acres, Black Walnut Plain, 105 acres, Dickason's Chance, 50 acres, Waters Purchase, 52 acres, Waters Lot, 38 acres. (Advertised in Maryland Gazette, May 9, 1789.)

(*A.A. Co. Deeds N.H. No. 4*, f. 260)

The will of Henry Ridgely made on May 8, 1791 and probated September 7, 1791 reads:

> Desire real and personal estate to be sold after my decease for purpose of satisfying my just debts and the sale of my land hereafter or of any land heretofore sold and remaining unconveyed. I hereby do empower my son Henry Ridgely to execute as good and sufficient conveyances for same to all purchasers to all intents and purposes as if they had been executed by me in my lifetime.
>
> Appoint my beloved friends Charles Alexander Warfield and Thomas Snowden and my son joint executors. (*A.A. Co. Original Will*, Box R, Folder 30)

The testamentary bond was signed by Henry Ridgely and Nicholas Watkins, October 14, 1791. (*A.A. Co. Test. Papers*, Box. 21, Folder 51)

Between the years 1792 and 1800, Henry Ridgely Jr., who was made trustee with sufficient authority to sell all of the real estate of his deceased father Henry Ridgely, sold his father's lands and personal property and paid his debts. (*A.A. Co. Deeds, N.H. No. 5*, folios 233, 473; *Deeds N.H. No. 6*, folios 358, 473)

JOHN DORSEY SON OF EDWARD

6. JOHN[3] DORSEY (Col. Edward,[2] Edward[1])

b. June 15, 1688 (*A.A. Co. Land Commissions I.B. No. 1*, f. 158)

d. 1764 at First Discovery, Anne Arundel County

m. Apr. 8, 1708 Honor Sta——(Stafford) (*St. A.*), b. Oct. 12, 1689; d. c 1757 (See page 51)

John, who signed his name as John Dorsey son of Edward, outlived his brothers, and all but one of his sisters. In 1700 he received by deed of gift from his father 100 acres of Major's Choice, and in 1704 he was left by his father's will, 148 acres of land called Long Reach, one new gun and two silver spoons to be delivered to him at the age of 16 years.

In 1730, as John Dorsey son of Edward, he was paid for 3 day's attendance as Juryman in the May Provincial Court. (*Arch. of Md.* XXXVII, 125) When an act was passed for laying out the town of Elk Ridge Landing in 1732, he was appointed one of the commissioners for Anne Arundel County. (*Arch. of Md.* XXXIX, 125)

He became vestryman of Christ Church in Queen Caroline Parish in December, 1728, and served in this capacity from time to time until April 8, 1761. In 1736 he occupied pew No. 3.

COLONEL EDWARD DORSEY

On October 7, 1720, a tract of 632 acres called Brother's Partnership was surveyed for John and Joshua Dorsey on the west side of Good Range, Anne Arundel County. (*Patents E.I. No. 4, f.* 221) The next year, Dorsey's Grove, which consisted of 1,080 acres in Baltimore County, was surveyed for John Dorsey son of Edward, (*Patents P.L. No. 5, f.* 489) and on February 21, 1722, with his brother Joshua Dorsey, he took up a tract of 135 acres called Gore, which they sold on April 26, 1725 to Caleb Dorsey of Anne Arundel County for 30 pounds Sterling. Honor, wife of John, and Ann, wife of Joshua, consented to the sale. (*Balt. Co. Deeds I.S. No. H, f.* 41)

He bought a tract of 500 acres for the sum of 105 pounds Sterling called the First Part of the Discovery, on November 26, 1734, from Elizabeth Beale of Anne Arundel County, widow and executrix of John Beale late of Anne Arundel County, planter. (See page 175A)
(*A.A. Co. Deeds R.D. No. 2, f.* 175)

Deeds of gift made by John Dorsey of Edward to his children are from time to time recorded.

On August 2, 1735, he gave to his son Michael Dorsey the tract bought of Josias Jones March 6, 1724, called Pushpin containing 200 acres, and 100 acres of the adjoining tract, the Discovery. To his daughters Hannah Barnes, Ruth Lawrence, Sarah Howard, and Susanna Dorsey he gave all that tract called Dorsey's Grove containing 1,080 acres, except 247 acres, which had been sold to Edward Bronson, to be equally divided. Witnesses were Abel Browne and Samuel Norwood.
(*Ibid., f.* 269)

This tract was divided among the four daughters and their husbands on November 7, 1750, and the deed was signed by Henry Howard and Sarah Howard, Levin Lawrence and Susan Lawrence, Adam Barnes and Hannah Barnes, and Benjamin Lawrence and Ruth Lawrence.
(*A.A. Co. Deeds R.B. No. 3, f.* 316)

On May 18, 1744, John Dorsey son of Edward purchased from Mary Higginson of the Kingdom of Great Britain, daughter and heir of John Tailor of said Kingdom, part of a parcel of land containing 1,500 acres called Tailor's Park on the south side of the main falls of the Patapsco River, for 100 pounds Sterling. (*A.A. Co. Deeds R.B. No. 2, f.* 21) On March 29, 1744, she sold him for 100 pounds Sterling, Belt's Hills, a tract of 800 acres at the main falls of the Patapsco River in Baltimore County. (*Ibid.*, 57)

On October 27, 1747, he gave to his grandson Samuel Howard a negro girl called Rachel, when he shall arrive at age of 21 years. Should he die, the negro girl to go to his brother John Howard. In event of both their deaths, girl to go to son Vachel Dorsey. Onour Dorsey, wife of John, gave up all her rights of dower. (*Ibid., f.* 499)

John Dorsey son of Edward gave to his son Michael Dorsey, on December 27, 1750, the tract called Good Range containing 333 acres and also one-half of the tract called Brother's Partnership of 316 acres; to his son Vachel Dorsey, the tract called Belt's Hills containing 800 acres and also seven negroes, names Sam, Robin, James, Rose, Abigail, Sam the son of Rose, and Fanney; to his son Edward Dorsey, the tract called Tailor's Park containing 740 acres and also seven negroes, names Sam, Sampson, Toby, Jack, Hagar, Charles, and Jenny. Onour Dorsey, wife of John, gave up all her right of Dowry. (*A.A. Co. Deeds R.B. No. 3, f.* 338)

On April 24, 1750, John Dorsey of Edward bought for 100 pounds Sterling from Daniel Carrol of Prince George's County, a tract called Mistake, lying in Anne Arundel County, adjoining Ranter's Ridge and containing 500 acres. (*Ibid., f.* 250) He also bought from William Ryan for 146 pounds Sterling, 152 acres called Brown's Chance and 150 acres of Dorsey's Friendship lying in Anne Arundel County. (*Ibid.*, 720)

A tract called Dispute Ended containing 200 acres was surveyed for him on April 25, 1752, and on December 10, 1755, he sold to Charles Carrol of Anne Arundel County for 50 pounds Sterling, the tract called Half Pone containing 50 acres, which he had bought from Zachariah Barlow on March 9, 1754, beginning at McCubbin's part of said tract on the Patuxent River continuing down the river to the landing. Onor Dorsey, wife of John, signed.

(*A.A. Co. Deeds B.B. No. 1*, f. 126)

John Dorsey son of Edward gave to his son Nathan Dorsey, April 5, 1756, land called Mistake containing 500 acres, and a tract called Dispute Ended containing 200 acres, also 7 negroes, Peter, Robin, Joe, Ben, Hagar, Pol, and Jenny, and all cattle, Hoggs, & Sheep on the plantation where he now lives. At the same time, Onour Dorsey, wife of John, gave up her right of dower. (*Ibid.*, f. 16)

On January 11, 1757, he bought from Henry Howard, his son-in-law, for 15 pounds Sterling, part of a tract called Land Resurveyed adjoining Pushpin and Discovery. (*Ibid.*, f. 270) On the same day, John Dorsey sold to Henry Howard the tract called Chance containing 86 acres, which he bought from Charles Carrol Esq. of the City of Annapolis on May 29, 1744. No wife signed. (*A.A. Co. Deeds B.B. No. 2*, f. 230)

The will of John Dorsey son of Edward made September 24, 1764 and proved November 13, 1764 follows:

MARYLAND SST.
In the name of God Amen, I John Dorsey, son of Edward, of Ann Arundel County of the Province aforesaid Gentleman being Sick and weak in Body but of sound and perfect Memory Praise be given to God for the same, and knowing the uncertainty of this Life on Earth and being desirous to settle Things in order Do Make this my Last Will and Testament in Manner and form following Vizt.
First and principally I Commend my Soul to Almighty God that gave it and my Body to the Earth from whence it was taken to be buried in such decent and Christian Manner as to my Executors hereafter named shall be thought meet and Convenient

Item - I give... to my loving son Michael Dorsey my Dwelling plantation Containing four hundred acres of Land part of the first Discovery to him and his heirs forever

Item - I give...to my grandson John Dorsey son of Michael one hundred & fifty two Acres of Land being part of a Tract of Land called Browns Chance & Dorseys friendship to him and his heirs forever

Item - I give...to my Grandson John Barnes Son of Adam my negro boy named Sock to him and his heirs forever

Item - I give...to my Grandson John Elder my negro boy named Robin to him and his heirs forever

Item - I give...to my Grandson John Lawrence my negro boy named Harry to him and his heirs forever

Item - I give...to my Grandson John Howard son of Henry my negro Girl named Hager to him and his heirs forever

Item - I give...to my Grandson John Dorsey Son of Nathan my negro Boy named Ben to him and his heirs forever

Item - I give...to my Grand Daughter Onour Elder Daughter of Michel Dorsey the following Negroes Vizt. Sue, Jane, Rachel, Nace, Beal, Jeffery, Mol, they and their Increase during her natural Life, and after her Decease, to her two Sons Joshua and Michel, and in Case they should die before they arrive to the Age of twenty one years then they and their Increase to Elizabeth Burgess and her Children forever

Item - I give...to my Grand Daughter Onour Warfield my negro girl named Nan Daughter of Jenney to her and her heirs forever

Item - I give...to my Grand Daughter Onour Elder my negro Girl named Ester to her and her heirs forever

Item - I give...to my loving Daughters hereafter named Vizt. Hannah Barnes, Ruth Rumney, Sarah Howard, Susannah Lawrence, Jemima Hobbs, twenty Pounds Current Money each, to be paid by my Executors in full of their part of my Estate

Item - I give...to my Grand Daughter Sarah Berry one hundred Pounds Current Money to be paid by my Executors out of my Estate at ten pounds per Year until the whole be paid

Item - I give...all the remainder and residue of my Personal Estate after my Just Debts & Legacies are paid, to be equally divided amongst my four Sons Vizt. Michael Dorsey, Vachel Dorsey, Edward Dorsey, and Nathan Dorsey, willing and Requiring that my negro Man Ben, after Appraisment be allowed to Choose his Master out of my four Sons aforesaid and the one he Chooses to take him and allow out of his part of my Estate the Sum he is appraised to, I do hereby Will that All just Debts Bequeaths and Legacies be paid according to the true Intent and meaning of this my Will

Lastly I Constitute appoint and Ordain my loving Sons Michael & Vachel Dorsey to be my Executors of this my last Will and Testament and I do hereby Revoke and Disallow all former and other Wills by me made ratifying and Confirming this and no other to be my last Will and Testament in Witness whereof I have hereunto set my hand and affixed my Seal this twenty fourth Day of September One thousand seven hundred and sixty four

In presence of
Cornelius Howard
Robert Davis
Ely Dorsey

John Dorsey (Seal)
son of Edward

(A.A. Co. Original Wills, Box D, Folder 48)
(Wills 33, f. 44)

The inventory of the estate of John Dorsey of Edward was appraised November 27, 1764, by Henry Ridgely and Henry Griffith. It included:

Wearing Apparel
Cash in house 10 pounds
5 Feather Beds and furniture
Couch and Mattress
Parcell of Chests and Trunks
2 cases of bottles
1 desk and some tables
2 Looking glasses
Sheets, Table Linen and Towels
Hand Irons, Tongs and Shovel
2 doz chairs and one Spice Box
Knives and Forks, Books and papers
gun and stool
Tin, glass, copper, Earthen Stone
and glass ware, Flax Hatchet
Plantation Utensils
Spitts, frying pans, Grind stone, Ladle
6 Wheels, and Reels, Cooper and Carpenters
and Joiners Tools, Trays, Tubs, Sifters
parcell of pewter, Iron Potts and Hooks

Rum Cyder 14/12/4
Sundry articles of new goods 147/6/11
Sundry kinds of grain 91/12
Tobacco worth 157/0/0
Bacon and tallow
Negroes -
George and Cesar, Leath, Timothy
Sam, Will, and Robin a legacy
Jacob, Alice, Sarah, Jane, William
and Buck, Leach, Tom, Charles,
Nich, Jane, Little Jack, Ben
and Bett
47 Sheep, 80 hoggs & piggs
13 cows, 8 cows, 16 cattle
3 young steers
Negro bedding
Tarr and Lumber

(Invts. 95, f. 141)

A later account of Michael and Vachel Dorsey, executors of John Dorsey of Edward, shows the value of the estate to be £3023/11/2½. *(Bal. Bk. 5,* f. 158)

The St. Anne's Parish Register *(Liber 1,* f. 1) records the marriage of John Dorsey to Honor Sta_____. The last letters of the name have been lost because the corner of the page has crumbled. A copy of the record appears below.

Aprill 8 1708 Was Maried John Dorsey to Honor
Do Was Maried Richard [illegible] Katherine

Honor Sta_____ is thought to have been the Honor Stafford who was left personalty in the will of Honor Marriarte, March 25, 1701. *(Wills 11,* f. 21)

Honor Marriarte was the mother of Rachel, who m. (1) Benjamin Lawrence, and (2) John Norwood, nephew of John Dorsey. (See page 29)

Honor Marriarte and her husband Edward, were left personalty in the will of Richard

Russel in Lower Norfolk County, Virginia, in 1667. (*Norfolk Co., Va. Wills E, f.* 29)

It is also thought that Honor Sta——(Stafford) Dorsey was related to William Stafford who married Sarah Todd, widow of Thomas. (See page 193)

Honor Dorsey was living in 1756 when she signed a deed of gift to her children. Since her name does not appear on later deeds, or in the will of her husband, it seems probable that she died soon after this date.

Children of John and Honor Sta——(Stafford) Dorsey:
(Names and dates from J.H.C. Watt's Bible said to be the oldest Dorsey Bible in existence)

1. Hannah^{4} Dorsey, b. Aug. 26, 1709, m. Adam Barnes
2. Ruth Dorsey, b. Oct. 15, 1710, m. (1) Benjamin Lawrence
   (2) Nathaniel Rumney
3. Michael Dorsey, b. Mar. 15, 1712, m. Ruth Todd (See page 80)
4. Sarah Dorsey, b. Oct. 15, 1715, m. Henry Howard
5. Susannah Dorsey, b. Dec. 15, 1717, m. Levin Lawrence
6. Jemima Dorsey, b. Dec. 6, 1720, m. (1) John Elder
   (2) Joseph Hobbs
7. Patience Dorsey, b. May 7, 1722, m. Samuel Howard
8. Vachel Dorsey, b. Oct. 20, 1726, m. Ruth Dorsey
9. Edward Dorsey, b. Oct. 25, 1728, m. Elizabeth Gillis
10. Nathan Dorsey, b. Aug. 11, 1731, m. Sophia Owings

1. HANNAH^{4} DORSEY (John,^{3} Col. Edward,^{2} Edward^{1})
b. Aug. 26, 1709; d. 1789 at Dorsey's Grove, Anne Arundel County
m. c 1732 Adam Barnes; d. 1779

In 1735 Hannah Barnes, the eldest daughter of John and Honor Dorsey, received by deed of gift one-fourth of the tract Dorsey's Grove, adjoining the plantation where she and her husband, Adam Barnes, were then living.

Adam Barnes was a vestryman of Christ Church in 1738, and he signed the inventory of Peter Hanks in 1739. His signature appears below.

On June 13, 1734, Adam Barnes, who was the son of James and Keturah (Shipley) Barnes, took up a tract called John's Lott containing 100 acres, which he increased to 640 acres by resurvey October 20, 1752 under the name of Cumberland. (*Patents B.Y.& G.S,* f. 368)

On September 21, 1741, he resurveyed a tract and patented the same under the name of Adam's Forrest, October 4, 1743. This consisted of 287 acres, 150 acres obtained by warrant from his brother Richard Barnes, and 137 acres of vacant land adjoining. (*Patents E.I. No. 6,* f. 674) On May 27, 1745, he resurveyed this tract and increased it to 1,187 acres and patented it as Invasion. (*Patents B.T.& B.Y. No. 3,* f. 465) He purchased from John Hood 105 acres of Conclusion, originally called Barn's Hunt, on December 20, 1752. The same day he conveyed 111 acres of Invasion to Vachel Dorsey. (*A.A. Co. Deeds R.B. No. 3,* folios 565, 599)

Adam Barnes gave to his five daughters, Susannah Linthicum, Patience Norwood, Ruth Stephens, Sophia Petticoate, and Hannah Barnes, a negro each and a portion of land, on October 22, 1764. (*A.A. Co. Deeds B.B. No. 3,* folios 282, 340, 342) The same date, he also gave to his son Henry Barnes 94 acres of Invasion. (*Ibid.,* f. 271)

On July 27, 1765, Adam Barnes conveyed to his son John Barnes, 1263/4 acres of Invasion and 46 acres, a part of Conclusion, (*Ibid.*, f. 416) The part of Invasion adjoining Dorsey's Grove, he deeded to his son James Barnes. (*A.A. Co. Deeds I.B. No. 5*, f. 256)

The will of Adam Barnes, Yeoman, made November 19, 1768 and probated February 16, 1779 left:

> To wife Hannah Barnes, dwelling plantation with all my personal Estate except 2 negro boys Viz: Simon, I give to son James, and Yarrow, to son Michael Barnes, when he shall arrive at age of 21 years
> To wife Hannah during her natural life, household goods, movables, and stock and after her decease same to be equally divided amongst my children, Henry, John, Sophia, Ruth, Susannah, James, Patience, Hannah, and Michael Barnes
> To son James Barnes, part of a tract called Dorsey's Grove and part of Invasion
> To son Michael Barnes, part of Cumberland with my plantation after the decease of my wife Hannah
> Exrs: wife Hannah, son James Barnes. (*A.A. Co.Wills E.V. No. 1*, f. 82)

Hannah Barnes, widow of Adam, on November 2, 1786, conveyed to her son James Barnes, her share of Dorsey's Grove. (*A.A. Co. Deeds N.H. No.2*, f. 544)

Hannah Barnes died in 1789 intestate. (*A.A. Co. Adm. Bond J.G.* f. 149) The inventory of her estate was dated June 10, 1791. (*A.A. Co. Test. Papers*, Box, 24, Folder 37)

Children of Adam and Hannah (Dorsey) Barnes:
(Named in father's will and in deeds)

1. Henry[5] Barnes, d. bef. 1790. Moved to Washington Co. Md.
   Named as eldest son. (*Abstracts of Deeds, A.A. Co.* Vol. 1, f. 446)
2. John Barnes, d. 1800 intestate (*Balt. Co. Accts. B. No. 3*, f. 17) (See page 213)
   m. Hammutal Tivis, dau. of Robert (*Balt. Co. Wills 5*, f. 475)
   (*A.A. Co. Deeds N.H. No. 8*, f. 486)
3. Sophia Barnes, m. (1) William Petticoat, d. 1779 (*A.A. Co. Deeds I.B. No. 5*, f. 525)
   m. (2) Thomas Greenwood (*Balt. Co. Adm. Acct. 10*, f. 281) (See page 32)
4. Ruth Barnes, m. Dawson Stephens (*A.A. Co. Deeds I.B. No. 4*, f. 42)
5. Susannah Barnes, m. ________ Linthicum
6. James Barnes, m. Elizabeth Shipley, dau. of George and Catherine
   (*Chanc. Papers* No. 4874)
7. Patience Barnes, m. John Norwood (*A.A. Co. Debt Book*, 1768, f. 38)
8. Hannah Barnes, m. John Hood
9. Michael Barnes, underage 1778

2. RUTH[4] DORSEY (John,[3] Col. Edward,[2] Edward[1])

b. Oct. 15, 1710; d. 1782 Anne Arundel County

m. (1) Benjamin Lawrence, b. Jan. 27, 1704/5; d. Jan. 4, 1755

In 1735 Ruth and Benjamin Lawrence were given by Ruth's father one-fourth of Dorsey's Grove. In 1736 Benjamin Lawrence, who was the son of Benjamin and Rachel Lawrence, was a pew holder at Christ Church, Queen Caroline parish.

On June 27, 1747, Benjamin Lawrence exchanged with John Talbot, a tract of 115 acres called the Favor on the draughts of West River for 200 acres of Talbott's Resolution at Elk Ridge. (*A.A. Co. Deeds R.B. No. 2*, f. 552)

Benjamin Lawrence died intestate in 1755. The Maryland Gazette gives the information that

> "While walking across a Field with a pipe in his mouth, he fell down, forward, and run the pipe stem into the Roof of his mouth of which he died January 4, 1755."
> (*Md. Hist. Mag.* XVIII, 33)

The inventory of Benjamin Lawrence's estate, amounting to £478/12/1, was filed December 29, 1755. (*Invts. 61, f. 236*)

In 1756 Benjamin Lawrence's heirs paid taxes on 196 acres of Dorsey's Grove and 505 acres of Benjamin's Addition. (*A.A. Co. Debt Books*)

Ruth Lawrence, widow of Benjamin, m. (2) as his second wife, Nathaniel Rumney, d. 1773.

On May 11, 1758, Nathaniel Rumney and Ruth, his wife, signed a quit-claim deed to Susannah Lawrence, widow of Levin Lawrence, for all interest Ruth had in Benjamin Lawrence's land. (*A.A. Co. Deeds B.B. No. 2, f.* 157)

Nathaniel Rumney in his will made October 25, 1772 and probated May 4, 1773 left:

To wife Ruth Rumney Exrx., tracts Holland's Choice, Leaf's Forrest during her life or widowhood provided my daughters Elizabeth and Rebecca shall live there while single, also land purchased from William Mills and personalty during her life or widowhood provided daughters live with her as long as single, at her death to my daughters equally
To daughter Elizabeth Rumney, one-half of tract Leaf's Forrest, 100 acres, 4 negroes
To daughter Eleanor Boone, other half of Leaf's Forrest, 100 acres, 2 negroes
To daughter Rachel Rumney, part of Holland's Choice, 100 acres, 2 negroes
To daughter Rebecca Rumney, part of Holland's Choice, 160 acres residue of tract bought of Jacob Holland with dwelling house, 4 negroes and personalty (*Wills 39, f.* 260)

Ruth Rumney, widow of Nathaniel, in her will made October 7, 1782 and proved November 1, 1782, left her negroes to her niece Sophia Peddicort and nephew John Howard of Samuel Howard deceased. She appointed her nephew John Howard executor. (*A.A. Co. Wills T.G. No. 1, f.* 78)

4. SARAH[4] DORSEY (John,[3] Col. Edward,[2] Edward[1])

b. Oct. 15, 1715; d. 1791 Anne Arundel County

m. c 1731 Henry Howard, b. Jan. 14, 1703; d. 1773 (See page 33)

Sarah and Henry Howard received by deed of gift from Sarah's father a portion of Dorsey's Grove in 1735, and the next year Henry Howard was willed by his father Joseph Howard, a tract of land called Kilhenny at Elk Ridge, Howard's Package, and Second Discovery. (*Wills 21, f.* 623)

In 1736 Henry Howard held pew No. 12 with Nicholas Gassaway in Christ Church, and in 1750 he was a vestryman.

In 1738 Henry Howard bought from his brother Ephriam Howard 500 acres of Discovery, which lay southeast of Carrol's Manor. (*A.A. Co. Deeds R.D. No. 3, f.* 76)

Other tracts of land owned by Henry Howard are shown in his will made June 15, 1772 and probated October 29, 1773. He left:

To son Ephriam Howard, part of Dorsey's Grove that lays south side road that leads to Poplar Spring Chapel
To son John Beal Howard, Pheasant Ridge, Safe Guard, lands from Levin Lawrence, and lands called Windsor. Should he die without issue land to go to Onner Wilkins. Also negro man, stock and plantation whereon he dwells
To son Vachel Denton Howard, remaining part of Howard's Resolution, North Hills, remainder part of Second Discovery, 50 acres Dorsey's Grove, 3 tracts Costly Finish, and Little Worth, also Building in Elk Ridge Landing, negro girl and boy and stock
To son James Howard, 40 acres of land, part of Dorsey's Grove
To son Joshua Howard, dwelling plantation with all my land adjoining after mother's decease, negro boy and stock
To grandson Benjamin Nelson, lands in Frederick County
To daughter Onner Davidge, one negro boy and girl
To granddaughter Ann Warfield, daughter of Onner, to Grandson Henry Davidge, to granddaughters Sarah Nelson and Sarah Warfield, daughter of Onner, a negro each
To daughter Onner Davidge, part of land from Benjamin Lawrence, and during her widowhood to have use of 100 acres adjoining land given to son John
After decease of wife, estate to be divided among 5 children or their survivors, Vachel Denton Howard, Joshua Howard, Rachel Warfield, Sarah Green, Onner Davidge. (*Wills 39, f.* 458)

Sarah Howard outlived her husband eighteen years. In her will made March 4, 1790 and proved May 11, 1791, she left:

To granddaughter Rachel Dorsey (daughter of Vachel Dorsey Jr.) a negro boy and seal skin trunk
To granddaughter Maria Dorsey (daughter of Vachel Dorsey Jr.) a negro girl
To two granddaughters, feather beds, furniture marked S.H., my riding horse etc.
To grandson Charles Dorsey (son of Michael Jr.) a negro girl
To granddaughter Sarah Warfield, daughter of Oner Wilkins, negro girl
To grandson Henry son of John Beal Howard, a negro boy
To grandson Henry son of Dr. Ephriam Howard, my silver shoe buckles
To granddaughter Anne Slade Howard daughter John Beale Howard, saddle and furniture and my large gilt looking glass
To granddaughter Sarah Howard daughter of Joshua Howard, a negro girl
To son Joshua Howard, 20 shillings
To three daughters, Rachel Warfield, Sarah Green, Oner Wilkins, wearing apparel and the residue of my estate to be equally divided
Children to divide estate. (*A.A. Co. Wills J.G. No. 1, f.* 234)

Children of Henry and Sarah (Dorsey) Howard:
(Births recorded in Queen Caroline Parish Register)

1. Rachel[5] Howard, b. Apr. 2, 1732; d. 1792 (*A.A. Co. Wills J.G. No. 1, f.* 304)
   m. Aug. 6, 1751 Dr. Joshua Warfield
2. Sarah Howard, b. Feb. 28, 1733; d. Mar. 21, 1815, (Tombstone)
   m. (1) Burgess Nelson, d. 1765 (*Wills 33, f.* 270)
   m. (2) Richard Green, b. 1742; d. July 36, 1818 (Tombstone) (*Mont. Co. Wills L, f.* 88)
3. Onner Howard, b. Mar. 27, 1740; d. 1792 (*A.A. Co. Accts. J.G. No. 1, f.* 343)*
   m. (1) Rezin Warfield, d. 1767 (*Wills 36, f.* 115)
   m. (2) John Davidge, d. 1770 (*Wills 38, f.* 75)
   m. (3) Joseph Wilkins, d. 1785 (*A.A. Co. Wills T.G. No. 1, f.* 262)
4. James Howard, b. July 15, 1744; d. 1795 (*A.A. Co. Wills T.G. No. 1, f.* 267)
   m. Mary Rumney, dau. of Nathaniel.
5. Dr. Ephriam Howard, b. Dec. 3, 1745; d. 1788 (*A.A. Co. Wills J.G. No. 1, f.* 46)
   m. Achsah Dorsey, d. 1799, dau. of John
6. John Beal Howard, b. Nov. 30, 1748; d. c 1799 (*A.A. Co. Test. Papers,* Box 45, Folder 12), m. Rebecca Boone, d. 1824 (*A.A. Co. Wills J.G.E.V. No. 1, f.* 203)
7. Capt. Vachel Denton Howard, b. Apr. 30, 1751; d. 1777/8 unm. (*A.A. Co. Wills E.V. No. 1, f.* 68)
8. Joshua Howard, b. Nov. 28, 1752
   m. Rebecca Owings, d. bef. 1803 (*Chano. Papers* No. 5350)

5. SUSANNAH[4] DORSEY (John,[3] Col. Edward,[2] Edward[1])
b. Dec. 15, 1717; d. after 1769 at Dorsey's Grove, Anne Arundel County
m. Levin Lawrence, d. 1756

Before her marriage, Susannah Dorsey received from her father one-fourth of the tract called Dorsey's Grove. She and Levin Lawrence lived upon this land, which bordered on Poplar Spring Branch.

Levin Lawrence was a vestryman of Christ Church from 1749 to his death.

On November 7, 1750, he sold to the Rector and Vestry of Queen Caroline Parish, one acre of Poplar Spring Garden for 50 pounds. Susannah, wife of Levin, gave her consent. (*A.A. Co. Deeds R.B. No. 3, f,* 310) In February 1753, he agreed to

"under Pinn the chapel and saw planks for flooring the same for 10 pounds, and to gett the sleapers, put in the Lites and finish the chapel for £3/9/10." (*Vestry Proc.*)

* This record shows that the thrice-widowed Honor (Howard) Wilkins did not marry Michael Dorsey II, as was stated by Warfield in his book, *Founders of Anne Arundel and Howard Counties.* Michael Dorsey II married Honor Elder, who died in 1818. (See pages 95 and 97)

In 1756 Levin Lawrence, son of Benjamin and Rachel Lawrence, paid taxes on 196 acres of Dorsey's Grove, and 272 acres Poplar Spring Garden. (*A.A. Co. Debt Book*)

Levin Lawrence died as the result of a fall from his horse on the hunting field.

His will made February 27, 1756 and proved November 9, 1756 left:

To son Benjamin Lawrence, 156 acres land called Benjamin's Addition and also 1 negro boy named Tury to him and his heirs
To son John Lawrence, all that part of a tract of land called Poplar Spring Garden that lies on the side of a branch called the Poplar Spring Branch and also 1 negro
To son Leaven Lawrence, all the remaining part of that tract of land called Poplar Spring Garden and also 1 negro boy named Peter
To daughter Rachel Lawrence, 1 negro girl named Nan
To daughter Ruth Lawrence, 1 negro girl named Sander
To daughter Betsy Lawrence, 1 negro girl named Kate
To daughter Peggey Lawrence, 1 negro girl named Nan
To unborn child, negro boy named Israel
My will is that if either of my above mentioned sons should die before they arrive to the age of 21 years that the above mentioned lands shall be equally divided between the surviving brothers and the negro left to the Deceased Son shall be divided among surviving sons and daughters
I give and bequeath all the rest of my estate real and personal when my wife's thirds is deducted and my just Debts paid to be equally Divided among my children Benjamin, John, Leaven, Rachel, Ruth, Betsy, Peggey, Lawrence, and the child my wife now goes with, and I do hereby constitute and appoint my loving wife, Susannah Lawrence sole executrix.
Witnesses: Henry Howard Vachel Dorsey
Michael Dorsey John Dorsey son of Edward

(*Wills 30, Pt. 2, f.* 287)

On May 11, 1758, Susannah Lawrence, widow of Levin, was given a quit-claim deed by Nathaniel Rumney and Ruth, his wife, for the interest Ruth had in Benjamin Lawrence's land. (*A.A. Co. Deeds B.B. No. 2, f.* 157)

Susannah Lawrence, executrix of Levin Lawrence deceased, on March 13, 1760, submitted her account of his estate, which was valued at £549/6/4. (*Accts. 44, f.* 238)

In 1769 Susannah Lawrence paid taxes on 196 acres of Dorsey's Grove, 90 acres of Poplar Spring Garden, and in 1774, on those two pieces of land and also 55 acres of Poplar Spring Garden, the 90 acres being called Spring Garden. (*A.A. Co. Debt Book*)

Children of Levin and Susannah (Dorsey) Lawrence:
(Named in father's will)

1. Rachel[5] Lawrence, b. May 3, 1739
   m. (1) Dec. 13, 1759 as 2nd wife, Capt. Philemon Dorsey, d. 1771
   m. (2) Nathan Harris (See page 43)
2. Benjamin Lawrence, b. May 17, 1741; d. 1814 (*Jefferson Co. Ky. Wills 2*)
   m. Jan. 28, 1762 Urith Owings, dau. of Samuel
3. John Lawrence, m. Martha West
4. Capt. Levin Lawrence, m. May 23, 1775 Sarah Dorsey, dau. of Caleb and Rebecca. Moved to Jefferson Co., Ky.
5. Elizabeth (Betsy) Lawrence, d. 1785 unm.
6. Margaret Lawrence
7. Ruth Lawrence, b. Dec. 22, 1745, m. Nov. 27, 1760 Thomas Owings, d. 1830 (*A.A. Co. Wills T.T.S. No. 1, f.* 80)
8. Richard Lawrence, b. 1757 after father's death
   m. Mar. 22, 1780 Ann Warfield, dau. of Rezin and Honor (Howard) Warfield

6. JEMIMA[4] DORSEY (John,[3] Col. Edward,[2] Edward[1])
   b. Dec. 6, 1720; d. bef. 1773 at Tailor's Park, Anne Arundel County
   m. (1) John Elder Jr., bapt. Oct. 14, 1708 (*St. A.*); d. 1762

On November 15, 1739, John Elder Jr. received from his father two tracts of land, Addition to Huntington Quarter and Laxford, in all 150 acres. (*A.A. Co. Deeds B.B. No. 3, f.* 205) (See page 196)

John Elder purchased from Margaret Higginson of the Kingdom of Great Britain, daughter and heir of John Tailor of said Kingdom, part of a tract called Tailor's Park, on May 8, 1744. (*A.A. Co. Deeds R.B. No. 2, f.* 25)

John Elder Jr. was a vestryman in 1744 in St. Anne's Church.

On September 1, 1755, John Elder, gentleman, and Jemima, his wife, sold 199½ acres of a former grant called Elder's Plague. (*Balt. Co. Deeds B.B. No. 1, f.* 447)

The will of John Elder Jr. made September 20, 1762 and proved November 9, 1762 named his lands. He devised:

To wife Jemima, slaves and personal estate, she to live on dwelling plantation
To my five sons, John, Owen, Charles, Ely, Elijah Elder, all my lands, namely my dwelling plantation, part of Tailor's Park, 660 acres, two tracts in fork of the Patuxent River, Addition to Huntington Quarter & Laxford. Land in Baltimore County, Adam's Garden, 397 acres, Elder's Puzzel, 160 acres, Elder's Plague, 125 acres, if any son die before reaching age of 21 years, land to surviving sons
To eldest daughter Elizabeth Elder, 10 pounds, to 2 daughters Honor and Jemima Elder, 30 pounds, at age of 16 years or marriage
Exrs: sons John and Owen Elder (*Wills 31, f.* 844)

Jemima Elder did not long remain a widow. A deed dated June 10, 1763, shows that a marriage is intended to take place between Jemima Elder, widow, and Joseph Hobbs. Jemima, therefore, made over to James Elder, greatest creditor, all real and personal estate of her late husband John Elder deceased. (*A.A. Co. Deeds B.B. No. 2, f.* 791)

On November 12, 1763, Joseph Hobbs, and Jemima, his wife, executrix of John Elder late of Anne Arundel County, deceased, paid to daughter Elizabeth, who married Joseph Gist, her part of the estate. (*Accts. 50, f.* 34) On November 23, 1764, John Elder of Baltimore County and Vachel Dorsey were bound unto Joseph Hobbs and Jemima, his wife, administratrix of John Elder deceased, for 1,000 pounds. The names of John Elder's children are given in this deed. (*A.A. Co. Deeds B.B. No. 3, f.* 383)

A deed made October 17, 1770 shows that Jemima's health was failing and she conferred to Joseph Hobbs her personal estate during her natural life. Her name does not appear on later records or in his will in 1773. (*A.A. Co. Deeds I.B. No. 2, f.* 219)

Children of John and Jemima (Dorsey) Elder:
(Named in father's will)

1. John[5] Elder, d. 1794
   m. (1) c 1759 Honor Dorsey, b. 1737; d. 1771, dau. of Michael (See page 84)
   m. (2) Sarah ________
2. Charles Elder, m. Feb. 14, 1769 Ruth Howard, d. 1827 (*Balt. Co. Wills 12, f.* 409)
3. Owen Elder, d. 1774, m. Apr. 10, 1766 Ann Dorsey, dau. of Michael
   She m. (2) Mar. 25, 1775 Charles Dorsey (See page 90)
4. Ely Elder, d. bef. 1788 unm. (*A.A. Co. Test. Papers*, Box 13, Folder 54)
5. Elizabeth Elder, b. 1742; d. Apr. 6, 1814
   m. Nov. 12, 1763 Joseph Gist (See pages 57 and 59)
6. Honor Elder, b. after 1746; d. 1817. m. c 1764 Michael Dorsey (See page 95)
7. Elisha Elder, m. July 28, 1778 Mary Davidge
8. Jemima Elder, m. (1) Jan. 8, 1778 Samuel Howard, d. 1788 (See page 59)
   m. (2) Daniel Elliot

5. ELIZABETH ELDER[5] (Jemima[4] (Dorsey) Elder, John,[3] Col. Edward,[2] Edward[1])
b. 1742; d. Apr. 6, 1814 Brooke County, West Virginia
m. Aug. 30, 1759 Major Joseph Gist, b. Sept. 30, 1738; d. Jan. 22, 1803

Major Joseph Gist was the son of William and Violetta (Howard) Gist of Baltimore County, Maryland; the grandson of Richard and Zipporah (Murray) Gist; and the greatgrandson of Christopher Gist, the immigrant and his wife, Edith (Cromwell) Gist.

On April 3, 1767, there was laid out for Joseph Gist of Baltimore County, 120 acres of land called Gistsylvánia. (*Patents B.C.& G.S,* f. 53) In 1773 Gist's Hope and Gist's Contrivance containing 26½ acres were patented to Joseph Gist, (*Ibid.,* f. 342) which he transferred to Thomas Renbottom in 1779. (*Balt. Co. Deeds W.G. No. D,* f. 27) .

Joseph Gist secured his commission as Quartermaster of the Soldier's Delight Battalion, Militia of Baltimore County, Maryland, May 25, 1776. (*Arch. of Md.* XI, 443) He was promoted to First Lieutenant, June 6, 1776, and to Major, September 10, 1777. (*Ibid.,* folios 467, 368) In November, 1781, Major Joseph Gist of Col. Hammond's Battalion resigned.
(*Arch. of Md.* XLVII, 560)

On June 18, 1793, Joseph Gist bought from Samuel Owings part of two tracts called Harrison's Meadows and Gist's Enlargement. (*Balt. Co. Deeds W.G. No. L.L,* f. 339)

On August 24, 1794, Joseph Gist sold to Charles Carnan for 423 pounds, parts of 4 tracts, Gist's Enlargement, Addition to Harrison's Meadows, Gist's Den, and Gist's Hope, 140½ acres. Elizabeth, his wife, signed the deed. (*Balt. Co. Deeds W.G. No. O.O,* f. 575)

Shortly after this Major Joseph Gist and some of his family moved to Ohio County, Virginia (now Brooke Co., W. Va.) He paid taxes in 1797 in Brooke County, the first year the county was legally organized. (*Brooke Co. Tax Records* Vol. 174, Va. Archives, Richmond, Va.)

On March 24, 1801, Major Joseph Gist purchased 400 acres of land on Buffalo Creek, Brooke County, West Virginia, from George McCullock. (*Brooke Co. W. Va. Deeds 2,* f. 363)

The will of Joseph Gist made November 16, 1801 and probated in 1803 bequeathed:

To son in law John Dorsey, 50 acres of land and a part of a tract of land I now live on
To son James Gist and his heirs, 200 acres of land, part of my tract of land aforesaid, brothers Samuel and George be permitted to make sugar at sugar camp now in use by family
To son Samuel Gist and heirs, 130 acres of above tract adjoining John Dorsey's land
To wife Elizabeth, residue of my tract of land and after her death to son George Gist and heirs
To daughters Elizabeth and Ann Gist, personalty
To wife Elizabeth, remainder of personal property during her life and after her death to be divided equally between 5 children now living, James, Samuel, George, Elizabeth, and Ann Gist
Sons James, Samuel, and George Gist to pay to Cornelius Gist of Baltimore County Maryland, balance of a bond due from me
Exrs: son James Gist and wife Elizabeth Gist
Wit: George Hammond, James Thompson, Henry Harvey
(*Brooke Co. W. Va. Wills 1,* f. 18)

Joseph and Elizabeth Gist are buried on the old Gist farm in Brooke County, West Virginia. The burying ground was ploughed over about 25 years ago and some of the stones used inside the old spring house. In the fall of 1946, the stones of Joseph and Elizabeth Gist were removed to the Franklin Cemetery, where three generations of Gists are buried.

The sugar grove mentioned in Joseph Gist's will, stands across the road from the site of the old home, which burned some years ago.

Children of Joseph and Elizabeth (Elder) Gist:

(Births of first eleven children are recorded in St. Thomas' Parish Register, Baltimore. Last three children are mentioned in father's will)

1. John Elder Gist, b. Jan. 1, 1761, m. Nov. 13, 1783 Frances Trippe (*St. Paul's*)
2. Cecil Gist, b. Nov. 12, 1762, m. Dec. 12, 1790 Abraham Cole
3. Joseph Gist, b. Aug. 12, 1764; d. Dec. 15, 1786 (*St. Paul's*)
4. Jemima Gist, b. May 4, 1766, m. John Dorsey (See page 108)

5. Joshua Howard Gist, b. Mar. 3, 1768; d. bef. 1801
6. Cornelius Howard Gist, b. Jan. 25, 1770; d. 1830, m. Clara Reinecker
7. William Gist, b. June 6, 1772; d. Aug. 13, 1773
8. Violetta Gist, twin d. Oct. 13, 1773
9. Elizabeth Gist, b. Mar. 21, 1774
10. James Gist, b. Feb. 29, 1776; d. Mar. 20, 1839
    m. Nov. 24, 1799 Rachel Hammond, b. 1780; d. July 20, 1844, Shannon, Ohio
11. Owen Gist, b. Jan. 9, 1778; d. bef. 1801
12. Samuel Gist, b. Dec. 27, 1779
    m. (1) July, 1804 Ann Baxter, d. 1811
    m. (2) Apr. 11, 1816 Sarah Baxter, b. c 1792; d. Mar. 21, 1870 Shannon, Ohio
13. Anne Gist, b. Oct. 11, 1781, m. Nov. 24, 1807 Thomas Haney
14. George Gist, b. 1783; d. 1857, m. Rachel Jones, b. 1789; d. July 9, 1870
    George Gist lived in Brooke County, W. Va., except the last three years of his life, which he spent with his daughter Alice and her husband, Joshua Butler, Muskingum County, Ohio.

7. PATIENCE^4 DORSEY (John,^{3} Col. Edward,^{2} Edward^1)
   b. May 7, 1722; d. Apr. 5, 1747 (*St. A.*) Anne Arundel County
   m. Jan. 29, 1740 Samuel Howard (*St. A.*). b. 1711; d. 1766/7

On July 7, 1744, Samuel Howard of Anne Arundel County, planter, sold to Richard Warfield, Jr. for 70 pounds Sterling a tract of 180 acres called Lancaster Plains on the south side of Anne Arundel River. His wife, Patience, signed the deed. (*A.A. Co. Deeds R.B. No. 1, f.* 407)

He was a vestryman of St. Anne's Church in 1755, and again in 1763.

Children of Samuel and Patience (Dorsey) Howard:
(Births recorded in St. Anne's Parish Register)

1. Samuel^5 Howard, b. Jan. 26, 1744/5; d. 1788
   m. Jan. 8, 1770 Jemima Elder, who m. (2) Daniel Elliot (See page 57)
2. John Howard, b. Jan. 22, 1746/7, living in 1782, when he was named as executor of the will of his aunt Ruth Rumney. (*A.A. Co. Wills T.G. No. 1, f.* 78)

Samuel Howard, m. (2) c 1748 Ann Harvey, d. 1774

In his will made December 1, 1766 and probated 1767 he bequeathed:

To son Benjamin Howard and his children, negroes Jenny, Dick, Tom, and James. He to pay or cause to be paid to each person 20 sh yearly during his natural life, if he does not pay, negroes to son Samuel Harvey Howard
To son Benjamin Howard, negro Lennon, and my will is that my son Benjamin continue with his brother Samuel Howard and said negroes until he is at age
To son Samuel Howard and his heirs, my Dwelling Plantation and all lands, should he die without issue, plantation and lands to my son John Howard's son John and heirs
To son Samuel Howard, negro Rachel and her 4 children, as they ought to by his grandfather giving him negro Rachel
To son John Howard, negroes, Hagar, Bett, Poll, Benj, Robin, Little Nan, Joe, Rose
If my son John Howard shall die without issue, negroes to go to his brother Samuel Howard
To son Samuel Harvey Howard, negroes Harry and Esther
To daughter Ann Howard, negroes Beck and Lydia
To sons Phillip, Charles, Thomas, 5 pounds each
Exrs: sons Samuel and John Howard (*Wills 35, f.* 335)

Ann Howard, widow of Samuel, was the daughter of Samuel and Elizabeth Harvey. She was not named in the will of her husband, but in 1774 the will of Ann Howard of Annapolis, widow, was probated. Her estate was to be divided amongst all of her children, Samuel, Harvey, Anne, Phillip, Charles, Benjamin, and Thomas Howard.

(*Wills 40, f.* 45)

Children of Samuel and Ann (Harvey) Howard:
(Named in parent's wills)

1. Samuel Harvey Howard, b. Aug. 23, 1750 (*St. A.*)
2. Anne Howard, b. Jan. 21, 1752 (*St. A.*)
3. Phillip Howard
4. Charles Howard
5. Benjamin Howard
6. Thomas Howard

8. VACHEL[4] DORSEY (John,[3] Col. Edward,[2] Edward[1])
b. Oct. 20, 1726; d. 1798 Anne Arundel County
m. Ruth Dorsey, d. 1814

In 1750 Vachel Dorsey received a gift from his father of a tract of 800 acres called Belt's Hills and seven negroes.

On December 20, 1752, Vachel Dorsey bought 111 acres of Invasion from John Hood of Anne Arundel County. (*A.A. Co. Deeds R.B. No. 3, f.* 599)

A tract called Anything was patented to Vachel Dorsey in 1759, and in 1762 and 1763, The Addition, Dorsey's Industry, Addition to Vachel's Purchase, Young Man's Folly, and Dorsey's Interest were patented to him. (*Patents B.C.& G.S. No. 10, f.* 237; *No. 17, f.* 257; *No. 20,* folios 47, 60)

On December 1, 1763, Vachel Dorsey sold Dorsey's Thicket of 300 acres to John Dorsey, Ruth his wife, signed. (*A.A. Co. Deeds B.B. No. 3, f.* 91) In 1770 Vachel Dorsey and his brother Edward Dorsey bought 3 tracts of land, Mistake, Dispute Ended, and Yate's Contrivance from Nathan Dorsey. (*A.A. Co. Deeds I.B. and J.B. No. 1, f.* 322)

In 1786 Vachel Dorsey gave to his son Johnsa Dorsey 500 acres of land, and to his son Elias Dorsey, Industry, containing 473 acres. (*Balt. Co. W.G. No.* ᵛ, folios 297, 344) In 1790 he also gave to his son Johnsa Dorsey, Baltimore County, 564 acres, including tracts, John's Chance, Polly's Inheritance, Addition, Vachel's Part of Dorsey's Thickett. (*Balt. Co. Deeas W.G. No. EE, f.* 464)

Vachel's will made March 26, 1790 and probated March 9, 1798 left:

To son Levin Dorsey, Dorsey's Interest, 30 acres, Salophia, 100 acres and Lost Sheep, which lies partly in Baltimore County and partly in Anne Arundel County
To son Edward Dorsey, Belt's Hills, 790 acres, part of Invasion, 111 acres
To daughter Ruth Owings, tracts Dexterity, 580 acres, Young Man's Folly, 44 acres, Vachel's Purchase, 24 acres, Addition to Vachel's Purchase, 25 acres, Ely's Lot, 50 acres. If no issue to descend to granddaughters Ruth and Maria, daughters of sons Elias and Vachel Dorsey
To daughter Ruth Owings, 5 negroes. To granddaughter Elizabeth Frost, a negro boy
Rest of estate to be divided equally among children, Johnsa, Elias, Vachel, Edward, and Ruth Owings.
Exrs: sons Johnsa and Elias Dorsey (*A.A. Co. Wills J.G. No. 2, f.* 37)

Ruth Dorsey, who outlived her husband, was the daughter of Edward and Sarah (Todd) Dorsey. (See page 145) In her will made December 24, 1813 and proved May 27, 1814 she left:

To son Johnsa Dorsey, silver spoons
To daughter Ruth Owings, wearing apparel, bed and furniture
To granddaughter Eliza Owings, a negro boy in case her father will pay 30 pounds to assist in the maintenance of son Levin
To son Levin Dorsey, 30 pounds for his maintenance
To granddaughter Ruth Maria Dorsey a negro in case her father Johnsa Dorsey will pay 30 pounds to assist in the maintenance of son Levin
To granddaughters Maria and Caroline, and May Dorsey, a negro each in case their fathers will assist in the maintenance of son Levin
To granddaughter Rachel Dorsey, 15 pounds
To granddaughter Elizabeth Frost, residuary legatee
All money from Samuel Owings and all property to be used in Maintenance of son Levin
Exr: Edward Dorsey (*A.A. Co. Wills J.G. No. 3, f.* 63)

Children of Vachel and Ruth (Dorsey) Dorsey:
(Named in father's will)

1. Johnsa[5] Dorsey, d. 1821 (*Jefferson Co., Ky. Wills 2*) (See page 233)
m. Mar. 5, 1788 Sarah Hammond, dau. of Rezin (*Fred. Co. Mar. Rec.*)
2. Vachel Dorsey, d. 1814 intestate, (*Balt. Co. Adm. Bk. 20, f.* 611)
m. (1) Apr. 9, 1783 Sarah Nelson
m. (2) Mar. 19, 1798 Elizabeth Dorsey (*St. Paul's*)
3. Edward Dorsey, b. May 4, 1762; d. 1808 Jefferson Co., Ky. (*Balt. Co. Wills 8, f.* 436)
m. Feb. 21, 1786 Susannah Lawrence (See pages 224,229,230)
4. Ruth Dorsey, m. Feb. 18, 1790 Beal Owings
5. Elias Dorsey, d. 1794 (*Balt. Co. Wills 5,f.* 193)
m. (1) June 2, 1779 Susannah Snowden
m. (2) Feb. 13, 1788 Mary Lawrence
6. Levin Dorsey, b. 1755. He applied for a pension 1833, Jefferson Co., Ky.
78 years old.

9. EDWARD[4] DORSEY (John,[3] Col. Edward,[2] Edward[1])
b. Oct. 25, 1728; d. after 1788
m. July 29, 1750 Elizabeth Gillis, b. Sept. 9, 1730, living in 1763

In 1750 Edward Dorsey received by deed of gift from his father a tract called Tailor's Park, containing 740 acres, and 7 negroes.

In 1768 he paid taxes on 1,906 acres of land in Anne Arundel County. (*A.A. Co. Debt Book*)

Edward Dorsey and his brother Vachel Dorsey bought three tracts of land, Mistake, Dispute Ended, and Yates Contrivance from their brother Nathan Dorsey in 1770.
(*A.A. Co. Deeds I.B.& J.B. No. 1, f.* 322)

He was a member of the Committee of Observation for Anne Arundel County, 1775, and he took the Oath of Fidelity and Support to the state of Maryland, 1778.

On March 5, 1779, as Edward son of John of Elk Ridge, Anne Arundel County, he sold to Peter Barnes son of Peter for 230 pounds Sterling, a tract of land called Invasion, and also a tract called Woodford. No wife signed. (*A.A. Co. Deeds N.H. No. 1, f.* 73)

In 1783 Edward Dorsey of John paid taxes on 450 acres of Mistake, 200 acres Dispute Ended, 325 acres New Year, and 24 acres of Neglect. (*A.A. Co. Tax List,* 1783)

Edward Dorsey son of John, and his son Ezekiel John Dorsey, transferred to Edward Dorsey, son of Edward of John, Progress, Additional Progress, and Dorsey's Dilemma, 448 acres in 1786. They also sold to William Patterson, Cheney's Neglect, 221 acres.
(*Balt. Co. Deeds W.G. No. Y,* folios 548, 579)

This same year he sold to John Gillis, 223 acres called Addition to Greenberry's Grove Enlarged. (*Ibid.,f.* 546)

He was administrator of his brother Nathan's estate February 13, 1786, (*Balt. Co. Adm. Bk, f.* 246) and on January 14, 1788, Edward Dorsey son of John, and John Odle were administrators of the estate of Samuel Baker. (*Balt. Co. Accts. 9, f.* 145)

Edward Dorsey, son of John, died after 1788 intestate.

Elizabeth Dorsey, wife of Edward, was the daughter of Ezekiel and Mary Gillis. She received from her father a legacy of 10 pounds Sterling, her portion of the two-thirds of her father's personal estate, and 5 pounds to be paid by her brother in 1763. (*Wills 26, f.* 140) She was left personalty in the will of her grandmother, Mary Gillis in 1763
(*Wills 38, Pt. 1, f.* 78)

Children of Edward and Elizabeth (Gillis) Dorsey:

1. Ezekiel[5] John Dorsey, b. Nov. 5, 1751; d. 1827 (*Balt. Co. Wills 12, f.* 350)
   m. Rebecca Maccubin
2. Joseph Dorsey, b. Aug. 29, 1753; d. 1837 (*Washington Co., Pa. Wills 5, f.* 306)
   m. July 7, 1780 Amelia Gillis
3. Edward Dorsey, b. Apr. 8, 1760; d. 1839 (*Balt. Co. Wills 17, f.* 266)
   m. June 8, 1781 Deborah Maccubin
4. Mary Hill Dorsey, b. July 23, 1764
5. Elizabeth Dorsey, b. Oct. 24, 1766

10. NATHAN[4] DORSEY (John,[3] Col. Edward,[2] Edward[1])
    b. Aug. 11, 1731; d. July 10, 1773/4 Baltimore County
    m. Sophia Owings

In 1756 Nathan Dorsey received by deed of gift from his father a tract of 500 acres called Mistake, and a tract called Dispute Ended containing 200 acres, and also 7 negroes.

He bought of Samuel Yates, Yate's Contrivance, a tract of 75 acres on February 27, 1758, and also 100 acres more from John Sellman and Daniel Roller. (*A.A. Co. Deeds B.B. No. 2, f.* 322)

Nathan Dorsey and Sophia, his wife, on May 26, 1764, sold to John Cord part of Mistake on the west side of the main wagon road. On September 26th, he mortgaged Mistake, Dispute Ended, and Yate's Contrivance to Henry Griffith: He sold to William Hall of Elk Ridge, merchant, on December 11, 1766, negroes Charles, Trice, Phill, Ben, young Ben, Sarah, Jenny, young Jenny, Poll, Hagar, Fanny, William, Jesse, Peter, Cloe, and Benjamin. (*A.A. Co. Deeds B.B. No. 3,* folios 188, 322, 641)

On September 26, 1770, Nathan Dorsey, because of indebtedness, conveyed to his brothers, Edward Dorsey and Vachel Dorsey, Mistake, 500 acres, Dispute Ended, 200 acres, Yate's Contrivance, 75 acres, and his other lands. (*A.A. Co. Deeds I.B. and J.B. No. 1, f.* 322; *Deeds I.B. No. 3, f.* 142)

Nathan Dorsey died in 1774 intestate. His brother Edward Dorsey served as his administrator with William Noke and Nicholas Dorsey his securities. (*Test. Proc. 46, f.* 56) His estate was appraised June 15, 1775. The nearest of kin were Michael Dorsey and Nathaniel Dorsey. (*Invts. 123, f.* 201)

Sophia Dorsey, wife of Nathan, was the daughter of John and Asenah Owings. She was left 5 pounds in the will of her father in 1765. (*Wills 33, f.* 347)

Children of Nathan and Sophia (Owings) Dorsey:

1. John[5] Dorsey, heir in grandfather John Dorsey's will
2. Vachel Dorsey, d. bef. 1814. (*A.A. Co. Test. Papers,* Box 112, Folder 57)
   m. Mar. 14, 1786 Clementina Ireland (See page 223)
   On Aug. 13, 1816, the estate of Vachel Dorsey was distributed in A.A. Co. by John Ireland Dorsey, son and administrator. (*A.A. Co. Test. Papers,* Box 130, Folder 16)
3. Dr. Nathan Dorsey, d. 1806 Philadelphia, Pa.
   m. May 7, 1783 Ann Sword (First Pres. Ch., Philadelphia)
   Surgeon on Ship Defense in 1776 (Naval Rolls, *Arch. of Md.* XVII)
   Member of Society of Cincinnatti.
4. Priscilla Dorsey, heir in will of Priscilla Dorsey, wife of Caleb in 1782.
   (*A.A. Co. Wills T.G. No. 1, f.* 75)
5. Dr. Samuel Dorsey
   m. (1) Feb. 12, 1795 Marie Josett Bows m. (2) June 12, 1800 Elizabeth Thompson

NICHOLAS DORSEY

7. NICHOLAS^{3} DORSEY (Col. Edward,^{2} Edward^{1})

b. c 1690; d. 1717 at Major's Choice, Baltimore County

buried Sept. 25, 1717 Elk Ridge (*A.H.*)

m. Dec. 20, 1709 Frances Hughes (*St. A.*), b. May 18, 1692 (*St. A.*)

Nicholas Dorsey received by deed of gift in 1700 from his father, 100 acres of Major's Choice, and by his father's will in 1704, he was left 100 acres of Long Reach, 2 silver spoons, one new gun, and a horse named Dick to be delivered to him at the age of 16 years.

In 1707 he chose his brother Joshua Dorsey as his guardian, (*Prov. Ct. Judg. P.L. No. 1, f.* 90) and the next year, he received his share of his brother Edward's estate.

Nicholas Dorsey died at the age of 27 years. His will made September 16, 1717 and probated February 13, 1717/8 bequeathed:

To sons Thomas, Nicholas, Benjamin, and Edward Dorsey and heirs, personalty at age of 21 years. Sons to have liberty to choose guardians at 18 years. Should any of said sons die before coming of age, their portion to be divided among other survivors
To son Thomas Dorsey and heirs, 50 acres of Long Reach near the Patuxent River
To son Nicholas Dorsey and heirs, 50 acres of Long Reach
To son Benjamin Dorsey and heirs, dwelling plantation at decease of wife
Exrx: Frances Dorsey and residuary legatee
Test: Henry Ridgely, John Dorsey son of Edward, Joshua Dorsey, Timothy Regan, Thomas Smith, John Dorsey

(*Balt. Co. Original Wills*, Hall of Records, Annapolis)
(*Wills 14*, f. 478)

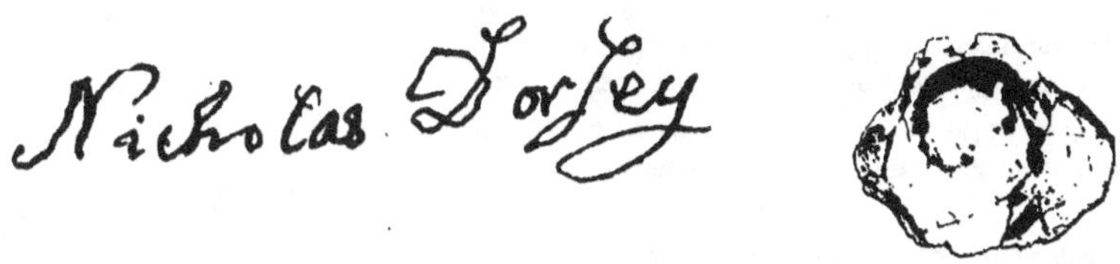

SIGNATURE AND SEAL FROM THE ORIGINAL WILL OF
NICHOLAS DORSEY
Filed in the Hall of Records, Annapolis, Maryland

The estate of Nicholas Dorsey was appraised July 4, 1718 by John Israel and Edward Norwood. The inventory included a Bible, testament, spelling book, psalter, money scales, pocket book, 2 small deal boxes, chest, lock and key, negroes, Tom, Hagar, Jenny & child, Isaac, Esther, Maria. The nearest of kin were Joshua Dorsey and John Dorsey son of Edward. The estate was valued at £347/15/9½ (*Invts. 1, f.* 40)

The second additional account of Frances Dorsey, executrix of Nicholas Dorsey deceased, filed September 4, 1721, included rent (Yearly tax) due on part of Major's Choice and Long Reach. (*Accts. 4, f.* 15) The third additional account of Frances Dorsey filed July 30, 1725, stated the funeral expenses ought not to have been allowed, the necessary £4/10/0 for his burial being of his own estate. (*Accts* 7, f. 43)

Frances Dorsey, widow of Nicholas, was the daughter of Thomas and Lydia Hughes (*St. A.*)

Children of Nicholas and Frances (Hughes) Dorsey:

(Named in father's will)

1. Thomas^{4} Dorsey, b. c 1710; d. bef. 1732
2. Nicholas Dorsey, b. c 1712, m. Sarah Griffith

3. Benjamin Dorsey, b. c 1713, bapt. Sept. 17, 1717 (*A.H.*), m. Sophia ______.
4. Edward Dorsey, b. c 1715, bapt. Sept. 17, 1717 (*A.H.*); d. bef. 1732

2. COLONEL NICHOLAS[4] DORSEY (Nicholas,[3] Col. Edward,[2] Edward[1])
b. c 1712; d. 1780 Baltimore County
m. bef. 1732 Sarah Griffith, b. May 13, 1718; d. Sept. 1, 1794

Nicholas Dorsey inherited 50 acres of Long Reach from his father in 1717, which was to be his at the age of 21 years. On June 20, 1732, Nicholas and Benjamin Dorsey, both being of age, exchanged 100 acres of Long Reach with Mr. John Dorsey Jr., for part of Dorsey's Search on the eastermost side of the Patuxent River. Sarah, wife of Nicholas, gave her consent.
(*A.A. Co. Deeds R.D. No. 2*, f. 430)

The above exchange of land indicates that 100 acres of Long Reach had come into the possession of Nicholas and Benjamin Dorsey, suggesting that Thomas Dorsey, their eldest brother, who was left 50 acres of Long Reach, had died before coming of age, and that Edward Dorsey had also died young.

In 1736 Nicholas Dorsey occupied pew No. 8, with Capt. John Howard and Orlando Griffith, in Christ Church, Queen Caroline Parish.

He was on the Committee of Observation January, 1775, was commissioned Ensign, 1776, and later promoted to Colonel, (Muster Rolls, Maryland, *Arch. of Md.* XVI, 263; XXI, 241) He also served as Judge of the Orphan's Court of Baltimore County.

The estate of Nicholas Dorsey Sr. was long in being settled. On the 8th of September, 1741, Phillip Hammond, merchant, appeared in court and presented a debt due him from the unadministered portion of the estate. Since Frances, wife of Nicholas Dorsey, had failed to complete the administration, he demanded that notice to pay this debt be sent to his sons, Nicholas and Benjamin Dorsey. (*Test. Proc. 32*, f. 34)

On October 21, 1754, Nicholas Dorsey of Baltimore County, planter, sold to John Dorsey Jr. Dorsey's Search. Sarah, wife of Nicholas, gave her consent.
(*A.A. Co. Deeds B.B. No. 1*, f. 1)

The will of Nicholas Dorsey made March 1, 1769 and probated May, 1780 left:

To the elder children, Rachel, Lydia, Nicholas, Charles, Catherine, and Sarah Dorsey, who had all ready received their portion of the estate 1 sh each
To son Henry Dorsey 15 pounds Sterling
To grandson Charles Dorsey, son of Nicholas, Forest Level
To younger children; Vachel, Lucretia, Frances, Orlando, and Achsah Dorsey, the rest of the estate.
(*Balt. Co. Wills 3*, f. 344)

Sarah Dorsey, widow of Nicholas, outlived her husband 20 years. She was the daughter of Orlando and Katherine (Howard) Griffith, and was left 10 pounds in her father's will of 1757.
(*Wills 30*, f. 301)

Children of Nicholas and Sarah (Griffith) Dorsey:
(Named in father's will)

1. Rachel[5] Dorsey, b. 1737; d. 1805, m. Anthony Lindsay, b. 1736; d. 1808
Moved to Kentucky
2. Lydia Dorsey, m. Charles Dorsey, son of Edward. Moved to Nelson County, Kentucky before 1796 (See page 145)
3. Nicholas Dorsey Jr., b. 1741; d. 1796 (*Balt. Co. Invts. 19*, f. 238)
m. Feb. 14, 1765 Ruth Todd, d. 1815
4. Charles Dorsey, b.1744; d. Sept. 12, 1814
m. Mar. 25, 1775 Nancy (Dorsey) Elder, widow of Owen (See page 90)
5. Catherine Dorsey, m. Oct. 13, 1763 Robert Wood, Fred. Co. Moved to Ross Co. Ohio

6. Sarah Dorsey
7. Henry Dorsey
8. Vachel Dorsey
9. Lucretia Dorsey, b. June 4, 1754, m. John Welsh, d. 1820 (*A.A. Co. Wills T.H.H. No. 1,* f. 13)
10. Frances Dorsey, m. Feb. 17, 1792 Eli Warfield
11. Orlando Dorsey, d. 1816 Balt. Co., m. Martha Gaither
12. Achsah Dorsey, m. July 25, 1785 Beal Warfield

3. BENJAMIN[4] DORSEY (Nicholas,[3] Col. Edward,[2] Edward[1])
b. c 1713, of age 1732; d. 1747 Anne Arundel County
m. c 1739/40 Sophia _____; d. 1788 Baltimore County

On February 3, 1741, Benjamin Dorsey sold to John Hammond son of Charles, 100 acres, part of Major's Choice, which he had inherited from his father. Sophia Dorsey, wife of Benjamin, gave her consent. (*A.A. Co. Deeds R.B. No. 1,* f. 111)

On August 24, 1741, Benjamin Dorsey, Anne Arundel County, bought of Thomas Colegate, Baltimore County, Talbot's Last Shift lying in Anne Arundel County near the main falls of the Patapsco River. (*Ibid.,* f. 81)

Benjamin Dorsey died intestate in 1747. (*Test. Proc. 31,* f. 278) The inventory of the estate of Benjamin Dorsey, son of Nicholas, wife Sophia Dorsey, administratrix, was appraised by Richard Shipley and John Talbott on April 12, 1750. Nearest of kin were John Dorsey of Edward and Nicholas Dorsey. (*Invts. 42,* f. 34)

Children of Benjamin and Sophia Dorsey:

1. Benjamin[5] Dorsey, b. c 1741; d. 1775 unm. and intestate
   Letters of administration were issued to Elisha Dorsey on the estate of Benjamin Dorsey deceased of Baltimore County, intestate, 1775. No representatives and no claimants. (*Balt. Co. Accts. 3,* f. 68) His inventory was taken April 14, 1778. Nearest of kin were Cassandra Dorsey and John Talbott.
2. Elisha Dorsey, b. c 1743, m. Mary Slade (See below)
3. Cassandra Dorsey, b. bef. 1747; d. after 1804 unm. at that time

Sophia Dorsey, widow of Benjamin, m. (2) John Talbott, on whose estate she with John Talbott, Benjamin Shipley, and Elisha Dorsey gave bond, September 9, 1771. (*Test. Proc. 44,* f. 262)

Sophia Talbott died before February 21, 1788, for on this date the administration bond on her estate was given by John Talbott, son of John of Mine Run Hundred, Greenberry Wyle, and Richard Colegate Talbott. (*Balt. Co. Adm. Bond Bk. 7,* f. 50) The inventory of the goods of Sophia Talbott, taken April 16, 1788, gave as kin, Henry and Jeremiah Talbott.

Children of John and Sophia Talbott:

1. John Talbott
2. Richard Colegate Talbott, b. 1762, m. 1788 Drucilla Grove, Moved to Kentucky
3. Jeremiah Talbott - the 1783 tax list names him with 4 in family
4. Henry Talbott
5. Sophia Talbott, unm. in 1804

2. LIEUT. ELISHA[5] DORSEY (Benjamin,[4] Nicholas,[3] Col. Edward,[2] Edward[1])
b. c 1743; d. 1801/2 at Dorsey's Plains, Baltimore County
m. Dec. 15, 1768 Mary Slade (*St. Jn. and St. Geo.*); d. 1782

DORSEY FAMILY

In 1772 Elisha Dorsey of Baltimore County bought from Thomas Marshall, 123 acres of a tract called Climna Lina.. (*Balt. Co. Deeds A.L. No. F, f.* 92) He also owned land called Dorsey's Plains.

On January 21, 1771, Elisha Dorsey, son and heir of Benjamin Dorsey of Anne Arundel County, deceased, and Sophia Talbott, his mother, formerly widow of said Benjamin Dorsey, sold Talbott's Last Shift to Joshua Griffith. Mary, wife of Elisha, relinquished her third of this land. (*Prov. Ct. Rec. D.D. No. 5, f.* 121)

On November 30, 1774, Jeremiah Johnson and Elisha Dorsey were chosen to serve on a committee from Baltimore County, North Hundred. At a meeting of the Baltimore County Committee, it was resolved that the Enrollment and Association Papers be lodged with the following gentlemen for the greater convenience of the Freeman in their respective Hundreds to sign, viz... North Hundred, Nicholas Merryman of Nicholas, Elisha Dorsey and Thomas Stansbury. (*Amer. Arch. 4th Series,* IV, 1691, 1742)

Elisha Dorsey was appointed first Lieutenant of Capt. Christopher Owing's Company in Soldier's Delight Battalion, Baltimore County, on September 11, 1777. (*Arch of Md.* XVI, 369)

Elisha Dorsey d. in 1801/2 intestate. His estate was appraised October 16, 1802. His son William Dorsey served as administrator and Cassandra Dorsey and Cassandra Jones signed as kin. (*Balt. Co. Invts. 22, f.* 327)

The account of his estate shows that Cassandra Dorsey was paid in full her share of the deceased's estate, Mary Dorsey, her part, Elisha Dorsey, his part, and Thomas Marshall, guardian of Nicholas Dorsey in full for his ward's portion. (*Balt. Co. Accts. 16, f.* 167) At the sale of his personal estate, Cassandra Dorsey and Sophia Talbott bought several articles.

Mary Dorsey, wife of Elisha, was the daughter of Josias and Mary (Day) Slade. She died in 1782 when her son Nicholas was born.

Children of Elisha and Mary (Slade) Dorsey:

1. William[6] Dorsey, m. Elizabeth ________
2. Cassandra Dorsey, m. Apr. 15, 1805, Benjamin Parker, Balt. Co.
3. Mary Dorsey, d. unm.
4. Elisha Dorsey, living in 1802
5. Nicholas Slade Dorsey, b. 1782, m. Mary Anderson (See below)

5\. NICHOLAS SLADE[6] DORSEY (Elisha,[5] Benjamin,[4] Nicholas,[3] Col. Edward,[2] Edward[1])

b. 1782; d. Feb. 3, 1867 Baltimore County

m. Aug. 1, 1809 Mary Anderson, b. 1790, dau. of Thomas and Ruth (Sparks) Anderson

Nicholas Slade Dorsey served in the war of 1812. His death was recorded in "The Sun," Baltimore, Maryland, February 23, 1867 as follows:

> "Dorsey - On Saturday, February 23, at his residence on the York turnpike, 17 miles from Baltimore, Nicholas Dorsey, one of the Old Defenders in 1812, in the 85th year of his age," He signed his will, Nicholas S. Dorsey.

Children of Nicholas Slade and Mary (Anderson) Dorsey:
(From Family Records)

1. Thomas Anderson[7] Dorsey, b. July 4, 1810, m. Maria Sweetser Hance
2. Eliza Dorsey, b. 1814, d. unm.
3. John Dorsey, b. 1823, d. unm.
4. Sophia Talbott Dorsey, b. 1825, d. unm.
5. Maria Dorsey, b. 1829, d. unm.
6. Owen Dorsey, b. 1830, d. unm.

1. THOMAS ANDERSON[7] DORSEY (Nicholas Slade,[6] Elisha,[5] Benjamin,[4] Nicholas,[3] Col. Edward,[2] Edward[1])
   b. July 4, 1810; d. 1852 Baltimore County
   m. December 24, 1847 Maria Sweetser Hance, b. July 17, 1826; d. 1899, Washington D.C. dau. of James and Ann (Sweetser) Hance. She m. (2) Levin Stanforth

Thomas Anderson Dorsey was educated at St. James Academy, Baltimore County. He became senior partner in the dry goods firm of Dorsey and Ross, Baltimore, Maryland.

Children of Thomas Anderson and Maria (Hance) Dorsey:

1. Rev. James Owen[8] Dorsey, b. Oct. 31, 1848, m. Clara Virginia Wynkoop
2. Thomas Anderson Dorsey, m. Mar. 21, 1883 Bettie Claybaugh

   Children:

   1. George Brent[9] Dorsey, m. Jessie Dean Twyman

      Children: Bettie Dean[10] Dorsey
      Dorothy Burke[10] Dorsey
   2. James Owen Dorsey, d.y.
   3. Lawrence Dorsey, m. Ethel Virginia Gale

1. REV. JAMES OWEN[8] Dorsey (Thomas Anderson,[7] Nicholas Slade,[6] Elisha,[5] Benjamin,[4] Nicholas,[3] Col. Edward,[2] Edward[1])
   b. Oct. 31, 1848; d. Feb. 4, 1895 Washington D.C.
   m. Apr. 18, 1876 Clara Virginia Wynkoop, b. Nov. 8, 1851; d. Oct. 10, 1926 dau. of Garrett and Julia A. (Mountz) Wynkoop

James Owen Dorsey, American ethnologist and anthropologist, was educated at Baltimore City High School and the Theological Seminary of Virginia, from which he went as a missionary in 1871 to the Ponka Indiana in the Dakota Territory.

He was Rector of the historic old St. John's Episcopal Church, Broad Creek, Maryland from 1874 to 1878. He was then appointed an ethnologist of the U.S. Geological and Geographic Survey of the Rocky Mountain Region, from which he was transferred in 1879 to the Bureau of American Ethnology of the Smithsonian Institution, where he remained until his death.

Children of Rev. James Owen and Clara Virginia (Wynkoop) Dorsey:

1. Virginia[9] Dorsey, d. inf.
2. Virginia Dorsey, m. June 18, 1901 James Herndon Lightfoot, d. Nov. 17, 1942, son of Col. Charles Edward Lightfoot, C.S.A., and Georgiana (Chapin) Lightfoot. Attorney at law; on the Board of Supervising Examiners, U.S. Patent Office, having served in the Patent Office for more than 50 years. (*Ency. of American Biography, New Series*, 1944, pages 308-310) (See page 216)

   Children:

   1. James Herndon[10] Lightfoot, d. inf.
   2. James Owen Dorsey[10] Lightfoot, d. inf.
   3. Virginia Dorsey[10] Lightfoot, m. Fitzhugh Maclean

      Children: Anne Fitzhugh[11] Maclean
   4. Georgiana Chapin[10] Lightfoot

BENJAMIN DORSEY

8. BENJAMIN[3] DORSEY (Col. Edward,[2] Edward[1])
   b. c. 1692; d. 1717 unm. Baltimore County

DORSEY FAMILY

Benjamin Dorsey, the youngest son of Edward and Sarah Dorsey, received in 1700 by deed of gift from his father, 100 acres of Major's Choice. In 1704 he was willed 100 acres of land called Long Reach, with two silver spoons and the little gun to be delivered to him at the age of 16 years.

On November 1, 1709, he bound himself to Matthew Beard of Anne Arundel County, Carpenter, for five years to learn the trade of carpentry. During this time his clothing and washing were to be furnished and he was to be given a good suit after the first year's work. (*A.A. Co. Deeds P.K.* f. 112) On November 8th, he chose Matthew Beard as his guardian. (*A.A. Co. Judg. T.B. No. 2,* f. 95)

He was of age on May 8, 1714, for on this date he sold for 40 pounds Sterling to Joshua Dorsey, 100 acres of Major's Choice given him by his father, which he hath full power to sell. (*Balt. Co. Deeds T.R. No. A,* f. 338) On May 30th, he sold to Thomas Worthington of Anne Arundel County, 200 acres of land, being a part of Long Reach lying near the Patuxent River in Baltimore County, 100 acres thereof being by will bearing date 1704 bequeated by Col. Edward Dorsey to his son Benjamin Dorsey, the other 100 acres sold and conveyed by Joshua-Dorsey of Baltimore County to said Benjamin. (*Ibid.,* f. 340) On July 2, 1719, as heir at law to Benjamin Dorsey deceased, Samuel Dorsey confirmed this sale. (*Balt. Co. Deeds T.R. No. DS,* f. 3)

Benjamin Dorsey died intestate in 1717. His brother, John Dorsey, signed his administration bond on June 4, 1717. (*Test. Proc. 23,* f. 280)

LACON DORSEY

9. LACON^3 DORSEY (Col. Edward,^{2} Edward^1)
b. c 1694; d. c 1712 Baltimore County

Lacon Dorsey, the eldest son of Col. Edward Dorsey and his wife Margaret, was willed the parcel of land lying near the Maine Falls of the Patapsco River known by the name Hockley containing 100 acres, servants, furniture, stock and feed to be his at the age of 21 years. With his brothers Charles, Francis, and Edward, he was given all of his father's land on the north side of the Patapsco River, to be equally divided as soon as either of them shall come of age, and in case either of them die before coming of age, the land was to be equally divided amongst the rest of the sons.

In June 1710 he chose his brother-in-law, John Petticoat as his guardian.
(*Balt. Co. Ct. Rec. I.S.B.*)

He died before coming of age and his three brothers divided his lands to each of their interests and satisfaction as was provided in their father's will.
(*Balt. Co. Deeds I.S. No. 1,* f. 139)

FRANCIS DORSEY

10. FRANCIS^3 DORSEY (Col. Edward,^{2} Edward^1)
b. c 1696; d. 1749 Baltimore County
m. c 1724 Elizabeth Baker, d. bef. 1749

Francis Dorsey inherited by the will of his father in 1704 one-fourth of his father's land on the north side of the Patapsco River, and also stock, feed, furniture, and a negro boy named Charles to be his upon coming of age.

On June 10, 1728, Francis Dorsey and his brother Edward sold to Hyde Haxton, the tract called United Friendship containing 150 acres, which had been made over to them by their brother Charles Dorsey, after the death of their brother Lacon Dorsey. Elizabeth, wife of Francis, signed the deed. Both signed with their marks.
(*Balt. Co. Deeds I.S. No. 1,* f. 156)

The will of Francis Dorsey made June 5, 1749 and probated February 17, 1749/50 left:

To son Francis Dorsey, all my right and title to 100 acres of Scotchman's Desire in Baltimore County, north side main falls of Patapsco River, also 50 acres of Dorsey's Addition and one negro by name of Tom about 4 years old
To son Lacon Dorsey, my interest in land on the northern branch of great falls of the Patapsco River called White Oak Bottom, also 50 acres of Dorsey's Addition, Lacon to have the upper part, and a negro girl named Sue 1½ years old
Should Francis or Lacon die without issue, real estate to the survivor
Remainder of personal estate after just debts are paid to be divided among my daughters. If negro woman has any children they are to be sold and money put to the use of my daughters
To daughter Venitia Dorsey, Mare Colt to be appraised and value deducted from her division
Exr: Son-in-law, William Murphy
Wit: John Hurd, Dorsey Petticoart, Jacob Rowles Jr. (*Wills 27*, 132)

On June 17, 1752, William Murphy, son-in-law of Francis Dorsey, administered on his estate. (*Bal. Bk.* 1, f. 21) Th administration account shows that the deceased left 8 children, his daughters Priscilla and Keziah being dead. In his account William Murphy claimed one year's allowance for dieting and clothing 4 of the children of the deceased, they being young and naked. (*Accts. 33*, f. 312)

At the March Court 1765, Charles Wells and Sarah, his wife, Morris Baker and Elizabeth, his wife, Margaret Dorsey, Francis Dorsey, and Lakin Dorsey issued a citation against William Murphy executor of Francis Dorsey. (*Test. Proc. 41*, folios 35, 70)

Elizabeth Dorsey, wife of Francis, was not mentioned in his will. She was the daughter of Maurice Baker, who bequeathed to his grandson Francis Dorsey, 100 acres called Scotchman's Desire in Baltimore County. (*A.A. Co. Wills 31, Pt. 2*, f. 672)

Children of Francis and Elizabeth (Baker) Dorsey:
(Births recorded in St. Paul's Register, Baltimore)

1. Priscilla[4] Dorsey, b. Mar. 22, 1725/6; d. bef. 1752, m. William Murphy

   Children: (St. Thomas Register)

   Elizabeth Murphy, b. 1743
   Priscilla Murphy, b. 1746
   William Murphy, b. 1748
   Benjamin Murphy, b. 1750

2. Venitia Dorsey, b. Oct. 16, 1728
3. Sarah Dorsey, b. Jan. 28, 1730, m. Charles Wells
4. Elizabeth Dorsey, b. Aug. 16, 1733, m. Morris Baker
5. Kezia Dorsey, b. Apr. 25, 1735; d. bef. 1752
6. Margaret Dorsey, b. June 18, 1738/9
7. Francis Dorsey, b. June 23, 1741; d. 1769, m. Ann ______ (See below)
8. Lacon Dorsey, b. Feb. 15, 1747 (St. Thos.) m. bef. 1770 Lucy_____
   On October 3, 1770, Leakin Dorsey sold to Nathan Petticord 10½ acres of Dorsey's Addition beginning at a line of Scotchman's Desire.
   (*Balt. Co. Deeds A.L. No. F*, f. 66)

7. FRANCIS[4] DORSEY (Francis,[3] Col. Edward,[2] Edward[1])

b. June 23, 1741; d. 1769 at Scotchman's Desire, Baltimore County
m. Ann ______

Francis Dorsey inherited from his father in 1749 his right to 100 acres of Scotchman's Desire, and also 50 acres of Dorsey's Addition in Baltimore County.

His will dated March 1, 1769 and proved September 5, 1769 left:

To son Basil John Dorsey, 100 acres Scotchman's Desire, he to be of age at 18 years
To wife Ann, Dorsey's Addition and life interest in negro named Tom
To daughter Priscilla Dorsey, remainder interest in negro named Tom and one young horse
To unborn child, one feather bed and furniture
To Patience Davis, a cow and calf
Lands not to be cut except for use of plantation
Exrx: wife Ann (*Wills 37, f.* 301)

Children of Francis and Ann Dorsey:
(Named in father's will)

1. Basil John[5] Dorsey, b. c 1762; d. 1807, Franklin County, Georgia (*Franklin Co., Ga. Wills & Invts.* 1804-07 f. 89)
   m. Mary Robinson, Lincoln County, North Carolina
   In 1780 he chose ann Ousler as his guardian. In 1782 he enlisted in the 2nd Maryland Regiment. (*Arch. of Md.* XVIII, f. 680) (See pages 243,244)
2. Priscilla Dorsey

CHARLES DORSEY

11. CHARLES[3] DORSEY (Col. Edward,[2] Edward[1])
    b. c 1698; d. 1733 at Owen's Adventure, Anne Arundel County
    m. bef. 1725 Ann ________

Charles Dorsey received by the will of his father in 1704 one-fourth of his father's land on the north side of the Patapsco River, and also stock, feed, furniture, and a negro boy named Dick to be his when he comes of age.

In 1718 he chose Samuel Dorsey as his guardian. (*Balt. Co. Ct. Rec. 2, I.S.B, f.* 36)

Upon the death of Lacon Dorsey, Charles Dorsey and his brothers divided the land left them by their father, On June 10, 1728, Charles made over to Francis and Edward Dorsey all of his part of United Friendship. Charles and Francis signed the deed with their marks, Edward Jr., with his name. In December, 1732, Francis and Edward Dorsey recorded a deed to show that Owen's Adventure containing 225 acres, in their aforesaid division, fell to and became the property of Charles Dorsey and is the land on which he lives. (*Balt. Co. Deeds I.S. No. 1,* folios 139, 149)

On August 13, 1729, Charles Dorsey conveyed to Richard Snowden of Anne Arundel County the tract called Major's Fancy, which had formerly belonged to his brother Samuel. Ann, his wife, signed. (*A.A. Co. Deeds T.I. No. 1, f.* 44)

Charles Dorsey died intestate in 1733. His estate was appraised January 10, 1733/4. (*Invts. 17, f.* 468) His administration account was recorded July 20, 1733, with Ann Dorsey as his administratrix, and Francis and Edward Dorsey Jr., son of John as kin. (*Accts. 15, f.* 118)

Ann Dorsey, widow of Charles, whose maiden name is unknown, m. (2) before November 19, 1735 John Martin.. On this date John Martin, who had intermarried with Ann Dorsey administratrix of Charles Dorsey, under oath swore to an additional inventory. (*Invts. 21, f.* 172)

Children of Charles and Ann Dorsey:
(Births recorded in Queen Caroline Parish Register)

1. Margaret[4] Dorsey, b. Apr. 28, 1725
2. Jane Dorsey,. b. Sept. 22, 1726
3. Ann Dorsey, b. June 22, 1728
4. Aquilla Dorsey, b. Mar. 23, 1729, m. Ann Griffith (See page 240)
5. Ellis Dorsey, b. Jan. 28, 1731/2

EDWARD DORSEY

12. EDWARD[3] DORSEY JR. (Col. Edward,[2] Edward[1])
    b. c 1700; d. 1753 at Thomas' Lott, Anne Arundel County m. Phebe ________

COLONEL EDWARD DORSEY

Edward Dorsey Jr. was the second son of Col. Edward bearing this name, the eldest son having died in 1703. He was left by his father, one-fourth of his land on the north side of the Patapsco River, furniture, cattle, feed, the value of all his wearing clothes and the value of a horse named Sparke, his best gun, largest silver Tankard, silver Tobacco box, his seal Gold ring, and a seal skin trunk marked E.D. to be his when he comes of age.

On July 10, 1728, Edward Dorsey Jr. and his brother Francis Dorsey, planters sold to Hyde Haxton part of the tract called United Friendship containing 150 acres, which was a portion of the land the four sons inherited from their father. (*Balt. Co. Deeds I.S. No. I*, f. 156)

On April 17, 1739, Edward Dorsey Jr. bought from Capt. John Howard for 9/7/6 pounds, Thomas' Lott, a tract of 60 acres laid out by Thomas Reynolds of Anne Arundel County. (*A.A. Co. Deeds R.D. No. 3*, f. 138) He also purchased an adjoining tract of land called Dorsey's Addition to Thomas' Lott. In 1747 he was a witness to the will of Ruth Howard, whose first husband was Edward Dorsey, son of Hon. John Dorsey. (*Wills 25*, f. 108)

The will of Edward Dorsey Jr. made June 13, 1753 and probated March 15, 1753 bequeathed:

To wife Phebe during her natural life, my dwelling plantation with 201½ acres of land, it being a part of a tract Thomas' Lott alias Dorsey's Addition to Thomas' Lott. After debts are paid, negroes named Colleum, Harry, Tom, Abigail
To son Lacon Dorsey, 112½ acres of land out of the said above land, he to have the west side thereof and also a negro girl Isabelle and her increase
To son Edward Dorsey, 100 acres out of the above mentioned land and also negro Nan and her increase
To son Joshua Dorsey, 100 acres of a tract Dorsey's Addition to Thomas' Lott and negro Jem and her increase
To daughter Rachel Dorsey, negro Lucy
To Benjamin Gaither, son of John and his heirs, 45 acres and ½ of land being a part of a tract called Dorsey's Addition to Thomas' Lott agreed to by bond July 5, 1750
If Laton, Edward, or Joshua dye before they come of age 21 years, their estate real and personal to be divided between brothers that survive.
Exrs: wife Phebe and Michael Dorsey
Wit: Phil Dorsey, Benj. Lawrence, Samuel X Norwood (*Wills 28*, f. 437)

Children of Edward and Phebe Dorsey:
(Named in father's will)

1. Lacon[4] Dorsey
2. Edward Dorsey
3. Joshua Dorsey, d. 1777 Frederick Co., Va. (*Fred. Co. Va. Wills 4*, f. 559), m. Rachel ________ (See page 239)
4. Rachel Dorsey

ANN DORSEY

13. ANN[3] DORSEY (Col. Edward,[2] Edward[1])

b. c 1702; d. 1785/6 at Major's Choice, Anne Arundel County

m. John Hammond, b. 1701/2 (*A.A. Co. Land Commissions I.B. No. 1*, f. 271) d. 1753

Ann, the youngest daughter of Col. Edward and Margaret Dorsey, received by her father's will in 1704, one negro girl named Jenny, one feather bed and furniture, 50 pounds Sterling, one silver cup size of a quart and two silver spoons to be delivered to her at the age of sixteen or the day of marriage. She later came into possession of 250 acres of Major's Choice in Anne Arundel County, on which she paid taxes in 1750 as Ann Dorsey Hammond. (*A.A. Co. Debt Book*)

In 1713 John Hammond was left by the will of his father Maj. Charles Hammond 238 acres of Phelp's Luck on Elk Ridge in Baltimore County, later Howard County. (*Wills 13*, f. 608)

On November 15, 1736, John's Lott containing 152 acres, originally called Major's Choice was surveyed for John Hammond and patented April 20, 1748. (*Patents T.I. No. 4*, f. 192) On February 1, 1741, he bought from Benjamin Dorsey, son of Nicholas Dorsey of Anne Arundel County for 30 pounds Sterling, 100 acres, part of Major's Choice, originally patented to Edward Dorsey, Baltimore County, adjoining John's Lott. (*A.A. Co. Deeds R.B. No. 1*, f. 115)

DORSEY FAMILY

In 1732 John Hammond was appointed one of six commissioners for Anne Arundel County to buy land and lay out the town of Elk Ridge Landing. (*Arch. of Md.* XXXIX, 125)

The will of John Hammond made October 2, 1753 and probated November 12, 1753 left:

To wife Ann, dwelling plantation of 700 acres, 5 negroes, 3 feather beds, two tables, one dozen chairs, one looking glass
To daughter Hannah, wife of John Welsh, 20 shillings and negroes
To daughter Ann, wife of Francis Davis, 20 shillings and negroes
To son and heir John Hammond, the benefit of a resurvey on a tract of land called Hammond's Contrivance and 100 acres of a common warrant, and 2 negroes
To son Charles Hammond, after his mother's death, my dwelling plantation with all the lands adjoining thereto, and 2 negroes
To daughter Hamutel Hammond, 2 negroes
To daughter Rachel Hammond, 1 negro
To son-in-law Henry Griffith, 25 pounds Sterling money
To Sarah Ann Dorsey, daughter of Vachel Dorsey, 5 pounds Sterling to be paid her at age of 16 years
It is my desire that my executors convey to my beloved brother Phillip Hammond the following tracts of land Vizt: The Marsh, John's Chance, Old Man's Folly
It is my desire that William Jean pay my executors the sum of 20 pounds Sterling money with legal interest according to the terms of his land now in my hands, then that my executors make over and convey to William Jeans his heirs tract of land called Weaver's Lott containing 80 acres
I desire all my back lands under cultivation after rights are paid to his Lordship, be sold by my executors and money applied to the use of my estate
What remains of my estate, not before mentioned, after payment of all just debts, be added to my estate and equally divided between my children Hannah Hammond, Ruth Griffith, Rachel Hammond, John Hammond, Charles Hammond and their heirs.
Exrs: wife Ann Hammond and son-in-law Henry Griffith (*Wills 28,* f. 536)

The will of Ann Hammond made December 1, 1779 and probated July 1, 1786 left:

To daughter Hamutel Welsh, Major's Choice (except part whereon son Charles Hammond now lives) during her natural life after which to son Charles Hammond, also 4 negroes
To son Charles Hammond, 2 negroes
To daughters Hannah Welsh, Ruth Griffith, and Rachel Mackelfresh, each 10 pounds Sterling
To daughter Hamutel Welsh, remainder after legacies are paid
(*A.A. Co. Wills T.G. No. 1,* f. 338)

On February 27, 1787, Hamutel Welsh advertised in the Maryland Gazette for the settlement of debts due the estate of the late Ann Hammond, her mother.

Children of John and Ann (Dorsey) Hammond:
(Named in parent's will)

1. Hannah[4] Hammond, b. Apr. 26, 1723 (*A.H.*), m. John Welsh
2. Ann Hammond, m. Francis Davis
3. John Hammond, d. unm.
4. Charles Hammond, m. Rachel ______
5. Hammutel Hammond, m. ______ Welsh
6. Ruth Hammond, b. 1733, m. Henry Griffith
7. Rachel Hammond, m. John, McElfresh

1. HANNAH[4] HAMMOND (Ann[3] (Dorsey) Hammond, Col. Edward,[2] Edward[1])
b. Apr. 26, 1723 (*A.H.*), living in 1779
m. bef. 1742 John Welsh, b. Feb. 3, 1719/20 (*A.H.*); d. bef. 1784

John Welsh, who was the son of Col. John Welsh and wife Rachel, inherited in 1733 the dwelling plantation, Arnold Gray, and two other tracts, The Neglect and Addition to Arnold Gray, about 400 acres, and 2 negroes when 18 years old. (*Wills 21,* f. 102)

On May 18, 1742, Rachel Welsh of Arnold Gray released her dower rights in 2 tracts The Enlargement and Neglect, to her son John Welsh, and on the same day John Welsh sold the tracts to Henry Hall. His wife, Hannah, signed the deed. (*A.A. Co. Deeds R.B. No. 1,* f. 145)

On September 6, 1749, John Welsh sold to Benjamin Welsh, Prince George's County, 300 acres of land, a part of a tract called Arnold Gray. Hannah, his wife, signed.
(*A.A. Co. Deeds R.B. No. 3, f.* 180)

In 1755 John Welsh deeded 295 acres of Hopson's Choice to Richard Welsh, and in 1766 he transferred part of the same tract to John Welsh Jr., his son. (*A.A. Co. Deeds B.B. No. 1, f.* 101; *B.B. No. 3, f.* 604)

John Welsh was Justice of the Peace, Anne Arundel County in 1774 and 1775. In 1778 he signed the Oath of Allegiance and was commissioned captain. (*Com. Bk. Md. Hist. Soc, f.* 207)

John Welsh died intestate before 1784.

The approximate date of his death is shown in the will of his brother Henry Welsh, dated December 16, 1784, in which Henry Welsh, son of John Welsh deceased was bequeathed a negro boy. (*A.A. Co. Wills J.G. No. 1, f.* 399)

Children of John and Hannah (Hammond) Welsh:

1. John[5] Welsh, d. 1820 (*A.A. Co. Wills T.H.H. No. 1, f.* 13)
   m. Lucretia Dorsey
2. Charles Welsh, d. 1814 (*A.A. Co. Wills J.G. No. 3, f.* 26), m. Sarah ______
3. Rezin Welsh, m. Ruth Davis
4. Henry Welsh, m. Jan. 25, 1786 Mary Davis, Fred. Co.
5. Samuel Welsh, m. Rachel Griffith, dau. of Henry
6. Hamutel Welsh
7. Sarah Welsh, m. Mar. 1792 James Holland, Fred. Co.
8. Nancy Welsh, d. 1825 (*Mont. Co. Wills O, f.* 461), m. Lewis Duval
9. Ruth Welsh
10. Rachel Welsh
11. Phillip Welsh, m. Elizabeth Davis ?

2. ANN[4] HAMMOND (Ann[3] (Dorsey) Hammond, Col. Edward,[2] Edward[1])
   d. after 1763
   m. bef. 1753 Francis Davis, d. 1778 Baltimore County

Ann Davis, wife of Francis, was left 20 shillings in her father's will in 1753.

On January 9, 1755, John and Francis Davis served as administrators of Thomas Davis Sr. late of Anne Arundel County. (*Bal. Bk. 1, f.* 124)

On December 31, 1763, Francis Davis, Baltimore County, sold to Phillip Hammond, 700 acres of land, parts of 2 tracts called Buck Bottom and Valley of Strife, also part of Diamond, 150 acres, and part of Grinisston, now called Davises' Addition, Anne Arundel County. Ann, wife of Francis, signed the deed. (*A.A. Co. Deeds B.B. No. 3, f.* 88)

Francis Davis, m. (2) Katherine ______

The will of Francis Davis made March 22, 1778 and proved April 2, 1778 left:

To daughter Ruth Welsh, wife of Rezin Welsh, 50 pounds current money
To daughter Mary Ann Davis, 50 pounds
To wife Katherine Davis, bay mare called Lightfoot, side saddle etc.
To son Rezin Davis, loom that he now uses
To son Matthais Davis, loom and land Favour and Ease, part of land alloted to son Rezin
To wife Katherine to live at my dwelling house and have liberty of any part of my land during her life or widowhood except 95 acres
Residue among my 7 children, 5 sons and 2 daughters, Viz: Rezin, Matthias, Samuel, Zachariah, Thomas, Lucy, and Nancy Davis.
(*Balt. Co. Wills 3, f.* 370)

Children of Francis Davis:
(Named in will)

1. Ruth Davis, m. Rezin Welsh
2. Mary Ann Davis, m. Jan. 25, 1786 Henry Welsh, Fred. Co.
3. Thomas Davis
4. Rezin Davis
5. Matthias Davis
6. Samuel Davis
7. Zachariah Davis
8. Lucy Davis
9. Nancy Davis

3. JOHN[4] HAMMOND (Ann[3] (Dorsey) Hammond, Col. Edward,[2] Edward[1])
d. unm.

John Hammond was left Hammond's Contrivance by the will of his father and he seemed to have had surveyed for himself a tract called, Sept. 14, I was Born John Hammond son of John. He was not mentioned in his mother's will of 1779 and it is thought that he died without issue, because the above tracts of land came into the possession of his brother Charles Hammond.

4. CAPTAIN CHARLES[4] HAMMOND (Ann[3] (Dorsey) Hammond, Col. Edward,[2] Edward[1])
b. c 1740; d. Nov. 29, 1796 at Hammond's Elk Ridge, Anne Arundel County
m. Rachel ________

Charles Hammond of John was on the Committee of Observation, 1775; Capt. 1777 in 22d Battalion, Anne Arundel County; Capt. in Elk Ridge Battalion, 1778. (*Arch. of Md.* XVI, 347, 525)

On April 21, 1778, Charles Hammond son of John conveyed the tract called Hammond's Contrivance, left to him by his father, to Phillip Hammond. Rachel, wife of Charles, signed the deed. (*A.A. Co. Deeds I.B. No. 5,* f. 495)

He also came into possession of a tract which evidently belonged to his brother John, called Sept. 14, 1739 I was Born John Hammond son of John. This tract joined Hammond's Chance, a tract surveyed for Charles Hammond, Sept. 14, 1792.

On August 23, 1794, he sold for five shillings one acre of Major's Choice situated near Bellows Spring to Charles White, Elizabeth Dorsey, and Achsah Howard, for the purpose of erecting a meeting house thereon for the society of Methodists. (*A.A. Co. Deeds N.H. No. 7,* f. 293)

On December 2, 1794, Charles Hammond obtained a special warrant to resurvey the following land in Anne Arundel County and contiguous to each other (vizt) Phelps Luck, The Addition to Phelps Luck, The Recovery, John's Lott, and part of Major's Choice into one entire tract called Hammond's Elk Ridge Connexion, found to contain 702 acres. Beginning at a bounded rock stone marked with the letters C.H. 17- standing in a valley... (*Patents I.B. No. 2,* f. 212)

A deed of June 30, 1854 states that William B. Dorsey's land goes to Charles Hammond's gate, it being a boundary to Major's Choice, Phelp's Luck, and New Year's Gift from a rock marked C.H., 1795, the beginning of Hammond's Elk Ridge and going to a hickory stump of the Bellow's Spring Meeting House lot. (*Howard Co. Deeds 14,* f. 324)

Charles Hammond's will made July 20, 1796 and probated September 24, 1796 left:

To John Hammond, all my land in Frederick County
To son Charles Hammond, my plantation Hammond's Elk Ridge, on which I now dwell resurveyed last fall correction beginning at a bounded stone in valley marked C.H., 1795
To son Rezin Hammond, tract called Sept. 14, 1739 I was Born John Hammond son of John
To daughters Polly, Deborah, Nancy, Sally, Betsy Hammond, 50 pounds each
Exrs: son John Hammond and son-in-law John Deborah (*A.A. Co. Wills J.G. No. 1,* f. 585)

Children of Charles and Rachel Hammond:
(Named in father's will)

1. John[5] Hammond, b. 1768; d. Apr. 21, 1796 (*Md. Gazette*)
2. Charles Hammond, m. Nov. 4, 1809 Catherine Gassaway, b. 1781; d. 1836
3. Rezin Hammond, went to Tennessee, but returned for the settlement of father's estate
4. Mary (Polly) Hammond, m. John Deborough
5. Ann (Nancy) Hammond, m. William Woods, d. 1826 (*Balt. Co. Wills 12*, f. 298)
6. Sarah (Sally) Hammond, b. 1779; d. 1841, m. Dec. 2, 1806 John Dorsey b. 1773; d. 1820 (See page 241)
7. Betsy Hammond, m.____ Woods

5. HAMUTEL[4] HAMMOND (Ann[3] (Dorsey) Hammond, Col. Edward,[2] Edward[1])
d. 1815 Montgomery County
m. after 1753______ Welsh, d. bef. 1779

Hamutel Welsh was left by the will of her mother in 1779, a part of Major's Choice during her natural life, after which it was to go to her brother Charles Hammond. Her husband had no doubt died before that time. In the 1790 census she is given as head of her family and was then living in Montgomery County.

On December 5, 1810, she gave Thomas Riggs, son of Samuel, 8 negroes for a term of years to provide her support for and during her natural life in his family.
(*Mont. Co. Deeds P*, f. 101)

The will of Hamutel Welsh made November 15, 1811 and probated July 18, 1815 left:

Freedom to slaves given to Thomas Riggs at the expiration of their term
To grand daughter Caroline Eleanor Riggs, daughter of Thomas Riggs, a negro boy William and girl Susannah for certain terms and then to be free; also wearing apparel and furniture, and if she die before 16 or marriage, all property given her to be divided between grandchildren Sarah H. Riggs and Samuel Riggs, son and daughter of aforesaid Thomas Riggs
To grandson John Hammond Riggs, 2 negro boys in possession of Joshua Cocoran, freedom at age of 30, residue of estate as a compensation for the trouble he may be at in seeing that my negroes are freed at the term to each affixed.
Exr: grandson John Hammond Riggs.
A codicil made in 1813 revoked part of the will. (*Mont. Co. Wills* 1, f. 434)
(Grandchildren named in will are great-grandchildren)

______ and Hamutel (Hammond) Welsh had one child:
Caroline Eleanor[5] Welsh, d. 1777
m. Elisha Riggs, d. 1777 (*A.A. Co. Wills E.V. No. 1*, f. 6)

6. RUTH[4] HAMMOND (Ann[3] (Dorsey) Hammond, Col. Edward,[2] Edward[1])
d. Jan. 29, 1782 Montgomery County
m. June 4, 1751 as 2nd wife of Henry Griffith, b. Feb 14, 1720; d. Sept. 28, 1794

Henry Griffith, eldest son of Orlando Griffith, was a large landowner in both Anne Arundel and Montgomery Counties, He was a commissioner in the formation of Montgomery County and one of the Justices in its organization in 1777.
(J. Thomas Scharf, *History Western Maryland*, f. 651)

Henry Griffith m. (1) Apr. 9, 1741 Elizabeth Dorsey, dau. of Edward (*Q. Car.*) (See page 145)

Their children were:
1. Sarah Griffith, b. Jan. 25, 1741/2, m.______ Todd
2. Henry Griffith, b. Mar. 16, 1744/5
3. Ruth Griffith, b. May 18, 1747, m. Amos Riggs
4. Rachel Griffith, b. Nov. 28, 1749, m. Samuel Welsh

The will of Henry Griffith made October 10, 1794 and proved January 14, 1794 left:

To son Henry Griffith, two plantations whereon his two sons now live containing 600 acres, provided he conveys to brothers Samuel and Joshua, Ward's Pleasure, but if otherwise 50 acres within limits to be deducted from his part
To son Samuel Griffith, plantation where he now lives, 500 acres
To son Joshua Griffith, my dwelling plantation, 500 acres, negroes, furniture, stock, and a bond of Charles Welsh which he now has in his possession
To 4 grandchildren, William Ridgely Griffith, Juliet Griffith, Pheby Griffith, John Griffith, sons and daughters of son John Griffith deceased, the sum of 900 pounds current money to be divided equally as they come of age
To grandchildren, sons and daughters of Amos Riggs and wife Ruth, tract of land called Griffith's Park in Allegheny County
To grandchildren, sons and daughters of Samuel Welsh and late wife Rachel, land called Sherwoods Forest
To grandchildren, sons and daughters of Nicholas Hall and late wife Ann, 50 pounds current money to be divided equally amongst them when of age
To grandson Lyde Griffith, 25 pounds at age of 21 years
Grant power to executor to sell following land and mill and undivided part of Turulum, adjoining mill lands, 200 acres, and all that part of Turulum which is undivided and lies on main road and called New Design, and also land in Anne Arundel County known as Honlip Place, 250 acres. Also land in Frederick County
Remaining estate to be divided into 10 parts and paid sons and daughters or their representatives Henry, Samuel, Philemon, Joshua, to child of Sarah Todd, to Amos Riggs for his wife's part, to Samuel Welsh's children, to Nicholas Hall's children, to John Burgess for his wife's part, to Joale Water for his wife's part
Exrs: sons Philemon and Joshua Griffith (*Mont. Co. Wills C,* f. 153)

Children of Henry and Ruth (Hammond) Griffith:
(Births recorded in Queen Caroline Parish Register)

1. Capt. Samuel[5] Griffith, b. May 7, 1752, m. (1) Rachel Warfield
   m. (2) Ruth Berry, dau. of Richard
   (See page 86)
2. John H, Griffith, b. Apr. 20, 1754; d. bef. 1794, m. Elizabeth Ridgely
3. Col. Philemon Griffith, b. Aug. 29, 1756, m. Eleanor Jacob
4. Lieut. Charles Griffith, b. Dec. 16, 1758
5. Ann Griffith, b. Feb. 24, 1762; d. Apr. 27, 1791, m. Nicholas Hall
6. Joshua Griffith, b. July 25, 1764, m. Elizabeth ______
7. Eleanor Griffith, b. Mar. 9, 1766, m. John Burgess
8. Elizabeth Griffith, b. Dec. 16, 1768; d. Sept. 13, 1770

7. RACHEL[4] HAMMOND (Ann[3] (Dorsey) Hammond, Col. Edward,[2] Edward[1])
d. bef. 1799, living in 1786
m. John McElfresh (Mackelfresh) d. 1799 Frederick County

The will of John McElfresh made May 3, 1799 and probated September 13, 1799 left:

To son Phillip McElfresh, land called Land of Promise
To son Charles McElfresh, land called Principle
To son Henry McElfresh, land called Cowman's Manor
To son Joseph McElfresh, part of Hobb's Purchase
To daughter Sarah Wood, personalty
To daughter Rachel Smith, personalty
To grandsons Lloyd and John McElfresh, a farm each
(*Fred. Co. Wills G.M. No. 3,* f. 317)

Children of John and Rachel (Hammond) Mc Elfresh:
(Named in father's will)

1. Phillip McElfresh, m. Feb. 22, 1781 Lydia Griffith
2. Charles McElfresh, m. Nov. 25, 1789 Ann Smith
3. Henry McElfresh, m. Arianna Hammond
4. Joseph McElfresh, m. Jan. 19, 1792 Sarah Howard
5. Sarah McElfresh, m. Henry Wood
6. Rachel McElfresh, m. Apr. 4, 1792 John Smith

MICHAEL DORSEY I

and

SOME OF HIS DESCENDANTS

FAMILY LINES

of

MAXWELL J. AND JOHN MUIR DORSEY

Urbana, Illinois

NANNIE BALL NIMMO

Baltimore, Maryland

HERBERT GROVE DORSEY

Washington, D. C.

CHART
SHOWING LINE OF DESCENT OF
MAXWELL J. DORSEY AND JOHN MUIR DORSEY
Urbana, Illinois

EDWARD DORSEY 16 -1659 m. Ann ______

Sarah m. Matthew Howard | COL. EDWARD 16 -1705 m. 1 Sarah Wyatt | Joshua m. Sarah Richardson | Hon. John m. Pleasance ______

Edward unm. | Sarah m.1 John Norwood m.2 John Petticoat | Samuel m. Jane ______ | Hannah m. Joseph Howard | Joshua m. Ann Ridgely | JOHN 1688-1764 m. Honor Sta ______ (Stafford) | Nicholas m. Frances Hughes | Benjamin unm.

Hannah m. Adam Barnes | Ruth m.1 Benj. Lawrence m.2 Nathaniel Rumney | MICHAEL 1712-76 m. Ruth Todd | Sarah m. Henry Howard | Susannah m. Levin Lawrence | Jemima m.1 John Elder m.2 Joseph Hobbs | Patience m. Samuel Howard | Vachel m. Ruth Dorsey | Edward m. Elizabeth Gillis | Nathan m. Sophia Owings

John m. Ann Dorsey | Elizabeth m. Joseph Burgess | Honor m. John Elder | Sarah m. Richard Berry | Ruth m. Ely Dorsey | MICHAEL 1745-1812 m. Honor Elder | Lancelot m. Sarah Warfield | Ann m.1 Owen Elder m.2 Charles Dorsey | Lydia m. Richard Talbot

Michael m. Amelia Green | JOHN 1770-1835 m. Jemima Gist | Owen m. Henrietta Dorsey | Lloyd m. Anna Green | Jemima m. Alexander Warfield | Elizabeth * m. William Ball | Cecelia m. Michael Dunn | Honor m. Joshua Jones

Honor m. James McGee | JOSEPH 1796-1845 m. Johannah Foster | Michael m. Hannah Ellis | Owen m. Elizabeth Foster | William m.1 Rebecca Gorsuch m.2 Eliza Cooksey | Jemima m. Moses Cole | Elizabeth m. James McClintock | John** m. Prudence Means

BENJAMIN 1821-94 m. Martha McCann | Jemima m. Harvey Compton | John m. Jane McCann | Elizabeth m. Joseph Spencer | Abraham m. Isabelle Lane | Johanna m. Dr. Hendren | Joseph m. Anna Cresap | Naomi m. Samuel Hendren | Permelia unm. | Ciscil m. John Shaw

SAMUEL 1850-1927 m. Martha Magruder | Maxwell m. Olive Jane Lane | Margaret m. Lyman Fulks | Johanna m. Harvey Wright | Joseph m. Cora Divan | Carrie m. U. Grant Porter

Sarah m. John Beal | Frank M. m. Margaret Treat | MAXWELL J. m. Jean Muir | Mary m. Carl Parkinson | Benjamin m. Lillie German | Bertha m. Walker King | Elmer m. Mary Pine | Ernest | Ciscil

JOHN MUIR DORSEY m. Marguerite Shaw

NORMA JEAN DORSEY

* Line of Descent of Nannie Ball Nimmo
** Line of Descent of Herbert Grove Dorsey

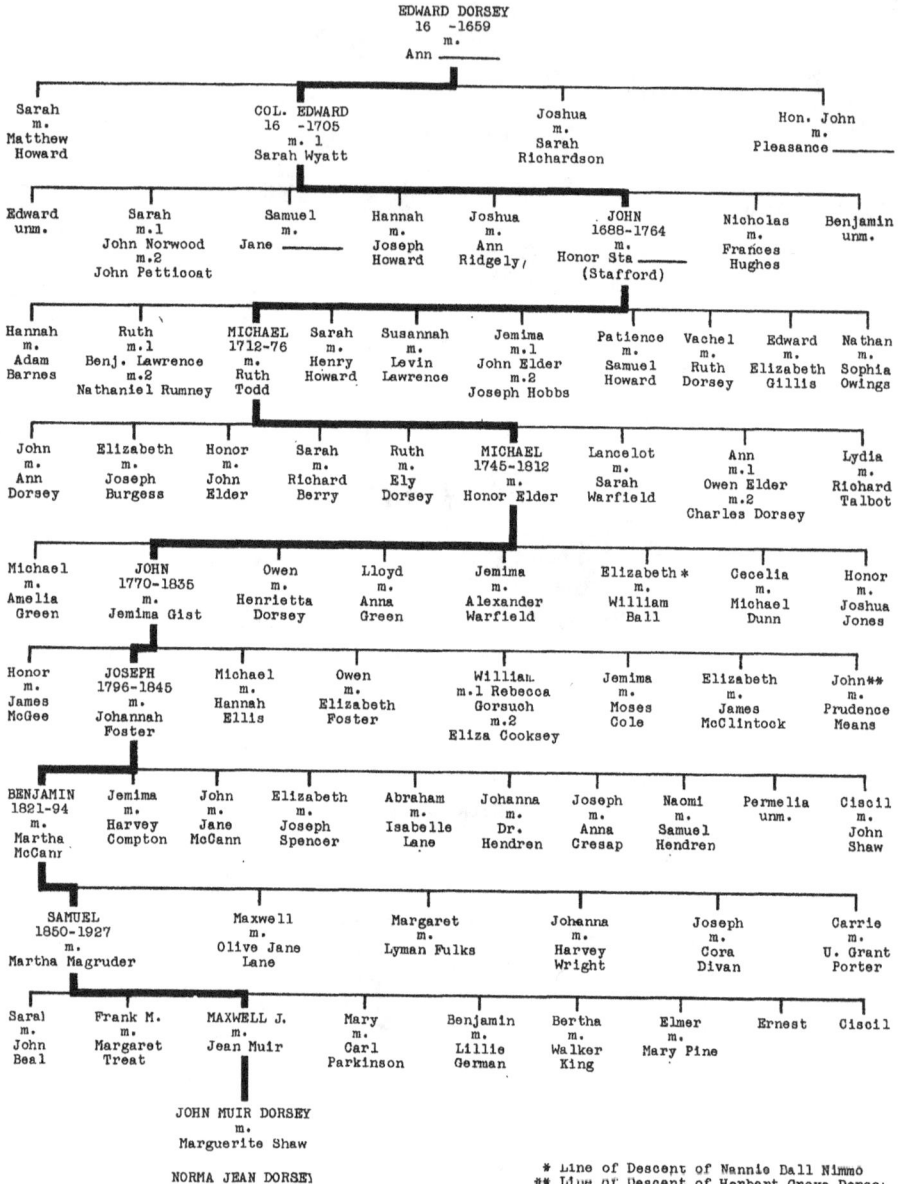

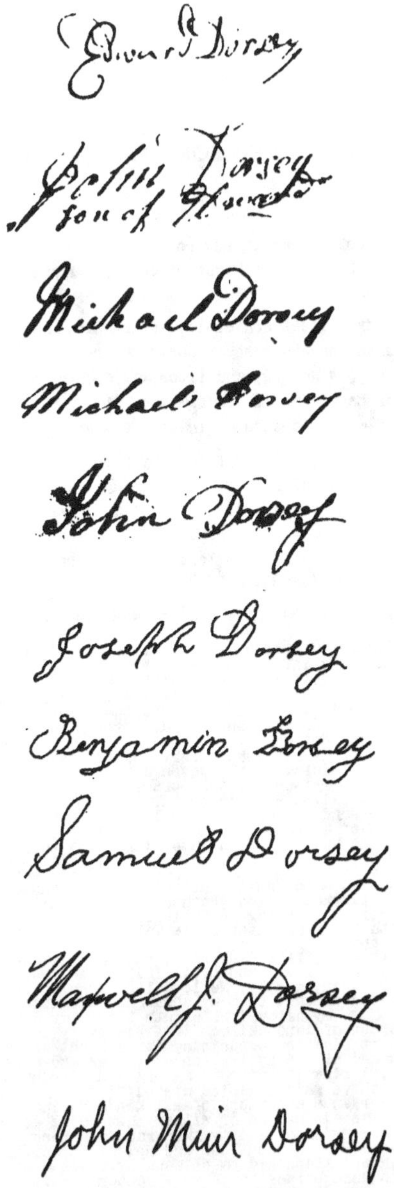

SIGNATURES OF TEN GENERATIONS

In the Line of Descent of Maxwell J. Dorsey and John Muir Dorsey

MICHAEL DORSEY I AND SOME OF HIS DESCENDANTS

3. MICHAEL[4] DORSEY I (John,[3] Col. Edward,[2] Edward[1])

b. Mar. 15, 1712; d. Dec. 20, 1776 at First Discovery, Anne Arundel County
m. Aug. 10, 1733 Ruth Todd; d. Nov. 1789

The name of Michael Dorsey, eldest son of John of Edward, seldom appeared on the records. On May 6, 1735, he qualified as churchwarden in Christ Church, Anne Arundel County (now Howard County), occupied side seat on pew No. 29, and later was elected vestryman. When an acre of Poplar Springs Garden was purchased from Levin Lawrence in 1750 for a Chapel of Ease, Michael Dorsey and Alexander Warfield were witnesses. (*Christ Church Records*, folios 65, 73, 158)

On August 2, 1735, he received from his father by deed of gift a tract called Pushpin containing 200 acres, and 100 acres of Discovery adjoining, (*A.A. Co. Deeds R.D. No. 2, f.* 269) and on December 27, 1750, he received 330 acres of Good Range and 316 acres of Brother's Partnership. (*A.A. Co. Deeds R.B. No. 3, f.* 389)

By the will of his father in 1764 he was left the dwelling plantation called First Discovery containing 400 acres. (See page 175A)

Michael Dorsey's will made July 20, 1774 and probated June 3, 1777 follows:

Maryland In the Name of God Amen, I Michael Dorsey of Anne Arundell County and Province aforesaid being infirm in health but sound of mind and memory blessed be God therefore, and knowing it is appointed for men once to die, do make this my last will and testament in manner and form following Vizt.

Imp- First and principally I give my soul to God that gave it me and my body to the earth to be buried in a decent manner and as to my worldly goods I dispose of them in the manner following

Item- I give and bequeath to my son John Dorsey and his heirs forever one tract of land called Toddy containing twenty seven acres

Item- I give and bequeath to my son Michael Dorsey and his heirs forever the land whereon he now lives called Pushpin containing two hundred acres, part of first Discovery two hundred acres, to be laid off across the said land adjoining Pushpin, & part of a tract of land called First Division containing twenty five acres. Also one hundred pounds Sterling money to be paid him by my executor hereafter mentioned out of my estate in full for his part thereof

Item- I give and bequeath to my son Lancelot Dorsey and his heirs for ever, part of a tract of land called Good Range containing three hundred and thirty three acres, and part of a tract called Brother's Partnership containing three hundred and sixteen acres, it being in full for his part of my estate

Item- I give and bequeath to my daughter Lydia Talbot and her heirs forever one negro girl named Nan

Item- I give and bequeath to my five daughters, namely, Elizabeth Burgess, Sarah Berry, Ruth Dorsey, Ann Elder, and Lydia Talbot and their heirs forever the following negro children, namely, Nell, Caleb, Dennis, Sam, Dinah, and Basil to be equally divided amongst them my abovesaid daughters

Item- I give and bequeath to my beloved wife Ruth Dorsey my dwelling plantation being part of a tract of land called first Discovery containing three hundred acres, part of first Division containing forty eight acres during her natural life or widowhood and at the expiration of either, to my son John Dorsey and his heirs forever, I likewise give to my beloved wife Ruth Dorsey (after all my just debts and above said legacies are paid) all my negroes, on the said plantation white servants and stock of all kinds during her natural life or widowhood, and at the expiration of either then to be equally divided among my daughters above mentioned, and my two granddaughters (the daughters of Onor Elder deceased) Providence Elder and Helenia Elder to have one equal part with my daughters aforesaid to be equally divided between them

Lastly- I appoint my son John Dorsey to be my executor in witness whereof I set my hand and seal this twentieth day of July one thousand seven hundred and twenty four.

In presence of
Brice Howard
James Riggs
Joshua Howard

Michael Dorsey (seal)

(*A.A. Co. Original Wills*, Box D, Folder 63)
(*A.A. Co. Wills E.V.* No. 1, f. 8)

MICHAEL DORSEY AND SOME OF HIS DESCENDANTS

The inventory of the estate of Michael Dorsey was taken June 18, 1777 by his sons, Michael and Lancelot Dorsey. It included:

Wearing apparel
6 beds with furniture
5 trunks, case with bottles
6 chests, Sheep and garden shears
4 Tables, 2 Rings, Griddle & Seve
Woolen and Linnen Wheels, Bottles
Jugs and Chamber potts
Sheets, Table Cloths, Linnen
7 yds Cloth, close stool
Warming pan, Sifter, Desk, Spice Box
Looking glasses, Hand Irons, Candle Sticks
Tongs, Shovels, Iron Hooks, China Delph Stone
Glass Ware, Tin Ware and spoons
Books, Scales, Rule and square
Couch and chairs, Gun, Scythes, Sickles
Still, Hoes, Axes, Mall & Wedges, Pitch fork
frying pans, Marking Irons, Iron Basons
Cake Irons, Ladle, flesh forks, potts & Hooks
Trammels, Spit and Hook, Candle snuffers
Old lumber and Soap Jars, Cask, Vinegar casks
Runlet; Grind stone, Kettles, Mortar & pestle
Skillet, Tubbs, peggen, Wooden Tray, 5 bottles wine
Cyder Mill, Hand Mill, cart & wheelbarrow, Spades
Bending Irons, Carpenter & coopers tools
Bee hives, Wool, Cards
Pewter Plates, Bottles, Collar for Horses
Cart, Saddle and Bridle, six traces, Iron Tooth
8 hanks of Silk, Hone Strap, 2 pr Spectacles
Bed pan, bag with feathers, cards, Knives and forks
Six Medicines, Blocks with rope, Dryed Beef, Bacon
8 pounds of thread, Towels, Raw Hides, Negro bedding
Candles, Cut saw, Wheat, Rye, flax, oats, corn Meal
55 Head of Cattle, 41 head Sheep, 70 Hoggs, 14 Horses of different ages

1 servant negro Jack, Pomp, Cesar, Else, Fan, Will, Ben, John
Bill, Shadrock, Nell, Dinah, Sam, Caleb, Basil, Nan, Dennis

The value of the estate was £1302/18/8. *(A.A. Co. Invts. E.V. No. 1, f. 38)*

Because of the death of John Dorsey, executor of the will Michael Dorsey, Lancelot Dorsey (merchant) was administrator de bonis non of his father's will, The account of Lancelot Dorsey, May 8, 1790, lists payments to Ely Dorsey, legacy left to wife Ruth Dorsey, to Elizabeth Burgess, Sarah Berry, Lydia Talbot, Michael Dorsey, Ruth Dorsey, widow to Ely Dorsey Jr., Richard Talbot, Charles Dorsey, Joseph Burgess, Richard Berry, Nancy Dorsey. *(A.A. Co. Test. Papers, Box 20, Folder 2)*

Ruth Dorsey, widow of Michael, was the daughter of Lancelot and Elizabeth (Rockhould) Todd, and by deed of gift from her father, made October 22, 1733, received 250 acres of Altogether, the remaining acres of the 500 acre tract of land going to her sister Sarah, wife of Edward Dorsey. (See page 195)

(A.A. Co. Deeds R.D. No. 2, f. 8)

Ruth Dorsey died in November, 1789. The following record dated May 3, 1792 is of interest.

The petition of Lancelot Dorsey on behalf of himself and others hereby showeth that Ruth Dorsey died about the month of November 1789, entitled to one-half part of a tract of land Altogether lying in Anne Arundel County, the one-half part containing 250 acres, that said Ruth died intestate, whereby the said half part of said land descended to the Representatives of said Ruth, according to act of assembly entitled Acts to direct descendants, that the said Ruth Dorsey had nine children, to wit John Dorsey, now deceased, Elizabeth, now Elizabeth Burgess, Sarah, now Sarah Berry, Ruth, now Ruth Dorsey, Oner formerly Oner Elder, now deceased, Michael Dorsey, Ann Dorsey, Lancelot Dorsey, your petitioner, and Lydia Talbot deceased, that some of the children of the said John Dorsey and Lydia Talbot deceased are under age so that no division or agreement can be made respecting the said land among the representatives of the said Ruth Dorsey during the minority of said children, your petitioner therefore prays that 5 discreet men may be appointed etc...

Court appoints Charles Warfield guardian to Michael Dorsey and infant son of the representative of John Dorsey deceased, and Richard Talbot guardian of Michael, William, Elisha, Lloyd, Samuel, Pleasant, and George Talbot, his children minors.

(*A.A. Co. Guardians for Infants* 1791-1805, f. 50)

A commission appointed April 25, 1792 touching the moiety of land 500 acres Altogether, which Ruth Dorsey died entitled to, I do hereby certify that I have carefully surveyed and laid out part etc... made between Edward Dorsey, and Sarah, his wife, and Michael Dorsey, and Ruth, his wife, bearing date September 27, 1757. (*A.A. Co. Deeds B.B. No. 2*, f. 43)

Children of Michael and Ruth (Todd) Dorsey:
(Named in father's will and above document)
(Births from family records)

1. John[5] Dorsey, b. July 3, 1734, m. Ann Dorsey
2. Elizabeth Dorsey, b. Dec. 13, 1735, m. Joseph Burgess
3. Honor Dorsey, b. Nov. 3, 1737, m. John Elder
4. Sarah Dorsey, b. Sept. 25, 1739, m. Richard Berry
5. Ruth Dorsey, b. Mar. 17, 1743, m. Ely Dorsey
6. Michael Dorsey, b. Oct. 29, 1745, m. Honor Elder (See page 95)
7. Lancelot Dorsey, b. July 17, 1747, m. Sarah Warfield
8. Ann (Nancy) Dorsey, b. Jan. 29, 1748, m. (1) Owen Elder
   m. (2) Charles Dorsey
9. Lydia Dorsey, b. Feb. 6, 1750, m. Richard Talbot

1. JOHN[5] DORSEY (Michael,[4] John,[3] Col. Edward,[2] Edward[1])
b. July 3, 1734; d. 1779 Anne Arundel County
m. Ann Dorsey, b. Oct. 2, 1740, living in 1791

John Dorsey inherited from his grandfather, John Dorsey, two tracts of land, Brown's Chance and Dorsey's Friendship, and from his father Michael Dorsey, a tract called Toddy containing 27 acres, 300 acres first Discovery, and 48 acres of first Division.

On April 12, 1773, Major Henry Ridgely, Anne Arundel County, sold to John Dorsey son of Michael, part of a tract called Bite the Skinner containing 213 acres.

(*A.A. Co. Deeds I.B. No. 4*, f. 83)

The will of John Dorsey made January 8, 1779 and probated March 9, 1779 left:

To wife Ann Dorsey, tracts of land called Brown's Chance and Dorsey's Friendship during her natural life to be taken in lieu of her third of land
To son Philemon Dorsey, tracts of land Altogether containing 121 acres, Brown's Chance and Dorsey's Friendship containing 152 acres, and Toddy, 27 acres

To son Vachel Dorsey, tracts of land called Bite the Skinner, 213 acres, Pindon's Range, 50 acres, also those lands called Peace, with my part of tract called Seline and all the lands that Philemon Dorsey (my wife's father) left to me and my wife Ann Dorsey
To son Michael Dorsey, a tract called first Division containing 300 acres and one other tract called first Discovery containing 48 acres
To daughters Ruth Dorsey, Eleanor Dorsey, Elizabeth Dorsey, 200 pounds each
To sons Philemon Dorsey, Vachel Dorsey, and Michael Dorsey, 200 pounds each
It is my will that if either of my sons die without heirs that his lands be equally divided among other sons
Exr: brother Lancelot Dorsey (*A.A. Co. Wills E.V. No. 1*, f. 89)

The account of Lancelot Dorsey, December 2, 1789, executor of John Dorsey late of Anne Arundel County, deceased, paid to Philemon Dorsey guardian of Ruth and Eleanor Dorsey, to Basil Burgess guardian to Vachel Dorsey and Philemon Dorsey, to Charles Warfield of John, wife's part, to Gassaway Watkins, wife's part, to widow Ann Dorsey, and to Basil Dorsey guardian to Michael. (*A.A. Co. Test. Papers*, Box. 17, Folder 18)

The final distribution of the estate of John Dorsey deceased in 1791 named Ann Dorsey widow, Ruth Dorsey, Charles Warfield, who intermarried with Catherine Dorsey, Basil Burgess, who intermarried with Eleanor, Philemon, Vachel, Michael, and Elizabeth who had died. (*A.A. Co. Test. Papers*, Box 22, Folder 77)

Ann Dorsey, widow of John, was the daughter of Philemon and Katherine Dorsey. In 1771 Ann and John Dorsey inherited a portion of six tracts of land from Ann's father. (*Wills 38*, f. 605) (See page 42)

On May 15, 1779, Ann Dorsey, widow of John son of Michael, gave to Vachel Dorsey, her son, land left him in his father's will, which John and Ann had inherited from her father Philemon Dorsey. (*A.A. Co. Deeds I.B. No. 5*, f. 63)

Children of John and Ann Dorsey:
(Named in father's will)

1. Philemon[6] Dorsey, d. unm.
2. Vachel Dorsey, d. bef. 1798, m. Mar. 13, 1792 Anne Poole, Fred. Co., who m. (2) Lyde Griffith (*A.A. Co. Test. Papers*, Box 40, Folder 106)
3. Ruth Dorsey, m. Feb. 28, 1788 Gassaway Watkins
4. Eleanor Dorsey, m. Jan. 11, 1785 Basil Burgess
5. Elizabeth Dorsey, d. bef. 1791
6. Catherine Dorsey, m. Charles Warfield, son of John
7. Michael Dorsey, m. Sept. 6, 1796 Elizabeth Poole, Fred. Co.

2. ELIZABETH[5] DORSEY (Michael,[4] John,[3] Col. Edward,[2] Edward[1])

b. Dec. 13, 1735; d. after 1806 Anne Arundel County
m. June 13, 1751 Capt. Joseph Burgess, d. 1806

On April 17, 1754, Joseph Burgess and his brother William bought from James Dick 420 acres of land called Upland on the north branch of the Patuxent River, Anne Arundel County, which had been granted to Christian Geist in 1725. (*A.A. Co. Deeds R.B. No. 3*, f. 686)

Sarah Burgess, widow and executrix of William, sold 210 acres of this tract to John Botson on August 1, 1776, at which time Joseph Burgess released all claim in William's share. (*A.A. Co. Deeds I.B. No. 5*, f. 372)

Joseph Burgess enlisted on December 10, 1776, and as Capt. Joseph Burgess commanded a company of Elk Ridge Militia. He belonged to the 3rd Battalion, Maryland Flying Camp. On March 4, 1777, it was ordered that the Western Shore Treasurer pay to Capt. Joseph Burgess one thousand dollars for recruiting service. (*Arch. of Md.* XVIII, 160) In 1778 he signed a letter of Edward Norwood which showed the feeling of certain Continental officers toward Gen. Smallwood. (J. Thomas Scharf, *Chronicles of Baltimore*, f. 183)

On April 9, 1781, Michael Burgess bought from Lancelot Dorsey of Michael a certain part of a tract called Dispute Ended which Joseph Burgess Jr. late of Anne Arundel County deceased, some few years past, purchased from Michael Dorsey Sr. The said Burgess paid the said Michael Dorsey 60 pounds Sterling, but by the deaths of said Michael Sr. and Joseph Burgess Jr., the said land was not conveyed. Lancelot Dorsey therefore conveys to Michael Burgess as elder brother of Joseph Burgess Jr., the said land, 29 pounds yet to be paid was paid by Joseph Burgess Sr., April 9, 1782. (*A.A. Co. Deeds N.H. No. 1, f.* 237)

The will of Joseph Burgess made September 9, 1805 and proved May 19, 1806 left:

To wife Elizabeth Burgess during her natural life, 3 negroes, Jack, Moses, old Jenny
To son William Burgess, 100 dollars, horse called Marten, and after decease of said wife, negro called Moses
To son Joseph Burgess, furniture, horse called Fany, stock, 1/5 of money from sales of five Hhds of tobacco in warehouse in Baltimore, also 1/5 part of crop now growing, and 100 dollars
To daughter Sarah Burgess, negro woman, young Jeney and furniture
To wife Elizabeth Burgess, during her natural life, remainder of estate, and after her death to be equally divided between children, Philemon, William, Joseph Burgess and Lidey Barster or their heirs
Exrs: sons William and Joseph Burgess (*A.A. Co. Wills J.G. No. 2, f.* 357)

Children of Joseph and Elizabeth (Dorsey) Burgess:
(Named in father's will, deeds, and War Records)

1. Lieut. John[6] Burgess, m. Sarah Dorsey, dau. of Basil (See page 157)
2. Ensign Michael Burgess, d. 1818 (*A.A. Co. Invts. J.G. No. 9, f.* 519)
   m. Oct. 22, 1783 Sarah Warfield
3. Lieut. Joseph Burgess, d. c 1780 (*Arch. of Md.* XVIII, 88)
4. Capt. Vachel Burgess, d. 1824 (*A.A. Co. Invts. T.H.H. No. 3, f.* 502)
   m. Oct. 1, 1782 Rebecca Dorsey, dau. of Thomas
   (Vachel of Joseph) (*A.A. Co. Deeds N.H. No. 1, f.* 285)
5. Richard Burgess
6. Lieut. Joshua Burgess, b. 1760; d. 1831, m. Sarah Dorsey
   Moved to Mason Co, Ky. Pension June 29, 1830
7. Lidey (Lydia) Burgess, m. ______ Barster
8. William Burgess
9. Philemon Burgess, m. Mary Ridgely Dorsey, dau. of Thomas
10. Joseph Burgess
11. Sarah Burgess
12. Ruth Burgess, m. Aug. 6, 1778 Elisha Warfield

3. HONOR[5] DORSEY (Michael,[4] John,[3] Col. Edward,[2] Edward[1])
b. Nov. 3, 1757; d. June 19, 1771 Baltimore County
m. John Elder, d. 1794

In 1764 Onour Elder inherited from her grandfather John Dorsey, seven negroes and their increase during her natural life, and after her decease to go to sons, Joshua and Michael, Elder. In 1774 her father Michael Dorsey gave negroes to his two granddaughters, Providence and Helenia Elder, daughters of Onour Elder deceased.

John Elder, son of John and Jemima (Dorsey) Elder, inherited several tracts of land from his father in 1762. (*Wills 31, f.* 844) (See page 57)

Children of John and Honor (Dorsey) Elder:

1. Joshua[6] Elder, b. 1761
2. Michael Elder, b. 1763, m. Dec. 31, 1793 Pleasant Petticord
3. Helen Elder, b. 1765, m. Benjamin Tevis
4. Providence Elder, b. 1767, m. Feb. 27, 1786 Robert Shipley

John Elder, m. (2) 1791 Sarah______

John Elder died in 1794 intestate. His inventory taken July 12, 1794 included gold sleeve buttons, silver knee buckles, and silver shoe buckles. Elijah and Charles Elder signed as kin. (*Balt. Co. Invts. 17, f.* 179)

The first account of John Elder, administrator of John Elder late of Baltimore County, deceased, was filed November 21, 1795. (*Balt. Co. Adm. Accts. 12, f.* 69)

On February 16, 1796, the final account paid Robert Shipley, who married Providence Elder, wife's share, Benjamin Tevis, who married Helen Elder, wife's share, David Brown, who married Jemima Elder, wife's share, paid Michael Elder, paid Sarah Elder chosen guardian of Elizabeth and Mary Elder, their part of deceased's estate, 118/16/2 pounds, paid others 50/18/1 Paid Sarah her part in full. (*Ibid.*, 101)

In 1794 Owen Elder, orphan, son of John Elder, chose John Elder his guardian. (*Balt. Ct. Proc, 3,* year 1794)

Children of John and Sarah Elder:
(Births recorded in St. Thomas Parish Register)

1. John[6] Elder, b. June 5, 1772
2. Jemima Elder, b. Mar. 1, 1774, m. David Brown
3. Onour Elder, b. Feb. 21, 1776
4. Owen Elder, b. May 9, 1778
5. Elizabeth Elder, b. c 1781
6. Mary Elder

4. SARAH[5] DORSEY (Michael,[4] John,[3] Col. Edward,[2] Edward[1])
b. Sept. 25, 1739; d. bef. 1818 Montgomery County
m. Richard Berry, b. July 20, 1734; d. 1819

Before her marriage Sarah Dorsey was willed by her grandfather John Dorsey, 100 pounds current money to be paid by executors at 10 pounds per year until whole is paid.

In 1752 Richard Berry inherited part of a tract called Croome from his grandfather Richard Clagett. In 1769 he inherited part of Charles and Benjamin in Frederick County, from his father, Jeremiah Berry, and in 1792, silverware and part of a tract called Concord and Outlet from his mother Mary Berry. (See pages 146 and 152)

On December 15, 1778, Richard Berry bought of Thomas Owen, Montgomery County, the tract called Pig Park containing 67 acres. (*Mont. Co. Deeds A, f.* 207) On November 6, 1802, Richard Berry Sr., Montgomery County, conveyed to Nicholas Gassaway, Anne Arundel County, all of the tract called Addition to Charles and Benjamin, 31 acres. (*Mont. Co. Deeds K, f.* 500) On September 20, 1806, Richard Berry Sr., sold to William Kelly, Shepherd's Hard Fortune, 31½ acres. Sarah, his wife, signed the deed. (*Mont. Co. Deeds N, f.* 28)

In November 1815, Richard Berry sold to John Brown, Loudon County, Virginia, a parcel of land, containing part of Berry's Neglect and part of Shepherd's Hard Fortune. (*Mont. Co. Deeds S, f.* 19)

The will of Richard Berry made August 26, 1818 and probated November 30, 1819 left:

To daughters Mary Moody, Ruth Griffith, Elizabeth W. Beal, Eleanor Gittins, Amelia Gassaway, and Ann Thomas, 1 negro each
To daughter Deborah D. Berry, land in Montgomery County called Pig Park, also part of land called Charles and Benjamin adjoining and 4 negroes
To son Elisha D. Berry, remainder of Charles and Benjamin, also remaining land called Shepherd's Hard Fortune, negroes, bed, and furniture
To son Richard Berry (now in Kentucky) and my three grandchildren, Michael R. Berry, Sarah G. Berry, and Sarah B. Offutt, $20.00 to be divided among them.
Exr: son Elisha D. Berry (*Mont. Co. Wills L, f.* 110)

DORSEY FAMILY

Sarah Berry, wife of Richard, was living in 1806, when she signed a deed. Since her name is not found on later deeds or in the will of her husband, it appears that she died before 1818.

Children of Richard and Sarah (Dorsey) Berry:
(Births from Griffith Family)

1. Mary[6] Berry, b. June 4, 1760, m. Mar. 24, 1796 Thomas Moody
2. Ruth Berry, b. Mar. 5, 1762; d. 1846 (*Mont. Co. Wills Z*, f. 449) m. Apr. 1, 1779 Samuel Griffith (See page 76)
3. Elizabeth Berry, b. Aug. 11, 1766, m. Nov. 26, 1801 Samuel Beall
4. Elinor Berry, b. Apr. 7, 1768, d. bef. 1823 m. Kinsey Gittings (*Mont. Co. Minute Bk. O*, f. 70)
5. Amelia Berry, b. Feb. 22, 1770, m.——— Gassaway
6. Michael Berry, b. June 7, 1772
7. Ann Berry, b. Oct. 1, 1779, m. Nov. 19, 1798 John Thomas
8. Elisha Berry, b. Sept. 22, 1781
9. Richard Berry, married and moved to Kentucky
10. Deborah D. Berry

5. RUTH[5] DORSEY (Michael,[4] John,[3] Col. Edward,[2] Edward[1])
b. Mar. 17, 1743; d. May 17, 1805 Frederick County, Maryland
m. Dec. 1, 1765 Capt. Ely Dorsey, d. March 14, 1803

Ely Dorsey inherited from his father Edward Dorsey Jr., a part of Ely's Lot and part of Belly Ake Thickett in Anne Arundel County in 1767. (*Wills 36*, f. 109) (See page 144)

In January 1775 Ely Dorsey was appointed one of the members of the Council of Safety from Anne Arundel County. On December 10, 1776, he was commissioned Captain of the Second Maryland Regiment under Col. Thomas Price. He was taken prisoner at Staten Island on August 22, 1777. (*Arch. of Md.* XVIII, 177)

At the time of her death, Ruth Dorsey was living in Frederick County, where her will was probated on June 25, 1805. She left personalty to children Polly, Edward, Michael, Oner, Ruth, and Allen Dorsey. (*Fred. Co. Wills G.M.R.B. No. 1*, f. 125)

Children of Ely and Ruth Dorsey:
(Births from family records)

1. Polly (Mary)[6] Dorsey, b. Oct. 17, 1766
2. Edward Dorsey, b. Feb. 4, 1769, m. Mary Klein (See below)
3. Michael Dorsey, b. Dec. 19, 1770
4. Oner (Honor) Dorsey, b. Aug. 17, 1773, m. Feb. 7, 1791 Adam Poffenberger
5. Ruth Dorsey, b. Feb. 4, 1776, m. June 28, 1796 John Davey
6. Allen Dorsey, b. June 19, 1779; m. Elizabeth Smith (See page 89)

2. EDWARD[6] DORSEY (Ruth,[5] Michael,[4] John,[3] Col. Edward,[2] Edward[1])
b. Feb. 4, 1769; d. Mar. 29, 1848 Loudon County, Virginia
m. Mar. 27, 1802 Mary Klein, Fred. Co., Md.; d. Sept. 30, 1844

The will of Edward Dorsey made May 9, 1846 and probated April 10, 1848 reads:

I Edwd Dorsey of the County of Loudon State of Virginia, Ordain this my last will & Testament hereby revoking all other wills whatsoever. I desire amediately after decese that all my perishable property be sold and my just debts and funeral expenses be pade the balance of my estate be divided in the maner following to my Granson Edward H my Crudens concordance and a large family Bible and to my other three Gransons a large family bible that is to say Charles W. Jonathan E. Emery W and that the family record that is rite in my ould bibel be rote in each of them befor

they ar delivered to them as I think it is the best legesey that I cold leve them if they make a proper use of them
I will and bequeth to my son Alfrid twenty dollars to be sent to him out of the first money that is colected as a spesheal legsey and the balance of my estate to be Eaqutry devided among my four sons that is to say Presly K Alfred I Allen M and Hamilton M it is my wish that what part that would be coming to *Allen now deceased* shold be pad to his surviving children when they come to the yers of moturity and the interest of it be pade to thare Gordun anueley for thare support. It is my will that my son Presley K have the privelage of the House and lot that he know occupies for twelve months after my decese and that he shall not be compeled to pay any rent for it and at the experation of the above time that all of my real estate that I may die posed of be sold and divided as above stated I dow here consecute and appoint my son Presley K Dorsey Exectuar of my last will and testament and I desur that he may not be required to give security.
Edwd Dorsey (seal)
(*Loudon Co. Virginia Wills 2, D's*, f. 113)

Children of Edward and Mary (Klein) Dorsey:
(Births from family records)

1. Eliza[7] Dorsey, b. Nov. 26, 1804; d. Apr. 21, 1806
2. Presley H. Dorsey, b. June 6, 1806; d. 1859, m. Hannah Reed, b. 1810; d. 1880
3. Jonathan E. Dorsey, b. Aug. 3, 1808; d. Nov. 7, 1831
4. Alfred J. Dorsey, b. Feb. 8, 1810, m. Eleanor Moon (See below)
5. Allen M. Dorsey, b. Feb. 25, 1812; d. Apr. 13, 1846
6. Hamilton M. Dorsey, b. 1814; d. 1879, m. Sarah Catherine Polten, b. 1821; d. 1907 (See page 242)

4. ALFRED J.[7] DORSEY (Edward,[6] Ruth,[5] Michael,[4] John,[3] Col. Edward,[2] Edward[1])
b. Feb. 8, 1810; d. Mar. 7, 1884
m. Dec. 30, 1833 Eleanor Moon, Waterford, Va., b. June 1807 Manchester, England
d. Dec. 30, 1882 Kearney, Nebraska, at the home of her son Daniel A. Dorsey

Alfred Dorsey was left $20.00 in the will of his father, Edward Dorsey, in 1846. After the birth of their first three children, Alfred and Eleanor Dorsey moved to Kingston, Ross County, Ohio, where their last six children were born.

Their son Isaac Edward Dorsey, who enlisted at Leistville, Pickaway County, Ohio, August 15, 1861, stated that his mother and seven children were then living at Kingston, Ross County, Ohio.

Children of Alfred and Eleanor (Moon) Dorsey:
(Births from family records)

1. Edward H.[8] Dorsey, b. Mar. 31, 1835 Waterford, Va; d. Mar. 2, 1874, Illinois
   m. May 29, 1870 Sarah Rebecca Rust, Randolf, Ill., who m. (2) Isaac E. Dorsey, brother of Edward. (See page 88)
   Children:
   1. Lulu E.[9] Dorsey, b. Apr. 22, 1871; d. July 7, 1905 Terra Haute, Ind.
      m. ________ McCallister
   2. Anna May[9] Dorsey, b. Aug. 15, 1873
      m. (1) May 28, 1891 Grant Ulysses Farley, b. Apr. 10, 1863; d. Aug. 10, 1901
      Children:
      1. Glen[10] Farley, b. Dec. 12, 1893
      2. Cloe[10] Farley, b. Mar. 10, 1894, m. Maurice Lockwood, b. Feb. 15, 1894
         One child:
         Mary Louise[11] Lockwood, b. Mar. 29, 1918
         m. James Eppinger Cope, b. Feb. 22, 1913 Savannah, Ga.
         One child:
         Sally Lockwood[12] Cope, b. Mar. 4, 1944 Savannah, Ga.
      3. Clara[10] Farley, b. June 28, 1900
      m. (2) Henry Giese, b. Jan. 21, 1851; d. Jan 26, 1937 Bellflower, Ill.
   3. Sarah R.[9] Dorsey, d. Jan. 26, 1920 Heyworth, Ill. unm.

2. Thomas[8] Dorsey, b. Jan. 21, 1837; d. Feb. 9, 1839
3. Daniel Allen[8] Dorsey, b. Dec. 31, 1838 Waterford, Va.; d. 1913. Buried National Cemetery, Leavenworth, Kan.
   m. Mar. 1864 Annie Catherine Miller, b. Mar. 1840; d. July 14, 1908 Kearney Nebraska.
   Daniel Dorsey taught school in Fairfield County, Ohio, and also in Illinois, until about 1870, when he and his family went by wagon to Nebraska, first to Adams, then to Kearney, where he practised law and engaged in the real estate business.
   Children:
   1. Jessie Ellen[9] Dorsey, b. Dec. 21, 1865 Illinois; d. Mar. 24, 1932
   2. Edwin Stanton[9] Dorsey, b. July 1867, Illinois; d. June 10, 1907
   3. Clarence Arthur[9] Dorsey, b. Sept. 11, 1869, Illinois; d. 1938 San Jose, California
      m. Mabel Wells Parker, d. Jan. 27, 1945
      Children:
      1. Clarence R.[10] Dorsey, b. Oct. 11, 1898,
         m. Mar. 17, 1922 Mabel Ochsner, b. May 3, 1902
         Children:
         1. Virginia Gaile[11] Dorsey, b. Oct. 2, 1923, m. Oct. 17, 1943 Foster Campbell Hamlin, b. Nov. 27, 1921
         2. Lieut. David Wells Dorsey, b. Mar. 27, 1926 – d. Apr. 28, 1946
      2. David Wells[10] Dorsey, b. Dec. 8, 1903
   4. James Oscar[9] Dorsey, b. June 8, 1871 Illinois; d. Mar. 5, 1879
   5. Mabel L.[9] Dorsey, b. June 10, 1879 Kearney, Nebraska (See page 242)
      Founder - President of WOMEN, ASSOCIATED, Los Angeles, California
   6. George Emery[9] Dorsey, b. May 27, 1881; d. Mar. 6, 1945.
      Buried National Cemetery, El Paso, Texas
      m. Dec. 26, 1912 Etta Freeman
      One child:
      Susabel[10] Dorsey, b. Nov. 13, 1913 Sacramento, California
4. Mary Ellen[8] Dorsey, b. Jan. 9, 1840; d. Aug. 19, 1903 San Francisco, California
   m. I. Will B. Price
5. Isaac Edward[8] Dorsey, b. Nov. 26, 1842; d. Jan. 2, 1920. Buried National Cemetery, Dayton, Ohio
   m. Mar. 2, 1876 Sarah R. Dorsey, Illinois, widow of brother Edward Dorsey d. Jan. 26, 1920
   One child:
   1. Laura Ellen[9] Dorsey, b. Mar. 22, 1877
      m. Feb. 20, 1896 Adolph Christian Bauermeister
      One child:
      Harold Frederick Bauermeister, b. Mar. 7, 1903
6. Catherine E.[8] Dorsey, b. Apr. 16, 1846, m. Harlow Gilbert
7. Hamilton P.[8] Dorsey, b. Apr. 12, 1848; d. Feb. 5, 1865
8. Deborah Ann[8] Dorsey, b. Oct. 16, 1850; d. 1871
9. James Lyman[8] Dorsey, b. Apr. 10, 1852: d. Nov. 16, 1852

6. ALLEN[6] DORSEY (Ruth,[5] Michael,[4] John,[3] Col. Edward,[2] Edward[1])
b. June 19, 1779; d. Oct. 15, 1849
m. May 23, 1802 Elizabeth Smith, Frederick Co., b. Jan. 1, 1780; d. May 5, 1850

Children of Allen and Elizabeth (Smith) Dorsey:
(Births from family records)

1. George[7] Dorsey, b. Aug. 28, 1803
2. Alfred W. Dorsey, b. Jan. 8, 1805; d. 1876, m. Charlotte Heckrotten, b. 1810; d. 1874. Moved to Missouri
3. John Smith Dorsey, b. Oct. 25, 1806
4. William Dorsey, b. Nov. 12, 1808
5. Stephen Dorsey, b. May 4, 1811
6. Presley Dorsey, b. Nov. 27, 1812
7. Kitty Ann Dorsey, b. Dec. 23, 1814; d. June 14, 1885, m. June 3, 1850 Augustus Jethro Naylor, b. Apr. 29, 1821
8. Allen Dorsey, b. Dec. 26, 1816
9. Henry Dorsey, b. Feb. 11, 1819
10. Ruth Dorsey, b. Jan. 7, 1821
11. Mary Elizabeth Dorsey, b. Aug. 10, 1823

7. LANCELOT[5] DORSEY (Michael,[4] John,[3] Col. Edward,[2] Edward[1])
b. July 17, 1747; d. c March 1829 Anne Arundel County
m. Sarah Warfield, d. bef. 1829

Lancelot Dorsey inherited from his father in 1774 the tract called Good Range containing 333 acres and Brother's Partnership of 316 acres.

Lancelot Dorsey (Merchant) was the administrator de bonis non of the estate of his father, Michael Dorsey, and the executor of his brother John Dorsey's will, 1779.

In 1782 his name appears on the tax list of Upper Fork Hundred, Anne Arundel County, with 8 in the family.

On February 5, 1796, Lancelot Dorsey sold for 40 pounds to James Barnes, son of Adam Barnes, part of Brother's Partnership. (*A.A. Co. Deeds N.H. No. 8*, f. 58)

On January 3, 1797, he sold another part of this tract to Vachel Warfield, (*Ibid.*, f. 404) and the next year he conveyed the remainder of the tract to Christopher Treakle and his son Darius Dorsey. (*A.A. Co. Deeds N.H. No. 9*, folios 287, 619)

On October 18, 1797, he transferred part of Good Range to Nicholas Merriweather. Sarah, his wife, signed the deed. (*A.A. Co. Deeds N.H. No. 10*, f. 37)

On February 8, 1800, Lancelot Dorsey of Michael, being indebted to Charles Alexander Warfield for 294 pounds made over to him a negro, stock and furniture. (*Ibid.*, f. 178)

A case in Chancery September 4, 1829, to obtain a decree for the sale of real estate of Lancelot Dorsey deceased, who was possessed of a tract called Brother's Partnership containing 250 acres, records that Lancelot Dorsey died about March 1, 1829 intestate. His wife, Sarah Dorsey, died in the lifetime of her husband.

Dennis Dorsey, Dathan Dorsey, Owen Elder, and Ann, his wife, Nicholas Ridgely and Ruth, his wife, entered a complaint against Deal Dorsey, who was living in Kentucky, Darius Dorsey in Ohio (Belmont County), Philemon Dorsey, who had gone to Kentucky and died before 1829 and left heirs. (*Chanc. Rec. R.W. No. 140*, f. 847)

Sarah Dorsey, wife of Lancelot, was the daughter of Alexander and Sarah Warfield. On June 11, 1745, there was left to Lancelot Dorsey who had intermarried with Rachel, daughter of the deceased, her part of the estate.

(*Accts 21*, f. 287)

Children of Lancelot and Sarah (Warfield) Dorsey:
(Named in Chancery Record)

1. Deal[6] Dorsey, moved to Kentucky
2. Dennis Dorsey
3. Darius Dorsey, d. Feb. 29, 1848 Dover, Ohio
   m. Nov. 30, 1795 Mary Talbot, d. 1852
4. Philemon Dorsey, d. bef. 1829 in Kentucky. Left heirs.
5. Dathan Dorsey, d. 1857 Balt. Co., m. Dec. 22, 1809 Ann Johnson
6. Ann Dorsey, m. Sept. 1, 1794 Owen Elder, son of Owen (See below)
7. Ruth Dorsey, m. Aug. 21, 1821 Nicholas Ridgely

8. ANN (NANCY)[5] DORSEY (Michael,[4] John,[3] Col. Edward,[2] Edward[1])
b. Jan. 29, 1748; d. Sept. 30, 1806 Baltimore County
m. April 10, 1766 Owen Elder, d. 1774 (*St. Thos.*)

Owen Elder inherited from his father John Elder in 1762 parts of several tracts of land. (*Wills 31*, f. 844)

He died in 1774 intestate and letters of administration were granted to his widow Ann Elder, securities Joseph Burgess and Johnsa Dorsey. (*Test. Proc. 46*, f. 91)

Children of Owen and Ann (Dorsey) Elder:
(Births recorded in St. Thomas Parish Register)

1. Terrisha[6] Elder, b. Jan. 12, 1767, m. Nov. 8, 1788 Dennis Dorsey
2. Ruth Elder, b. Mar. 6, 1769
3. Owen Elder, b. Feb. 19, 1771, m. Sept. 1, 1794 Ann Dorsey (*St. Thos.*)

Nancy Elder, widow of Owen, m. (2) March 25, 1775 Charles Dorsey, d. 1814 (See pages 57,64)

On December 25, 1777, the inventory of Owen Elder was filed by Charles Dorsey, and Ann, his wife, executrix of Owen Elder deceased. (*Balt. Co. Invts. 12*, f. 24)

On May 23, 1792, Owen Elder, son and heir-at-law of Owen Elder, deceased, and Charles Dorsey of Nicholas, guardian and trustee of said Owen Elder under a decree of Chancery, sold land of Owen Elder to Elias Brown, Charles Dorsey son of Nicholas, having married widow of said Owen Dorsey deceased. (*Balt. Co. Deeds W.G. No. H.H*, f. 662)

Children of Charles and Ann (Dorsey) Dorsey:
(Births recorded in Baltimore Sun, March 22, 1908 by S.C.D.)

1. Hezekiah[6] Dorsey, b. July 12, 1776, m. Dec. 8, 1798 Mary Talbot
2. Charles Dorsey, b. Apr. 30, 1778; d. 1843, m. Feb. 3, 1807 Catherine Welsh
3. Zacchariah Dorsey, b. Aug. 20, 1780
4. Sarah Dorsey, b. Dec. 30, 1782, m. Jan. 1, 1817 John Litchfield
5. John Dorsey, b. July 5, 1785; d. 1861, m. Apr. 21, 1811 Jane Connor (See pages 232 and 246)
6. Nancy Dorsey, b. Jan. 3, 1788, m. Apr. 14, 1804 Zachariah Poulter

2. TERISHA[6] ELDER (Ann[5] (Dorsey) Elder, Michael,[4] John,[3] Col. Edward,[2] Edward[1])
b. Jan. 12, 1767; d. Apr. 9, 1843 Washington County, Pennsylvania
m. Nov. 8, 1788 Dennis Dorsey, b. 1769; d. Sept. 12, 1815 in western Pennsylvania

In 1807 Dennis moved from Maryland to Wellsburg, Virginia, then known as Charleston, with his wife and six children. In 1809 he moved across the state and located on a portion of the widow Wells farm, near the Forks, now the village of Independence. He remained there until 1813 and then moved to Fowlerstown. (Boyd Crumrine's History of Washington County, Pa. Independence Township, f. 827)

MICHAEL DORSEY AND SOME OF HIS DESCENDANTS

Family records indicate that Dennis Dorsey may have been the son of Henry Dorsey, the son of Nicholas and Sarah (Griffith) Dorsey, but no other records have been found to prove this fact.

A letter written by Dennis Basil Dorsey dated September 1834 to his mother, Mrs. Terisha Dorsey, New Independence, Washington County, Pennsylvania, is now in the possession of her great grandson, Lawrence Foster King, Pittsburg, Pennsylvania.

Children of Dennis and Terisha (Elder) Dorsey:
(Births from family records)

1. Samuel[7] Dorsey, b. Oct. 12, 1789 (See below)
   m. (1) Mary Costello, m. (2) Isabelle Rickey
2. Ruth Dorsey, b. Feb. 26, 1791; d. June 17, 1846 unm.
3. Matilda Dorsey, b. Dec. 24, 1794; d. Oct. 29, 1859 unm.
   She named her brother Dennis Basil Dorsey in her will
4. Elizabeth Dorsey, b. Mar. 1, 1797; d. Feb. 3, 1859
5. Martha Dorsey, b. 1802; d. 1899 (Tombstone) Lower Buffalo Cemetery, Brooke Co., W. Va., m. June 2, 1845 Michael Leetch. No issue.
6. Dennis Basil Dorsey, b. Dec. 28, 1799, m. Frances Purdue (See page 93)

1. SAMUEL[7] DORSEY (Terisha[6] (Elder) Dorsey, Ann[5] (Dorsey) Elder, Michael,[4] John,[3] Col. Edward,[2] Edward[1])
   b. Oct. 12, 1789; d. Apr. 22, 1886 Rutland, Marshall County, Illinois
   m. (1) Jan. 10, 1809 Mary Costello, Morgantown, W. Va., b. Oct. 6, 1788
   d. Nov. 11, 1818 Marshall County, Va,

Samuel Dorsey came to Brooke County, Virginia, with his parents in 1808 and after his marriage lived in what was then called "Flats of Grave Creek", Ohio County, Virginia, now Moundsville, Marshall County, West Virginia. About 1851 he moved to Rutland, Illinois, now in Marshall County, where he bought a tract of land.

Children of Samuel and Mary (Costello) Dorsey:
(Births from family records)

1. Sarah[8] Dorsey, b. Nov. 2, 1810, m. Elias Magess
2. Catherine Dorsey, b. June 2, 1812, d. unm.
3. Ruth Dorsey, b. Feb. 24, 1814, m. Walter McMillen
4. Harriet Dorsey, b. Nov. 21, 1816, m. Andrew Zook

Samuel Dorsey m. (2) July 1, 1819 Isabelle Rickey, Middletown, Pennsylvania, d. 1866

Children of Samuel and Isabelle (Rickey) Dorsey:

1. Mary[8] Dorsey, b. Aug. 30, 1820; d. Jan. 6, 1884
   m. Mar. 4, 1851 Seth Ingram
2. Rebecca Dorsey, b. Nov. 10, 1821, m. Thomas Dorsey (See page 92)
3. Dennis Dorsey, b. Mar. 5, 1823; d. July 3, 1880
   m. (1) Dec. 12, 1844 Elizabeth Mc Lean
   m. (2) Feb. 2, 1847 Elizabeth Allen
4. Samuel[8] Dorsey, b. Feb. 5, 1831; d. 1900 Blair, Nebraska
   m. Nov. 11, 1852 Rutland, Illinois, Joanna Holiday, b. 1828; d. 1916

Children: (All but youngest child were born in Virginia)

1. William[9] Dorsey, b. 1853; d. 1908 Wright Co., Ia.
   m. Maggie Scott
   Children:
   1. Orton Scott[10] Dorsey, m. May Mc Farland
      Children:
      1. Alta[11] Dorsey, b. 1906, m. Arthur Cavanaugh
      2. Vera Dorsey, b. 1907, m. Lawrence Stuedemann
      3. Howard Dorsey, b. 1909, m. Mariona Peterson
      4. Thomas Dorsey, b. 1911, m. Isla Sorensen (See page 234)
      5. Stanley Dorsey, b. 1912, m. Ilo Kramer
      6. Orville Dorsey, b. 1916, m. Geraldine Thompson
      7. Glenn Dorsey, b. 1921
      8. Ben Dorsey, b. 1921
      9. Betty Dorsey, b. 1927
2. Samuel James[9] Dorsey, b. Apr. 26, 1855
3. Fillmore[9] Dorsey, b. Sept. 21, 1857, m. Lydia Scott, Zanesville, Ohio
4. Mary Belle[9] Dorsey, b. Aug. 9, 1859
5. Orton[9] Dorsey, b. Aug. 5, 1866
6. Charles[9] Dorsey, b. Feb. 20, 1871

2. REBECCA[8] DORSEY (Samuel,[7] Terisha[6] (Elder) Dorsey, Ann[5] (Dorsey) Elder, Michael,[4] John,[3] Col. Edward,[2] Edward[1])
   b. Nov. 10, 1821; d. Nov. 26, 1906 Marshall County, West Virginia
   m. Mar. 22, 1838 Thomas Dorsey, b. Jan. 22, 1812; d. Nov. 24, 1868, son of Basil and Susannah (Lindsay) Dorsey who came from Maryland to Virginia.

   Children: (Births from family records)

   1. Isabelle[9] Dorsey, m. Frank Dowler
   2. Basil Dorsey, m. Saline Baird
   3. Thomas Dorsey, m. Matilda Gamble
   4. William Dorsey, m. Agnes Campbell
   5. Samuel[9] Dorsey, b. Dec. 26, 1846, m. Nov. 19, 1872 Sarah Ellen Pierce
      (See History of Marshall County)
      Children:
      1. Pearl[10] Dorsey, b. 1874 Moundsville, W. Va. (See page 234)
      2. Elmer William[10] Dorsey, b. June 1878; d. Nov. 28, 1938
         m. Carrie A. Hammond, b. Nov. 1878
         Children:
         1. Mary Ellen[11] Dorsey, m. 1920 William Beam
            Children:
            1. Buddy[12] Beam, b. 1934
            2. Mary Ellen[12] Beam, b. May 5, 1936
            3. William Dorsey[12] Beam, b. Nov. 9, 1938

2. Lloyd Elmer[11] Dorsey, m. Mary Margaret Barr

   Children:

   1. Sarah Jane[12] Dorsey, b. June 22, 1935
   2. Sylvia Alice[12] Dorsey, b. July 1, 1936
   3. William Lloyd[12] Dorsey, b. June 5, 1938

3. Samuel[10] Dorsey

6. DENNIS BASIL[7] DORSEY (Terisha[6] (Elder) Dorsey, Ann[5] (Dorsey) Elder, Michael,[4] John,[3] Col. Edward,[2] Edward[1])
   b. Dec. 28, 1799; d. Mar. 18, 1806 Fairmont, West Virginia
   m. Mar. 8, 1826 Center County, Pennsylvania, Frances Purdue, b. Nov. 18, 1806;
   d. June 16, 1854 Steubenville, Ohio

Between the years 1821 and 1827, Dennis Basil Dorsey served as a minister of the Methodist Episcopal Church in western Pennsylvania. In 1828 he studied medicine under Dr. S.K. Jennings, and on March 21, 1831 he graduated, as a Medical Doctor, from the Washington Medical College of Baltimore. In 1832 he settled in Wheeling, West Virginia and started to practice medicine. In 1835 he was president of the Methodist Protestant Church, (Pittsburg Conference). Between the years 1840 and 1857 he lived in Steubenville, Ohio, and Martinsville, Ohio, where he started a paper, The Independent Press. Soon after the death of his wife, he went to live with his son Dennis Basil Dorsey in Fairmont, West Virginia.

Children of Dennis Basil and Frances (Purdue) Dorsey:
(Births from family records)

1. Rev. Samuel Jennings[8] Dorsey
   b. June 2, 1828; d. Nov. 22, 1908 Scranton, Pa.
   m. (1) Mar. 1851 New Lisbon, Ohio, Louisa _____ ; d. Feb. 1860

   Children:

   1. Rebecca[9] Dorsey
   2. John Dennis[9] Dorsey, b. Johnston, Pa.; d. 1937 Alma, Ill.
      m. Philomene St. Pierre, d. Jan. 28, 1939, buried Vandalia, Ill.

      Children:

      1. Catherine Lois[10] Dorsey, d. Feb. 26, 1939 unm.
      2. Rupert M.[10] Dorsey, Grand Junction, Colorado (See page 235)
         m. Mattie Forester, Georgia
   3. Samuel[9] Dorsey, m. Callie _____ d. Apr. 1941, Sacremento, Calif.
   4. Paul[9] Dorsey, d. Gig Harbor, Washington

   m. (2) Terish Schoch, lived only a short time
   m. (3) Sarah Caroline Ellis, b. Oct. 8, 1838 Goshen, Orange Co., N.Y., d. Apr. 23, 1929 Clerdon, Va.

   Children:

   1. Alfred Ellis[9] Dorsey, b. June 25, 1865 Orange Co., N.Y.
      m. (1) Cecelia Schulz, Decatur, Ill.
      m. (2) Catherine Cameron, Ashley, Ill.

      Children:

      1. Cameron[9] Dorsey Sr., b. Mar. 28, 1903 Chicago, Ill.
         m. Alice Wilsberg

         Children:
         1. Cameron[10] Dorsey Jr., b. March, 1927.

2. Arthur Dorsey
3. Caroline Victoria Dorsey, m.________McClure, d. Albuquerque, N. Mex.
4. Eva Dorsey

2. Dr. Dennis Basil[8] Dorsey Jr., d. Braymer, Missouri.
m. Margaret Gray

Dennis B. Dorsey lived in Fairmount, Virginia, now West Virginia when he was first married and after serving in the Civil War, he moved to Braymer, Missouri.

Children: (Births from family records)

1. George[9] Dorsey
2. Dr. Jacob Gray[9] Dorsey, b. July 5, 1860 Fairmont, Va.; d. Nov. 15, 1929 Wichita, Kansas.
   m. Oct. 1, 1883 Etta Palmer, Chillicothe, Mo.
   He graduated from the College of Physicians and Surgeons, Keokuk, Ia. in 1890. He practiced medicine in several Missouri towns until 1893, when he went to Wichita, Kansas, where he became one of the early specialists in Eye, Ear, and Nose treatment.

   Children:

   1. Mabel[10] Dorsey, m. _____ Moore
   2. Helen[10] Dorsey, m. _____ Weaver
3. Dr. Frank Blinn[9] Dorsey, b. Fairmont, Va.; d. Keokuk, Iowa.
   m.
   He graduated from the College of Physicians and Surgeons, Keokuk, Ia., and after practicing in Missouri returned to Keokuk, where he and his son Dr. Frank Blinn Dorsey Jr., worked together.

   Children:

   1. Dr. Frank Blinn[10] Dorsey
      Perhaps others
4. Luella[9] Dorsey
5. Eva[9] Dorsey
6. Claude Purdue[9] Dorsey, b. July 11, 1874; d. Mar. 5, 1940 Clinton Co.·Mo.
   m. Mary Alice Lankford
   He was Editor of The Cameron Sun, Cameron, Mo.

   Children:

   1. Dr. Dennis Basil[10] Dorsey, m. Mar. 11, 1939, Chicago, Ill. Hazel Overly of Kansas City
   2. Claude Purdue[10] Dorsey
   3. Gray L.[10] Dorsey
   4. Mary Ruth[10] Dorsey
   5. Mrs. W.E. Wolf

3. John P.[8] Dorsey, m. Elvira Miller, Lived in New York City
4. Frances[8] Dorsey, m. Rev. W. Blake, Moved to Colorado
5. Victoria A.[8] Dorsey, m. Luther W. Blake, d. Moundsville, W. Va.
6. George Stockton[8] Dorsey, m. Rebecca Gray
7. Martha C. Dorsey, d. inf.
8. Charles W.[8] Dorsey, d. unm.
9. Michael Angelo[8] Dorsey, d.y.

10. Margaret (May)[8] Dorsey, b. 1854; d. 1929 Pittsburg, Pa.
m. Joseph V. King, b. 1864; d. 1918

One child:

Lawrence Foster[9] King, b. 1881, m. Verda Dorsey Carroll (See page 235)

One child:

Harry Dorsey Carroll[10] King, b. 1897, m. Gladys Oakley

One child:

June Oakley Carroll[11] King, b. 1920, m. Robert Lee Sughrue

11. Purdue[8] Dorsey, d.y.

9. LYDIA[5] DORSEY (Michael,[4] John,[3] Col. Edward,[2] Edward[1])
b. Feb. 6, 1750; d. bef. 1792
m. Richard Talbot

Children of Richard and Lydia (Dorsey) Talbot:
(Named in *A.A. Co. Guardians for Infants* 1791-1805, f. 50)

1. Michael[6] Talbot
2. William Talbot
3. Elisha Talbot
4. Lloyd Talbot
5. Samuel Talbot
6. Pleasant Talbot
7. George Talbot

MICHAEL DORSEY II

6. MICHAEL[5] DORSEY II (Michael,[4] John,[3] Col. Edward,[2] Edward[1])
b. Oct. 29, 1745; d. 1812 at Pushpin, Anne Arundel County
m. bef. 1769 Honor Elder, b. after 1746; d. 1818

By the will of his father made in 1776, Michael Dorsey inherited 200 acres of Pushpin on which he lived at that time, 200 acres First Discovery, 25 acres First Division, and 100 pounds Sterling. (See page 175A)

On March 26, 1789, he sold to Charles Carrol an adjoining neighbor, 3½ acres of First Division, and on May 10, 1792, Michael Dorsey of Ann Arundel County, farmer, for 421/5/5 current money, mortgaged to Brice Howard 425 acres viz: 200 acres Pushpin, 200 acres First Discovery, and 25 acres First and Second Division. (*A.A. Co. Deeds N.H. No. 2,* folios 293, 584)

This land he redeemed on March 12, 1799. (*A.A. Co. Deeds N.H. No. 9,* f. 675) Ann Howard acknowledged on April 15, 1800 that the mortgage had been paid. (*A.A. Co. Deeds N.H. No. 10,* f. 236)

Michael Dorsey bought 43/4 acres of First Discovery from Joshua Howard, August 31, 1796, (*Abstracts of Deeds, A.A. Co. Vol. 1,* f. 196) and on October 20, 1799 Michael Dorsey and his wife, Honor, sold to Owen Dorsey for 337 pounds, 10 sh, 150 acres of First Discovery clear of Doughregan Manor. On October 7, 1800, Michael Dorsey sold his interest in First Discovery to Michael Dorsey of John. (*A.A. Co. Deeds N.H. No. 10,* folios 234, 449)

The tax list of 1783 describes the house in which Michael Dorsey lived on Pushpin as a frame dwelling, 1 story, 44 by 24 feet. There was also a frame kitchen 24 by 16 feet, a smoke house 12 by 8 feet, and a log barn 24 by 20 feet. A log house 16 foot square stood on First Discovery.

Michael Dorsey took the Oath of Allegiance and Support from Anne Arundel County.
(*List of Oaths,* Md. Hist. Soc.)

DORSEY FAMILY

An old corner stone still stands near the east side of the Clarksville Road, six miles from Ellicott City, twelve miles from Elk Ridge Landing, and four miles from Clarksville, which bears the inscription, "Here stands The Beginning Trees of Doohoregan Pushpin and The Girls Portion, 1773."

CORNER STONE ERECTED NEARLY 175 YEARS AGO
By Michael Dorsey II and His Neighbors

At the May term 1793, Michael Dorsey came into Court to give a deposition as to the sanity of John Beal Howard.

I Michael of Mike, Summoned at the Instance of the Defendant Brice Howard.

Question - By the Defendant Brice Howard. Did you visit John Beal Howard during his last illness, if yes, what was the occasion of your visit and what was his Situation.

Answer - I did visit him once at Mr. Brice Howard's in consequence of a message by his father Mr. Brice Howard requesting me or my brother to come down, when I found the said John B. Howard poorly and asked him how he did, he answered, very poorly, after being there some time he asked this deponent to give him a Drink which I did. Sometime after the covering slipped down and he asked the deponant to cover him which he did and in the morning when the deponant was going away, he the deponant asked said John B. Howard how he found himself, he replied he thought he was much better - at that time the deponant believed him to be in weak low state of body but perfectly in his sense. (*Chanc. Rec. No. 27,* f. 148)

The will of Michael Dorsey Jr. made February, 1812 and probated April 13, 1812 follows:

In the name of God Amen I Michael Dorsey of Anne Arundel County do make and publish my last will and testament in manner following that is to say I give and devise to my wife Honor Dorsey during her natural life the use and benefit of my whole estate both real and personal for the purpose of supporting herself and my three daughters Honor, Elizabeth, and Cecil until they may severally marry

Item at the death of my wife I give and devise to my son Michael Dorsey his heirs and assigns forever my land and dwelling plantation whereon I now reside containing about two hundred and fifty acres of land with the buildings and appurtenances upon the express condition nevertheless that he or they shall pay within the term of four years after my wife's death in four annual payments to each of my daughters Jemima Warfield, Honor Dorsey, Elizabeth Dorsey and Cecil Dorsey or to their respective executors administrators or assigns the sum of five hundred dollars the payment of which amounting in the whole to the sum of two thousand dollars I expressly charge on my said land

Item after my wife's death I leave to my son Lloyd Dorsey the sum of two hundred and fifty dollars to be paid out of my personal estate also I give to my son John Dorsey the sum of ten pounds to be paid them out of my personal estate. I give to my son Owen Dorsey my gun and shot bag.

Item all the rest and residue of my personal estate I leave to be equally divided after the death of my wife between my son Michael Dorsey and my daughters Honor Elizabeth and Cecil Dorsey their executors administrators and assigns share and share alike.

Lastly I appoint my son Owen Dorsey executor of this my last will and testament hereby revoking all other wills given under my hand and seal the day of February eighteen hundred and twelve

Witness:
Abner Buckman
Caleb Dorsey
William Buckman

Michael Dorsey (Seal)

(*A.A. Co. Original Wills*, Box D, Folder 64)
(*A.A. Co. Wills J.G. No. 2*, f. 562)

On March 31, 1812, Owen Dorsey and Michael Dorsey signed a bond to pay debts of Michael Dorsey.

The residuary legatees of Michael Dorsey late of Anne Arundel County deceased certified that no inventory be made of the personal estate, but that Owen Dorsey the executor shall give bond and security to pay debts and legacies due from the deceased. Signed by Michael Dorsey, Honor, Elizabeth, Cecil Dorsey. (See page 98) (*A.A. Co. Test. Papers*, Box 104, Folder 13)

Honor Dorsey, widow of Michael, was the daughter of John and Jemima (Dorsey) Elder. By the will of her father made 1762, she was left 30 pounds to be hers at the age of 16 years or marriage. (*Wills 31*, f. 844) (See page 57)

Her will made January 31, 1817 and proved July 6, 1818 reads:

I, Oner widow of Michael Dorsey late of Ann Arundel County deceased do make and publish this my last will and Testament in manner following.

I give my daughter Jemima Warfield my mulatto boy called Jim aged three years & six months to serve until he is thirty years of age and then to be free

Item I give my daughter Oner Dorsey her Executors, administrators and assigns all the residue of my personal estate of every description with this exception that my small mulatto girl called Sall shall serve her until she is thirty years of age & then to be free also any issue she may have to serve during the same period. I do hereby appoint Owen Dorsey my son to be Executor of this my last Will and Testament and do hereby authorize him to make use of any part of the Stock or provisions that may be on hand which may be necessary for the support of the negroes and stock until a division thereof can be had among the residuary devisees of my late husband Given under my hand and seal the thirty-first day of January eighteen hundred & Seventeen.

Witnesses
Nicholas Harding
Henrietta Warfield

Her
Oner X Dorsey (Seal)
Mark

(*A.A. Co. Wills J.G. No. 3*, f. 220)

Michael and Honor (Elder) Dorsey are buried in a small cemetery called Elioak near the present house on Pushpin. Their graves are unmarked. (William Gaither is the present owner of Pushpin.)*

Children of Michael and Honor (Elder) Dorsey:
(Named in parent's wills)

1. Michael[6] Dorsey, b. Jan. 9, 1769, m. Amelia Green
2. John Dorsey, b. 1770, m. Jemima Gist (See page 108)
3. Owen Dorsey, b. Oct. 14, 1771, m. Henrietta Dorsey
4. Lloyd Dorsey, b. c 1774, m. Anna Green
5. Jemima Dorsey, m. Alexander Warfield
6. Elizabeth Dorsey, b. 1785, m. William Ball
7. Honor Dorsey, m. Joshua Jones
8. Cecelia Dorsey, m. Michael Dunn

---

* The information concerning the location of Elioak cemetery and the members of the Dorsey family buried there, as well as the location of the old corner stone of Pushpin, was given by Mr. Louis T. Clark, attorney, Ellicott City, a descendant of Michael Dorsey.

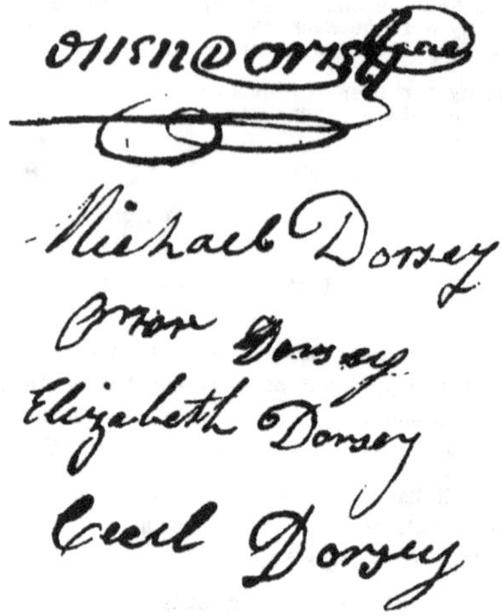

SIGNATURES OF FIVE CHILDREN OF MICHAEL AND HONOR DORSEY
From Testamentary Papers Filed in the Hall of Records, Annapolis, Maryland

1. MICHAEL^{6} Dorsey III (Michael,^{5} Michael,^{4} John,^{3} Col. Edward,^{2} Edward^{1})
b. Jan. 9, 1769; d. Apr. 26, 1843 at Pushpin, Anne Arundel County (now Howard Co.)
m. Jan. 2, 1808 Amelia Green, b. Dec. 28, 1779; d. Nov. 10, 1838

Michael Dorsey inherited the dwelling plantation of Pushpin containing 250 acres in 1812 when his father died.

Amelia Dorsey, wife of Michael, was the daughter of Richard and Sarah (Howard) Green. She inherited her share of the parental plantation in Montgomery County in 1818, (*Mont. Co. Wills L*, f. 88) which she and Michael Dorsey sold to Allan Green, Tyler County, Virginia. (*Mont. Co. Deeds U*, f. 381)

Michael and Amelia Dorsey are buried in Elioak Cemetery on Pushpin. Their graves are marked with rough field stones, which bear no inscriptions. (See page 175A)

Children of Michael and Amelia (Green) Dorsey:
(Records from Bible of Daniel Jones, brother of Eliza Jones, July 26, 1835)
In possession of Louis T. Clark, Ellicott City

1. John^{7} Dorsey, b. Jan. 12, 1809
2. Dr. Hanson Dorsey, b. Mar. 3, 1810; d. Jan. 21, 1879 near Front Royal, Va.,
   m. Amanda Castleman, b. Oct. 13, 1820; d. Apr. 28, 1901
3. Michael Green Dorsey, b. Oct. 11, 1813, m. Eliza Jones (See below)
4. Sarah Ann Dorsey, b. Feb. 27, 1819, m. Lemuel Jones, son of David
5. Honor Jane Dorsey, b. Jan. 3, 1823, m. Theophilus Jones, son of David

3. MICHAEL GREEN^{7} DORSEY IV (Michael,^{6} Michael,^{5} Michael,^{4} John,^{3} Col. Edward,^{2} Edward^{1})
b. Oct. 11, 1813; d. Dec. 1892 at Ravenswood, Howard County
m. Mar. 31, 1836 Eliza Jones, b. Aug. 21, 1807; d. Jan. 31, 1890

Michael Dorsey lived on Pushpin until 1845, when he sold the part he had inherited from his father and moved to Ravenswood. His wife was the daughter of David Jones, who died in 1845.

MICHAEL DORSEY AND SOME OF HIS DESCENDANTS

Michael and Eliza Dorsey are buried in Elioak Cemetery on Pushpin. Their graves are marked with engraved stones. (See page 175A)

Children of Michael and Eliza (Jones) Dorsey:
(Births from family records)

1. Theophilis Jones[8] Dorsey, b. Jan. 9, 1837; d. Jan. 1906 unm.
2. George Byron[8] Dorsey
3. Marian Bradford[8] Dorsey, b. Oct. 20, 1840; d. Mar. 7, 1920
   m. Mar. 4, 1802 Louis Gassaway

   Children:

   1. Louis[9] Gassaway, m. Oct. 1891 Mary Iglehart
   2. Ellen Brewer[9] Gassaway, m. Oct. 15, 1901 Co. Ronald Fisher

      Children:

      1. Dorsey G.[10] Fisher, unm. in American Embassy, London
      2. Martha Ellen[10] Fisher, b. Dec. 27, 1908, m. Sept. 10, 1934
         George Egerton May, Englishman, Bombay, India
      3. Marian[10] Fisher, b. Apr. 6, 1911, m. Apr. 18, 1942 George Maynard
4. Edwin[8] Dorsey, d.y.
5. Howard[8] Dorsey, d.y.
6. Caleb Lloyd[8] Dorsey, d.y.
7. Mary Frances[8] Dorsey, b. Apr. 2, 1846; d. May 25, 1906 at Ravenswood, Howard County
   m. Dec. 1870 James Thomas Clark, b. Mar. 31, 1846; d. Feb. 17, 1926
   He owned part of Pushpin, and was a splendid farmer and horseman.
   He also served as county treasurer.

   They had one son:

   Louis Thomas[9] Clark, b. Nov. 28, 1872
   m. Dec. 15, 1904 Desiree Branch, b. Dec. 30, 1878, daughter of Rev. Dr. Henry Branch (Presbyterian) and Melissa Jarvis, daughter of Nathan and Ellen (Chinn) Jarvis.

   Louis Thomas Clark, who is an attorney, owns the historic home of Mt. Ida in Ellicott City. He formerly owned Walnut Hill near Christ Church, and Judge Edward Hammond's Font Hill, where all his children were born. (See page 161)

   Children of Louis Thomas and Desiree (Branch) Clark:

   1. Lieut. USNR Louis Dorsey[10] Clark, b. Sept. 26, 1905
      m. Dec. 24, 1931 Helen Gambrill, dau. of Prof. J. Montgomery Gambrill of Columbia, N.Y. City, and Johns Hopkins Universities, and Maud (Mayfield) Gambrill

      One child:

      Michael Dorsey[11] Clark, b. Nov. 5, 1937
   2. Henry Branch[10] Clark, b. Oct. 21, 1906, Executive, C. and P. Tel. Co.
      m. Feb. 11, 1933 Charlotte Garrison Spence, dau. of John Mooreland and Nellie (Garrison) Spence
   3. Lieut. Commander USNR James Thaddeus[10] Clark, b. Jan. 25, 1908
      Lawyer

4. Millicent[10] Clark, b. June 7, 1909, m. July 17, 1929
John Rogers Hammond, son of Edward Mackubin and Mary Reubena (Rogers) Hammond, Colonel (U.S.A.) World War II

Children:

1. John Rogers[11] Hammond, b. May 23, 1930
2. Sally Millicent[11] Hammond, b. Mar. 3, 1932
3. James David[11] Hammond, b. Sept. 14, 1938

5. Mary Dorsey[10] Clark, b. July 11, 1910
6. Desiree Branch[10] Clark, b. Nov. 4, 1911, Business Executive, N.Y. City
7. Captain USMC Charles Branch[10] Clark, b. June 5, 1913
m. May 26, 1945 Adelaide Snowden Hodges Clark, dau. of Edward Talbott Clark and Adelaide (Snowden) Hodges Clark
8. Marian Gassaway[10] Clark, b. Nov. 18, 1914, m. Aug. 28, 1937
Robert Farnsworth Howard, son of General John and Helen Howard

Children:

1. Helen Melissa[11] Howard, b. Jan. 22, 1943
2. John Farnsworth[11] Howard, b. Sept. 3, 1945

9. Lieut. Commander USNR Nathan Jarvis[10] Clark, b. Apr. 13, 1916
m. Aug. 26, 1944 Marjory Davis Murphy, dau. of Herbert Hayes Murphy and Eva (Davis) Murphy
10. Lieut. USNR Basil Crawford[10] Clark, b. Oct. 16, 1917, m. Aug. 12, 1944
Joan Johnston, dau. of Lyle T. and Cecil Johnston
11. Betsey Chinn[10] Clark, b. May 31, 1920, m. Oct. 27, 1945 Lieut. Phillip Caldwell, son of Robert and Wilhemina Caldwell of Ohio

3. OWEN[6] DORSEY (Michael,[5] Michael,[4] John,[3] Col. Edward,[2] Edward[1])
b. Oct. 14, 1771; d. 1825 Baltimore County
m. Oct. 14, 1797 Henrietta Dorsey, b. 1776; d. 18--

On Oct. 20, 1799, Owen Dorsey bought from his father Michael Dorsey, 150 acres of First Discovery, and on August 25, 1800, he transferred this tract to Michael Dorsey of John.
(*A.A. Co. Deeds N.H. No. 10,* folios 234,449)

Owen Dorsey of Baltimore, Maryland, on June 14, 1813, bought of his brother John Dorsey and wife, Jemima, of Muskingum County, Ohio, 321 acres of land in Licking County, Ohio.
(*Licking Co. Ohio Deeds D,* f. 70)

On June 30, 1814, he conveyed to Vachel Dorsey part of two tracts, Discovery and First Discovery. (*A.A. Co. Deeds N.H. No. 2,* f. 528)

During the War of 1812, Owen Dorsey was lieutenant and paymaster of the 39th Maryland Regiment composed of recruits from Baltimore City. In 1815 he became Judge of the Orphan's Court of the City of Baltimore.

Owen Dorsey's will made January 1, 1819 and proved April 18, 1825 left:

To wife Henrietta Dorsey during her widowhood, the income from lands in Anne Arundel County, Maryland, and Ohio, to support and educate his children, sons Edwin, Owen, Lorenzo, and daughter Elizabeth Dorsey. In event of wife's marriage, then she was to receive only her third
On September 26, 1825, Edwin Dorsey, only son of Lawful age of the deceased Owen Dorsey, Andrew Adgate and Elizabeth Adgate, only daughter of Owen Dorsey deceased, renounced their rights to administer on the estate. (*Balt. Co. Wills 12,* f. 121)

Henrietta Dorsey, widow of Owen, was the daughter of Nicholas and Elizabeth (Worthington) Dorsey. She inherited from her mother in 1804, silver tablespoons and soup spoons. (*A.A. Co. Wills J.G. No. 2,* f. 273) (See page 46)

Children of Owen and Henrietta (Dorsey) Dorsey:
(Named in father's will)

1. Edwin[7] Dorsey
2. Elizabeth Owen[7] Dorsey, b. Oct. 15, 1805, m. (1) Andrew Adgate (See below)
   m. (2) Rev. James Higgins
3. Lorenzo[7] Dorsey, b. 1808, m. Anna Hanson McKenny, b. Washington D.C.

   Children:

   1. Louis Dorsey, d. unm.
   2. Clare Dorsey, m. Richard B. Mohun
   3. Angela Dorsey, m. Maj. Robert L. Eastman
   4. Florence Dorsey
   5. Ella Lorraine Dorsey, d. unm.
4. Owen Alexander[7] Dorsey, b. Oct. 23, 1811; d. July 2, 1880

2. ELIZABETH OWEN[7] DORSEY (Owen,[6] Michael,[5] Michael,[4] John,[3] Col. Edward,[2] Edward[1])
b. Oct. 15, 1805; d. Jan. 12, 1882, Baltimore
m. (1) Oct. 15, 1822 Andrew Adgate, b. 1794; d. Aug. 19, 1827, son of Andrew

They had one child:
Henrietta Dorsey[8] Adgate, b. 1826; d. Nov. 7, 1910, Baltimore
m. Sept. 9, 1845 John Duer, b. Aug. 16, 1816; d. Oct. 29, 1901 son of John and Susannah (Norris) Duer

Children:

1. Andrew Adgate[9] Duer, b. Dec. 3, 1846; d. Nov. 11, 1891
   m. Oct. 31, 1772 Margaret Marshall, b. Dec. 25, 1850; d. Nov. 26, 1937
2. Isabel[9] Duer, b. Apr. 28, 1848; d. 1937
3. Dr. Douglas Henry[9] Duer, b. Apr. 11, 1851; d. May 13, 1913
   m. Apr. 18, 1882 Genevieve Bloget, b. Dec. 23, 1852 Boston, Mass.

   Children:

   1. Leland[10] B. Duer, b. Feb. 21, 1883
      m. (1) Dorothy Tate, m. (2) Marjorie Driscoll
   2. Edith[10] Duer, b. Mar. 14, 1884, m. Riggin Buckler
   3. Edward N.[10] Duer, b. Mar. 20, 1891; d. June 26, 1891
   4. Henry T.[10] Duer, b. June 10, 1892
      m. Apr. 9, 1923 Anne Eugenia Levering, b. Nov. 30, 1888, dau. of Leonidas and Anna Riggs (Keys) Levering (See page 221)

      One child: Douglas[11] H. Duer, b. May 19, 1924
4. Edith[9] Duer, b. Jan. 5, 1853; d. 1921

Elizabeth Adgate, widow of Andrew, m. (2) Rev. James Higgins, b. Nov. 6, 1809; d. Feb. 13, 1879

4. LLOYD[6] DORSEY (Michael,[5] Michael,[4] John,[3] Col. Edward,[2] Edward[1])
b. 1772; d. May 7, 1815 Montgomery County
m. June 26, 1797 Anna Green (Pr. Geo, Parish Reg. Mont. Co.) b. 1770; d. Mar. 1851

On October 11, 1803, Lloyd Dorsey (son of Michael of Anne Arundel County) purchased from John Gartell a portion of two tracts, one called Addition to Brooke Grove and part called Gray's Lot. (*Mont. Co. Deeds L*, f. 82)

On April 8, 1806, he bought from Obed Leeke, parts of Gittings Hah, Hah, Leeks Venture, and Leeks Lot, adjoining Prospect Hill on road leading from Green's Bridge to Frederick Town. (*Mont. Co. Deeds M*, f. 602)

Lloyd Dorsey died intestate in 1815. Letters of administration were granted to his widow Anna Dorsey on May 30, 1815. (*Mont. Co. Docket 1798-1824*, f. 31) The final account was filed June 8, 1819. One-third of the estate was left to the widow and the remainder divided equally among the 8 children, Sarah, Richard, Onor, Anna, Lloyd, Washington, Mary, and William Dorsey. (*Mont. Co. Wills M*, f. 35)

Anna Dorsey, who was the daughter of Richard and Sarah (Howard) Green was willed a share of the parental estate called Pleasant Farm on September 17, 1818. (*Mont. Co. Wills L*, f. 88) On January 13, 1819, she conveyed her rights to this property to her brother Allan Green of Tyler County, Virginia. (*Mont. Co. Deeds U*, f. 380) She went to live with her daughter Mary Green, Zanesville, Ohio, where she is buried.

Children of Lloyd and Anna (Green) Dorsey:
(Births from family Bible Records)

1. Sarah[7] Dorsey, b. Nov. 17, 1797, m. June 14, 1826 Achilles Simpson
2. Richard Green Dorsey, b. Apr. 18, 1799, m. Mar. 7, 1825 Honor Warfield (See below)
3. Honor Dorsey, b. June 9, 1801, m. Dec. 1, 1820 Thomas Burgess, Balt. Co.
4. Anna Dorsey, b. June 10, 1803, m. Charles Barnes
5. Lloyd Dorsey, b. Nov. 7, 1805 Moved to St. Louis, Missouri
6. Dr. Washington Dorsey, b. Nov. 17, 1807; d. Sept. 22, 1864 Granville Co., N. Car.
   m. Camilla Yerrill Seabrook, Rockbridge Co., Va., d. Oct. 3, 1882
7. Mary Dorsey, b. Oct. 15, 1809, m. Lewis Hugh Green, Moved to Zanesville, O.
8. William Dorsey, b. Jan. 6, 1812, m. Lucy Harrison, Moved to Martinsburg, W. Va.
9. Artemas Dorsey, b. July 11, 1814; d. Apr. 30, 1815

2. RICHARD GREEN[7] DORSEY (Lloyd,[6] Michael,[5] Michael,[4] John,[3] Col. Edward,[2] Edward[1])
b. Apr. 18, 1799; d. Dec. 12, 1832 Frederick County, Maryland
m. Mar. 7, 1825 Honor Warfield, dau. of Alexander and Jemima (Dorsey) Warfield
They had one son: (See page 103

Dr. Alexander Warfield[8] Dorsey, b. Dec. 27, 1828; d. Jan. 2, 1868 Westminister, Md.
m. Mary R. Webster, b. 1830; d. 1892
He received his degree from the University of Maryland on Mar. 7, 1857, and practiced medicine in Gettsyburg, Pennsylvania, and Urbana, Maryland.

Children of Alexander W. and Mary (Webster) Dorsey:

1. Richard Green[9] Dorsey. Moved west, married and had four children
2. Lloyd[9] Dorsey, b. Mar. 10, 1856 St. Louis, Mo.; d. Aug. 29, 1942 Baltimore, Md.
   m. Feb. 6, 1884 Mary Augusta Canter, b. Feb. 22, 1859; d. May 12, 1942
   Children: (Born in Baltimore)
   1. Harry Warfield[10] Dorsey, b. Jan. 23, 1885
      m. June 20, 1908 May Richards Williamson, b. Feb. 10, 1888
      Realtor, Orlando, Florida
   Children:
   1. May Williamson[11] Dorsey, b. Aug. 22, 1912 Baltimore, Md.
      m. June 1, 1936 Walter Alfred Gielow, Orlando, Florida
      Children:
      1. Gayle Dorsey[12] Gielow, b. June 23, 1937
      2. Bonnie Ruth[12] Gielow, b. Nov. 12, 1943

2. Jessie Warfield[11] Dorsey, b. Aug. 1, 1918 Baltimore, Md.
m. Nov. 21, 1941 Capt. Warren Woodrow Bennett
3. Sara Jane[11] Dorsey, b. Jan. 17, 1924 Orlando. Fla.

2. Lloyd[10] Dorsey Jr., b. July 10, 1886
m. Dec. 10, 1921 Atlantis Rice Hull, b. June 11, 1886
Grain Elevator Agent, Pennsylvania Railroad

One Child:

John Lloyd[11] Dorsey, b. Nov. 22, 1924 (See Who's Who among Students in American Colleges 1945-6)

3. Jesse Hodgdon[10] Dorsey, b. May 23, 1893; d. Nov. 1908 Baltimore, Md.
4. Lieut. Commander USNR Frank Furst[10] Dorsey, b. June 11, 1895
m. Nov. 3, 1933 Margaret Bell Hicks
Vice-President and Secretary, Fidelity and Guaranty Fire Corporation, Baltimore, Md.

Children:

1. Frank Colston[11] Dorsey, b. Dec. 15, 1934
2. Carol Stephens[11] Dorsey, b. May 8, 1937

5. Arthur Gorman[10] Dorsey, b. Oct. 19, 1897
m. July 19, 1930 Elsie Anna Helmig, b. Nov. 8, 1905
Electrical Load Dispatcher, Pennsylvania Water and Power Company, Baltimore, Md.

Children:

1. Arthur Gorman[11] Dorsey Jr., b. Nov. 4, 1931
2. Herbert Warfield[11] Dorsey, b. Nov. 10, 1940

Honor Dorsey, widow of Richard, m. (2) Andrew Nicodemus

One child:

Cecelia Nicodemus, m. Rev. J.P. Hentz

5. JEMIMA[6] DORSEY (Michael,[5] Michael,[4] John,[3] Col. Edward,[2] Edward[1])
d. after 1835
m. Mar. 14, 1797 Alexander Warfield, d. 1835 at Pilgrim's Retreat, Frederick Co. Md.
(*Fred. Co. Wills G.M.E.Z*, f. 28)

Alexander Warfield represented Frederick County in the Maryland Legislature in the years 1818 and 1819.

Children of Alexander and Jemima (Dorsey) Warfield:
(Named in father's will)

1. Charles Alexander[7] Warfield, d. in Butte County, California
2. Joshua Warfield
3. Dr. Jesse Lee Warfield, b. Nov. 27, 1801; d. Feb. 9, 1887 Baltimore County
4. Honor Warfield, m. (1) Mar. 7, 1825 Richard Dorsey (See page 102)
(2) Andrew Nicodemus
5. Asbury O. Warfield
6. Cecilia Warfield, m. Aug. 4, 1834 Frederick A Davis
7. Sarah Warfield, m. Thomas H.W. Moore
8. Mary Catherine Warfield
9. Henrietta Warfield, m. Feb. 1, 1819 Thomas I. Worthington
10. Elizabeth Warfield, m. Apr. 25, 1827 Upton Higgins
11. Dennis Warfield
12. ________ Warfield, m. ________ Howard

6. ELIZABETH[6] DORSEY (Michael,[5] Michael,[4] John,[3] Col. Edward,[2] Edward[1])
b. 1785; d. 1857 Portsmouth, Virginia
m. Jan. 27, 1814 as 2nd wife, William Ball Jr., b. 1790, A.A. Co,
d. July 30, 1863 Baltimore

William Ball Jr. inherited from the estate of his mother Sarah Ball, Todd's Risque, part of Andover, and personal estate. (See page 46)

He acquired property in Baltimore City, and in 1815 assigned to Judge Owen Dorsey (his brother-in-law) part of Carter's Delight, lying in Baltimore County.

(*Balt. Co. Deeds W.G. 134*, folios 558, 559)

In the battle of Bladensburg, he was wounded in the leg. He also served in the War of 1812.

Children of William and Elizabeth (Dorsey) Ball:
(Births from family records)

1. Prudence Gough[7] Ball, b. Dec. 14, 1814, m. Jan. 23, 1832 Samuel Story, lived on the Eastern Shore of Maryland. Had issue.
2. Owen Dorsey[7] Ball, b. Feb. 17, 1817, m. Elizabeth Frances Boyd (See below)
3. John[7] Ball, b. Feb. 22, 1819; d. Jan. 15, 1850, m. Caroline Schmenke, Baltimore. One son, George Ball, who left son Robert Ball
4. Walter[7] Ball, b. Mar. 22, 1822; d. 1910
   m. Anna Schmenke, d. 1898
   He was treasurer for the Old Bay Steamship Company for 65 years
   Of his ten children, but one brought down heirs, vizt:
   Elizabeth Dorsey[8] Ball, b. Jan. 12, 1854
   m. James Boyce of Baltimore and New York Cities

   Children:

   1. Raymond[9] Boyce, b. Oct. 19, 1874; d. N.Y.C.
      m. (2) Natalie Graff

      Children:

      1. Raymond[10] Boyce
      2. Wallace[10] Boyce
   2. Walter[9] Boyce, no issue
   3. Arthur[9] Boyce, m. Edna Grandau

      One child: Elizabeth Boyce
5. Alexander[7] Ball, b. Dec. 16, 1825, d. unm.
6. Summerfield[7] Ball, b. May 12, 1828, d. unm.

2. OWEN DORSEY[7] BALL (Elizabeth[6] (Dorsey) Ball, Michael,[5] Michael,[4] John,[3] Col. Edward,[2] Edward[1])
b. Feb. 17, 1817 Baltimore City; d. Nov. 1898 Portsmouth, Virginia
m. Nov. 18, 1841 Elizabeth Frances Boyd, Frederick, Maryland, b. July 12, 1817;
d. 1904 Portsmouth, Virginia, dau. of David Boyd, Frederick, Maryland

Owen Dorsey Ball moved to Portsmouth, Virginia, in 1851, and became General Manager of the Seaboard and Roanoke Railroad. (See page 105)

Children of Owen and Elizabeth (Boyd) Ball:
(Births from family records)

1. William[8] Ball, b. Mar. 13, 1843, m. Mary Jordan, Norfolk, Va.
2. David Charles[8] Ball, b. Apr. 4. 1844, m. Anna DeVere (See page 106)

HOUSE BUILT IN PORTSMOUTH, VIRGINIA, 1784
Owned and Occupied by the Owen Dorsey Ball Family for over 50 Years

3. Elizabeth Prudence^{8} Ball, b. Nov. 5, 1845; d. Feb. 1931 Portsmouth, Va.
   m. John W.H. Porter, Portsmouth, Va.

   Children:

   1. Ridgely Ball^{9} Porter, m. Augusta Maupin

      Children:

      1. Sallie Macon^{10} Porter
      2. J. Ridgely^{10} Porter
      3. Augusta M.^{10} Porter

   2. Capt. J. Hunter^{9} Porter, d. unm.

4. Albert^{8} Ritchie Ball, m. Jeanette Minter, Portsmouth, Va. No issue
5. Samuel^{8} Boyd Ball, m. Lulu Blair, St. Louis, Mo. No issue
6. Helen^{8} Ball, b. 1849; d. July 1, 1895 unm.
7. Henrietta^{8} Ball, b. Aug. 25, 1851; d. July 20, 1917 unm.
8. Owen Davis^{8} Ball, b. Mar. 30, 1861

   Children:

   1. Harvey^{9} Ball, m. (1) Mary Barbee

      Children:

      1. Edward^{10} Ball 2. George^{10} Ball

      m. (2) Mildred San Souci
      One child: Constance^{10} Ball, m. Lt. George Standish Jr.

2. Elizabeth[9] Ball, m. Ross Nicholson

   Children:

   1. Betsy Ross[10] Nicholson
   2. Roberta Bruce[10] Nicholson
   3. Thomas[10] Nicholson
   4. Marie[10] Nicholson

3. Alexina[9] Ball, m. Richard Jones, Norfolk, Va.

   Children;

   1. Martha[10] Jones
   2. Richard[10] Jones

4. Raymond[9] Ball, d. inf.
5. Robert Owen[9] Ball, m. Thelma Hatch, Norfolk, Va.
   One child: Robert[10] Ball

2. DAVID CHARLES[8] BALL (Owen,[7] Elizabeth[6] (Dorsey) Ball, Michael,[5] Michael,[4] John,[3] Col. Edward,[2] Edward[1])
   b. Apr. 4, 1844, Frederick Co. Md.; d. Apr. 29, 1926 at DeVere Place, Baltimore Co.
   m. Anna Clay DeVere, b. May 5, 1844; d. Feb. 1931 Baltimore

David Charles Ball was educated at the Norfolk Collegiate Institute, Norfolk, Virginia. He left school at the age of 16 years to enter the Confederate Army, in which he served four years. At the conclusion of the war he went with the Bay Line Office in Norfolk, Virginia. He later became associated with the Clyde Line, known as the Chesapeake Steamship Line, and moved to Baltimore.

Anna Ball, his wife, daughter of Col. William and Sarah (Jones) DeVere of DeVere Place, Baltimore County, was educated at the Quaker School in Montgomery County, and The Misses Sappington's School for Girls, Baltimore, Maryland. Her father, William DeVere, was presideht of the first voluntary fire company of San Francisco, California.

Children of David and Ann (DeVere) Ball:
(Births from family records)

1. Eleanor DeVere[9] Ball, d. 1931
   m. June 6, 1893 Howard Stabler Milnor

   Children:

   1. William Ball[10] Milnor, m. July 22, 1946 Betty Joan Tosland of England
   2. Eleanor[10] Milnor, m. Gyfford Collins
      One child: Gyfford[11] Collins

2. Nannie Boyd[9] Ball (See pages 78 and 211)
   m. Dec. 23, 1896 Walden C. Nimmo, d. 1923
   One child:
   Ruth Natali[10] Nimmo, m. (1) James C. Harlan, m. (2) Calder Kirk
3. Owen Lester[9] Ball, d. 1930 unm.
4. Elizabeth Rogers[9] Ball, d. Sept. 16, 1933
   m. Dr. William Bull Stoddard
   Children:
   1. Mary[10] Stoddard, d.y.
   2. Eleanor[10] Stoddard, m. Otis Starkey. No issue
   3. William[10] Stoddard, m. Mary Weaver. No issue
   4. David[10] Stoddard, m. Ruth Steckman
      Children: David C.F.[11] Stoddard   William M.B.[11] Stoddard

5. Rosalia Barret[9] Ball
6. M. Virginia[9] (Virgie) Ball, d. Oct. 10, 1942
   m. T. Carroll Davis, d. 1942

   Children:

   1. Rosalia[10] Davis
   2. T. Carroll[10] Davis, m. Katherine Wood

      Children: Sally[11] Davis
      Sue[11] Davis

7. S. Janet[9] Ball)
8. Albert Day[9] Ball, d. inf.) twins

7. HONOR[6] DORSEY (Michael,[5] Michael,[4] John,[3] Col. Edward,[2] Edward[1])
   d. after 1836
   m. as second wife, March 30, 1819 Joshua Jones, d. 1836 Frederick County, Maryland
   (*Fred. Co. Wills G.M.E.Z,* f. 214)

   Joshua Jones m. (1) Susannah Gist, d. Oct. 8, 1817, dau. of Joshua

   Children of Joshua Jones:
   (Named in his will)

   1. Dr. Joshua Jones
   2. Edwin Jones
   3. Wesley Jones
   4. Awbray Gist Jones
   5. Harvey Gist Jones
   6. John R. Jones
   7. Mary Ann Jones
   8. Elizabeth Honor Jones
   9. Hannah Jones

   Besides the above children, Joshua Jones also named his grandson John Osborn Battee, and his nephew, Dorsey Dunn, son of Michael and Cecelia (Dorsey) Dunn

8. CECELIA[6] DORSEY (Michael,[5] Michael,[4] John,[3] Col. Edward,[2] Edward[1])
   d. probably in Ohio
   m. Aug. 22, 1814 Michael Dunn
   They moved to Ohio

   Children:

   1. Dorsey[7] Dunn, b. in Maryland, Named in the will of uncle Joshua Jones of Frederick County, who married Honor Dorsey
   2. Jemima Cecelia[7] Dunn, b. Oct. 9, 1830 near Zanesville, O. (Bible Rec.)
   3. Daniel Dunn, m. Annie ——
   4. Elizabeth Dunn, m. Newton Willis
   Perhaps others

2. JEMIMA CECELIA[7] DUNN (Cecelia,[6] (Dorsey) Dunn, Michael,[5] Michael,[4] John,[3] Col. Edward,[2] Edward[1])
   b. Oct. 9, 1830 near Zanesville, Ohio
   m. Joel Hinman, b. in Connecticut

Children:

1. Elizabeth[8] Hinman, b. Nov. 5, 1855; d. Aug. 31, 1930, Baltimore, Maryland m. J. Henry Sirich

   Children:

   1. Mary[9] Sirich, m. Charles B. Mann Jr., Baltimore, Maryland Other children

JOHN DORSEY OF MARYLAND AND OHIO

2. JOHN[6] DORSEY (Michael,[5] Michael,[4] John,[3] Col. Edward,[2] Edward[1])
   b. 1770 at Pushpin, Anne Arundel County, Maryland
   d. Feb. 5, 1835 near Shannon, Muskingum County, Ohio
   m. Dec. 2, 1792 Jemima Gist, Baltimore, Md., b. May 4, 1765; d. Dec. 15, 1834

A few years after their marriage, John and Jemima Dorsey moved to Ohio County, Virginia (now Brooke County, West Virginia). John Dorsey's name appeared on the first tax list for Brooke County in 1797, the year the county was legally organized.
(*Brooke Co. Tax Records*, Vol. 174, Va. Archives, Richmond, Va.)

John Dorsey was given 50 acres of land by his father-in-law, Joseph Gist in 1801, (*Brooke Co. W. Va. Wills 1*, f. 18) and on November 27, 1809 he bought 19½ acres on Buffalo Creek from his brother-in-law Samuel Gist and his wife, Ann. (*Brooke Co. W. Va. Deeds 4*, f. 306) (See page 58)

Some time before November 25, 1809, he made a trip to Ohio, for on that date John Dorsey of Brooke County, Virginia, bought 321 acres of land for $1,000 in Licking County, Ohio, from Noah Linsly of Ohio County, Virginia. (*Licking Co. Ohio Deeds D*, f. 70)

On June 24, 1811, John and Jemima Dorsey sold their land in Brooke County, West Virginia, (*Brooke Co. Deeds 4*, f. 443) and shortly after moved to Muskingum County, Ohio, where a patent was issued to John Dorsey on November 19, 1812, for the W½ Sec. 4, T. 2 N., R. 8 W., United States Military Survey, Ohio, being based on Zanesville credit entry 646 (prior). (*U.S. Land Office* Washington D.C.)

On June 13, 1813, John and Jemima Dorsey of Muskingum County, Ohio, sold their land in Licking County, Ohio, to John's brother, Owen Dorsey of the City of Baltimore, Maryland. (*Licking Co. Ohio, Deeds E*, f. 78)

The land patented by John Dorsey in Muskingum County was located about 12 miles north of Zanesville and 1 mile east of Shannon. With the help of his sons he cleared the land and built a comfortable log house for his family. The old stone-covered "Dorsey Spring" is still in use on this farm (now known as the Max Frazier farm) (See page 109)

The records of the Primitive Baptist Church at Shannon, Ohio, (known as Falls of Licking) state that John and Jemima Dorsey joined by letter March 6, 1813. John Dorsey was a deacon of the old School Baptist Church for many years, and both he and his wife are buried on the grounds of the Baptist Meeting House at the Cross Roads (Shannon).* (See page 109A)

* The Falls of Licking Church at Shannon, Ohio, was organized in September, 1808. The first church was built of logs in 1813; the second one of brick. The present church, which was erected about two blocks east of the original site, is a frame building. Services are still held at the church once a month. The records which cover a period of 136 years are now in the possession of Mr. Benjamin Dorsey, Dresden, Ohio, a great-great-grandson of John Dorsey, who has been the clerk of the church for the last 30 years.

THE OLD DORSEY SPRING

THE BURYING GROUND OF THE BAPTIST MEETING HOUSE, SHANNON, OHIO
Where Three Generations of Dorseys are Buried

THE OLD BAPTIST MEETING HOUSE, SHANNON, OHIO

DORSEY FAMILY

Jemima Dorsey died a year before her husband. She was the daughter of Major Joseph and Elizabeth (Elder) Gist, who moved from Baltimore, Maryland to Brooke County, Virginia about 1794/5. Joseph was the son of William Gist; grandson of Capt. Richard Gist; and great grandson of Christopher Gist, the immigrant.

The will of John Dorsey made in 1834 follows:

I John Dorsey of Muskingum Township and State of Ohio do make and publish this my last will and testament, hereby revoking and making void all former wills by me at any time heretofore made. And first I direct that my body be decently interred in the burying ground of the Baptist meeting house at the Cross Roads (Shannon) according to the rites and ceremonies of the said Church, and that my funeral be conducted in a manner corresponding with my situation in my life, and as to such worldly estate as it hath pleased God to intrust me with, I dispose of the same as follows:

First - I direct that all my debts and funeral expenses be paid as soon after my decease as possible out of the first money that shall come into the hand of my executors from any portion of my personal estate.

Second - I give and devise to my youngest son John Dorsey the farm on which I now reside situate in Muskingum township and on the waters of the Licking containing one hundred and forty one acres, to him the said John Dorsey his heirs and assigns forever, and further I bequeath unto my son John Dorsey all the farming utensils that shall be in my possession at my decease, to have and to hold forever, and further I give and bequeath unto my three daughters Honor, Elizabeth, and Jemimah all the house hold furniture, stock or goods and chattels of any description in my possession except the above mentioned to have and to hold the same to themselves their heirs and assigns forever.

And lastly I constitute my son Joseph Dorsey and my son John Dorsey to be the executors of this my last will and testament, revoking and annulling all former wills by me made, and ratifying and confirming this and no other to be my last will and testament. In testimony where of I have hereunto set my hand and seal this 27th of January A.D. 1834.

Signed published and declared in presence of John Dorsey
James Gist David Gist

A codicil added to his will the 18th of July, 1834 devised to his three daughters, Honor, Elizabeth, and Jemima all monies, notes of hand or proceeds of sales of stock and everything that may be in my possession at the time of my decease except otherwise disposed of.

(*Muskingum Co. Ohio Wills C*, f. 118)

Children of John and Jemima (Gist) Dorsey:
(Births from family records)

1. Honor[7] Dorsey
   b. Feb. 25, 1794; d. Aug. 2, 1844, Muskingum Co., Ohio. Buried at Shannon.
   m. Apr. 8, 1813 James McGee, b. Feb. 10, 1786; d. Aug. 3, 1835

   Children:

   1. John[8] McGee, b. Feb. 21, 1814
      m. (1) Oct. 5, 1857 Sarah Bainter; d. Oct. 2, 1861, Twelve children
      m. (2) Elizabeth Adams, Five children
   2. Elizabeth[8] McGee, b. Aug. 3, 1815; d. Apr. 5, 1895
      m. Jan. 4, 1838 William Butler Sr., b. July 20, 1810, Brooke Co. Va. d. June 16, 1885, buried in Baxter cemetery north of Zanesville, O., son of Henry and Charity (Baxter) Butler

      Children:

      1. Honor[9] Butler, b. Sept. 1838; d. Jan. 5, 1873
         m. Feb. 8, 1872 Downer Trimbley
      2. Henry[9] Butler, b. Apr. 13, 1841; d. May 8, 1905
         m. Feb. 9, 1864 Gratiot, O. Martha Winegardner, b. Nov. 20, 1839; d. Aug. 20, 1914
      3. Charity[9] Butler, b. Dec. 17, 1844; d. Mar. 17, 1925
         m. as his 2nd wife, William Beal, b. Nov. 3, 1841

3. Polly^{8} McGee, b. Jan. 13, 1817; d. 1819
4. Jemima^{8} McGee, b. Sept. 18, 1818, m. Oct. 13, 1836 John Younger

Children:

1. John^{9} Younger, b. Sept. 11, 1837
2. Mary^{9} Younger, b. Aug. 13, 1839, m. Mar. 9, 1862 John George
3. William^{9} Younger, b. Oct. 12, 1841
4. Fannie^{9} Younger

5. William^{8} McGee, b. Aug. 7, 1820; d. July 27, 1839 from an accident with a scythe in the hayfield
6. Martha^{8} McGee, b. Aug. 5, 1822, m. Jan. 2, 1842 Washington Haiselup
7. Samuel^{8} McGee, b. Feb. 10, 1825; d. Mar. 4, 1903 Galesburg
m. Jan. 31, 1851 Sarah Baxter, b. Jan. 1829; d. Dec. 14, 1893
dau. of Samuel and Actius Baxter
8. Mary Ann^{8} McGee, b. Jan. 1827, m. John Thrap
9. James^{8} McGee, b. Aug. 15, 1829, m. Mary Posey
10. Joshua^{8} McGee, b. July 20, 1831, m. Sarah Cassingham
11. Honor^{8} McGee, b. Aug. 31, 1833, m. Turner Haiselup

2. Joseph^{7} Dorsey
b. 1796, m. Johanna Foster (See page 113)

3. Michael^{7} Dorsey
b. 1799; d. Jan. 8, 1872, Dresden, Ohio
m. Mar. 20, 1823 Hannah Ellis, b. 1802; d. Apr. 30, 1880

Children:

1. Owen^{8} Dorsey, m. Hannah Fouts

Children: Susan,^{9} James, Thomas Dorsey

2. William^{8} Dorsey
3. Eliza^{8} Dorsey, d.y.
4. Jane^{8} Dorsey, d.y.
5. Thomas^{8} Dorsey, m. Sallie Jones

Children: Sue,^{9} Mark, Elias, Ellen, Helen Dorsey

4. Owen^{7} Dorsey
b. 1801; d. c 1912, Dresden, Ohio
m. Sept. 29, 1825 Elizabeth Foster, dau. of Benjamin, Wellsburg, W. Va.

Children:

1. Hannah^{8} Dorsey, m. Washington Campbell
2. Jemima^{8} Dorsey, m. David Welsh
3. Martha^{8} Dorsey, m. James Mansuer
4. Cromwell^{8} Dorsey, m. Ella Turner

Children: Addie,^{9} Xema, m. Rev. Holliday

5. John^{8} Dorsey, m. Eliza Welsh
6. Emily^{8} Dorsey, m. Charles Blaine
7. Adelaide^{8} Dorsey, m. Jacob Blaine
8. George^{8} Dorsey, d.y.
9. Pristley^{8} Dorsey

5. William^{7} Dorsey
b. 1803, m. (1) Aug. 4, 1825 Rebecca Gorsuch
m. (2) Eliza Cooksey
Children: Alfred,^{8} Joseph, Matilda Dorsey

6. Jemima[7] Dorsey
   b. 1805, m. Mar. 27, 1826 Moses Cole

   Children:

   1. Horace[8] Cole
   2. Bethia[8] Cole, m. Eliphet Vandenbark

      Children: Owen,[9] Gershom, Susan
   3. Eliza[8] Cole, m. David Vandenbark
   4. Samuel[8] Cole
   5. Robert[8] Cole
   6. William[8] Cole
   7. Josephine[8] Cole, d. unm.

7. Elizabeth[7] Dorsey
   b. 1807, m. James McClintock

   Children:

   1. Hannah[8] McClintock, m. Steve Compton
   2. Celia[8] McClintock, m. (1)——Campbell, (2) Peter Bainter
   3. William[8] McClintock, m. Letitia Cullins

      Children: Owen,[9] Isabelle, William, James

8. John[7] Dorsey
   b. Dec. 12, 1809; d. Aug. 10, 1877, buried at Shannon, Ohio
   m. Prudence Means, b. Jan. 3, 1810; d. June 9, 1878

   Children:

   1. Theodore H.[8] Dorsey, b. Apr. 14, 1832; d. Nov. 22, 1915
      m. Jan. 27, 1857 Louisa Davis, b. Aug. 22, 1838; d. Nov. 29, 1910

      Children:

      1. Adda Olive[9] Dorsey, b. Dec. 5, 1857; d. Dec. 23, 1925
         m. May 24, 1883 Robert Morton, b. July 30, 1858; d. Dec. 30, 1920

         One child:

         Walter Mervin[10] Morton, b. Nov. 3, 1895
      2. John Edward[9] Dorsey, b. Aug. 17, 1860
         m. Mar. 23, 1887 Pocahontas Cabbell, b. Oct. 29, 1863; d. Dec. 29, 1934, Quincy, Ill.

         Children:

         1. John E.[10] Dorsey, b. Jan. 22, 1888; d. Oct. 27, 1889
         2. Jane O.[10] Dorsey, b. Jan. 27, 1895, m. Max Zimmerman
         3. Theodore H.[10] Dorsey, b. June 15, 1897, m. May Shores
         4. Pocahontas C.[10] Dorsey, b. Aug. 26, 1901; d. Aug. 6, 1907
      3. Walter E.[9] Dorsey, b. June 24, 1875
         m. Oct. 21, 1903 Milly Deidesheimer, b. Mar. 6, 1875, Quincy, Ill.
   2. Edward Jackson[8] Dorsey, b. Jan. 12, 1835; d. Feb. 26, 1928, Granville, O.
      m. Apr. 30, 1867 Mary Elma Grove, b. Dec. 22, 1847; d. Mar. 20, 1932

      Children:

      1. George Amos[9] Dorsey, b. Feb. 6, 1868; d. Mar. 29, 1931, buried Granville, Ohio. Anthropologist and author. (See Who's Who)
         m. (1) Dec. 8, 1892 Ida Chadsey

Children:

1. Florence Dorothy Ann[10] Dorsey, b. May 23, 1894, m. Marston Cummings

   Children:

   1. Marcia Ann[11] Cummings, b. Oct. 1920
   2. John Marston Cummings, b. May 4, 1924

2. George C.[10] Dorsey, b. Dec. 25, 1896; d. Dec. 1935
   m. Ina Mattson, Three children

m. (2) Sue McLellan

2. Clarence Wilbur[9] Dorsey, b. July 6, 1872
   m. Dec. 28, 1899 Florence Juillard, b. Sept. 25, 1875

   Children:

   1. Louis J.[10] Dorsey, b. Sept. 6, 1901; d. Feb. 21, 1920
   2. Helen[10] Dorsey, b. May 28, 1906, m. Joseph Niles
   3. Aileen[10] Dorsey, b. Jan. 17, 1913, m. Dec. 10, 1934 William B. Coberly Jr.

      One child: Shirley[11] Coberly, b. Jan. 1936

3. Herbert Grove[9] Dorsey, b. Apr. 24, 1876 (See pages 78 and 215)
   m. June 21, 1906 Virginia Rowlett, b. Oct. 28, 1883
   Principal Electrical Engineer U.S. Geodetic Survey. Inventor of the dynamic speaker, the Dorsey Fathometer and the Sono-Radio buoys. (See Who's Who)

   Children:

   1. Herbert Grove[10] Dorsey II, b. Sept. 15, 1912
      m. Oct. 29, 1939 Elizabeth Copley Ballantine
      Meterologist with U.S. Weather Bureau. With Byrd's last South Pole Expedition. Capt. Army Air Force in Greenland.

      Children:

      1. Herbert Grove[11] Dorsey, III, b. May 27, 1940
      2. William Ballantine[11] Dorsey, b. Apr. 30, 1942
      3. Diana[11] Dorsey, b. Dec. 31, 1943

   2. Dr. William Rowlett Dorsey, b. July 11, 1919
      m. May 11, 1946 Swampscott, Mass., Eleanor Poor Jones
      Physician, Tampa, Florida

3. John Elmos[8] Dorsey, b. Nov. 1843; d. 1942
   m. Lizzie Magruder, b. 1851; d. 1930

JOSEPH DORSEY

2. JOSEPH[7] DORSEY (John,[6] Michael,[5] Michael,[4] John,[3] Col. Edward,[2] Edward[1])
   b. 1796; d. Aug. 18, 1845 Muskingum County, Ohio
   m. Apr. 4, 1820 Johanna Foster, Wellsburg, W. Va., b. 1796; d. May 22, 1869

Joseph Dorsey was about 15 years old when the family moved to Ohio. He returned to Brooke County, West Virginia, to marry Johanna Foster, who late in life often said that Joseph made five trips to Virginia to see her before they were married.

They lived in a log cabin on his father's farm about one-half mile south of Shannon. On April 14, 1837, Joseph Dorsey bought 156 acres of land for $872.99, in Muskingum County. The original deed is still in the possession of his grandson, Charles Dorsey, who lives on this land.

DORSEY FAMILY

Joseph Dorsey joined the Old School Baptist Church April 15, 1821, and later was a trustee. Both Joseph and Johanna Dorsey are buried near the Baptist Meeting House at Shannon. All of their children were members of the Old School Baptist Church except Dr. Joseph Dorsey.

The will of Joseph Dorsey made February 21, 1843 follows:

In the name of God Amen. I Joseph Dorsey of Muskingum County and State of Ohio being weak in body but of sound mind and memory do make and ordain this my last will and testament in manner and form following viz, first after my just debts and funeral expenses are paid I give and bequeath unto my beloved wife Johannah all my estate both real and personal for and during her natural life and at her death to be divided amongst my children so as to give Benjamin two hundred dollars more than any one of the others the rest all to have equal shares
2d I hereby ordain and appoint Mikeal Dorsey sole executor of this my last Will and Testament hereby revoking all other wills and parts of wills by me heretofore made and hereby ratifying and confirming this my last Will and Testament.
In Witness whereof I have hereunto set my hand and seal this twenty first day of February, one thousand eight hundred and forty three.
In presence of
John Crabtree
Henry Butter

Joseph Dorsey

(*Muskingum Co., Ohio Wills D,* f. 90)

Johanna Dorsey, widow of Joseph, was the daughter of Benjamin and Johanna Foster, Brooke County, West Virginia. She and her husband Joseph are mentioned in the settlement of her father's estate in 1829 in Brooke County. (*Brooke Co. W. Va. Deeds 9,* f. 311)

Johanna Dorsey, m. (2) Feb. 8, 1848, as his 2nd wife, John Van Voorhis, b. Mar. 3, 1781; d. June 28, 1874

Children of Joseph and Johanna (Foster) Dorsey:
(Births from family recrods)

1. Benjamin[8] Dorsey, b. Dec. 10, 1821, m. Martha McCann (See page 116)
2. Jemima[8] Dorsey
   b. Jan. 26, 1822; d. Dec. 15, 1885
   m. Sept. 8, 1840 Harvey Compton, moved to Whitley County, Indiana
   Children: Charles[9], Joseph, Johanna, Permelia, Andrew, Phebe, Theodore
3. John[8] Dorsey
   b. Nov. 30, 1825; d. Oct. 12, 1885 Dresden, Ohio
   m. Oct. 18, 1854 Jane McCann, b. July 10, 1831; d. May 21, 1904
   He lived on his father's farm

   Children:

   1. Emma[9] Dorsey, b. 1885; d. Feb. 4, 1904, m. Horace Lane
      Children: Alta[10], Harley, Vera Lane
   2. Joseph[9] Dorsey, b. Jan. 2, 1858, m. Dennis Archer, moved to Missouri
      Children: Clyde,[10] Letha Dorsey
   3. Howard[9] Dorsey, b. Feb. 26, 1860, m. Mary Lane, d. 1939
      Children: Walter[10], Edna, Velma, Bessie Dorsey
   4. Alva[9] Dorsey, b. Oct. 26, 1862; d. unm.
   5. Edward[9] Dorsey, b. June 16, 1866; d. Oct. 22, 1922
   6. Blanche[9] Dorsey, b. Oct. 3, 1868; d. July 26, 1944 unm.
   7. Charles[9] Dorsey, b. Nov. 3, 1871
   8. Addie[9] Dorsey, b. July 4, 1875, m. George Pryor
4. Elizabeth[8] Dorsey
   b. Mar. 1, 1828; d. June 2, 1882 Shannon, Ohio
   m. Joseph Spencer
   No issue

5. Abraham[8] Dorsey
   b. Apr. 23, 1830; d. May 28, 1900 Dresden, Ohio
   m. Nov. 1, 1855 Isabelle Lane, b. July 11, 1832; d. Apr. 20, 1896 dau. of Jacob, b. Huntington, Pa.; d. Feb. 19, 1872 and Achsah (Butler) Lane, who came to Ohio with parents Abraham and Mary (Robinson) Lane about 1808. When Abraham Dorsey was 23 years of age, 1852, he assisted in driving a herd of cattle from Dresden, Ohio, across the Allegheny Mountains to Philadelphia, and was from May 10th to July 1st in making the trip.

   Children:

   1. Salathiel[9] Dorsey, b. 1856, m. Sarah McCann
      Children: Nellie,[10] Lulu, Charlie Dorsey
   2. Flora[9] Dorsey, b. 1858, unm.
   3. James[9] Dorsey, b. 1860, m. Laura King
   4. Actius[9] Dorsey, b. 1863, m. John Wirick
   5. Johanna[9] Dorsey, b. 1866, m. Dec. 20, 1898 Edward Minner
   6. George[9] Dorsey, b. 1871, m. Lillie Quigley

6. Johanna[8] Dorsey
   b. June 28, 1832; d. Apr. 11, 1884
   m. 1856 Dr. Hendren, Columbus, Ohio, moved to Green County, Indiana

   Children: Gilbert[9] Hendren, m. Annie Hadley, Bloomfield, Ind.

7. Dr. Joseph[8] Dorsey
   b. Sept. 7, 1834; d. 1914 Dresden, Ohio
   m. Anna Cresap, b. 1852; d. 1922, dau. of Thomas B. Cresap
   He was a Civil War soldier under Thomas at Missionary Ridge and served in the famous 97th regiment until cessation of hostilities.

   Children:

   1. Clara[9] Dorsey, b. 1873; d. 1943 unm.
   2. Alice[9] Dorsey, m. Charles Stevenson
      Children:
      1. Dorothy[10] Stevenson, m. Maj. Lovewell, d. P.O.W. in Japan.
         Children: 2 daughters
      2. Elizabeth[10] Stevenson, m. Thomas O. Cresap, Los Angeles, Calif.

8. Naomi[8] Dorsey
   b. July 28, 1836; d. May 8, 1898
   m. May 10, 1860 Samuel Hendren, moved to Alton, Ill.

   Children:

   1. Clara[9] Hendren, b. Mar. 8, 1861, m. Edward McGlinchay
   2. John V.[9] Hendren, b. Apr. 29, 1862
   3. Cecil[9] Hendren, b. Apr. 14, 1867; d. Feb. 6, 1900
      m. Mar. 10, 1889 Orin King
      Children:
      1. Verna[10] King, d. unm.
      2. Walker[10] King, b. 1891, m. Bertha Dorsey
   4. Bertie Hendren, b. Jan. 28, 1878; d. Mar. 4, 1878

9. Permelia[8] Dorsey
   b. Sept. 12, 1839; d. Jan. 15, 1882 unm.

10. Ciscil[8] Dorsey
   b. Sept. 14, 1841; d. Sept. 30, 1914
   m. Nov. 27, 1888 as 2nd wife, John Deacon Shaw, b. Nov. 28, 1828; d. Jan. 6, 1898, buried at Shannon, Ohio

DORSEY FAMILY

BENJAMIN DORSEY

1. BENAJMIN[8] DORSEY (Joseph,[7] John,[6] Michael,[5] Michael,[4] John,[3] Col. Edward,[2] Edward[1])
   b. Dec. 10, 1821; d. Aug. 21, 1894 Muskingum County, Ohio
   m. Aug. 23, 1849 Martha McCann, b. Mar. 13, 1827; d. Nov. 9, 1898

Benjamin Dorsey lived on the parental homestead until 1865, when he and his wife Martha deeded their interest in the farm to his brother John Dorsey and his wife, Jane. They bought a nearby farm, adjoining the McCann homestead.

On April 11, 1869, Benjamin Dorsey was baptized and joined the Old School Baptist Church at Shannon. Both Benjamin and Martha are buried at Shannon.

Benjamin Dorsey's will made January 9, 1885 left:

To wife, personal and real estate during her widowhood, and at her death to be divided equally among the six children
A codicil attached to the will on August 10, 1892 left:
To daughter Johannah Dorsey, the homestead including the house, farm buildings, garden, orchard, together with fifty acres surrounding the same to be her home as long as she remain unmarried
To Johannah Dorsey after death of wife, household and kitchen furniture, and a good cow and horse
No real estate to be sold within 10 years after death, and if wife be living at that time, no sale until after her death
To son Joseph Dorsey, at death of wife, all agricultural implements and all stock
(*Muskingum Co., Ohio Wills 9, f.* 200)

Martha Dorsey, wife of Benjamin, was the daughter of Maxwell and Margaret (McDonald) Mc Cann, and granddaughter of James and Elizabeth (Sibbet) McCann, who came from Ireland in 1792. They first settled in Westmoreland County, Pennsylvania, and in 1816 moved to Muskingum County, Ohio.

Children of Benjamin and Martha (McCann) Dorsey:

1. Samuel[9] Dorsey
   b. Aug. 3, 1850, m. Martha Magruder (See page 117)
2. Maxwell[9] Dorsey
   b. Aug. 11, 1852; d. Apr. 16, 1926, buried Muskingum Presbyterian Church Cemetery
   m. Oct. 22, 1885 Olive Jane Lane, b. Apr. 21, 1858; d. Jan. 3, 1914
   No issue
3. Margaret[9] Dorsey
   b. Nov. 29, 1854; d. Aug. 29, 1925, Dresden, Ohio
   m. June 10, 1888 Lyman Fulks, b. Oct. 21, 1848; d. Mar. 7, 1925

   Children:

   1. Lela May[10] Fulks, b. Mar. 22, 1889, m. Oct. 30, 1912 Ray Dean, b. Mar. 19, 1886

      One child:

      First Lieut. A.A.F. Paul[11] Dean, b. Feb. 12, 1914, m. Jean Hall
   2. Ben Floyd[10] Fulks, b. Apr. 20, 1892
      m. Aug. 21, 1919 Bess Darling, b. Oct. 25, 1895
   3. Carl E.[10] Fulks, b. Apr. 13, 1894,
      m. Sept. 6, 1923 Doris Schumacher, b. Mar. 3, 1898

      One child: Joy Ann[11] Fulks, b. Dec. 30, 1929
   4. Max Milton[10] Fulks, b. Sept. 26, 1895
      m. June 16, 1934 Margaret Ulrich, b. Oct. 21, 1904

      One child: Nancy Ann[11] Fulks, b. June 21, 1935

4. Johannah[9] Dorsey
   b. Dec. 15, 1858; d. Dec. 17, 1922, Dresden, Ohio
   m. Jan. 29, 1902 Harvey Wright, b. 1869; d. 1918
   No issue
5. Joseph[9] Dorsey
   b. Nov. 23, 1862, living near Frazeysburg, Ohio
   m. Jan. 3, 1900 Cora E. Divan, b. Oct. 22, 1872

   Children:

   1. Everett[10] Dorsey, b. Jan. 3, 1901, m. June 15, 1930 Edna Marshall
   2. Paul[10] Dorsey, b. July 28, 1904, m. July 25, 1936 Virginia McKeown
   3. Robert[10] Dorsey, b. Aug. 3, 1909
6. Carrie May[9] Dorsey
   b. Nov. 20, 1865; d. Dec. 7, 1941 Hanover, Ohio
   m. June 10, 1891 Ulysses Grant Porter, b. May 24, 1863; d. June 21, 1945

   Children:

   1. Ralph[10] Porter, b. Nov. 15, 1893, living at Hebron, Ohio
      m. Dec. 1921 Lulu Geiger

      One child: David Porter
   2. Blanche[10] Porter, b. Feb. 11, 1896, m. Sept. 2, 1915 Edwin Montgomery

      Children:

      1. Jeanne Francis[11] Montgomery, b. May 28, 1919
      2. Mary Louise[11] Montgomery, b. July 25, 1920
      3. Ruth L.[11] Montgomery, b. July 25, 1922; d. July 5, 1932
      4. Donald Edwin[11] Montgomery, b. Nov. 13, 1934
   3. Grace Louise[10] Porter, b. May 11, 1899, m. Nov. 30, 1922 John R. Williams

      Children:

      1. Mary Ellen[11] Williams, b. Sept. 6, 1923
      2. Virginia Elizabeth[11] Williams, b. Mar. 10, 1925
      3. Dorothy Rose[11] Williams, b. Apr. 27, 1927
   4. Martha Francis[10] Porter, b. Jan. 23, 1902, m. Nov. 30, 1922 Hugh B. Cole

      Children:

      1. Miriam Jeanette[11] Cole, b. Oct. 22, 1923
      2. Mildred Carrie[11] Cole, b. Nov. 10, 1927
   5. Dr. Mary Roseamonde[10] Porter, b. Aug. 26, 1904

SAMUEL DORSEY

1. SAMUEL[9] DORSEY (Benjamin,[8] Joseph,[7] John,[6] Michael,[5] Michael,[4] John,[3] Col. Edward,[2] Edward[1])
   b. Aug. 3, 1850; d. Nov. 2, 1927 near Frazeysburg, Ohio
   m. Feb. 10, 1875 Martha Jane Magruder, b. Oct. 31, 1850; d. Jan. 10, 1936

Samuel and Martha Jane Dorsey lived for a number of years after their marriage in a small stone house on the Benjamin Dorsey homestead. From here they moved to 80 acres of hill land on the north side of the Wakatomika valley midway between Dredsen and Frazeysburg, which had been given to them by John Shaw. Other lands were added, which increased the homestead to 273 acres. Their first home was a log house. (See page 118)

Martha Jane Dorsey, who was the daughter of Hezekiah and Sarah Ann (Lake) Magruder, was left an orphan at the age of eight years. (*Year Book, American Clan Gregor Society,* folios

THE FIRST AND SECOND HOMES ON THE SAMUEL DORSEY FARM IN OHIO

58-87) She was reared by her uncle and aunt, John and Mary (Lake) Shaw, who lived on an adjoining farm.

Samuel and Martha Dorsey and their sons and daughters, all attended the Primitive Baptist Church at Shannon, and their son Benjamin is now serving as clerk of the church.

Children of Samuel and Martha Jane (Magruder) Dorsey:

1. Sarah Ann[10] Dorsey
   b. May 14, 1876; d. Feb. 29, 1928 at old Beal home near Dresden, Ohio
   m. Nov. 28, 1907 John William Beal, b. June 26, 1874, son of William,
   b. Nov. 3, 1841 and Charity (Butler) Beal.
   Farmer and fruitgrower

   Children:

   1. Mabel Elizabeth[11] Beal, b. Apr. 21, 1909, m. Oct. 3, 1931 John Little, son of Alexander Randall and Flora (Evans) Little

      Children:

      1. George Raymond[12] Little, b. Mar. 1, 1933
      2. Robert Lee[12] Little, b. Sept. 22, 1935
      3. Richard Beal[12] Little, twin
   2. Martha Eleanor[11] Beal, b. Sept. 15, 1910
   3. Capt. Annabelle[11] Beal, A.N.C., b. Aug. 1, 1912
      Volunteered in Army Nursing Corps, 1942. Commissioned 2nd Lieut. and sent overseas to Australian base hospital. Later transferred to New Guinea.
2. Col. Frank[10] Dorsey
   b. Jan. 22, 1878, d. Feb. 10, 1931 Cleveland, Ohio. Buried at Weedsport, N.Y.
   m. Apr. 30, 1917, Margaret Treat, dau. of Ernest J. and Nettie (Mack) Treat.
   Chemical engineer. Chief of the Development Division Chemical Warfare Service, World War I.

   Children:

   1. Robert Treat[11] Dorsey, b. Feb. 28, 1918, m. Dec. 29, 1944 Phyllis Swan, dau. of Hugo and Joy Swan, Dallas, Texas. Electrical engineer, Cleveland, O.
      One child: Carol[12] Dorsey, b. Nov. 28, 1945
   2. Jane Magruder[11] Dorsey, b. Jan. 30, 1920, m. Aug. 8, 1942, Capt. John H. Roehm, son of Charles L. and Carolyn (Koehn) Roehm, Detroit, Mich.
   3. Marian Center[11] Dorsey, b. Mar. 4, 1921, m. Feb. 17, 1945 M/Sgt. Charles S. Crawford, Dayton, Ohio
3. Dr. Maxwell Jay[10] Dorsey (See pages 78 and 210)
   b. May 3, 1880
   m. Dec. 9, 1914 Jean Muir, dau. of Robert James Watt Muir and Julia (Fuller) Muir, Winnebago, Minnesota
   Head of Department of Horticulture, University of Illinois (See Who's Who)

   One child:

   John Muir[11] Dorsey, b. Apr. 4, 1918 Minneapolis, Minn.
   m. Dec. 11, 1944 Marguerite Shaw, Chicago, Ill., dau. of Arthur and Eileen Mary (Perrin) Shaw, Akron, Ohio
   Electrical engineer, Chicago

   One child:

   Norma Jean[12] Dorsey, b. Sept. 10, 1946

4. Mary Elizabeth[10] Dorsey
   b. Sept. 9, 1882
   m. Dec. 24, 1914 Carl Parkinson, Newark, Ohio, b. Oct. 24, 1876 near Kirkersville, Ohio, son of Isaac, b. July 29, 1846, Pataskla, Ohio, and Lucetta (Hewitt) Parkinson, b. Jan. 3, 1849, Outville, Ohio
   Farmer, living near Newark

   Children:

   1. Daughter, b. and d. Apr. 24, 1916
   2. Samuel Dorsey[11] Parkinson, b. Apr. 30, 1917, m. Oct. 10, 1937, Greenup, Kentucky, Pearl Eva Gearheart, b. Dec. 17, 1921

      Children:

      1. Mary Jean[12] Parkinson, b. Sept. 26, 1942
      2. Ruth Ann[12] Parkinson, b. Mar. 30, 1944

5. Benjamin Hezekiah[10] Dorsey
   b. Oct. 22, 1884
   m. Feb. 15, 1913 Lillie German, b. June 22, 1884 near Hopewell, Ohio, dau. of William H. and Elizabeth Ann (Christman) German.
   Farmer and fruitgrower near Dresden, Ohio

   One child:

   Ruth Elizabeth[11] Dorsey, b. Sept. 27, 1916

6. Bertha May[10] Dorsey
   b. Oct. 14, 1886
   m. June 3, 1922 Walker James King, b. July 10, 1891, son of Orin R. and Cecil (Hendren) King, Columbus, Ohio
   Industrial Chemist, Geneva, Ill.

   Children:

   1. Mildred B.[11] King, b. Mar. 21, 1923 Cleveland, Ohio
      m. May 25, 1946, Joseph M. Bradley, Batavia, Ill.
   2. James Dorsey[11] King, b. Apr. 19, 1926 Cleveland, Ohio

7. Elmer Ray[10] Dorsey
   b. Oct. 21, 1888
   m. May 26, 1923 Mary Pine, b. Sept. 22, 1900, dau. of Richard Chaney and Alice (Robinson) Pine, Frazeysburg, Ohio
   Farmer, lives on part of Samuel Dorsey homestead

   Children:

   1. Sgt. John Richard[11] Dorsey, b. Mar. 15, 1924, killed in action Mar. 30, 1945, Bergmannsgluck, Germany. (20 miles east of Rhine River)
      Inducted Mar. 27, 1942 and received training in armored services at Camp Polk, La. Went overseas in November, 1944 in 80th Armored Reg., and saw combat between Siegfried and Rhine lines
   2. Martha Alice[11] Dorsey, b. Aug. 26, 1926
   3. Margaret Ellen[11] Dorsey, b. May 22, 1935

8. Dr. Ernest[10] Dorsey, b. June 3, 1891
   Instructor in Plant Breeding, Cornell University, Ithaca, N.Y.

9. Ciscil Louise[10] Dorsey, b. Nov. 11, 1893 unm.

JOSHUA DORSEY

II. JOSHUA[2] DORSEY (Edward[1])

d. 1688 Anne Arundel County

m. Sarah Richardson, d. 1705/6, who m. (2) Thomas Blackwell, d. 1700

In 1663 Joshua Dorsey was living with his brothers, Edward and John, on their plantation called Hockley in the Hole. On December 6, 1681, he sold his interest in this tract to his brother John Dorsey.

He came into possession of 180 acres of Howard's Interest, which had been granted to John Howard in 1664, (*Patents 7, f.* 252) and on May 27, 1680, two tracts, Burnt Wood and Upper Taunton were conveyed to him by Lawrence Richardson Jr. (*A.A. Co. Deeds P.K, f.* 7) This same year he was granted 50 acres of land called Dorsey's Addition, lying in the woods at a bounded hickory of John Howard's land. (*Patents N.S. No. B, f.* 433) (See page 175A)

In 1681, with Lancelot Todd, he appraised the estate of Robert Gudgeon. A copy of Joshua Dorsey's original signature and the seal used appear on page 6.

(*Test. Papers*, Box 4, Folder 59)

Joshua Dorsey seems to have held no position of state, but his early death may account for this. The inventory of his estate indicates that he was a man of means and a successful planter at the time of his death.

The will of Joshua Dorsey made February 20, 1687 and proved June 21, 1688 follows:

In the name of God Amen the Twentieth day of the year one thousand six hundred eighty and seaven, All though sick and weake of body, yet of perfect Memory Thanks be to God for the same, I Do make this my Last Will and Testament in Manner and form following..That is to say first I bequeath my soul and spirit unto the hands of All Mighty God My Heavenly father..... I will that all my just debts be truely paid and the rest of my estate be disposed of in manner and form following.

Item I give and Bequeath unto my Deare wife Sarah Dorsey one Third Part of my Personal Estate and one Third Part of my lands now in occupation During her natural life and my Bay Guilding also over and above

Item I give unto my loving cossin John Howard my gray guilding

Item I will That my servant boy named John Smith have one year off his Time of Servitude remitted

Item I give and bequeath to my Cossen Samuel Howard Two hoghds of Tobacco that Charles Stevens oweth me and I also give unto my Cossen Matthew Howard Two hoghds of Tobacco that Richard Evenywary oweth unto me and the other that Lawrence Draper Oweth to me

Item I give and bequeath unto my cossen Sarah Dorsey Twenty Shillings to Buy her a Ring

Item I give and bequeath all the Residue of my Reall and Personall Estate to my only Sonn John Dorsey and That my excs out of his estate allow him Two Thousand Pounds of Tobacco yearly from Sixteen years of age until he attains to the age of Twenty one

Item I do ordaine and appoint my two brothers Edward and John Dorsey my full and whole executors of this my last Will and Testament Requesting my said Executors to take unto their care and charge the Tuishon and Education of my said Sonn and that out of the Produce of this Estate he be brought up to such Lerning as our country will afford and until he attain to the age of sixteen years and if either of my sd Excs should decease before This my last will and Testament be dully and fully executed then the whole Power to continue in the survivor Requesting him to see that my last Will and Testament Dully and Truely executed ....

In presence of
John Rockhould
Thomas Blackwell
John Rockhould Jun
Joseph Robinson
Edward Houle

Joshua Dorsey (Seal)

(*A.A. Co. Original Wills*, Box D, Folder 50,
(*Wills 36*, f. 109)

In the name of God Amen

The twenty [illegible] day of February in the year of our Lord god one thousand six hundred Eighty
and seven, Although sick and weake of body, yet of perfect Memory thanks be to God for
the same, I doe Make this my Last will and Testament in Maner and forme following
That is to say first I bequeath my Soul and Spirit into the hands of All mighty God my
Heavenly father, by whome of his meare and only grace I trust to be saved, and Received into
Eternall Rest through the merrits of my saviour and Redeemer Jesus Christ, in whose
merrits [illegible] I put the whole and only hope of my salvation. My wretched Body in hope
of a Joyfull Resurrection I commit to the Earth, to be buryed in such sort and manner
as my Executors shall think fitt, and as touching the distribution of my Earthly goods
I dispose of them in Manner and forme following, first I will that all my just debts
be payed and the Rest of my Estate disposed of in manner and forme following

Item I give and bequeath unto my dear wife Sarah Dorsey one third part of my personall Estate and one third part of my Lands now in occupation during her
naturall life and my Boy [illegible] also over and above [illegible] worth [illegible]

Item I give to my loving [illegible] John Howard my gray gelding and the worth of [illegible] or [illegible]

Item I will that my servant boy named John Smith have one yeare of his time Remitted

Item I give and bequeath to my [illegible] Cornelius Howard two [illegible] of tobacco that Charles Stevens
oweth me. I also give unto my sister [illegible] Howard two [illegible] of tobacco one that
Richard [illegible] oweth unto me and the other that Laurance Draper oweth to me;

Item I give and bequeath unto my sister Sarah Dorsey twenty shillings to buy her a Ring

Item I give and bequeath all the Residue of my Reall and personall Estate to my
only sonne John Dorsey and that my Executors out of his Estate allow him two thousand
pounds of tobacco yearly from sixteen years of age untill hee attains to the age of twenty

Item I doe ordain and appoint my two Brothers Edward and John Dorsey my full and whole
Executors of this my Last will and testament Requesting my said Executors to take
into their care and charge the tuition and education of my said sonne and that out
of the produce of his Estate hee be brought up to such Learning as our Country will afford
untill hee attains to the age of sixteen years. And if either of my said Executors should
decease before this my last will and testament be duly and fully executed then the
whole power to continue in the survivor, Requesting them or [illegible] in the name of
God and as [illegible] of a brother to see this my last will & testament duly [illegible]
executed, and I doe utterly Revoke all former wills or testaments by me made any maner
of ways whatsoever In witness whereof I have hereunto set my hand and seale in the
presents of

John Rockhold
Thomas Blackwell
John Rockhould Junr
Joseph Robinson
Edward [illegible]

Joshua Dorsey

FACSIMILE OF THE ORIGINAL WILL OF JOSHUA DORSEY

Filed in the Hall of Records, Annapolis, Maryland

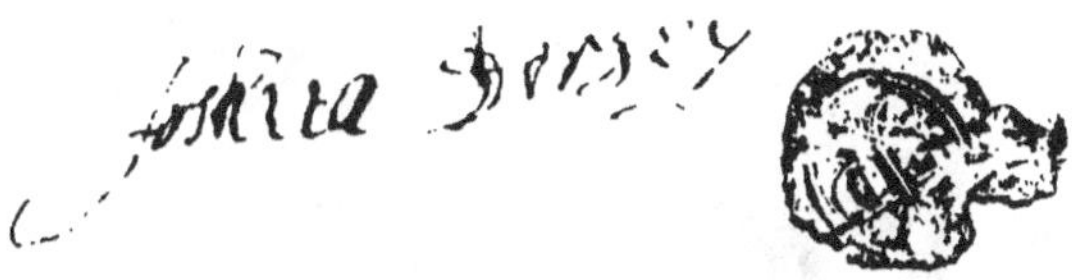

SIGNATURE AND SEAL FROM THE ORIGINAL WILL OF
JOSHUA DORSEY, 1688
Filed in the Hall of Records, Annapolis, Maryland

DRAWING OF TESTAMENTARY SEAL OF JOSHUA DORSEY
The initials indicate that this may have been the seal
of his father, Edward Dorsey

JOSHUA DORSEY

His estate was appraised July 6, 1688 by Richard Hill and John Hammond, and was valued at 199/15/11. His inventory included ruggs, printed curtains and valences, Table cloth and napkins, tables, 12 wooden bottom chairs, 12 leather chairs, chests, beds, a large hammock and cushion, a looking glass, a bible, garments of all kinds, yard goods, guns, pewter, and earthenware dishes, a chafing dish, kitchen utensils, tools, saddle, small boat, cattle, and tobacco shipped for Holland and England, price not known.

1 Man servant named Edward Hobb having to serve 8 months	£4/0/0
Joseph Robinson 7: months	3/0/0
Richard King 23: months	7/0/0
Edward Panck one yeare & ahalfe	4/10/0
M Adrian Rish 2: yeares & ahalfe	8/0/0
Katherine Man 2 yeares & ahalfe	4/0/0
Sarah Wild 3½ yeares	0/0/0
Phillip Broadshaw 3½ yeares	8/0/0
Thomas Johnson 6½ yeares	12/0/0
John Smith Seaven yeares & ahalfe	12/0/0

(*Invts. & Accts.* 10, 72)

Joshua

John and Sarah (Richardson) Dorsey left one son:

John Dorsey, b. c 1682, m. Comfort Stimpson

Sarah Dorsey, widow of Joshua, m. (2) bef. 1692 Thomas Blackwell, Innholder.

In 1692 Major Edward Dorsey, Mr. John Dorsey, Thomas Blackwell and Sarah, his wife, were appointed to make equal division of the late Joshua Dorsey's estate. The final settlement had not been reached when Col. Edward Dorsey died in 1705. (*Invts. & Accts. 10,* f. 314)

The will of Thomas Blackwell made October 31, 1700 and proved November 20, 1700 bequeathed to his wife's son John Dorsey and heirs all land, to Mrs. Mary Rockhold (persumed to be sister of Sarah) 15 pounds Sterling, and to wife Sarah Blackwell, executrix, residue of personalty. (*Wills 11,* f. 13) (See page 202)

Sarah Blackwell, widow of Thomas, was the daughter of Lawrence and Elizabeth Richardson. She died in 1705/6. Her son John Dorsey served as executor of her estate. (*Prov. Ct. Judg. P.L. No. 1,* f. 220) (*Md. Hist. Mag.* XXXII, f. 373)

COLONEL JOHN DORSEY

COLONEL JOHN[3] DORSEY (Joshua,[2] Edward[1])

b. c 1682; d. after 1736

m. Aug. 22, 1702 Comfort Stimpson (*A.H.*), b. 1686 (*Chanc. Rec.* 6, f. 128)

d. 1747 Baltimore County

In 1698 John Dorsey Jr. age 16 years petitioned the court to choose another guardian, stating that his father Joshua Dorsey left a good personal estate, leaving two thirds of it to your petitioner (his only son and heir) and appointed Maj. Edward Dorsey and Mr. John Dorsey, his brothers, executors, to pay your petitioner 2,000 pounds of tobacco, yearly until said petitioner became of full age, the payments to begin, when your petitioner should arrive at age 16 years, over and above his cloathing, that the said Edward and John Dorsey were to furish said petitioner out of his father's estate. They bound your petitioner apprentice to William Dent attorney at law, and were to furnish him sufficient cloathing, but they have stinted him, and for want of sufficient cloathing, he hath often fallen sick from being very much exposed following the said Dent's engagements.

The petitioner pleads to choose another guardian, and that said Edward and John Dorsey pay such guardian the 2,000 pounds of tobacco, as aforesaid, together with such yearly allowance for his cloathing as should be adjudged convenient and necessary. The petitioner was heard and ordered this day September 5, 1698 that the said Edward and John Dorsey, pay yearly on ye 25th of March during nonage of said John, 9 pounds Sterling for his cloathing and apparell. (*Proc. Ct. Judg. I.L,* f. 66)

On May 16, 1706, John Dorsey filed a suit against John Israel and his wife Margaret, administrators of Col. Edward Dorsey's estate for the remainder of his father Joshua Dorsey's estate not already turned over to him, stating that though he had repeatedly begged his uncles, when he became of age to settle upon him all of the goodly estate that he had been left by his father, his uncle Edward had demurred, though his uncle John had been willing.

On September 26, 1707, John Israel and Margaret, his wife, came to answer the charge, stating that they were strangers to John Dorsey Jr. and that it was a family affair and should be turned over to John Dorsey Sr., to which the court agreed.

John Dorsey Sr., brother of Col. Edward Dorsey and uncle of John Dorsey Jr., declared that he had left the matter with his brother Col. Edward Dorsey, never doubting that he would do the right thing, now, however, after his nephew John Jr. had brought to him papers showing what more was due unto him from his father's estate, he was proud of his nephew for the way he had worked out the papers, and did agree that the whole estate should be turned over to him. This the court decided should be done.

It is evident that Col. Edward Dorsey had thought his nephew too inexperienced to handle the estate. Later events suggest that his uncle may have been right.

(*Test. Proc. 19c,* f. 180)

John Dorsey Jr. was active in the affairs of state. He served as sheriff of Baltimore County from 1712 to 1715. He represented Baltimore County in the Lower House in 1715 and again in 1721. In 1715 he was appointed Captain of the County Militia, and by 1724 had been promoted to Colonel. (*Arch. of Md.* XXIX, 93; XXXIV, 278, 307; XXXVIII, 361)

When an act was passed for the encouragement of learning and erecting of schools in the Province, he was chosen as a member of the committee. In 1725 he signed his name as John Dorsey Gent., surveyor of Baltimore County, and complained of the small allowances that were appopriated by an act of the assembly for laying out the town of Joppa. (*Arch. of Md.* XXXIV, 741; XXV, 312)

John Dorsey Jr. inherited in 1700, by the will of Thomas Blackwell, two houses in the Town of Annapolis, which he sold for 10 pounds Sterling in 1704. (*A.A. Co. Deeds W.T. No. 2,* f. 156) Later he sold to Amos Garret 100 acres, part of Clarke's Enlargement, which he had previously purchased from Neil Clarke and Jane, his wife, (*Ibid.,* f. 673) and also three other tracts of land, Dorsey's Addition, Burnt Wood, and Upper Taunton, which he had inherited from his father. (*A.A. Co. Deeds P.K,* f. 7)

On July 5, 1718, John Dorsey Jr. of Baltimore County and Comfort, his wife, sold to Charles Hammond and his wife, Rachel, Merriton's Fancy and Stimpson's Choice, left to Comfort and Rachel in the will of their father John Stimpson, October 2, 1688. He had also left 600 acres of the 1,111 acres to his son John Stimpson, who had died soon after the making of the

will. His land then became the right of Rachel and Comfort, his sisters.
(A.A. Co. Deeds I.B. No. 2, f. 469)

In 1724 the following record appeared in relation to a deed of gift that was made by Mrs. Rachel Freebborne, mother of Comfort Dorsey, before her marriage to John Dorsey in 1702.

"Came before me the Subscriber, Chief Justice of Province, John Clark, who makes oath that at the request of Mrs. Rachel Freeborne he delivered to Coll John Dorsey and Comfort his wife to each of them a certain writing Signed by the said Rachel Freeborne and Sealed such said writing by the said John Clark Delivered as aforesaid, Viz: I hereby acquaint you that I Delivered you the money Herewith Sent, it being Twelve pounds Lawfull English Money by the hands of John Clark, and I doe Likewise here acquaint you That I Delivered you the said Money to make void and Frustrate so much of my Deed of Gift bearing date March 4, 1700/1 as relates to my daughter Comfort Stimpson als Dorsey according to the best Intent and Meaning of the Condition in the Deed aforesaid, and I do thereupon by these present Declare Make Void and Frustrate so much of the aforesaid Deed as Witness my hand and Seal this 1st day of April 1724.

her
Rachel Freeborne
mark
To John Dorsey and Comfort his wife

Test: Thomas Johnson
Charles Worthington

And the said John Clark Delivered the writing to said John Dorsey three severall times, but the said John Dorsey refused to accept thereof and the said John Clark Likewise declared upon his Oath that at the time of the Delivery of the writing aforesaid to the said Comfort, wife of the said John Dorsey, he tended her twelve pounds Lawful English Money which she accepted of and was accordingly by him to her delivered. The writing aforesaid was Delivered to the said John Dorsey and money tendered April 11th and writing and money to Comfort 9th instance. April 20, 1724"
(A.A. Co. Deeds R.C.W. No. 2, f. 245)

On July 21, 1724, John Dorsey sold to Phillip Norwood the tract called Desart, which had been devised to him by Thomas Blackwell in 1700. *(Balt. Co. Deeds I.S. No. H, f. 129)*

Col. John Dorsey, Baltimore County, on the marriage of his son Greenberry Dorsey to Mary Belt, daughter of John Belt, gave them as a deed of gift, on June 18, 1726, a white servant, one swing looking glass, two glass sconces, chairs, chest, such of my books as are marked G D - 1726, guns, 4 pieces of musick, Trumpett, hautboy, violin, and flute, plows and harness etc. *(Ibid., f. 377)*

In November, 1726, John Dorsey, Baltimore County, Gent. sold to John Hammond of Cecil County, Foosehold, Wingall's Rest, and Wee Bit containing 250 acres. *(Ibid., f. 284)*

He was later indebted to John Stokes, and possibly to avoid imprisonment left the Province, for a suit was brought against John Dorsey by Susannah, widow of John Stokes, claiming that John Dorsey had pretended to sell his plantation to John Hammond, to keep creditors from getting the land, and that said John had made an agreement with John Hammond of Cecil County for the land to come back to the wife and heirs of said John Dorsey. John Hammond testifying at Court in 1733 said that he had bought three tracts of land from John Dorsey and no agreement to make over said land had been made.

Comfort Dorsey, wife of John, being examined at court regarding his leaving the province and being in debt, testified on February 18, 1736 that she is 50 years of age, is the wife of Coll John Dorsey late of Baltimore County, that she had known him upward of 30 years, that it will be ten years ago since he left the province, that he went away in the day time and did not conceal his going from the neighbors. She further said that she had been informed that her husband was in debt, but did not know it for a certainty, and that she and her husband had been boarders at the Stokes home in 1726 and it was from there that her husband left the Province.

Joshua Dorsey age 24 years in 1736, admitted that he did know that his father was in debt when he left the province nearly eleven years ago, but that he was living on his father's plantation to which he had the right of possession. *(Chanc. Rec. 6, f. 128)*

The will of John Hammond of Cecil County, Maryland, made December 9, 1733 and proved June 7, 1737 bequeathed:

To Comfort Dorsey, 161 acres White Oak Spring, Anne Arundel County during her life, at her decease to her son Vincent Dorsey and heirs
To John Hammond Dorsey, son of John and Comfort Dorsey, 375 acres dwelling plantation Success, Wignalls Rest in fork of Gunpowder River, 200 acres Wey Bitt, and personalty
To Comfort Dorsey and her 4 children, viz: Vincent, John Hammond, Sarah, and Venesha Dorsey, residue of estate, boys to have their portions at 18, girls at 16, or day of marriage
Exrs: Comfort Dorsey and her son Vincent Dorsey (*Wills 22*, 78)

Comfort Dorsey was the daughter of John and Rachel Stimpson. She was left about 259 acres of land, part of Stinson's Choice and part of Meryton's Fancy, in the will of her father in 1688. (*Wills 6*, f. 49) Rachel, mother of Comfort, m. (1) Neale Clark, d. 1678; m. (2) John Stimpson, d. 1688; m. (3) Robert Proctor; m. (4) Thomas Freeborne, who died before 1724. (*Arch. of Md.* XXXVIII, 346)

In 1745 Comfort Dorsey was granted a license to keep an ordinary, and was known as an Inn Keeper. (*Balt. Co. Ct. Proc.* 1745, f. 803)

Comfort Dorsey's will made January 6, 1747 was proved January 23, 1747. She left:

To daughters Sarah and Venice and sons Joshua and Greenberry Dorsey, each 1 shilling
To sons Vincent and John Hammond Dorsey, and grandson John Dorsey, son of Greenberry Dorsey, estate to be equally divided
To Comfort Dorsey, daughter of Greenberry Dorsey, a pair of gold ear rings
To Elizabeth Dorsey, daughter of Joshua Dorsey, mortgage due from Joshua Dorsey value 41 pounds
To John Dorsey, son of Greenberry Dorsey, furniture
Exr: son John Hammond Dorsey (*Wills 25*, f. 204)

Children of John and Comfort (Stimpson) Dorsey:
(Named in mother's will)

1. Sarah[4] Dorsey, bapt. June 29, 1708 d.y. (*St. A.*)
2. Venetia Dorsey, bapt. June 29, 1708 d.y. (*St. A.*)
3. Comfort Dorsey, m. Joseph Cromwell
4. Greenberry Dorsey, b. 1710/11, m. Mary Belt
5. Joshua Dorsey, b. 1712, m. Flora Fitzimmons
6. Vincent Dorsey, m. Sarah Day
7. Sarah Dorsey, m. Alexander Cromwell
8. Venetia Dorsey, m. Woolquist Cromwell
9. John Hammond Dorsey, b. 1724, m. Frances Watkins

3. COMFORT[4] DORSEY (John,[3] Joshua,[2] Edward[1])

d. 1787 Baltimore County

m. Joseph Cromwell, d. 1769 at Deer Park, Baltimore County

Joseph Cromwell and his brother Woolquist inherited Deer Park from their father William Cromwell in 1735, (*Wills 21*, f. 492) and on November 11, 1740, Joseph Cromwell bought his brother's share of 110 acres. (*Balt. Co. Deeds H.W.S. No. IA*, f. 451)

In 1742 he donated 4 pounds for the erection of St. Thomas' Chapel, and in November 1754 the court appointed him overseer of certain roads in Harrison Park. (*Md. Hist. Mag.* XV, 220)

The will of Joseph Cromwell proved November 8, 1769 bequeathed:

To Richard Cromwell, youngest son, 300 acres of Deer Park, also all shop tools, joiner, carpenters, and smith tools
To sons Joseph and Stephen Cromwell, 580 acres of Nicholson's Manor bought from Kinsey Johns and a portion of Todds Forest purchased from John Murray
To daughters Ruth Towson, Chloe Cockey, Sarah Towson, residue of Deer Park
Exrs: Friend Thomas Taylor, sons Nathan and Joseph Cromwell (*Wills 37*, f. 427)

Comfort Cromwell, widow of Joseph, in her will of 1787 left her estate to her son Nathan and his daughter Comfort, and her daughters Ruth, wife of Ezekiel Towson, and Chloe, wife of John Cockey. (*Balt. Co. Wills 4,f.* 241)

Children of Joseph and Comfort (Dorsey) Cromwell:
(Named in parent's wills)

1. Nathan[5] Cromwell, d. 1813, m. Phoebe_____d. 1816
2. Ruth Cromwell, m. Ezekiel Towson
3. Joseph Cromwell, d. 1783 (*Balt. Co. Wills 3, f.* 453), m. Anne Orrick
4. Chloe Cromwell, m. John Cockey
5. Stephen Cromwell, d. 1783 (*Balt. Co. Wills 3, f.* 596)
   m. Elizabeth Murray, who m. (2) Oct. 6, 1785 Samuel Chenowith (*Balt. Co. Adm. Bk. 10, f.* 168)
6. Sarah Cromwell, m._____Towson
7. Richard Cromwell, m. Feb. 4, 1772 Rachel Cockey

4. CAPTAIN GREENBERRY[4] DORSEY (John,[3] Joshua,[2] Edward[1])
b. 1710/11 (*Balt. Co. Land Commissions H.W.S. No. 4,f.* 170)
m. (1) June 18, 1726 Mary Belt (*St. Paul's*)

On May 26, 1726, John Belt Sr., Baltimore County, in consideration of a marriage shortly to be celebrated between his daughter Mary and Greenberry Dorsey, Baltimore County, conveyed a tract of 112 acres called Belt's Point on the south side of the Patapsco River to his prospective son-in-law. (*Balt. Co. Deeds I.S. No. H, f.* 441)

Greenberry Dorsey also received a deed of gift of furniture, books, 4 pieces of musick, Trumpett, violin and flute, stock etc., from his father John Dorsey on the day of his marriage, June 18, 1726. (*Ibid., f.* 377)

On March 7, 1744, Greenberry Dorsey of Prince George's County conveyed to John Hammond Dorsey, Baltimore County, a tract called Wee Bitt, and in 1745 he sold to William Murphy 175 acres of Roborarium. (*Balt. Co. Deeds T.B. No. D,* folios 45, 66)

As Captain Greenberry Dorsey, he made a deposition in 1748, stating he was about 37 years old on March last, when he was proposing to purchase part of a tract of land called Morgan's Delight of William Barney. (*Balt. Co. Land Commission, H.W.S. No. 4, f.* 170)

Children of Greenberry and Mary (Belt) Dorsey:

1. John[5] Dorsey, d. 1785 (*Harf. Co. Wills A.J. No. 2, f.* 153)
   m. May 9, 1751 Elizabeth Gardner, dau. of John
2. Greenberry Dorsey Jr., b. Mar. 10, 1729/30 (St. Paul's); d. 1798 (*Harf. Co. Wills A.J. No. 2, f.* 187)
   m. (1) Frances Frisby, b. Aug. 4, 1741; d. bef. 1776
   m. (2) Sophia, widow of John Clark (*Test. Proc. 46, f.* 31)
3. Comfort Dorsey, heir in grandmother's will, 1747

The will of John Dorsey of Harford County made in 1785 named as heir a half-sister Mary Dorsey, who may have been the daughter of Greenberry Dorsey and his second wife Sarah.

Greenberry Dorsey, m. (2) bef. 1750 Sarah Fell, widow of William, d. 1746

On February 2, 1750, the account of Sarah Dorsey (lately) Fell and Joseph Taylors, executors of William Fell late of Baltimore County deceased, was filed. (*Accts. 29,f.* 154)

On March 6, 1752, Greenberry Dorsey sold to William Robinson a tract called Better Hope containing 100 acres. Sarah Dorsey, his wife, signed. (*Balt. Co. Deeds T.R. No. D, f.* 318) In 1754 he sold 100 acres of land called Three Sisters to William Oldham and in 1756 he conveyed part of this tract to John Hammond Dorsey. No wife signed.

(*Balt. Co. Deeds B.B. No. 1,* folios 513, 611)

Greenberry Dorsey conveyed Belt's Point to his son John on September 16, 1758. The next year John Dorsey, who was the *eldest son* and heir at law to Greenberry Dorsey and Mary his wife, daughter of John Belt, sold this tract to Thomas Harrison.

(*A.A. Co. Deeds B.B. No. 2,* folios 174, 245)

Greenberry Dorsey m. (3) Catherine Grimes, widow of William, Fairfax County, Va.

At a Court for the County of Fairfax on March 25, 1760, Greenberry Dorsey, who intermarried with Catherine Grimes administratrix of William Grimes deceased, exhibited his account.

(*Fairfax Co. Va. Wills C, No. 1,* f. 23)

Greenberry Dorsey owned land in Fairfax County, which he transferred to Patton and Butcher and to Thomas Conway. (*Fairfax Co. Va. Deeds N-1,* 1778-1783, folios 203-214)

5. JOSHUA[4] DORSEY (John,[3] Joshua,[2] Edward[1])

b. 1712 (*Chanc. Rec. 6,* f. 128); d. bef. 1784

m. Nov. 3, 1734 Flora Fitzimmons (*St. Mrgts.*), d. 1784 Anne Arundel County

In 1736 Joshua Dorsey and his wife were living on his father's plantation to which he had the right of possession. (*Chanc. Rec.* 6, f. 128) (See page 125)

On October 11, 1743, Flora Dorsey inherited from her father Nicholas Fitzimmons of Baltimore County, Knighton's Fancy and Mascall's Rest on the south side of the Patapsco River.

(*Wills 23,* f. 501)

The will of Flora Dorsey, widow of Joshua, made October 20, 1784 and proved December 29, 1784 left:

To six absent sons, Frederick, Peregrine, Greenberry, Joshua, John, James, 5 shillings each, if they be living
To son Nicholas Dorsey, 20 pounds
To daughter Providence Lane, 350 acres, Mascall's Rest
To son-in-law Richard Lane, tracts of land in Baltimore County
To daughter Rebecca Dorsey, residue of Mascall's Rest and Knighton's Fancy.

(*A.A. Co. Wills T.G. No. 1,* f. 230)

Children of Joshua and Flora (Fitzimmons) Dorsey:
(Births recorded in St. Margaret's Parish Register)

1. Frederick[5] Dorsey, b. Dec. 7, 1735
2. Peregrine Dorsey, b. Sept. 3, 1737
3. Providence Dorsey, b. Sept. 2, 1739 (See pages 129 and 212)
   m. (1) Richard Lane, d. 1785 Baltimore County (*Chanc. Papers* 2983)
   (2) Samuel Maccubbin Lane
4. Greenberry Dorsey, b. Apr. 13, 1741
5. Hamutel Dorsey, b. Jan. 12, 1742
6. Elizabeth Dorsey, b. Oct. 9, 1744
7. Joshua Dorsey, b. Mar 3, 1745; d. 1791 (*A.A. Co. Wills J.G. No. 1,* f. 255)
   m. Mar. 9, 1787 Margaret Watkins, dau. of Joseph (See page 222)
8. James Dorsey
9. John Dorsey
10. Nicholas Dorsey
11. Rebecca Dorsey

6. VINCENT[4] DORSEY (John,[3] Joshua,[2] Edward[1])

d. 1753 Baltimore County

m. Oct. 26, 1742 Sarah Day (*St. Jn. and St. Geo.*)

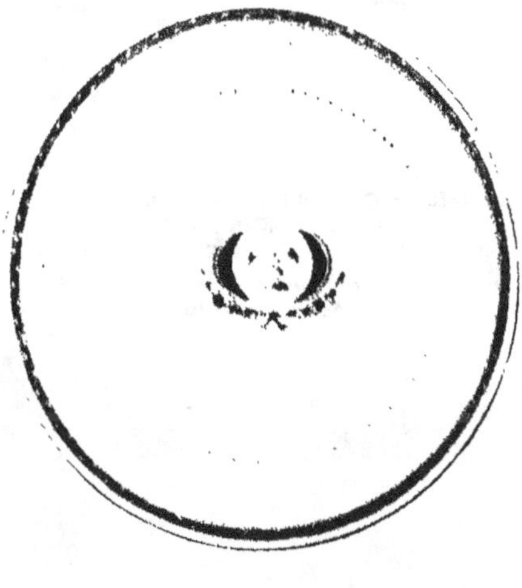

A TIP-TOP TABLE OF MAHOGANY
AND A SAUCER OF CHINESE LOWESTOFT CHINA
THAT BELONGED TO PROVIDENCE (DORSEY) LANE 1739-

Shown Through The Courtesy of Her Great-Great-Great Grandson
Dr. Caleb Dorsey, Baltimore, Maryland

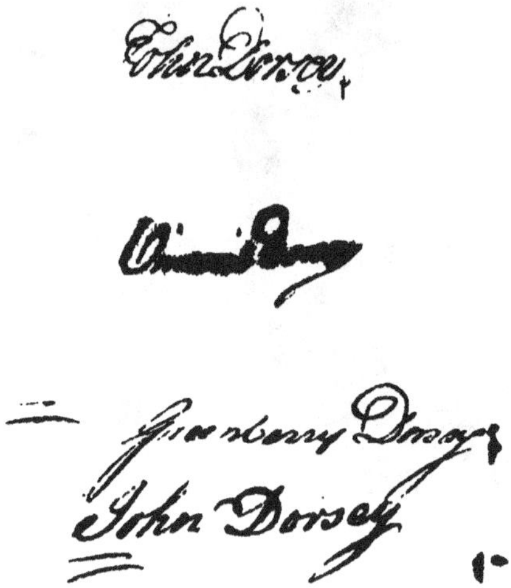

SIGNATURES OF JOHN DORSEY, SON OF JOSHUA
AND HIS SON VINCENT, AND TWO OF
HIS GRANDSONS, SONS OF GREENBERRY DORSEY

From Testamentary Papers Filed in the Hall of Records
Annapolis, Maryland

In 1737 Vincent Dorsey was bequeathed by John Hammond of Cecil County, the tract called White Oak Spring in Anne Arundel County, to be his at the death of his mother. (*Wills 22*, f. 78)

He was granted a license to keep an ordinary in 1744. (*Balt. Co. Ct. Rec.* 1744, f. 470)

The will of Vincent Dorsey made November 5, 1752 and proved February 5, 1753 left:

To wife Sarah Dorsey, gold buttons marked V.D.
To John Dorsey, son of Greenberry Dorsey, wearing apparel
To Greenberry Dorsey, son of John and Elizabeth, 1 negro girl
To Vincent Cromwell, son of Woolquist and Venesha Cromwell, 1 negro child
To wife Sarah, executrix, remainder of estate. (*Wills 28*, f. 437)

Vincent and Sarah (Day) Dorsey had:

Keturah[5] Dorsey, b. July 27, 1747; d. Oct. 3, 1747 (*St. Jn. and St. Geo.*)

Sarah Dorsey, wife of Vincent, was the daughter of Edward Day, who in his will of 1746 left to his son-in-law, Vincent Dorsey, all that he possesses, and to his daughter Sarah Dorsey, two lots in Joppa. (*Wills 25*, f. 4)

Sarah Dorsey, widow of Vincent, m. (2) June 24, 1754 Jacob Waters

7. JOHN HAMMOND[4] DORSEY (John,[3] Joshua,[2] Edward[1])
b. 1724 (*A.A. Co. Land Commissions I.B. No. 1*, f. 658), d. c 1774 Baltimore County
m. Feb. 16, 1743 Frances Watkins (*St. Jn. and St. Geo.*)

In 1737 John Hammond Dorsey inherited Success, the dwelling plantation of John Hammond of Cecil County, also 200 acres in Baltimore County on the fork of the Gun Powder River called Wignall's Rest and Wey Bit. (*Wills 22*, f. 78)

He was a vestryman of St. John's Parish at Joppa in 1747, and again in 1762.

He died in 1774 intestate. John Hammond Cromwell rendered an account of his estate March 7, 1778. (*Balt. Co. Accts. 8*, f. 9)

Frances Dorsey, wife of John Hammond Dorsey, was the daughter of John and Mary (Warman) Watkins. She was named in her mother's will in 1768. (*Wills 36*, f. 307)

Children of John Hammond and Frances (Watkins) Dorsey:
(Births recorded in St. John's and St. George's Parish Register)

1. John Hammond[5] Dorsey Jr., b. Feb. 12, 1744; d. May 1, 1748
2. Stephen Dorsey, b. Nov. 29, 1747; d. 1749
3. Mary Hammond Dorsey, b. Feb. 21, 1749, m. John Hammond Cromwell (See page 132)
4. Rebecca Dorsey, b. May 22, 1752, m. John Lane
5. John Hammond Dorsey, b. Feb. 14, 1754, m. Feb. 20, 1772 Anne Maxwell
6. Francis Dorsey, b. Apr. 19, 1756
7. Stephen Dorsey, b. Mar. 7, 1758, m. Rachel Ewing

8. SARAH[4] DORSEY (John,[3] Joshua,[2] Edward[1])
d. bef. 1788 Edge Combe County, North Carolina
m. Apr. 17, 1733 Alexander Cromwell (*St. Mrgts.*), b. 1772 (*A.A. Co. Land Commissions I.B. No. 1*, f. 102); d. 1788 Edge Combe County, North Carolina

On March 2, 1759, Alexander Cromwell, Anne Arundel County, petitioned the assembly for his share of John Hammond's estate through his intermarriage with Sarah Dorsey; according to the accounts of Comfort Dorsey, executrix of the estate, the balance due the four legatees amounted to 1,000 pounds 18 sh., which was never paid; the executrix sold a tract of land Borens Forrest in Cecil County, but did not give the money to the heirs; in 1747 Comfort died, but her executor, John Hammond Dorsey, has refused to settle with John Hammond's heirs. (*Black Books XI*, 16, Hall of Records)

On March 8, 1774, John Hammond Dorsey of Baltimore County sold to Thomas Cromwell, Alexander Cromwell, and Sarah, wife of Alexander of Edge Combe County in the Province of North Carolina, part of Paradise in Harford County, on the west side of the Susquehannah River. On October 4th, Alexander and Sarah Cromwell of Edge Combe County, North Carolina, sold this tract to Thomas Cromwell. (*Harf. Co. Deeds A.L. No. 1, f.* 64)

The will of Alexander Cromwell made August 19, 1788, Edge Combe County, North Carolina left:

To sons Alexander and Thomas Cromwell, joiners and carpenters tools
To daughter Comfort Laurence, personalty
To granddaughters Sarah and Mary Laurence, 30 pounds current money each, to be paid at the day of marriage
To daughters Mary Hodges, Sarah Ballard, Providence Marlow, and son Bolling Bowling Cromwell, 5 shillings each. To daughter Venetia Boothe, personalty
To grandson Vinson Smith, personalty and dwelling plantation to be his at the age of 21 years
To son-in-law Robert Boothe and wife Venetia, the use of my horses, cattle, hogs and sheep till my grandson Vinson Smith comes of age and what remains, to him
Exrs: son-in-law Robert Boothe and Venetia his wife
(*Edge Combe Co., N. Car. Wills C, f.* 66)

Children of Alexander and Sarah (Dorsey) Cromwell:
(Births recorded in St. Margaret's Parish Register)

1. Comfort[5] Cromwell, b. May 19, 1738, m.______ Laurence
2. Mary Cromwell, b. Sept. 1, 1740, m.______ Hodges
3. Elisha Cromwell, b. Nov. 4, 1742
4. Alexander Cromwell, b. Dec. 26, 1744
5. Sarah Cromwell, b. Jan. 20, 1746, m.______ Ballard
6. Thomas Cromwell
7. Venetia Cromwell, m. Robert Boothe
8. Bolling Cromwell
9. Providence Cromwell, m.______, Marlow
10. ______ Cromwell, m.______ Smith

9. VENETIA[4] DORSEY (John,[3] Joshua,[2] Edward[1])
m. Feb. 10, 1740 Woolquist Cromwell (*St. Mrgts.*), b. 1715 (*A.A. Co. Land Commissions I.B. No. 1, f.* 610)

In 1735 Woolquist Cromwell inherited from his father William Cromwell 110 acres of Deer Park, (*Wills 21, f.* 492) which, on November 11, 1740, he sold to Joseph Cromwell of Baltimore County. (*Balt. Co. Deeds H.W.S. No. IA, f.* 451)

His mother Mary Cromwell, widow of William, on November 17, 1758 conveyed her personalty to her son Woolquist Cromwell providing he support her in her old age.
(*A.A. Co. Deeds B.B. No. 1, f.* 190)

On January 3, 1771, Venetia Cromwell leased her dwelling plantation to John Davidson, (*Balt. Co. Deeds A.L. No. C, f.* 280) It is probable that her husband Woolquist Cromwell had died before this date.

Children of Woolquist and Venetia (Dorsey) Cromwell:
Births recorded in St. Margaret's Parish Register)

1. John Hammond[5] Cromwell, b. Nov. 28, 1741
   m. June 10, 1770 Mary Hammond Dorsey (*St. Jn. and St. Geo.*) (See page 131)
2. Joshua Cromwell, b. Mar. 6, 1742; d. Mar. 2, 1745
3. Joseph Cromwell, b. Feb. 11, 1744
4. Rebecca Cromwell, b. Feb. 10, 1746
5. Vincent Cromwell, b. 1752

HON. JOHN DORSEY

III. HON. JOHN^{2} DORSEY (Edward^{1})
d. 1714 at Troy, Baltimore County
m. Pleasance ______ ; d. bef. Aug. 1734, who m. (2) Thomas Wainwright, d. 1729

John Dorsey, the youngest son of the immigrant, outlived his brothers with whom he made his home on Hockley in the Hole in 1663. During his life he held many important positions of state, and was a highly respected man in the province. He is usually referred to as Hon. John Dorsey or Captain John Dorsey.

In 1692 and 1693 he served as a member of the Lower House of the Assembly. He was appointed Justice of Anne Arundell County in 1694 and again in 1696; Capt. of Baltimore County Militia, 1696; member of the Upper House, 1700; the Lower House from 1701 to 1704; and from 1711 to 1715, a member of the Upper House. (*Arch. of Md.* VIII,XIII,XIX,XX,XXIV,XXIX)

In 1694 he was appointed one of the commissioners to lay out lots for the Town and Port of Ann Arundell in Ann Arundell County, and on May 17, 1695, he petitioned the assembly for a boat to carry the Burgesses of Ann Arundell County to St. Marys. (*Arch. of Md.* XIX,111,199)

He was a member of a commission to oversee and direct the building of the Provincial prison at Annapolis. Later he served on a commission to inquire into the aggrievances of the province and to report on repairs of the house bought of Maj. Edward Dorsey for a store house to lodge the public arms. (*Arch. of Md.* XXIV,181,198)

John Dorsey was an extensive landowner in Ann Arundell and Baltimore Counties. On August 4, 1679, he purchased a tract of 150 acres called Howard's Heirship from Cornelius and Elizabeth Howard, and in 1681 he took over Edward and Joshua's rights in Hockley in the Hole, a resurvey of which in 1683 increased this tract to 842 acres. On March 10, 1697, he bought a nearby tract called Orphan's Addition. These lands he gave to his son Caleb Dorsey on August 6, 1702. (*A.A. Co. Deeds W.T. No. 1, f.* 288)

Dorsey's Adventure, a tract of 400 acres lying on a ridge between the Patuxent and Patapsco Rivers called Elk Ridge, was granted to John Dorsey on February 30, 1688, and on December 6, 1694, he took up another tract of 479 acres called Dorsey's Search. (*Patents 22, f.* 346; *Patents C, No. 3, f.* 352) In 1695 his name appears on the bond of Robert Maine. (See page 6)

Shortly before 1700 he moved with his family to his plantation called Troy, a grant of 763 acres lying at Elk Ridge, Baltimore County, which had been surveyed for him on October 12, 1694. (*Patents B- 23,f.* 290. In 1699 his name appears among the taxables on the South side of Patapsco Hundred with 5 slaves. (*Md. Hist. Mag.* XII,9) (See page 175A)

As Capt. John Dorsey, he took up White Wine and Claret, a tract of 1,400 acres in the Great Fork of the Patuxent River in Ann Arundell County adjoining Carrol's Mannour and Worthington's Chance, on January 6, 1702. (*Patents E.I. No. 3, f.* 490)

In 1704 he bought a tract of 79 acres called Whitaker's Purchase from James Bayley. (*Balt. Co. Deeds H.W. No. 2, f.* 371) On February 14, 1705, a tract of 100 acres called Roper's Increase was conveyed to him by Cornelius Howard and Mary, his wife. (*Balt. Co. Deeds R.M. No. H.S, f.* 569) The next year he took up 245 acres of Mt. Gilboa. (*Patents P.L. No. 2, f.* 5) On August 5, 1707, Capt. John Dorsey transferred these lands to Richard Colegate. (*Balt. Co. Deeds R.M. No. H.S, f.* 569)

He also acquired property in Annapolis, for on October 8, 1703 he sold to Amos Garret for 50 pounds Sterling the dwelling house where Christiana Barbara Guyther now lives with lands adjoining in the Town of Annapolis, and lot No. 10 adjoining land of Maurice Baker.

(*A.A. Co. Deeds W.T. No. 2, f.* 86)

On April 8, 1706, the widow Ridgely and her father Capt. John Dorsey were summoned in the interest of State affairs to appear before the assembly. In the same year he served as one of the commissioners for the advancement of trade and erecting ports and towns in the province.

(*Arch. of Md.* XXVI, 578, 638)

On January 18, 1714, the Hon. Samuel Young and Capt. John Dorsey being lame and indisposed, wrote asking to be excused from attending a meeting. The next year, on September 3rd the Council was said to consist of twelve of the most able and discreet gentleman of the Province. Among the list was Hon. John Dorsey Esqr lately deceased.

(*Arch. of Md. XXV*, 294, 319)

The will of John Dorsey and the inventory of his estate which follow, give a picture of his plantation home in Baltimore County and the way in which he divided his lands among his children.

WILL OF HON. JOHN DORSEY

MARYLAND. IN THE NAME OF GOD AMEN. I John Dorsey of Baltimore County Esqr being of sound disposing mind and memory thanks be to God for the same Do therefore hereby make my last will and testament in manner and forme following Vizt, Imp. I give and bequeath my soul to God in hopes to enjoy everlasting life through the merrit of my blessed Saviour and Redeemer and my body I comitt to the earth to be decently buried by the discretion of my executor hereafter named, ITEM I give and bequeath unto my wife Pleasance Dorsey one full third part of my estate real and personal, after my just debts are satisfied (that is to say) she may have either my plantation on South River or my own dwelling plantation on Elk Ridge at her choice if she thinks fit to accept - thereof in full of her dower of my real estate and likewise I give unto my said wife in part of her thirds of my personal estate if she thinks fit to accept thereof, four negroes Vizt. Jacob and his wife Jenny and one negro man named Lyman and one other negro named Sambo. ITEM I give and bequeath unto my grandson John Dorsey son of my sonn Edward Dorsey decd my Patuxent Plantation and the land thereunto adjoining called Dorsey's Search lying in Baltimore County to hold to him during his natural life, and from and after his decease then I give devise and bequeath my afsd land and plantation given him as aforesaid unto the heirs of the body of my said grandson John Dorsey, to be begotten forever and for want of such issue, then I do hereby devise and bequeath the samé unto my grandson Edward Dorsey, son of my sonn Edward Dorsey decd to hold the remainder of his natural life and after his decease I give and bequeath the same land and plantation unto the heirs of the body of my said grandson Edward Dorsey lawfully to be begotten for ever, But in case my said two grandsons should happen to dye without issue then I do hereby give and bequeath the afsd land and plantation called Dorsey's Search unto my three youngest grandchildren of my daughter Deborah to them and their heirs forever to be equally divided between them. ITEM I give and bequeath unto my said grandson Edward Dorsey one plantation called Dorsey's Adventure lying on Elk Ridge in Baltimore County, and one other small tract adjoining to the same which I bought of James Bailey called Whitaker's Purchase to hold to him during his natural life and from and after his decease, then I give devise and bequeath my afsd two last tracts of land given my said son Edward Dorsey as aforesd unto the heirs of the body of my said grandson Edward Dorsey to be begotten for ever and for want of such issue, then I do hereby give devise and bequeath the same two tracts of land unto my grandson John Dorsey sonn of Edward Dorsey to hold to him during his natural life and from and after his decease I give and bequeath the same two last tracts of land unto the heirs of the body of my said grandson John Dorsey lawfully to be begotten for ever But in case my said two grandsons should happen to die without issue then I doe hereby give and bequeath the afsd tracts of land unto my said three youngest grandchildren of my said daughter Deborah to them and theirs forever to be equally divided between them. ITEM I give and bequeath unto my two grandsons Charles Ridgely and William Ridgely sons of my said daughter Deborah one tract of land called White Wine and Clarret lying on the south side of middle branch of Patuxent River in Baltimore County to be equally divided between them, to hold to them during their naturall lives and from and after their decease then I give devise and bequeath the said tract of land called White Wine and Clarret unto the heirs of the bodys of my said two grandsons Charles Ridgely and William Ridgely to be begotten for ever and for want of such issue then I do hereby give devise and bequeath the same tract of land called White Wine and Clarret unto my three grandchildren Martha

Elinor and Edward Clegatt daughters and sonn of my said daughter Deborah to be equally divided between them and their heirs forever. ITEM I give and bequeath unto my two grandsons Samuel Dorsey and Richard Dorsey sons of my son Caleb Dorsey my plantation called Southriver Quarter being the remainder of a tract of land heretofore given my son Caleb Dorsey by deed of gift lying in Annarundell County to be equally divided between them, to hold to them during their naturall lives (after the decease of my wife in case she makes choice thereof for her thirds) and from and after the decease of my said two grandsons Samuel and Richard, then I give devise and bequeath my said plantation called Southriver Quarter given them as afsd unto the heirs of the body of my said two grandsons Samuel and Richard to be begotten for ever and for want of such issue then I doe hereby give and devise and bequeath the same Plantation called Southriver Quarter unto my two granddaughters Achsah and Sophia equally to be divided between them and their heirs lawfully to be begotten for ever. ITEM I give and bequeath unto my grandson Bazill Dorsey, son of my said sonn Caleb Dorsey my plantation lying on Elkridge called Troy lying in Baltimore County to hold to him during his natural life (after the decease of my wife in case she makes choice thereof for her thirds) and from and after the decease of my said grandson Bazill Dorsey, then I give devise and bequeath my said plantation called Troy given him afsd unto the heirs of the body of my said grandson Bazill to be begotten for ever, and for want of such issue then I do hereby give devise and bequeath the same plantation called Troy unto my two grandsons John Dorsey and Caleb Dorsey sons of my said son Caleb Dorsey equally to be divided between them and their heirs lawfully to be begotten for ever. ITEM I give and bequeath unto my afsd grandson John Dorsey son of my said son Edward Dorsey decd one negro called Solomon which I have already given him and now in possession of his mother and four cows and calves to be delivered him by my executor hereafter named when he shall arrive to the age of twenty one years. ITEM I give and bequeath unto my aforesd grandson Edward Dorsey son of my said son Edward Dorsey decd one negro boy called Roger four cows and calves to be delivered him by my executor hereafter named when he shall arrive to the age of twenty one years. ITEM I give and bequeath unto my aforesaid grandson Charles Ridgely second son of my aforesaid daughter Deborah one negro boy named Saxon four cows and calves and thirty pounds Sterling, the said negro cows and calves and money to be delivered and paid him when he shall arrive to the age of twenty one years by my executor hereafter named. ITEM I give and bequeath unto my aforesaid grandson William Ridgely son of my aforesd daughter Deborah one negro girl named Juno four cows and calves and thirty pounds Sterling the said negro and cows and calves and money to be delivered and paid him by my executor hereafter named when he shall arrive at the age of twenty one years. ITEM I give and bequeath unto my three grandchildren that is to say Martha Clegatt Elinor Clegatt and Edward Clegatt daughters and son of my afsd daughter Deborah one negro girl to each of them that is to say to Martha one negro girl called Sarah to Elinor one negro girl called Hager to Edward one negro girl called Beck to be delivered at some convenient time after my decease by my executor hereafter named. ITEM I give and bequeath unto my daughter Deborah fifty pounds Sterling to be paid by my executor hereafter named for her own proper use for her support to be paid at eight pounds a year as he shall see occasion serves. ITEM I give and bequeath unto my son Caleb Dorsey all the remainder of my real and personal estate that I shall die possest of to him and his heirs for ever and do hereby consitute ordaine and appoint my said son Caleb Dorsey full and sole executor of this my last will and testament hereby revoking all former wills by me heretofore made and declaring this to be my last will and testament.

IN TESTIMONY whereof I have hereunto set my hand and seal this twenty sixth day of November - in the first year of the reigne of our Sovereigne Lord GEORGE by the grace of God of Great Britain France and Ireland King defender of the faith Annoque Domini 1714

In presence of
Joseph Howard Thomas Roger — Jno Dorsey
his
Thomas Higgins
mark
John Beale Vachel Denton
Sam^{ll} Dorsey

(Balt. Co. *Original Will*, Hall of Records, Annapolis)
(*Wills 14*, f. 26)

FACSIMILE OF THE ORIGINAL WILL OF HONORABLE JOHN DORSEY
Filed in the Hall of Records, Annapolis, Maryland

SIGNATURE AND SEAL FROM THE ORIGINAL WILL OF
HONORABLE JOHN DORSEY
Filed in the Hall of Records, Annapolis, Maryland

DORSEY FAMILY

The inventory of the goods of John Dorsey Esq[r] of Baltimore County deceased was taken and appraised April 25, 1715 by Thomas Hammond and John Israel.

At the Home Plantation

In cash
1 Silver Tankard
1 Silver Spoon
1 Cloak
1 old Sealskin trunk
1 Doz old leather Chairs
1 warming pan
1 Gun
1 Small looking glass etc.
1 Feather bed canvas tick, Rug Blankett Sheets Bedstead and pillows
1 Feather bed Covering, only coarser
1 Table, 1 Case very old Knives and forks
1 Chest
1 pair tongs, fireshovel and Gridirons
1 pair Andirons Weighing 62 lbs
1 pair Taylors Shears, Tobacco box, Brand Irons and Spurrs
1 pair money Scales and weights
1 pot rack
4 Doz and 10 pr flatts
1 pair mans Shoes
1 old brass Candlestick
1 pair old small Stylyards

In the New Room

1 Feather bed and furniture, Curtains and Vallens
1 Escruitore
6 new Leather Chairs
2 Chests
1 small trunk
1 parcel of new books
2 razors 1 horn case
1 pr Spectacles and Case
8 small Brushes, 3 old combs, 3 pr Scissors
1 Grater and Hourglass
a parcel of old table linen
1 pr old Marking Irons
¼ lb Gunpowder
1 paper Inkpowder and Parcel needles
1 lb black beads
1 parcel Spice
2 Doz and 10 pr mens Shoes
3 pr womens Shoes
13 pr of Large Wove Stockings
1 pr Motheaten Stockings
20 pr of 4 thread worsted hoes
1 pr small yarn hoes
5 pr womens thread Stockings
8 pr mens worsted hoes
1 pr large Wove Stockings
6½ Lbs Colour'd thread
4 Turkey workt chairs
3 lbs Whited brown thread coarse
2 lbs finer thread
2 lbs finer
1 lb Brown thread
1½ lb White and Brown thread
¼ lb fine white Thread
about 1 lb of Silk
6 gross Coat Buttons
6½ gross Vest Buttons
about 5 gross fine thread
2 Carolina Hatts
21 pr mens Shoes
2 felt hatts
7 Doe Skins
1 Spinning Wheel
4 bushels English Salt
2 lb Great Salt
35 lbs old pewter
1692 lbs Bacon

In Kitchen

1 Hand Mill, Spitt, frying pan, negro bedding etc.	
1 negro girl 2 yrs old named Beck	val £ 8/0/0
1 negro boy 6 yrs old named Sambo	12/0/0
1 negro boy 4 yrs old named Roger	10/0/0
1 negro girl 10 yrs old named Sarah much hurt by fire	9/0/0
1 Dropsical negro man named Jack	14/0/0
1 negro man named Roger	28/0/0
1 negro woman named Beck & young girl with child	26/0/10
1 negro man named Tom	28/0/0
1 negro man named -	28/0/0

At Elk Ridge House

5 new Ruggs	
10 pr Blanketts	
10 lbs old pewter	
1 punch bowl	
1 negro man Simon	Val £28/0/0
1 negro man Sambo	28/0/0
1 negro woman Jenny	25/0/0
1 negro girl Hagar, 1 years old	10/0/0
1 negro man Jack	28/0/0
1 negro man Toby	28/0/0
1 negro girl Juno	10/0/0

Other items-At Pattuxant Quarter, At South River, and At the New Design.
(*Invts. & Accts. 36B*, f. 279)

The second additional account of Caleb Dorsey executor of the last will of John Dorsey late of Baltimore County esq., deceased mentions cash in hands of sundry merchants in England...
(*Accts. 1*, f. 231)

The maiden name of Pleasance Dorsey, who outlived her husband, is unknown. On December 17, 1717, a warrant was granted Pleasance Dorsey for 200 acres of land called the Isle of Ely adjoining the home plantation Troy. (*Pat. Bk. F.F. No. 7*, f. 279) This same year she bought a tract of 100 acres, called Oldman's Folly from Samuel Leatherwood. (*Balt. Co. Deeds T.R. No. A*, f. 547) In 1720 she purchased from Otho Holland and wife, 200 acres of Roper's Increase and 50 acres of Howard's Addition, and from John and Sarah Petticoat, Poplar Spring Garden, a tract of 120 acres lying in Baltimore County at the head of the Patapsco River adjoining Howard's Ridge. (*Balt. Co. Deeds T.R. No. DS*, folios 157, 185)

Children of John and Pleasance Dorsey:
(Named in father's will)

1. Edward[3] Dorsey, d. 1700/1, m. Ruth ______
2. Deborah Dorsey, m. (1) Charles Ridgely, m. (2) Richard Clagett
3. Caleb Dorsey, b. 1685, m. Elinor Warfield

Pleasance Dorsey, widow of John, m. (2) November 30, 1722 Thomas Wainwright. (*St. A_1*). He died in 1729 leaving his widow the greater portion of his estate. (*Wills 20*, f. 90)

Pleasance Wainwright died before ~~August 14~~, 1734, when her estate was appraised by Benjamin Howard and John Hammond, son of Charles. Nearest of kin were Caleb and Edward Dorsey. The inventory of her estate included: wearing apparell, a silver tankard and cups, a silver spoon, thimble and buckles, 3 silk hankerchiefs, Taylors shears, 2 small punch bowls, 4 ivory handle knives and forks, peper box, one Caster, 1 tin baster, one flesh fork, 1 Cutting knife, 1 pen knife, 2 chests, pair spectacles, 2 Turkey workt chairs, 6 old books, furniture and kitchen utensils, stock and feed, 1 old negro man Tom, one old woman Beck, 1 negro ladd George.
(*Invts. 20*, f. 126)

The account of John Dorsey Jun. administrator of the estate of Pleasance Wainwright was presented July 30, 1737. Total value, £104/9/2. (*Accts. 14*, f. 269)

EDWARD DORSEY

1. EDWARD[3] DORSEY (John,[2] Edward[1])
   d. 1700/1 Anne Arundel County
   m. Ruth ______; d. 1747, who m. (2) John Greniffe
   (3) John Howard

DORSEY FAMILY

In 1694 Edward Dorsey with his father's consent, bound himself to Richard Hill as a mariner for four years. (*Prov. Ct. Rec. W.R.C. No. 1, f.* 774) At a court held October 18, 1695, Capt. Hill Jr. appeared and brought Edward Dorsey second mate. (*Arch. of Md.* XX, 325)

His death occured before March 25, 1701, at which date Ruth Dorsey widow of Edward Dorsey late of Anne Arundel County deceased, asked for letters of administration on his estate. (*Test. Proc. 19A, f.* 32)

The inventory of the estate of Edward Dorsey Jr. deceased was taken November 28, 1701 by Samuel Young and Cornelius Howard. It included wearing apparel, ½ dozen leather chairs, looking glass, chests, trunks, tables, linens, kitchen utensils, tools, stock, and 6 servants. (*Invts. & Accts. 21, f.* 301)

Children of Edward and Ruth Dorsey:
(Named in grandfather John Dorsey's will)

1. John[4] Dorsey, b. c 1699, m. Elizabeth ________
2. Edward Dorsey, b. c 1701, m. Ruth Todd

Ruth Dorsey, widow of Edward, m. (2) c 1703 John Greniffe, d. 1708; (See page 199)

On November 4, 1703, John Grenif of Baltimore and Ruth, his wife, administratrix of Edward Dorsey deceased, presented an account of his estate. (*Invts. & Accts. 24, f.* 178)

John Greniffe in his will made October 30, 1708 and probated January 18, 1708/9 left:

To his daughter Katherine Greniffe, Quarter, plantation on the south side of Patapsco River, and 500 acres, part of Andover, adjoining, also 100 acres called Little Worth at head of Stony Run on south side of Patapsco River
To unborn child, his dwelling plantation, Harbor, also 300 acres, part of Andover. Should aforesaid Katherine and unborn child die without issue, the estate to be equally divided between John and Edward Dorsey, sons of wife Ruth
To Thomas Hammond and Rebecca his wife, personalty
To wife Ruth, dwelling plantation, Harbor
Exrx: wife Ruth (*Wills 12, f.* 323)

Children of John and Ruth Greniffe:

1. Katherine[4] Greniffe, b. c 1706/7; d. bef. Jan. 1730
   m. Lemuel Howard, who m. (2) c. 1730 Ann Ward, widow of Edward
   Lemuel and Katherine Howard had:
   John[5] Greniffe Howard, m. Elizabeth ________
2. Ruth Greniffe, b. 1708/9; d. June 5, 1735
   m. May 26, 1730 Lawrence Hammond (*St. Mrgts.*); d. c 1755, who m. (2) Dec. 5, 1736 Margaret Hughes (*St. Mrgts.*)
   Lawrence and Ruth had:
   Elizabeth[5] Hammond, b. Feb. 8, 1733; d. after 1747
   Heir in grandmother's will in 1747

Ruth Hammond and her husband Lawrence Hammond received the plantation Harbor as a deed of gift from her mother Ruth Howard and her husband John Howard on April 7, 1732.

On July 5, 1755, an act was passed to empower John Greeniffe Howard of Baltimore County Planter to dock the Entail of 249 acres of land part of a tract called Harborough lying in Anne Arundel County and to sell and convey the same in fee simple and to entail other lands of equal value.

Whereas the said John Greenif Howard by his humble petition to Assembly set forth that John Grenif late of Baltimore County Deceased being in his lifetime Possessed of sd tract now in Anne Arundel County, he the said John Greenif by his last will dated October 30, 1708 gave his wife Ruth Grenif during her natural life and after her decease to the unborn child to him or her forever, if child should die without issue or heir, said lands to be equally divided between John and Edward Dorsey, sons of the said Ruth. That the unborn child of the said Ruth was a female and christened by the name of Ruth to whom the tract legally descended after death of her mother. Ruth the daughter took possession thereof and intermarried with a certain Lawrence Hammond of Anne Arundel County by whom she had 2 children who both died under age without issue. That by virtue of sd marriage said Lawrence Hammond holds and enjoys part of sd tract as the sd John Greeif Howard is informed has a right to hold and possess during his natural life and that he as son of Catherine Greniff eldest daughter of said John Greniff has a right as heir at law after the death of said Hammond to the said tract of land and the said John Grenif Howard by his said petition sets forth he is desirous to sell the said land. (*Arch. of Md.* LII, 212)

Ruth Greniffe, widow of John, m. (3) bef. 1713 John Howard, d. 1746, (See page 178)

On July 14, 1713, Hopkin's Plantation and Howard's Addition were sold by John Howard and Ruth, his wife, and Matthew Howard to John Brice, merchant, Anne Arundel County. (*A.A. Co. Deeds I.B. No. 2*, f. 53)

In his will probated in April, 1746 John Howard left:

To wife Ruth Howard, dwelling plantation by name of Valley of Oren and 25 acres called Little Worth and at her decease to John Greniffe Howard and heirs
To Jassen Frizelle, Frizell's Choice. Should Jasen die, land to fall to John Griniff Howard
To wife's granddaughters Elizabeth Hammond and Ruth Todd, personalty
To Mary Coohoon, 5 pounds
To wife Ruth and her grandson John Greniffe Howard, balance of estate
To John Greniff Howard, land called Mt. Gilboa except my wife's thirds in the afsd tract during her natural life
Exrs: wife Ruth Howard and her grandson John Greniffe Howard (*Wills 24*, f. 369)

The maiden name of Ruth Howard, who was thrice married, is unknown. Her will made August 3, 1747 and probated August 12, 1747 left:

To granddaughter Elizabeth Hammond, my saddle horse called Stump and my saddle and one-half of my wearing apparel, the other half to Mary Cohoon
To sons John and Edward Dorsey, all personal estate and all my crop of Tobacco now in the ground
To my grandson John Greniff Howard, 20 shillings
Exrs: sons John Dorsey and Edward Dorsey (*Wills 25*, f. 108)

1. CAPTAIN JOHN^4 DORSEY JR. (Edward,^{3} John,^{2} Edward^1)

b. c 1699; d. 1761 at Dorsey's Search, Anne Arundel County

m. Elizabeth ______, d. 1777

John Dorsey Jr. inherited from his grandfather John Dorsey in 1714, the Patuxent Plantation, and the land adjoining called Dorsey's Search, and also 200 acres of Roper's Increase and 150 acres of Howard's Addition, which he sold to John Taylor on August 4, 1749. (*Balt. Co. Deeds T.R. No. C*, f. 268)

On January 20, 1736, John Dorsey Jr. conveyed to Thomas Gassaway the tract of 100 acres called Old Man's Folly, and the 20th of June, 1737, he sold to Bazil Dorsey the tract called Isle of Ely containing 200 acres lying formerly at Elk Ridge, Baltimore County, but now in Anne Arundel County, said tract having descended to John Dorsey Jr., as heir at law to Pleasance Wainwright (his grandmother). Elizabeth, his wife signed both of these deeds. (*A.A. Co. Deeds R.D. No. 2*, folios 455, 506)

In 1742 he was Captain of Elk Ridge Militia and as Capt. John Dorsey, he was a commissioner for Baltimore and Anne Arundel Counties in 1748. The next year he helped run lines between that part of Frederick County which was formerly included in Prince George's and Baltimore Counties. (*Arch. of Md.* XXXIX, 125; XLVI, 11, 299)

The following letter from a Baltimore merchant to his uncle in London is of interest.

"Mr. John Dorsey desires that I recommend your pay of his son's draft for £50. He has six hogsheads of tobacco in Spencer (Captain Spencer's ship), and you will be right to pay it, *as great umbrage to that family would be given otherwise.* Ely

Dorsey desired that I would write that Robert Izard's draft for £10 and Benj. Brown's for £9 be paid, which pray do..... Ely and the old man are very serviceable to you, and you must be very careful to oblidge them. In short, they are very powerful among the people." (Helen West Ridgely, *Old Brick Churches of Maryland* f. 91)

Capt. John Dorsey was a vestryman of Christ Church, Queen Caroline Parish, and occupied pew No. 3.

The will of John Dorsey Jr. made May 15, 1761 and probated September 8, 1761 left:

To son Samuel Dorsey, 456 acres Dorsey's Search, 128 acres Sam's Lott, and 25 acres Pleasant Valley
To son Benjamin Dorsey, 100 acres of Long Reach, and also all land taken by a warrant of Resurvey adjoining Dorsey's Search, and 248 acres, part of a tract called Partnership as laid out by Joseph Plummer
To son John Dorsey, 50 acres Good Luck
To William Hall of Elk Ridge, all the residue of Partnership
To daughter Rachel Hall, 10 pounds current money in full for her part
To daughter Lucy Dorsey, 1 negro boy
To Lucy, Samuel, and Benjamin Dorsey, as much of my estate as will make their parts equal to the part I have already given my daughters that are married
To wife, her thirds. Remainder to be equally divided
Exrs: wife Elizabeth and son Bazil Dorsey (*Wills 31*, f. 460)

The maiden name of Elizabeth Dorsey, widow of Capt. John, is unknown.

Her will made January 25, 1775 and proved March 23, 1777 left:

To daughter Lucy Dorsey, 2 negroes and personalty
All personal estate to be sold and debts paid and remainder of money divided equally among nine children, Ely, Basil, Benjamin, John, Samuel, Deborah, and Lucy Dorsey, Ruth Talbot, and Rachel Ridgely
Exrs: daughter Lucy Dorsey and nephew John Dorsey
Test: Samuel Brown Jr., Sarah Brown, Rachel Todd (*Wills 41*, f. 421)

Children of John and Elizabeth Dorsey:
(Named in parent's wills)

1. Ely[5] Dorsey, d. 1794 (*A.A. Co. Wills J.G. No. 1*, f. 384)
   m. (1) Jan. 24, 1744 Mary Crockett, dau. of John (*St. Paul's*) (See page 231)
   m. (2) Deborah Dorsey, dau. of Caleb (See page 167)
2. Samuel Dorsey, d. 1779 (*A.A. Co. Wills E.V. No. 1*, f. 110) (See pages 226 and 245)
   m. Eleanor Woodward, dau. of Henry, d. bef. 1779
3. Benjamin Dorsey, b. 1741 (*Western Shore General Court, Judg, J.G. No. 53*, f. 244)
   m. Sarah Dorsey, dau. of Henry (*Wills 40*, f. 699) (See page 39)
4. John Dorsey
   m. Mary Cummings, dau. of Wm and Margaret (*A.A. Co. Wills J.G. No. 2*, f. 300)
5. Basil Dorsey Jr. d. 1799 (*Fred. Co. Wills G.M. 3*, f. 306) (See pages 144 and 223)
   m. (1) Hannah Crockett, dau. of John (*Balt. Co. Deeds T.R. No. D*, f. 180)
   m. (2) Mar. 25, 1782 Tabitha Richardson, d. 1816 (*Fred. Co. Wills H.S. No. 1*, f. 22)
6. Rachel Dorsey, d. 1792 (*A.A. Co. Wills J.G. No. 1*, f. 300)
   m. (1) William Hall, d. 1770 (*Wills 38*, f. 152)
   m. (2) 1773 Henry Ridgely as 2nd wife (See page 47)
7. Lucy Dorsey, d. 1808 unm. (*A.A. Co. Wills J.G. No. 2*, f. 435)
8. Ruth Dorsey
   m. (1) John Todd
   m. (2) bef. 1750 Richard Talbot (*Accts. 28*, f. 237)
9. Sophia Dorsey, d. bef. 1760, m. Caleb Dorsey, son of John (See page 158)
   Their daughter Elizabeth was left personalty in the will of her aunt Rachel Ridgely, 1792, and a plantation in the will of her aunt Lucy, 1808.
   Caleb Dorsey, m. (2) Nov. 23, 1762 Rebecca Hammond
10. Deborah Dorsey, d. unm.

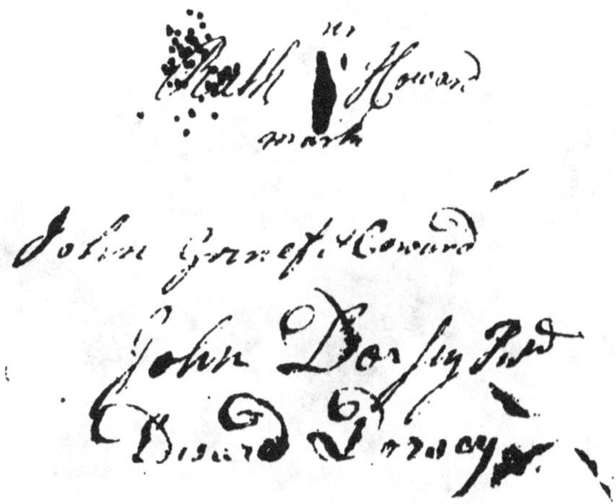

MARK OF RUTH HOWARD AND SIGNATURES OF HER GRANDSON AND TWO SONS

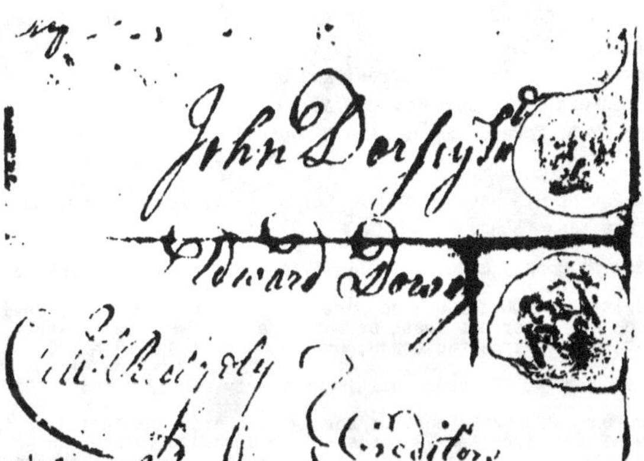

SIGNATURES AND SEALS OF THE TWO SONS OF EDWARD AND RUTH DORSEY

From Testamentary Papers Filed in the Hall of Records
Annapolis, Maryland

OLD BASIL DORSEY HOME, NEW MARKET DISTRICT, FREDERICK COUNTY, MARYLAND

2. EDWARD[4] DORSEY (Edward,[3] John,[2] Edward[1])

b. c 1701; d. 1767 at Dorsey's Inheritance, Anne Arundel County

m. Sarah Todd, d. after 1767

Edward Dorsey inherited from his grandfather Hon. John Dorsey in 1714, two tracts of land, Dorsey's Adventure and Whitaker's Purchase.

In 1732 two tracts of land, Dorsey's Inheritance and Belly Ache Thicket were surveyed for Edward Dorsey. (*Patents P.L. No. 8*, f. 668; *Patents Y.& S. No. 8*, f. 33)

Dorsey's Thicket, a tract of 655 acres, was surveyed for him in 1758, and in 1764 Ely's Lot Enlarged was laid out. (*Patents B.C.& G.S. No. 13*, f. 344; *No. 21*, f. 311)

On December 5, 1745, Edward Dorsey gave 2 negro girls to his daughter Elizabeth Dorsey. (*Balt. Co. Deeds T.B. No. E*, f. 3)

In the settlement of his estate, Edward Dorsey is called Captain, but no record of his military services has been found.

The will of Edward Dorsey made April 14, 1764 and probated in 1767 left:

To son Edward Dorsey, 200 acres land part of Dorsey's Inheritance devised to wife Sarah, to be his after her death or marriage, and wearing apparell, and on condition that he discharge two bonds, one to Charles Carrol and the other to John Brice

To son Lancelot Dorsey, 50 acres, Baltimore County, which I had of his brother Edward

To son John Dorsey, 230 acres part of Dorsey's Inheritance including the plantation where he now lives and 79 acres before deeded to him which adjoins his plantation, his mother to have use of the small meadow and Tobacco house which is on the land

To son Charles Dorsey, 40 acres of land in Baltimore County, adjoining his plantation taken up in a survey made by his father (the testator), John Gillis and Edward Dorsey of John

To sons Ely Dorsey and Richard Dorsey, remainder of lands lying in Baltimore County being part of Ely's Lot and part of Belly Ache Thicket to be equally divided between them, appoint Vachel Dorsey to divide same

To daughter Ruth Dorsey, 1 shilling

To daughter Sarah Gassaway, 1 shilling

To Ely Dorsey, one negro boy named Will

To Richard Dorsey, one negro boy named Jem
To wife Sarah, personal estate, during widowhood, but if she should marry then to be equally divided between 3 youngest sons, Charles, Ely, Richard.
Whereas I have reason to believe there is a great deal of iron ore on the 200 acres devised to son Edward, and if so, the profits of the ore are to be divided amongst the six sons
Exrs: sons John and Ely Dorsey (*Wills 36*, f. 109)

The inventory of the estate of Capt. Edward Dorsey was taken November 30, 1767. The relations were Richard Dorsey and Thomas Dorsey. (*Invts. 99*, f. 155)

Sarah Dorsey, widow of Edward, was the daughter of Lancelot and Elizabeth (Rockhould) Todd. (See page 195) In 1735 she received from her father a gift on one-half of a tract of 500 acres called Altogether. (*A.A. Co. Deeds R.D. No. 2*, f. 268)

Children of Edward and Sarah (Todd) Dorsey:
(Named in father's will)

1. Edward[5] Dorsey Jr., d. 1782 (*Balt. Co. Wills 3*, f. 483)
   m. Deborah Macubbin, dau. of Zachariah
2. Lancelot Dorsey, d. intestate
   m. Deborah Ridgely, dau. of William (*Wills 30*, f. 429) (See page 149)
3. John Dorsey, b. 1736 (*Chanc. Rec. 13*, f. 837)
   m. Mary Hammond, dau. of William (*Invts. 80*, f. 284)
   John Dorsey is given as nearest of kin
4. Charles Dorsey, moved to Nelson Co., Ky.
   m. Lydia Dorsey, dau. of Nicholas and Sarah (See pages 64,236,237)
5. Capt. Richard Dorsey
6. Ruth Dorsey, d. 1814 (*A.A. Co. Wills J.G. No. 1*, f. 63)
   m. Vachel Dorsey, son of John, d. 1798 (See page 60)
7. Elizabeth Dorsey, d. 1749, m. Apr. 9, 1741 Henry Griffith (*Q. Car.*)
   who m. (2) June 1751 Ruth Hammond (See page 75)
8. Sarah Dorsey
   m. Thomas Gassaway (*A.A. Co. Deeds N.H. No. 1*, f. 235)
9. Ely Dorsey, m. Ruth Dorsey, dau. of Michael, d. 1805 (See page 86)

DEBORAH DORSEY

2. DEBORAH[3] DORSEY (John,[2] Edward[1])
   b. 168-; d. bef. 1752 Prince George's County
   m. (1) Charles Ridgely, d. 1705 Prince George's County

Charles Ridgely died soon after his marriage to Deborah. After his death, Deborah went to live with her parents in Baltimore County. The administration account on the estate of her husband Charles Ridgely, late of Prince George's County was given by Deborah, his widow, in Baltimore County, October 14, 1705. (*Invts. & Accts. 25*, f. 48)

Charles Ridgely had inherited from his father, Robert Ridgely, the Gentleman's Gift and Timberly, at the head of the Patuxent River in Calvert County, which land became a part of Prince George's County, when that county was erected in 1695. (*Wills 2*, f. 162)

On April 12, 1705, George Harris, merchant, creditor to the estate of late Charles Ridgely, Prince George's County deceased, presented a petition to the Council showing that the said Charles Ridgely in his lifetime was possessed of considerable real estate and particularly 1,100 acres of land in Prince George's County, and at the time of his death owed the petitioner 69 pounds and 9 shillings, which his wife Deborah was unable to pay unless some of the real estate of her said husband be sold to answer the petitioner's demands. On April 8, 1706, the widow Ridgely and her father Capt. John Dorsey were summoned to appear before the Assembly,

and on the 13th of April the petition of George Harris was rejected by the House.
(*Arch. of Md.* XXVI, 574, 578, 591, 594)

The two sons of Deborah Ridgely inherited from their grandfather, Hon. John Dorsey, the tract White Wine and Claret, containing 1,400 acres lying on the Great Fork of the Patuxent River in Anne Arundel County.

Children of Charles and Deborah (Dorsey) Ridgely:
(Named in grandfather John Dorsey's will)

1. Charles[4] Ridgely, b. c 1700/1, m. (1) Rachel Howard
   m. (2) Lydia Stringer, widow of Samuel
2. William Ridgely, b. c 1702/3, m. Elizabeth Duvall

Deborah Ridgely, widow of Charles, m. (2) in 1706/7 Richard Clagett, d. 1752

Deborah and her husband lived on Croome, a large estate in Prince George's County, which Richard Clagett had inherited from his father Capt. Thomas Clagett, the immigrant, who died in 1703.

On April 3, 1707, George Harris again prayed leave to bring in a bill of sale for some lands of the late Charles Ridgely, Prince George's County, for the satisfaction of the debt to the said Harris. Notice was sent to the late wife of Charles Ridgely, now called Deborah Clagett to appear to make her defense, and on the 8th of April, Mrs. Deborah Clagett als Ridgely and her husband made their defense against the petition, but not being acquainted in these affairs prayed that her council might be admitted. After a debate the petition was again rejected. (*Arch. of Md.* XXVII, 24, 87, 100)

In 1722 Richard Clagett signed the testamentary bond of John Talbott. His signature is reproduced below.

The name of Richard Clagett was on the tax list in Mt. Calvert Hundred, Prince George's County, 1733, (*Black Books 11*, f. 117, Hall of Records)

The will of Richard Clagett made October 27, 1752 was proved December 7, 1752. He bequeathed:

To son Edward Clagett and heirs, 200 acres of land whereon he now lives being a part of a tract called Greenland
To Edward, Samuel, and Richard Clagett and grandson Richard Berry son of Jeremiah and Mary Berry, an equal share of land called Croome, Prince George's County
To daughters Eleanor Eversfield and Mary Berry and sons Edward, Richard, and Samuel Clagett, an equal part of personal estate
Exrs: sons Samuel and Richard Clagett (*Wills 28*, f. 422)

Deborah Clagett is not mentioned in the will of her husband and in all probability had died before this date.

The account of Samuel Clagett of Charles County, surviving executor of Richard Clagett late of Prince George's County deceased, was presented October 10, 1753. The estate was valued at £691/16/10. (*Accts. 35, f. 222*)

The second additional account of Samuel Clagett of Charles County, executor of Richard Clagett deceased late of Prince George's County listed the following children, Samuel Clagett, Richard Clagett Jr., one of the representatives, Edward Clagett, Mr. John Eversfield who intermarried with Elinor daughter of deceased, Jeremiah Berry who intermarried with Mary daughter of deceased, Lucy Clagett, widow of Richard Clagett Jr., son of deceased, November 20, 1755. (*Accts. 36, f. 281*)

Children of Richard and Deborah (Dorsey) Clagett:
(Named in grandfather John Dorsey's will and in father's will)

1. Martha[4] Clagett, b. bef. 1714; d. bef. 1752
2. Elinor Clagett, b. bef. 1714, m. Rev. John Eversfield
3. Edward Clagett, b. bef. 1714, m. Eleanor Brooke, widow of Benjamin
4. Richard Clagett, b. after 1714; d. bef. Dec. 7, 1752, when father's will was probated.
   m. Lucy Keene, dau. of Richard and Margaret Keen (*Wills 29, f. 198*)
   Lucy Clagett, widow and administratrix of Richard Clagett late of Prince George's County presented his account August 28, 1754. (*Accts. 36, f. 388*)
5. Samuel Clagett, b. after 1714, m. (1) Elizabeth Gantt
   m. (2) Ann Brown
6. Mary Clagett, b. after 1714, m. Jeremiah Berry

1. COLONEL CHARLES[4] RIDGELY (Deborah[3] (Dorsey) Ridgely, John,[2] Edward[1])
b. c 1702; d. 1772 at Northampton, Baltimore County
m. (1) c 1722 Rachel Howard, d. bef. 1753

Charles Ridgely and his brother William inherited from their grandfather, Hon. John Dorsey, the tract called White Wine and Claret containing 1,400 acres lying on the Great Fork of the Patuxent River in Anne Arundel County. In 1742 they made a division of this land, Charles taking what was called the Upper Body. (*A.A. Co. Deeds R.B. No. 1, f. 240*) (See page 135)

In 1725 Charles and Rachel Ridgely were living on a tract called Timber Neck, one-half of which Rachel had inherited from her father Col. John Howard Jr. in 1704.
(*Arch. of Md.* XXXVIII, 378)

Charles Ridgely was active in military and state affairs. He was Colonel of Militia, commissioner of Baltimore County, one of the Justices of the Quorum from 1748 to 1753, and a member of the House of Delegates in 1757.

He became an extensive landowner and from time to time made gifts to his children. On June 27, 1752, Charles Ridgely gave to his son-in-law Lyde Goodwin and wife Pleasance Goodwin a tract called Howard's Invitation. (*Balt. Co. Deeds T.R. No. D, f. 382*)

On December 27, 1735, he gave to his daughter Achsah Holliday, Wilkinson's Lott, 89 acres, and a part of Ridgely's Whim and Tayler's Purchase. No wife signed.
(*Balt. Co. Deeds T.R. No. D, f. 210*)

The tract of Northhampton containing 316 acres was surveyed for him in 1758. Iron mines were opened up and the Northhampton Furnaces established on this land.
(*Patents B.C.& G.S. No. 8, f. 332*)

On July 15, 1770, Charles Ridgely Sr. and Charles Ridgely Jr. of Baltimore County in the Province of Maryland, Iron Masters, petitioned the Council for aid in the recovery of two vessels of iron which had been seized and taken into the Colony of Virginia. (*Arch. of Md.* XXII,371)

Col. Charles Ridgely, m. (2) bef. 1757, Lydia (Warfield) Stringer, widow of Dr. Samuel Stringer. (*Accts. 41, f.* 134)

The will of Charles Ridgely made April 1, 1772 and probated in 1772 left:

To son Charles Ridgely, Silver_____, silver Salver, and all land that joins Northampton which I took in a resurvey and that lies to the northward of that part of Northampton that is in my will given to my grandson John Robert Holliday and bound on the north by east line of the original Tract and also one other tract called Ridgely's Good Will, one other tract Charles' Discovery, one other tract lying near Delaware Bottom in Anne Arundel County, which I bought of Phillip Edwards called Edward's Lot, containing 50 acres and all my right and title to that part of Boreing's Gift which is included within the fences of the plantation of my said son Charles Ridgely as they now stand, and also my right and title to an undivided 3rd part of such pieces or parcels of land as are included within the fences of my said plantation as they now stand which have been parts of Sundry tracts I have conveyed to my said son Charles Ridgely and my son John Ridgely for the line of the Northampton, all my rights in said land I give to my son Charles Ridgely, also $2,000, conveyed by deed in the year 1760, and land conveyed to sons Charles and John for use of Northampton Furnace, and 1/3 of John's land by purchase both right of son Charles
To daughter Pleasance Goodwin, negro during her life, at her death to go to granddaughter Rachel Goodwin, negro Tom also to daughter Pleasance to go at death of Pleasance to grandson Wm Goodwin, another negro to Pleasance to go at her death to granddaughter Susannah Goodwin, negro Punch to Pleasance to go to grandson Lyde Goodwin
To daughter Pleasance Goodwin, negroes, land, cattle, household furniture that her husband Lyde Goodwin, deceased made over to me and recorded in Baltimore County Records
To daughter Achsah Chamier, negro, at her death to go to granddaughter Elizabeth Carnan, another negro to Achsah, to go to granddaughter Prudence Gough, another negro to Achsah to go to grandson Charles R. Carnan
To daughter Rachel Lux and heirs, land called Addition to Larces Tw___ containing 19 acres Ridgely's Whim, already made over to daughter Achsah Chamier (as daughter Achsah Carnan) Todd's Purchase on Gunpowder Falls, should grandson Wm Lux die before 21 years of age, Todd's Purchase to granddaughters Ann and Rachel Lux
To grandson John Robert Holliday, Northampton, not already given by deed to sons Charles and John Ridgely, to grandson John Robert Holliday, 40 pounds Sterling to purchase silver plate, to him gold watch and negroes, land Shadrach's last Shift
To son Charles Ridgely and grandson Charles Ridgely son of John, Grist Mill
To grandson Charles Ridgely Carnan, negroes
To grandson William Ridgely of John, John of John, granddaughters Deborah Sterret and Mary Nicholson, grandson Edward Ridgely son of John, negroes
To Prudence Gough, 150 pounds her indebtedness to John Ridgely, deceased
To Charles Ridgely Carnan, Prudence Gough and Elizabeth Carnan, children of daughter Achsah Chamier, negroes and personalty
To son-in-law Darby Lux
To son Charles Ridgely, daughter Pleasance Goodwin, Achsah Chamier, and Rachel Lux, 20 acres Setter's Hill, Ridgely's Second Addition for use of Northampton Iron
To John Hidden, 10 pounds Sterling
To my four children, Charles, Pleasance, Achsah, and Rachel and the grandchildren, children of son John Ridgely, deceased 1/5 part
To children of daughter Pleasance her 1/5 part, her children, William Goodwin, Susannah, Rachel, Pleasance, and Lyde Goodwin, after her death
To children of daughter Achsah her 1/5 part, her children, Prudence Gough, Elizabeth Carnan and Charles Ridgely Carnan. Also land, Bosely's Delight
Marriage contract between me and my wife Lydia, children to respect and carry out according to stipulations. (*Wills 38, f.* 569)

Children of Charles and Rachel (Howard) Ridgely:

(Births recorded in Baltimore Sun, March 8, 1908)

1. John[5] Ridgely, b. June 14, 1723; d. 1771, m. Mary Dorsey (See page 168)
2. Pleasance Ridgely, b. Nov. 24, 1724; d. 1777 (*Balt. Co. Wills 3, f.* 354)
   m. Lyde Goodwin, d. bef. 1772
3. Charles Ridgely, b. Apr. 21, 1727
4. Achsah Ridgely, b. July 22, 1729; d. 1789 (*Balt. Co. Wills 4, f.* 96)
   m. (1) bef. 1753 John Holliday
   (2) John Carnan, d. bef. 1765 (*Balt. Co. Adm. Bk. 6, f.* 162)
   (3) Daniel Chamier, d. 1779 (*Balt. Co. Wills 3, f.* 595)
5. William Ridgely, b. May 20, 1731

6. Capt. Charles Ridgely, b. Sept. 17, 1733; d. June 28, 1790
   m. Nov. 18, 1760 Rebecca Dorsey, b. 1739; d. 1812, dau. of Caleb. (See page 162)
   Charles Ridgely was the builder of Hampton. In his will he leaves his estate to his nephew Charles Ridgely Carnan and his son, also nephew William's son Charles, Lyde Goodwin's son Charles, and John Sterret's son Charles, upon the condition they assume the Ridgely name. (*Balt. Co. Wills 4*, f. 450)
7. Rachel Ridgely, b. Dec. 5, 1734; d. 1831 (*Balt. Co. Wills 9*, f. 294)
   m. Darby Lux, d. 1795 intestate

2. WILLIAM[4] RIDGELY (Deborah[3] (Dorsey) Ridgely, John,[2] Edward[1])
   b. 1702/3; d. 1769 at White Wine and Claret, Anne Arundel County
   m. Elizábeth Duvall, b. Aug. 4, 1723 (*A.H.*) dau. of Lewis and Eleanor Duvall

William Ridgely and his brother Charles inherited from their grandfather Hon. John Dorsey, the tract called White Wine and Claret containing 1,400 acres lying in the Great Fork of the Patuxent River in Baltimore County. On May 16, 1742, they made a division of this tract, William taking what was called the Lower Body. (*A.A. Co. Deeds R.B. No. 1*, f. 240) (See page 135)

In his will made June 15, 1755 and probated 1769 William Ridgely bequeathed:

To son Samuel Ridgely, 20 shillings
To son William Ridgely, part of White Wine and Claret on which my dwelling Plantation now stands, 50 acres Make Delight, tract called Silence in Frederick County
To son Charles Ridgely, part of White Wine and Claret, called Lower Body, also 5 other tracts in Frederick County, Hobson's Choice, Jone's Addition, Round about Hills, Paccoson, and Ridgely's Ridge
To daughters Martha, Margaret, Deborah, Elizabeth, now wives of Henry Gaither, Samuel Farmer, Lancelot Dorsey, Aquilla Duvall, 5 pounds current money
Rest of estate not disposed of to be valued and divided among 9 children namely: William, Charles, Rachel, Mary, Eleanor, Ann, Sarah, Delilah, and Asenah,
Exrs: John Ridgely and wife Elizabeth (*Wills 30*, f. 429)

Children of William and Elizabeth (Duvall) Ridgely:
(Named in father's will)

1. Samuel[5] Ridgely
2. William Ridgely, m. Elizabeth Dorsey, dau. of Philemon (See page 42)
3. Martha Ridgely, M. Henry Gaither
4. Margaret Ridgely, m. Samuel Farmer
5. Deborah Ridgely, m. Lancelot Dorsey (See page 145)
6. Elizabeth Ridgely, m. Aquilla Duvall
7. Rachel Ridgely, m. Joseph Howard (*Accts. 43*, f. 286)
8. Charles Ridgely, m. Mar. 22, 1774 Ruth Norwood, dau. of Samuel (*Wills 39*, f. 406)
9. Mary Ridgely, d. c 1763 unm. (*Accts. 80*, f. 344)
10. Eleanor Ridgely
11. Ann Ridgely, d. 1801 (*A.A. Co. Wills J.G. No. 2*, f. 185), m. Brice Howard
12. Sarah Ridgely
13. Delilah Ridgely, d. 1798 unm. (*A.A. Co. Wills J.G. No. 2*, f. 59)
14. Asenah Ridgely
15. John Ridgely

2. ELINOR[4] CLAGETT (Deborah[3] (Dorsey) Clagett, John,[2] Edward[1])
   b. bef. 1714; d 1781 Prince George's County
   m. Rev. John Eversfield, b. 1701; d. Nov. 8, 1780

John Eversfield was a distinguished Episcopal Rector and upon his emigration to America in 1727 received from Lord Baltimore the large Parish of St. Paul's in Prince George's County, where he was rector for nearly 50 years. (*Arch. of Md.* XXXVIII, 451) (*Black Books* VIII, 7, 54, Hall of Records)

He owned land in both Prince George's County and Charles County.

His will made March 12, 1768 and probated March 3, 1781 bequeathed:

To wife Elinor, all personal property for her natural life, consisting of slaves, live stock and furniture, and at her death, ½ to go to son Matthew Eversfield and ½ to son Charles Eversfield, and also to each son certain books in library
To grandson John Eversfield, certain books
To daughters Eleanor Eversfield, Mary Brooke, Elizabeth Bowie, and Deborah Berry, 5 pounds and a guinea, each

Codicil of will of Rev. John Eversfield, dated June 16, 1772 and probated 1781:
To son Charles Eversfield, lands called Renchard Adventures, Gardiner's Purchase and Pheasant's Neck, all located in Charles County.
Exrs: wife Elinor and Fielder Bowie

(*Pr. Geo. Co. Wills T, No. 1,* f. 131)

Children of John and Elinor (Clagett) Eversfield:

1. John[5] Eversfield, b. July 29, 1731, d. bef. 1769 (*Accts. 63,* f. 3)
2. Eleanor Eversfield, b. June 18, 1733, m. William Eversfield, d. 1769 (*Wills 37,* f. 337)
3. Mary Eversfield, b. Feb. 26, 1739, m. Benjamin Brooke Jr.
4. Matthew Eversfield, b. Sept. 18, 1742, m. Susanna Bowie
5. Elizabeth Eversfield, b. May 6, 1745, m. Fielder Bowie
6. Deborah Eversfield, b. Apr. 31, 1748, m. Benjamin Berry
7. Charles Eversfield, b. Apr. 15, 1750, m. Elizabeth Gantt
8. William Eversfield, b. Aug. 11, 1755, d.y.

3. EDWARD[4] CLAGETT (Deborah[3] (Dorsey) Clagett, John,[2] Edward[1])
d. after 1775
m. after 1728 Eleanor (Bowie) Brooke, widow of Benjamin, d. 1728

The name of Edward Clagett was on the tax list in Mt. Calvert Hundred, Prince George's County in 1733. On October 16, 1742, he signed a petition for a division of Prince George's County, and on the 7th of September, 1750, he was appointed with 5 others for the warehouse at Nottingham. (*Black Books* II, 117; III, 9, 7, Hall of Records)

In 1752 Edward Clagett inherited from his father 200 acres of land called Greenland and 200 acres of Croome.

On May 5, 1756, Edward Clagett, Prince George's County, conveyed to his son John Clagett, 100 acres called William and Elizabeth which he had purchased from Abraham Green, Frederick County. (*Fred. Co. Deeds E,* folios 983, 1052)

On September 26, 1757, Edward Clagett sold to Benjamin Brooke, Fowler's Delight, Prince George's County, and on January 27, 1759, he conveyed to his son John Clagett the tract called Greenland and one negro. (*Pr. Geo. Co. Deeds P.P.* folios 35, 249)

Edward Clagett, on the 30th of December 1759, sold 604 acres of land to Colmore Beanes, Frederick County. Eleanor, his wife, signed. (*Fred. Co. Deeds F,* f. 675)

Edward Clagett was a testator in the will of Martha Keen in 1775. (*Wills 40,* f. 422)

Eleanor Clagett, wife of Edward, was the daughter of John Bowie. She m. (1) Benjamin Brooke Sr., who died before 1728. (*Accts. 9,* f. 138) They had one son, Benjamin. John Bowie, in his will of 1759, named his grandson Benajmin, and left the tract called Croome, which he had purchased from Edward Clagett, to be held in trust by his sons for the support

of grandchildren Nicholas, Eleanor, Margaret, and Wiseman Clagett. (*Wills 30, f.* 692)
Eleanor Clagett was living in 1759 when she signed a deed.

Children of Edward and Eleanor (Bowie) Clagett:
(Named in deeds and in the will of John Bowie)

1. John[5] Clagett, d. 1801 (*A.A. Co. Wills J.G. No. 2, f.* 182)
   m. Cassandra White
2. Richard Clagett, d. 1799 (*Charles Co. Wills A.K. No. 11, f.* 541)
   m. Ann ______
3. Nicholas Clagett
4. Eleanor Clagett, m. John Berry
5. Margaret Clagett
6. Wiseman Clagett, m. Jan. 16, 1779 Priscilla Lyles

5. SAMUEL[4] CLAGETT (Deborah[3] (Dorsey) Clagett, John,[2] Edward[1])
b. c 1710; d. 1756 Charles County
m. (1) Elizabeth Gantt, dau. of Thomas

In 1752 Samuel Clagett inherited from his father Richard Clagett part of a tract called Croome.

Rev. Samuel Clagett was rector of Christ Church, Calvert County, later going to parishes in Prince George's County and Charles County. (*Arch. of Md.* XXVIII, 528)

Children of Samuel and Elizabeth (Gantt) Clagett:
(Named in father's will)

1. Thomas John[5] Clagett, b. Oct. 7, 1743; d. 1816 at Croome
   m. Mary Gantt

   Thomas Clagett was the first Episcopal Bishop consecrated in America. In 1808 his remains were removed to the Episcopal Cathedral, Washington, D.C.

2. Priscilla Clagett, m. as 2nd wife, Samuel Chew, b. 1737; d. 1790 (See page 218)

Rev. Samuel Clagett m. (2) Ann Brown, dau. of Gustavius Brown. (*Charles Co. Deeds O, No. 3, f.* 607) They had:

3. Dr. Samuel Clagett, b. 1756; d. 1820 Warrenton, Va.
   m. Aug. 22, 1786 Annie Jane Ramey, Fauquier Co. Va.

The will of Rev. Samuel Clagett, Charles County, made August 12, 1756 and proved September 17, 1756 left:

To son Thomas Clagett, tract in Prince George's County called Croome, 500 acres
To daughter Priscilla Clagett, tract in Prince George's County called Pitch Croft, 28 acres
To unborn child, tract called Brook State, 270 acres
To wife Ann Clagett, for use of unborn child, tract of 80 acres called New Alford, William and Mary Parish
To wife Ann, to son Thomas, daughter Priscilla and unborn child, 2 negroes each
To wife Ann, stock, Money on hand to be divided among children
Thomas and daughter Priscilla to be left to the care and direction of their grandfather Thomas Gantt of Prince George's County until they come of age
To Dr. Gustavius Brown, money for the use of wife Ann
To son Thomas, wearing apparel, saddle and bridle, and that part of Croome which he bought
To son Thomas and unborn Child, books
Exrs: wife Ann, Edward Gantt, brother-in-law (*Wills 30,* 157)

6. MARY[4] CLAGETT (Deborah[3] (Dorsey) Clagett, John,[2] Edward[1])
b. after 1714; d. Oct. 15, 1792 at Marlborough Plains, Prince George's County
m. Jeremiah Berry, b. 1712; d. Apr. 3, 1769

Jeremiah Berry inherited from his father Benjamin Berry in 1719, the tract Charles and Benjamin and also 340 acres, a part of Levell. (*Wills 15*, f. 289)

His name was on the tax list of Mt. Calvert Hundred in 1733, and on a petition for the division of Prince George's County in 1742. In 1750 he was nominated for the warehouse at Nottingham. His indented servant was listed as one of the schoolmasters of Prince George's County in 1754. (*Black Books* XI, 177; VII, 7; X, 39 Hall of Records)

The will of Jeremiah Berry made April 2, 1769 and probated May 3, 1769 left:

To son Jeremiah Berry, 500 acres of a tract called Charles and Benjamin that he now lives on lying in Frederick County (now Montgomery County)
To son Benjamin Berry, 300 acres of land in Prince George's County, tract called Rover's Content alias Good Luck and Father's Gift
To son William Berry, all that tract in Prince George's County, called Good Luck
To son Zachariah Berry, 900 acres of land, Good Will Rovers and the Hogg Pen
To two daughters Mary and Amelia Berry, all land lying in Hanson Branch, Prince George's County to be equally divided
To wife Mary Berry, tract I now live on called Marlborough Plains, Prince George's County, and all other tracts I have adjoining it during her natural life and at her death to go to Elisha Berry
To wife Mary, all negroes and household furniture
To son Richard Berry, all remaining part of a tract called Charles and Benjamin lying in Frederick County
Exrs: wife Mary Berry and son William Berry (*Wills 30*, f. 392)

Mary Berry, widow of Jeremiah, in her will made July 12, 1787 and proved November 27, 1792 left:

To sons Richard, Benjamin, Zachariah, and Elisha Berry, and daughter Mary Williams silverware and an equal portion of land called Concord and Outlet
To grandsons William Berry, William Osborn Sprigg, and Jeremiah Williams, slaves, and to granddaughters Mary Douglas and Mary Berry, slaves
(*Pr. Geo. Co. Wills T, No. 1*, f. 317)

Children of Jeremiah and Mary (Clagett) Berry:
(Named in parent's wills)

1. Jeremiah[5] Berry, m. Sarah Clagett
2. Richard Berry, b. July 20, 1734, m. Sarah Dorsey, dau. of Michael (See page 85)
3. Benjamin Berry, b. July 16, 1739, m. Deborah Eversfield
4. William Berry, b. May 29, 1742 unm.
5. Mary Berry, b. Aug. 24, 1746, m. Thomas Williams
6. Zachariah Berry, b. July 11, 1749, m. Mary Williams
7. Amelia Berry, b. July 18, 1752, m. William Sprigg
8. Elisha Berry, b. Jan. 19, 1755, m. Eleanor Eversfield

CALEB DORSEY

3\. CALEB[3] DORSEY (John,[2] Edward[1])

b. Nov. 11, 1685 (*A.A. Co. Land Commissions I.B. No. 1*, f. 153)

d. 1742 at Hockley in the Hole, Anne Arundel County

m. Aug. 24, 1704 Elinor Warfield (*St. A.*), b. July 10, 1683; d. 1752

On August 6, 1702, Caleb Dorsey received by deed of gift from his father John Dorsey, 442 acres of the home plantation, Hockley in the Hole, and two adjoining tracts, 85 acres called Orphan's Addition, 150 acres part of Howard's Heirship, and a number of negroes. He was the executor of his father's will in 1714 and residuary legatee of the estate. In 1713 he was a vestryman at St. Anne's Church. (See page 175A)

Caleb Dorsey purchased another 150 acres of Howard's Heirship from Stephen Bently November 13, 1709, (*A.A. Co. Deeds P.K*, f. 119) and on June 16, 1718, he bought 272 acres called Crouchfield and 50 acres of Howard's Discovery from Benjamin Howard. (*A.A. Co. Deeds I.B. No.2*, f. 491) On July 2, 1719, he bought 200 acres of Long Reach from Thomas Worthington.
(*Balt. Co. Deeds T.R. No. DS*, f. 3)

HON. JOHN DORSEY

On April 28, 1720, Caleb Dorsey purchased from James Carroll for 500 pounds Sterling all that parcell of land formerly granted to Charles Carroll, February 20, 1706, called New Year's Gift containing 1,300 acres lying at Elkridge in Baltimore County and by the said Charles Carroll resurveyed and made over to said James Carroll on June 18, 1711, Beginning at a bounded poplar standing in a branch being a bounder of the land called Major's Choice and running thence to a bounded Spannish oak of John Crosses land and thence to Walter Phelps land and to the beginning bounded poplar of Major's Choice. (*Balt. Co. Deeds T.R. No. A*, f. 166) (*Prov. Ct. Rec. P.L. No. 5*, f. 82)*

Caleb Dorsey, on March 20, 1739, received a grant of 210 acres called Addition to New Year's Gift lying in Baltimore County but now Anne Arundel County between Elk Ridge and the Eastermost main Branch of the Patuxent River. (*Patents P.L. No. 8*, f. 84)

On April 26, 1725, Caleb Dorsey bought a tract of 135 acres called Gore from Joshua and John Dorsey, (*Balt. Co. Deeds I.S. No. H*, f. 491) and on June 2, 1729, he asked for a resurvey of Crouchfield on the south side of the Severn River near a creek called Marshes creek, which he had formerly bought from Benjamin Howard. (*A.A. Co. Deeds R.D. No. 2*, f. 117)

In March 1728, Caleb Dorsey was bequeathed a house, lot and household goods in the City of Annapolis by Jane Burnell, a spinster, who also appointed him executor of her will. (*Wills 19*, f. 784)

On November 16, 1734, he purchased from Elizabeth Beale, widow of John Beale, two tracts of land on the south side of the Severn River and on the south side of Hockley Creek, one called Howard's Hill containing 200 acres, and the other, 60 acres of Howard's Heirship. (*A.A. Co. Deeds R.D. No. 2*, f. 170)

Other lands and property owned by Caleb Dorsey are shown in deeds of gift to his children, and in his will.

Caleb Dorsey gave his daughters Achsah, Sophia, Elinor, Mary, and Deborah Dorsey, 2 negroes each on December 17, 1727. (*A.A. Co. Deeds S.Y. No. 1*, f. 425)

In 1731 Caleb Dorsey deeded to his son Basil Dorsey a tract of land containing 1,255 acres called Caleb's Purchase lying on Elk Ridge formerly in Baltimore County and now in Anne Arundel County. The next year he gave Basil Dorsey 100 acres called Addition to Troy lying next to the tract he had inherited from his grandfather, John Dorsey. (*A.A. Co. Deeds I.H.T.I*, folios 330, 377)

In 1732 he gave to his son John Dorsey 700 acres of New Year's Gift. (*Ibid.*, f. 379) At the same time he deeded to his son Caleb Dorsey Jr., two tracts, Moore's Morning Choyce containing 1,368 acres and Dorsey's Chance of 200 acres adjoining and lying on Elk Ridge now Anne Arundel County. (*Ibid.*, f. 382)

On March 25, 1732, Caleb Dorsey deeded the remainder of his land through his trustee John Beale to his five sons, who were all underage.

To Edward Dorsey he gave part of New Year's Gift and the Addition to New Year's Gift. To Samuel Dorsey he gave part of Chew's Resolution Mannor, The Gore, part of Long Reach and part of the Vineyard. To Joshua Dorsey he gave part of Chew's Resolution Mannor, and part of the Vineyard. To Richard Dorsey he gave Hockley in the Hole, Orphan's Addition, part of Howard's Heirship, and Howard's Hope. To his youngest son, Thomas Beale Dorsey, he gave Howard's Discovery, Crouchfield, and part of Howard's Heirship. (*Ibid.*, folios 415-424)

In 1736/7 he gave several lots in the City of Annapolis to his daughter Achsah Woodward, gentlewoman, widow of Amos Woodward, merchant, deceased, and her four children. (*A.A. Co. Deeds R.D. No. 2*, f. 437)

---

* The original deeds are in the possession of Mrs. Hammond Dorsey of Howard County.

DORSEY FAMILY

The will of Caleb Dorsey, Gentleman, made January 7, 1742 follows:

Item- To wife Elinor, ten negroes, Toby, Premus, Roger, Hannah, Peter, Flora, Hannah, Frank, Hagar, and Jenny
Item- To sons Basil, John and Caleb whom I have sufficiently provided for and advanced in the world, five pounds Sterling each. To son John my largest silver tankard marked E.D. on the bottom
Item- To son Richard, one mulatto man named Jack by trade a shoemaker, one negro boy Charles, and one negro man Peter
Item- To son Edward, one negro man Harry, one negro boy Phil, one negro girl Rachel, one negro girl Sarah and one negro boy Roger. Also to son Edward my small silver tankard marked P.E.D., twenty head of Cattle, twenty head of sheep and twenty head of hoggs
Item- To son Joshua, one negro man Jacob, two negro boys Joe and Will and negro girl Moll
Item- To son Thomas Beale Dorsey, one negro man Tom, two negro boys Joe and Solomon and one negro boy Sampson. Also to son Thomas Beale Dorsey, twenty head of cattle, twenty head of sheep and twenty head of hoggs
Item- To daughter Elinor Lynch, who for her disobedience, I exclude from any part of my estate, five shilling Sterling
Item- To wife Elinor, those two lots I purchased of Thomas Higgins, part of New Year's Gift containing 100 acres and Higgins Choice and Dorsey's Friendship containing 187½ acres for and during her natural life and after her death to son Edward. To son Edward, my house and lot in the city of Annapolis which was devised to me by Mrs. Jane Burnell deceased by paying son Richard thirty pounds
Item- To wife Elinor, those two tracts with the houses and appurtenances thereon which I purchased of Elizabeth Beale executrix of John Beale deceased namely Howard's Hills, 200 acres, and a part of Howard's Heirship, 60 acres, for and during her natural life and after her death to son Thomas Beale Dorsey, but if he should die without issue, then to son Richard providing he pays fifty pounds each to daughters Sophia, Deborah, and Mary
Item- One third part of the residue of my personal estate to wife Elinor and the other two thirds to be divided between son Thomas Beale Dorsey and daughters Sophia, Deborah, and Mary
Item- To grandson Caleb Dorsey, son of Basil, one negro girl named Sue
Item- To grandson Caleb Dorsey, son of John, one negro boy named Tom
Exrs: sons Richard and Edward Dorsey
Witnesses
Richard Warfield, Senior
Thomas Gough
Samuel Howard
Cadwallader Edwards (*A.A. Co. Original Wills*, Box D, Folder 37½)
(*Wills 23*, f. 239)

His estate was appraised May 12, 1743. It included wearing apparell, 21 Russian leather chairs, 21 napkins, books, 2 cases knives and forks, brass chafing dish etc., and 34 negroes. Value £2,436/7/8½. (*Invts. 28*, f. 245)

The account of Richard and Edward Dorsey, executors of Caleb Dorsey late of Anne Arundel County deceased was filed January 28, 1744. Payments were made to Mr. Thomas Gough who intermarried with Sophia daughter of the deceased, to Deborah Dorsey daughter of the deceased, to Mary Dorsey daughter of the deceased, to Elinor Dorsey as guardian of Thomas Beale Dorsey son of the deceased. Legacies were paid to the deceased's grandson Caleb, son of Basil, to grandson Caleb, son of John, and to the deceased's sons, John, Edward, Caleb, Basil, and to his son Joshua, since deceased. (*Accts. 21*, f. 29)

An additional account presented by Richard and Edward Dorsey included money paid to John Ridgely husband of the deceased's daughter Mary. (*Accts. 27*, f. 242)

Elinor Dorsey, wife of Caleb, was the daughter of Richard and Elinor (Brown) Warfield, nearby neighbors of the Dorsey family. Her father in his will of 1703/4 gave his daughter Elinor the use of the dwelling plantation while she remained unmarried and also a part of Warfield's Range and personalty. (*Wills 11*, f. 409)

Elinor Dorsey's will made May 14, 1752 and probated July 15, 1752 left:

To son Edward Dorsey, personalty to be held in trust, profits of which should be paid yearly to daughter Sophia Gough
To daughter Deborah Dorsey, 2 negroes
To grandson Henry Woodward, a negro
To granddaughter Mary Todd, 10 pounds current money

To granddaughter Elinor Dorsey, daughter of John, a negro
To son Thomas Beale Dorsey, 2 negroes and 10 pounds Sterling
To grandson Caleb Dorsey and granddaughters Ann Dorsey, Elinor Dorsey, Elizabeth Dorsey and Mary Dorsey, son and daughters of son Richard Dorsey, 10 pounds Sterling each
Residue to children living at time of my death, except my daughter Sophia Gough
(*Wills 28*, f. 411)

Children of Caleb and Elinor (Warfield) Dorsey:
Births recorded in St. Anne's Parish Register)

1. Achsah[4] Dorsey, b. July 25, 1705, m. (1) Amos Woodward
(2) Edward Fotterell
2. Basil Dorsey, twin, m. Sarah Worthington
3. Sophia Dorsey, b. Mar. 20, 1707, m. Thomas Gough
4. John Dorsey, b. Oct. 7, 1708, m. Elizabeth Dorsey
5. Caleb Dorsey, b. July 18, 1710, m. Priscilla Hill
6. Samuel Dorsey, b. Mar. 1712; d. 1739 unm.
7. Richard Dorsey, b. June 10, 1714, m. Elizabeth (Beale) Nicholson, widow of Wm.
8. Elinor Dorsey, b. Jan. 4, 1715/6, m. (1) Thomas Todd, (2) William Lynch
9. Edward Dorsey, b. Sept. 1718, m. Henrietta Maria Chew
10. Joshua Dorsey, b. July 13, 1720; d. 1744 unm.
11. Deborah Dorsey, b. Nov. 25, 1722, m. as 2nd wife Ely Dorsey
12. Mary Dorsey, b. May 18, 1725, m. John Ridgely
13. Thomas Beale Dorsey, b. Jan. 18, 1727, m. Ann Worthington

1. ACHSAH[4] DORSEY (Caleb,[3] John,[2] Edward[1])
b. July 25, 1705; d. 1741 Anne Arundel County
m. (1) April 3, 1728 Amos Woodward (*St. A.*); d. c 1735

Before his marriage to Achsah Dorsey, Amos Woodward received from his uncle Amos Garrett wealthy merchant and mayor of Annapolis, 500 pounds Sterling, six tracts of land and 2 lots in Annapolis. In 1734 his mother Mary Woodward of Surry, England, willed her son Amos Woodward, merchant, Annapolis, Maryland, 10 pounds. (Wills 19, f. 353)

He died soon after this, for in 1736, Achsah Woodward, then widow of Amos Woodward, former merchant of Annapolis, and her son Henry and three daughters, Mary, Elizabeth, and Elinor were given several lots in the city of Annapolis by her father Caleb Dorsey.

Children of Amos and Achsah (Dorsey) Woodward:

1. Mary[5] Woodward
2. Elizabeth Woodward, b. Dec. 12, 1730; d. 1758 (*Wills 30*, f. 603)
3. Henry Woodward, b. Nov. 1733; d. bef. 1767, m. Mary Young, who m. (2) John Hesselius (*Accts. 56*, f. 163)
4. Eleanor Woodward

Achsah Woodward, widow of Amos, m. (2) Edward Fotterell

The account of Edward Fotterell of Baltimore County and Achsah, his wife, administratrix of Amos Woodward late of the city of Annapolis, deceased was filed July 22, 1741.
(*Accts. 18*, 310)

They had one daughter, Achsah Fotterell, named in the will of her sister, Elizabeth Woodward.

2. CAPTAIN BASIL[4] DORSEY (Caleb,[3] John,[2] Edward[1])
b. July 25, 1705; d. Aug. 20, 1763 at Troy, Anne Arundel County
m. Sarah Worthington, d. 1774

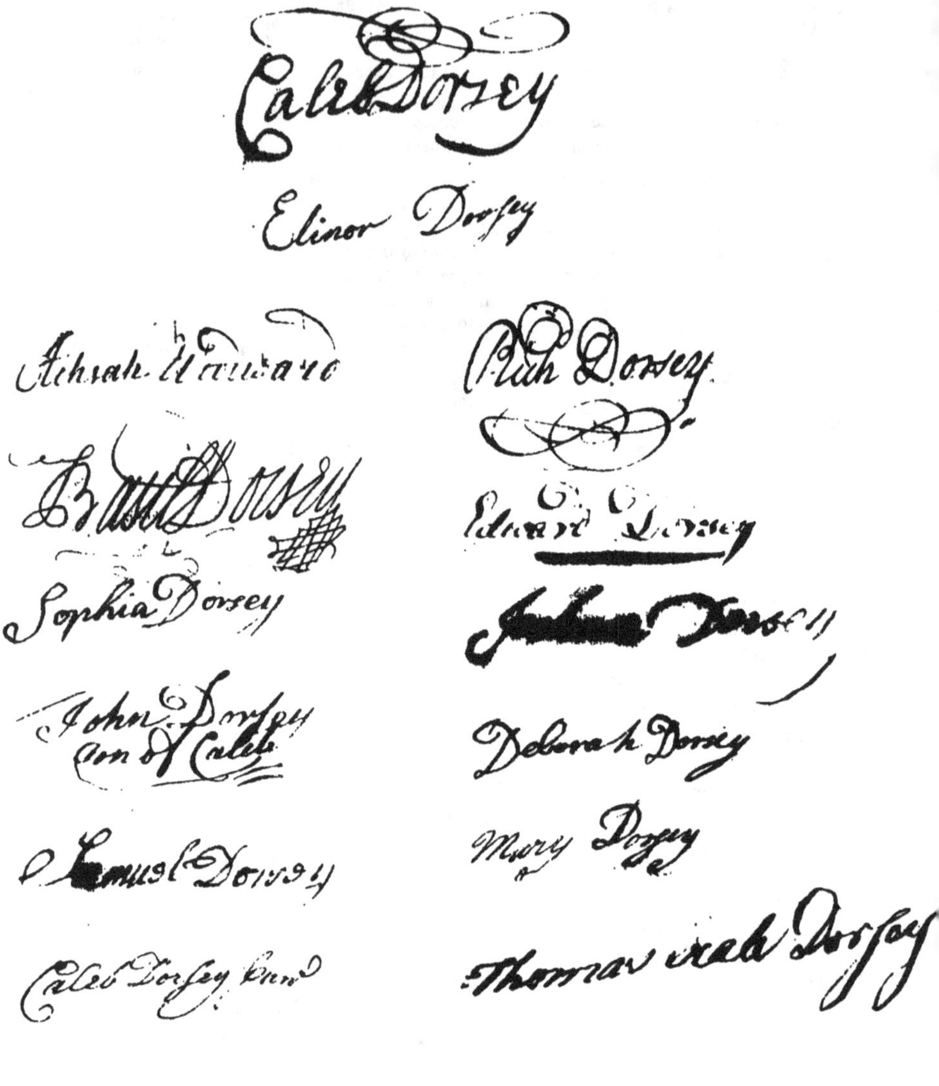

SIGNATURES OF CALEB AND ELINOR DORSEY
AND TWELVE OF THEIR CHILDREN

From Testamentary Papers Filed in the Hall of Records
Annapolis, Maryland

Basil Dorsey was left his grandfather's plantation of 763 acres called Troy, and in 1732 his father deeded him an adjoining tract of 100 acres called Addition to Troy, and also a tract called Caleb's Purchase containing 1,255 acres. (See page 175A)

He occupied pew No. 2, Christ Church, Queen Caroline Parish in 1736.

The Maryland Gazette gives the information that Capt. Basil Dorsey died at his plantation at Elk Ridge on August 20, 1763, a Gentleman of a fair, honest, and upright character much esteemed by his neighbors and acquaintances.

His will made May 30, 1763 and probated September 29, 1763 left:

To wife Sarah, one-third part of lands I now live on, also one-third of lands I hold adjacent during her natural life, also 11 negroes
To son Thomas Dorsey, land and houses at Elk Ridge Landing and at his death to go to my son Dennis Dorsey and his heirs
To son Dennis Dorsey and heirs, the following tracts, but for want of lawful heirs, to my daughters that may survive him and their heirs, one tract called Hobson's Choice and part of a tract called Altogether bought from son Thomas Dorsey and purchased by him of Lancelot Dorsey, and also 7 negroes
To daughter Sarah Burgess, 7 negroes
To granddaughters Achsah Burgess and Sarah Burgess and grandson Basil Burgess, one negro each
To daughters Ariana, Eleanor, and Elizabeth Dorsey, 6 negroes each, also all the land I bought of John Howard called Howard's Range and the Resurvey of Howard's Range and the lands I bought of brother Edward called Middleway and Howard's Rest to be equally divided between them
Remainder of my estate to my executor, son Thomas Dorsey
Remainder of personal estate to children, Thomas, Dennis, Ariana, Eleanor, and Elizabeth
Exr: son Thomas Dorsey (*Wills 31*, f. 1,007)

Sarah Dorsey, widow of Basil, was the daughter of Thomas and Elizabeth Worthington. In 1753 Sarah Dorsey inherited from her father 368 acres called Worthington's Range. (*Wills 28*, f. 445) (See page 183)

The will of Sarah Dorsey made March 12, 1769 and proved in 1774 left:

To son Thomas Dorsey, 20 pounds
To son Dennis Dorsey, 20 pounds and negroes
To grandchildren Achsah, Sarah, Basil, and John Burgess, 50 pounds Sterling
To grandson Thomas Sollers, 1 negro
To niece Elizabeth Watkins daughter late sister Ariana, personalty
To Mary Nichols, 10 pounds Sterling
One-fifth remainder of estate to 4 grandchildren, Achsah, Sarah, Basil, John Burgess, children of late daughter Sarah Burgess to be equally divided
Four-fifths of estate to children, Ariana Sollers, Eleanor Sheridine, Elizabeth Howard, Dennis Dorsey to be equally divided
Exrs: Thomas Dorsey and son-in-law John Burgess (*Wills 39*, f. 840)

Children of Basil and Sarah (Worthington) Dorsey:
(Named in parent's wills)

1. Col. Thomas[5] Dorsey, d. 1790 (*A.A. Co. Wills J.G. No. 1*, f. 192)(See pages 238 and 244) m.(1) Elizabeth Ridgely, d. 1763; m.(2) Elizabeth Ridgely, d. 1815
2. Basil Dorsey Jr., b. 1738; d. Feb. 17, 1761 at his father's house in Elk Ridge of a confirmed consumption in 23 years of his age - attorney at law, a young gentleman of great hope. (*Md. Hist Mag.* XVIII, 162)
3. Caleb Dorsey Jr., d. Feb. 7, 1762 (*Ibid.*, 168)
4. Dennis Dorsey d. 1778 unm. (*A.A. Co. Wills E.V. No. 1*, f. 77)
5. Sarah Dorsey, d. bef. 1769, m. John Burgess (See page 84)
6. Arianna Dorsey, m. Thomas Sollers
7. Eleanor Dorsey, m. Upton Sheridine
8. Elizabeth Dorsey, m. Ephriam Howard

3. SOPHIA[4] DORSEY (Caleb,[3] John,[2] Edward[1])
b. Mar. 20, 1707; d. after 1762 Anne Arundel County
m. June 23, 1743 Thomas Gough (*St. A.*); d. bef. 1762

Elinor Dorsey, mother of Sophia Gough, made provision for her maintenance in her will of 1752 with the understanding that her present husband Thomas Gough have no claim on her property. In 1760 Sophia Gough was left the plantation she now lives on by the will of her brother Edward Dorsey, and in 1762, his widow Henrietta Dorsey left to Mrs. Sophia Gough, widow of late Thomas Gough, a silver salver and silver ladle and 20 pounds.

Thomas and Sophia (Dorsey) Gough had one child:

Harry Dorsey Gough, b. Jan. 28, 1745; d. May 8, 1808
m. May 2, 1771 Prudence Carnan, b. Jan. 16, 1755, dau. of John

On August 13, 1746, Thomas Gough mortgaged his negroes to Edward Dorsey, and on September 18, 1746, he sold his household furniture, cattle etc., to Anoris Razolin and Thomas Walker to pay a debt of 76 pounds. (*A.A. Co. Deeds R.B. No. 2*, folios 244, 272)

4. JOHN[4] DORSEY (Caleb,[3] John,[2] Edward[1])
b. Oct. 7, 1708; d. July 22, 1765 (*Q. Car.*) at New Year's Gift, Anne Arundel County
m. Elizabeth Dorsey, b. Mar. 6, 1719/20; bur. Dec. 8, 1803 Montgomery County

John, who signed his name, John Dorsey son of Caleb, received from his father in 1732 a tract of land containing 700 acres called New Year's Gift. In 1735 John Dorsey and his father Caleb deeded two acres of this tract for a site for Christ Church of which John was a member. (*Arch. of Md.* XXXIX, 167, 229) He bought other tracts of land and lots in Frederick Town. (See pages 160 and 175A)

The will of John Dorsey made April 8, 1765 and proved in 1765 left:

To sons John Dorsey, Richard Dorsey and their heirs to be equally divided, the tracts Dorsey's Range, the Addition to Dorsey's Range, Duvall's Range, the Defendant, Mineral Hill, and part of a tract What's Left, and also a parcel of land that Philemon Dorsey is to convey to me, and if either die without heirs, the whole to go to survivor and if both should die without heirs to be divided among other children
To son Caleb Dorsey, 3 negroes
To daughters Elinor Stringer, Achsah Dorsey, Ann Dorsey, Elizabeth Dorsey, and sons John Dorsey and Richard Dorsey, 150 pounds Sterling and 1 negro each
To granddaughters Elizabeth Dorsey and Mary Stringer, 1 negro each
To wife Elizabeth, 200 pounds Sterling, 8 negroes, one-third of estate
Exrs: wife Elizabeth and son Caleb Dorsey, empowered to sell house and lot in Frederick Town. (*Wills 33*, f. 258)

Elizabeth Dorsey, widow of John, was the daughter of Joshua and Ann (Ridgely) Dorsey. She inherited 20 pounds Sterling from her father in 1747, (*Wills 25*, f. 315) and a portion of her mother's estate, 1771. (*Wills 38*, f. 444) (See page 38)

The will of Elizabeth Dorsey made May 3, 1802 and proved December 10, 1803 left:

To son Richard Dorsey, one-half of a tract of land in Anne Arundel County
To orphan children of son John, remainder of tract of land
To son Richard Dorsey in trust, all lands in Montgomery County, which I derive from my brother Joshua Dorsey, to be held by said Richard for the use and benefit of daughter Elizabeth Boggess during her natural life and after her death to granddaughter Elizabeth Dorsey Boggess
To grandchildren Mortimer and Eliza Anne, children of son Richard, Caleb and Peggy Dorsey, children of son John, and Ellen Stringer, daughter of daughter Eleanor, personalty
To son Richard Dorsey, all other property
Exr: son Richard Dorsey (*A.A. Co. Wills J.G. No. 2*, f. 259)

Children of John and Elizabeth (Dorsey) Dorsey:
(Births recorded in Queen Caroline Parish Register)

1. Caleb[5] Dorsey, b. July 8, 1740; d. 1795 (*A.A. Co. Wills J.G. No. 1*, f. 506)
   m. (1) Nov. 1, 1759 Sophia Dorsey, d. bef. 1760, dau. of John (See page 142)
   m. (2) Nov. 23, 1762 Rebecca Hammond, b. 1741; d. 1797, dau. of William (See pages 214 and 241)
2. Eleanor Dorsey, b. Sept. 5, 1743, m. Dec. 16, 1762 Richard Stringer (*Q. Car.*)

3. Achsah Dorsey, b. May 17, 1746, m. Dr. Ephriam Howard
4. Ann Dorsey, b. Dec. 11, 1748, m. Aug. 16, 1770 Philemon Dorsey (See page 42)
5. Col. John Dorsey, b. Mar. 31, 1751; m. Mar. 19, 1782 Margaret Boone, who m. (2) William Gaither (*Chanc. Rec.* 130, f. 565)
6. Elizabeth Dorsey, b. Sept. 27, 1753, m. Samuel Boggess (See page 217)
7. Col. Richard Dorsey, b. Dec. 6, 1756; d. 1826 intestate (*Chanc. Rec.* 135, f. 173) m. Feb. 22, 1796 Ann Wayman

5. CALEB[4] DORSEY JR. (Caleb,[3] John,[2] Edward[1])
b. July 18, 1710; d. June 28, 1772 at Belmont, Anne Arundel County
m. Feb. 10, 1735 Priscilla Hill, b. May 9, 1718 (*Md. Gazette*); d. Mar. 8, 1782

On May 25, 1732, Caleb Dorsey Jr. received as a deed of gift from his father Caleb Dorsey a tract called Moore's Morning Choice containing 1,368 acres and Dorsey's Chance, an adjoining tract of 200 acres. Some of this land was rich in iron ore, and Caleb Dorsey opened mines, built forges, erected furnaces, and shipped the output from the port of Elk Ridge Landing.

In 1738 he built a mansion which he called Belmont. The rambling two-story house, now covered with yellow plaster, is still owned by his descendants. (See pages 161 and 175A)

Caleb Dorsey's brother, Edward Dorsey, in his will of 1760, left all the land he held as tenements in common with Alexander Lawson and Caleb Dorsey, and his share of the personal stock in the iron works with the said Caleb Dorsey and Alexander Lawson, he to pay his wife, 100 pounds Sterling.

On September 18, 1761, Caleb Dorsey transferred to John Owings, 130 acres, part of Taylor's Forest. His wife, Priscilla, signed. (*Balt. Co. Deeds B. No. 1,* f. 301)

The will of Caleb Dorsey of Anne Arundel County, Ironmaster, made May 21, 1772 and probated June 12, 1772 left:

To daughter Rebecca Ridgely, 1,000 pounds Sterling to be paid 12 months after my decease
To daughter Mary Pue, 1,500 pounds Sterling to be paid 12 months after my decease
To daughter Milcah Goodwin, 2,000 pounds Sterling and 1 negro woman, also for her two eldest children to be paid ½ at 12 months and other ½ at 2 years after my decease
To daughter Eleanor Dorsey, 2,000 pounds Sterling and 3 negroes, said money to be paid ½ at 12 months and other ½ at 2 years after my decease
To daughter Peggy Hill Dorsey, 2,000 pounds Sterling, 3 negroes, said money to be paid ½ at 12 months, ½ at 3 years after my decease
To daughter Priscilla Dorsey, 2,000 pounds, 3 negroes, 1,000 pounds to be paid at day of marriage or when 21 years old and my desire is that her mother pay her as much
To granddaughter Priscilla Pue, 1 negro girl
To granddaughter Elizabeth Goodwin Dorsey, 500 pounds Sterling at day of marriage
To son Edward Dorsey, 2 negroes, desire he continue at school until he is 18 and education and maintenance be paid
Residue of personal estate to sons Samuel and Edward, equally divided between them
To Samuel Dorsey, Chew's Resolution Manor Resurveyed, Gore, Chew's Vineyard, Taylor's Forest in Baltimore County, part of Millfrog, Timber Ridge, Caleb's Delight, Lots at Elk Ridge Landing, and all my part of the Furnace Works at Curtises Creek together with all my lands purchased and taken up for use of the furnace.
If Samuel marries Magaret or Peggy Sprigg, Will revoked, except 500 acres, part of Caleb's Choice Enlarged in Frederick County
To Edward Dorsey, Moore's Morning Choice Enlarged, Caleb's Pasture, Valley of Owings, Little Worth, Caleb's and Edward's Friendship, Caleb's Vineyard, Taylor's Forest, Baltimore County
To daughter Mary Pue, Long Reach
Exrs: sons Samuel and Edward Dorsey, Dr. Michael Pue (*Wills 38,* f. 819)

Priscilla Dorsey, widow of Caleb, who was the daughter of Henry and Margaret Hill, survived her husband by ten years. She received a legacy from her father's estate in 1740. (*Accts. 18,* f. 2)

CHRIST CHURCH
QUEEN CAROLINE PARISH
Remodeled in 1809

In 1735 John Dorsey and his father Caleb Dorsey deeded two acres of New Year's Gift for a site for Christ Church in Anne Arundel County (now Howard County), Maryland.

ELKHORN, HOWARD COUNTY, MARYLAND
Built between 1740 and 1795 by Caleb Dorsey, who married Rebecca Hammond.

OAK HALL, HOWARD COUNTY, MARYLAND
Built about 1830 by Richard Dorsey, son of Caleb. Near Christ Church. Present home of Mrs. Hammond Dorsey.

FONT HILL, HOWARD COUNTY, MARYLAND
Built by the Howards
Home of Louis T. Clark from 1905 to 1927, and where his eleven children were born.

MOUNT IDA, ELLICOTT CITY, MARYLAND
Built by the Ellicotts in early 19th Century. Present home of Louis T. Clark.

BELMONT, HOWARD COUNTY, MARYLAND
Home of Caleb and Priscilla (Hill) Dorsey
Built by them in 1738.

In her will made February 6, 1777 and probated October 10, 1782, she left personalty to her granddaughter Priscilla Pue, and Priscilla Dorsey, daughter of Nathan and Sophia Dorsey. She named Dr. Michael Pue and William Goodwin Executors. (*A.A. Co. Wills T.G. No. 1*, f. 75)

Children of Caleb and Priscilla (Hill) Dorsey:
(Births recorded in Queen Caroline Parish Register)

1. Henry[5] Dorsey, b. Mar. 3, 1735/6; d. 1772 (*Wills 38*, f. 825)
   m. Elizabeth Goodwin, dau. of Lyde
2. Rebecca Dorsey, b. June 8, 1739; d. Sept. 22, 1812, m. Charles Ridgely, d. 1790
   (See page 149)
3. Samuel Dorsey, b. Dec. 7, 1741; d. Sept. 11, 1777
   m. Margaret Sprigg, d. 1781 (*A.A. Co. Wills T.G. No. 1*, f. 120)
4. Mary Dorsey, b. June 9, 1744; d. 1833, m. Dr. Michael Pue
5. Milcah Dorsey, b. Mar. 30, 1747; d. 1829, m. Mar. 30, 1773 William Goodwin, d. 1809
6. Eleanor Dorsey, b. Dec. 28, 1749; d. 1813 unm. (*Balt. Co. Wills 9*, f. 291)
7. Margaret (Peggy) Dorsey, b. June 20, 1752; d. 1797
   m. Nov. 26, 1772 William Buchanan
8. Priscilla Dorsey, b. June 26, 1754; d. 1756
9. Edward Dorsey, b. Sept. 2, 1758; d. 1799 (*A.A. Co. Wills J.G. No. 2*, f. 73)
   m. Mar. 25, 1786 Elizabeth Dorsey
10. Priscilla Dorsey, b. July 12, 1762; d. 1814
    m. Oct. 14, 1782 Charles Carnan (Ridgely) - one-time governor of Maryland
    (See page 219)

6. SAMUEL[4] DORSEY (Caleb,[3] John,[2] Edward[1])
b. Mar. 1712; d. 1739 Anne Arundel County

In 1732 Samuel Dorsey received by deed of gift from his father, 500 acres of Chew's Resolution Mannor, 135 acres called the Gore, 200 acres part of Long Reach, and 387 acres part of the Vineyard, to be his when he arrived at the age of 21 years.

His will made August 26, 1739 and probated November 15, 1739 left his personal estate after his debts were paid to be divided amongst brothers Basil, John, Caleb, Richard, Edward, Joshua, Thomas Beale Dorsey, and sisters Sophia Dorsey, Elinor Todd, Deborah Dorsey and Mary Dorsey. Executor, brother Richard. (*Wills 22*, f. 102)

7. RICHARD[4] DORSEY (Caleb,[3] John,[2] Edward[1])
b. June 10, 1714; d. Sept. 2, 1760 at Hockley in the Hole, Anne Arundel County
m. bef. 1736 Elizabeth (Beale) Nicholson, b. June 8, 1711 (*St. A.*); d. 1776

Richard Dorsey and his brother Samuel inherited from their grandfather John Dorsey the plantation on South River called South River Quarter.

On March 25, 1732, Richard Dorsey received by deed of gift from his father Caleb Dorsey, 442 acres, part of the home plantation, Hockley in the Hole, 85 acres called Orphan's Addition, 150 acres, part of Howard's Heirship purchased from Stephen Bently, 100 acres called Howard's Hope and 100 acres more part of Howard's Heirship bought by Caleb Dorsey of Cornelius Brooksby, to be held in trust until he came of age. (*A.A. Co. Deeds I.H.T.I. No. 1*, f. 419)

On February 22, 1736, Richard Dorsey and others brought suit against Daniel Dulany, guardian of Beal Nicholson, son of Mrs. Elizabeth (Nicholson) Dorsey, wife of Richard of Hockley in the Hole. (*Chanc. Rec. I.R. No. 3*, f. 97)

Richard Dorsey was a vestryman of St. Anne's Church from 1743 to 1745. He was an attorney in Annapolis and for a number of years served as clerk of the Committee of Aggrievances and Courts of Justice. (*Arch. of Md.* XXXIX, 155, 225; LV, 19)

Old Name Plate found about twenty years ago in one of the fields of Hockley in the Hole. The original is one-and-a-half inches in diameter and about three-eighths of an inch in thickness, and is made of hard vitreous material of a brownish color. The date indicates that it belonged to Richard Dorsey, who inherited the family plantation from his father, Caleb Dorsey. Shown through the courtesy of Dr. Caleb Dorsey of Baltimore, Maryland.

According to the Maryland Gazette, Richard Dorsey died early Tuesday morning, September 2, 1760, at his plantation near town of the gout of his Stomach, Head, and Bowels, aged 47 years, Clerk, the Paper Currency Office for about 20 years past, a very worthy magistrate of this county. (*Md. Hist. Mag.* XVIII, f. 159)

He died intestate, and on June 8, 1765 an account was rendered by Elizabeth Dorsey administratrix of Richard Dorsey late of Anne Arundel County deceased. Payments were made to son Caleb Dorsey, daughter Ann, who had married Benjamin Beall, and daughters Elinor and Elizabeth Dorsey. (*Accts. 49,* f. 208)

In a later account payments were made to Elizabeth who had married Elisha Harrison and to Mary Dorsey. (*Accts. 56,* f. 187)

Elizabeth Dorsey, widow of Richard, was the former wife of William Nicholson, who died in 1731, (*Wills 20,* f. 306) and a daughter of John and Elizabeth (Norwood) Beale. (*Wills 21,* f. 114) (See page 206)

The will of Elizabeth Dorsey (widow), of City of Annapolis, made May 26, 1772 and proved February 19, 1776 left:

To daughter Ann Beall, executrix, 1 negress over her share of my estate
To daughter Mary Dorsey, all household furniture, all stock, 150 pounds over her part of my estate
To daughter Elizabeth Dorsey, 20 pounds
To four daughters Ann Beall, Elinor Hall, Elizabeth Harrison, Mary Dorsey, residue of estate equally
Test: Frances Bryce, Margaret Ruth, Brice T.B. Worthington (*Wills 40,* f. 700)

Children of Richard and Elizabeth (Beale) Dorsey:
(Named in settlement of father's estate and in mother's will)

1. Caleb[5] Dorsey, d. 1770 (Test. Proc. 43, f. 417)
   m. Mary Rutland, d. 1815 (*A.A. Co. Wills J.G. No. 1,* f. 82)
   who. m. (2) ——— Watson
2. Ann Dorsey, d. 1787 (*A.A. Co. Wills T.G. No. 2,* f. 27)
   m. Benjamin Beale, d. 1765 (*Wills 33,* f. 268)
3. Elizabeth Dorsey, d. 1787 (*A.A. Co. Wills T.G. No. 2,* f. 28)
   m. (1) Elisha Harrison, d. 1773 (Wills 39, f. 451), m. (2) ——— McGowan
4. Elinor Dorsey, d. 1805 (*A.A. Co. Wills J.G. No. 2,* f. 339)
   m. Aug. 27, 1767 (*Md. Gaz*) John Hall, d. 1797 (*A.A. Co. Wills J.G. No. 1,* f. 607)
5. Mary Dorsey, d. 1816 (*A.A. Co. J.G. No. 3,* f. 145)
   m. John Weems, d. 1794 (*A.A. Co. Wills J.G. No. 1,* f. 454)

8. ELINOR[4] DORSEY (Caleb,[3] John,[4] Edward[1])
   b. Jan. 4, 1715/16; d. Oct. 16, 1760 Baltimore County
   m. (1) Thomas Todd, d. 1738

The will of Thomas Todd made December 9, 1738 and probated April 21, 1739 left:

To 3 daughters, Elizabeth, Elinor, and Frances and their heirs, Shawan Hunting Ground, divided equally
To youngest daughter Mary Todd and heirs, Todd Industry in Patapsco Neck, Thirels, Chuckels Poynt, where Thomas Jones now lives and Todd Islands
To son Thomas Todd and 4 daughters, personal estate after deducting wife's part to be divided equally
Exrs: wife Eleanor, Bazell Dorsey, Caleb Dorsey Jr. (*Wills 22,* f. 37)

Children of Thomas and Elinor (Dorsey) Todd:
(Named in parent's wills)

1. Thomas[5] Todd, m. Sarah Wilkinson
2. Eleanor Todd, m. John Ensor
3. Elizabeth Todd, m. John Cromwell

4. Frances Todd, m. George Risteau
5. Mary Todd, m. John Worthington

Elinor Todd, widow of Thomas, m. (2) Sept. 6, 1740 William Lynch

The will of Elinor Lynch proved July 23, 1760 left:

To son William Lynch, 80 acres bought of Thomas Gough called Harleston
To son Joshua Lynch, 2 lots, Baltimore Town with houses and building thereon
If he dies before he is 21, lots to go to daughters, Sarah, Deborah, Polly, and Ann Lynch
To son Joshua Lynch, 100 pounds Maryland currency
To daughters Sarah, Deborah, Polly, and Ann Lynch, negroes
To son Thomas Todd and daughters Elizabeth Cromwell, Eleanor Ensor, Frances Risteau, Mary Worthington, 10 pounds each
To granddaughter Eleanor Cromwell, a negro
Remainder of estate to be divided between sons and daughters, William, Joshua Lynch, Sarah, Deborah, Polly, and Ann Lynch
Exr: son-in-law John Ensor Jr. (*Wills 31*, f. 46)

The account of John Ensor Jr. executor of the last will of Elinor Lynch named legacies left by deceased to Thomas Todd, John Worthington's wife, John Cromwell's wife and George Risteau's wife, March 9, 1763. (*Accts. 49*, f. 169)

Children of William and Elinor (Dorsey) Lynch:
(Named in mother's will)

1. William[5] Lynch
2. Joshua Lynch
3. Sarah Lynch
4. Deborah Lynch, m. Samuel Owings
5. Polly Lynch
6. Ann Lynch

9. EDWARD[4] DORSEY (Caleb,[3] John,[2] Edward[1])

b. Sept. 1718; d. Mar. 20, 1760 at New Port, Rhode Island

m. Feb. 18, 1748 Henrietta Maria Chew, b. 1730; d. May 17, 1762 Anne Arundel County

Edward Dorsey was given 500 acres of New Year's Gift and 210 acres called Addition to New Year's Gift by his father Caleb Dorsey in 1732, to be held in trust until he was of age. In 1742 his father willed him 2 lots bought from Thomas Higgins, 100 acres of New Year's Gift, Higgin's Choice, and Dorsey's Friendship, containing 187½ acres to be his at his mother's death, and also 5 negroes, cattle, sheep, and hogs, and a house and lot in the City of Annapolis, where Edward lived and practiced law. He also was a large landowner in Frederick County.

Edward Dorsey was appointed Clerk of the Committee of Aggrievances in 1744, which office he held for a number of years. (*Arch. of Md.* XLII, 506; XLVI, 70) From 1758 to 1760 he was a delegate to the Lower House for Frederick County. (*Arch. of Md.* LVI, 13, 318) He was a member of the old Tuesday Club of Annapolis, and served as speaker of the Club for a number of years.

On October 9, 1760, the Maryland Gazette published the following statement:

"By the last Post from the Northward, we had the Advice of the Death of Mr. Edward Dorsey, an Eminent Attorney of this City, one of our common council and a representative for Frederick County. This Gentleman went from Home in Maryland, for the Recovery of his Health, had been as far as Boston, and on his Return Died at New-Port in Rhode Island, the 20th of last March." (*Md. Hist. Mag.* XVIII, f. 159)

The will of Edward Dorsey, City of Annapolis, Attorney at Law, proved May 5, 1760 left:

To my wife Henrietta Maria, my houses and lots in City of Annapolis, and my land near Annapolis called Dorsey, slaves cattle etc.
To sister Sophia Gough, the plantation she now lives on
To nephew Bazil Dorsey, my law books

To daughters, Henrietta Maria Dorsey and Eleanor Dorsey, balance of lands
To brother Richard Dorsey, executor, guardian of my children, his part of the following tracts, Chew's Resolution Mannor, Vineyard, Part of Long Reach, Gore
To brother Caleb Dorsey, all the land as I hold as tenements in common with Alexander Lawson and Caleb Dorsey and my share of the personal stock that I have in iron works with the said Caleb Dorsey and Alexander Lawson, he to pay my wife 100 pounds Sterling
To nephew Bazil Dorsey, lands in Frederick County
To sister Mary Ridgely and heirs, lands in Baltimore County
If my children should die underage, personal estate to children of sister Deborah Dorsey, sister Mary, brother Richard Dorsey, brother Thomas Beale Dorsey
Exr: brother Richard Dorsey *Wills 31*, f. 80)

Henrietta Maria Dorsey, widow of Edward, died in the 32d year of her age. She was the daughter of Samuel Chew and his wife Henrietta Maria (Lloyd) Chew, who m. (2) H.M. Dulany. (*Md. Hist. Mag.* XVIII, 166)

The will of Henrietta Maria Dorsey made April 26, 1762 and probated May 28, 1762 devised:

To mother Henrietta Maria Dulany, 1,000 pounds Sterling, wearing apparel, and a negro woman
To Ann Norwood Spinster, 20 pounds Sterling, Mrs, Grason, widow, 20 pounds
To each daughter of Richard Dorsey late deceased, 25 pounds except my god daughter Mary, 30 pounds Sterling
To unclè Francis Chew's children, 50 pounds to be divided
To Mrs. Sophia Gough, widow late Thomas Gough, silver salver and silver ladle and 20 pounds Sterling
To daughter Henrietta Maria Dorsey, my slaves, but if she should die before coming of age 21, then to my mother. My daughter who is under 8 years to be under mother's care
To sister Mary Chew, negroes
To mother Henrietta Maria Dulany, all estate in case of daughter's death
To my brothers and sisters and other friends, personalty
To the vestry of Annapolis, Parish, sum of 50 pounds Sterling for a pulpit Cloth and Cushion for the church and 100 pounds for poor of said parish
Exrs: brother Samuel Chew, Beal Bordley (*Wills 31*, f. 80)

In 1763 the account of Mr. Samuel Chew acting executor of Mrs. Henrietta Maria Dorsey late of the city of Annapolis, Anne Arundel County, deceased was filed. In addition to other legacies to brothers and sisters, one was left to the deceased's daughter Henrietta Maria Dorsey and paid to Mrs. Henrietta Maria Dulany guardian. (*Accts. 50*, f. 36)

On May 25, 1764, an account of the estate of Edward Dorsey deceased of the city of Annapolis was presented by Benjamin Beale acting person for Mrs. Henrietta (Chew) Dulany, mother of widow Henrietta Maria Dorsey deceased, Administratrix, de bonis non of estate of Edward Dorsey deceased. Value of estate, £13,607/10/¾. (*Accts. 51*, f. 90)

Children of Edward and Henrietta (Chew) Dorsey:
(Named in father's will)

1. Henrietta Maria[5] Dorsey, b. July 20, 1754 (*St. A.*); d. Oct. 12, 1766, only child of the late Edward Dorsey Esq. Deceased. By her death her fortune supposed to be 30,000 pounds falls to her father's relatives. (Maryland Gazette, *Md. Hist. Mag.* XVIII, 179)
2. Eleanor Dorsey, d. bef. 1766

10. JOSHUA[4] DORSEY (Caleb,[3] John,[2] Edward[1])
b. July 13, 1720; d. 1744 Anne Arundel County

Joshua Dorsey was given 500 acres of Chew's Resolution Mannor and part of The Vineyard by his father in 1732, to be his at the age of 21 years.

He died c 1744 intestate. The estate of Joshua Dorsey was appraised in 1744. (*Invts. 30*, f. 223) The account of his estate was filed by his administrators, Caleb Dorsey and Edward Dorsey, January 29, 1749. (*Accts. 27*, f. 248)

11. DEBORAH[4] DORSEY (Caleb,[3] John,[2] Edward[1])
b. Nov. 25, 1722; d. 1806/7 Anne Arundel County
m. as 2nd wife, Ely Dorsey, d. 1794

Ely Dorsey, son of Capt. John Dorsey, married first, January 1, 1744 Mary Crockett, (St. Paul's) by whom he had John Crocket Dorsey mentioned in his will, and Mary Dorsey named in the will of her uncle John Crockett in 1747. (*Wills 38,* f. 171)

In 1751 Mary, wife of Ely, came into possession of 650 acres of land, being a part of a tract called the Isle of Capere surveyed and patented to John Crockett who died without a will. The tract became the right of his son John Crockett Jr. as heir at law and when he died without a legal will, Mary and her sister Hannah, who married Bazil Dorsey, became co-heirs to the said tract of land. (*Balt. Co. Deeds T.R. No. D,* f. 182)

In 1748 Ely Dorsey and his wife Mary sold 410 acres of the Isle of Capere to John Greniffe Howard, (*Balt. Co. Deeds T.R. No. C,* f. 268) and on September 5, 1751, he sold the remainder of the tract to Thomas Miles. (*Balt. Co. Deeds T.R. No. D,* f. 188)

Deborah Dorsey m. Ely Dorsey soon after 1751. (See page 142)

Deborah Dorsey, wife of Ely, acting as administrator of the estate of her brother Edward Dorsey and Henrietta Maria Dorsey, entered a case against the executors of Caleb Dorsey, late partner of Edward Dorsey in the iron forges of Elk Ridge. The wife and daughter of Edward Dorsey had both died soon after his death in 1760, and Deborah hoped to get her part of his estate. (*Chanc. Rec. 32,* f. 249)

The will of Ely Dorsey made October 2, 1789 and probated February 3, 1794 left:

To grandson Caleb Dorsey, son of Caleb Dorsey, dwelling plantation and sundry tracts containing 700 acres with all personal property that belonged to his father Caleb Dorsey deceased, which I caused to be valued after his death and an inventory taken to be paid in kind, also his share of my estate,also my clock
To my executors for purpose of selling the tract called Dorsey's Search, whereon my father (John Dorsey) lived, containing 479 acres, same to be sold and equally divided between children of my two daughters, Elizabeth and Eleanor
To wife Deborah, one-third personal estate and her thirds in dwelling plantation also my carriage and horses and use of household for her natural life
To son Eli Dorsey, watch, sleeve buttons, wearing apparel
To grandsons Eli Dorsey, the son of John Crockett Dorsey, and Eli Dorsey, son of Ely 100 pounds each
Residue of personal estate to be equally divided between son Amos Dorsey, grandson Caleb Dorsey, and children of my two daughters, Elizabeth Ridgely and Eleanor Dorsey
Exrs: wife Deborah, son Amos, son-in-law Daniel Dorsey
Codicil - appoints wife sole executrix, son Amos having died leaving 4 children
Witness: Richard Dorsey (*A.A. Co. Wills J.G. No. 1,* f. 384)

The will of Deborah Dorsey made March 21, 1796 and proved May 27, 1807 left:

To grandson Caleb Dorsey, stock etc., dozen chairs, which were his father's.
Whereas I expect to be entitled to a considerable sum of money when the lawsuit with Caleb Dorsey's executors is finally settled, bequeath out of this 600 pounds money to be divided equally among 4 children of my son Amos deceased, daughters at 16 and son at 21 years.
To daughters Elizabeth and Eleanor, estate equally divided
Codicil was made because grandson Caleb Dorsey had died. (*A.A. Co. Wills J.G. No. 2,* f. 402)

Children of Ely and Deborah (Dorsey) Dorsey:
(Named in parent's wills)

1. Caleb[5] Dorsey, d. bef. 1789, m. Dinah Warfield, dau. of Joshua
2. Ely Dorsey, m. Sept. 5, 1778 Sarah Worthington
3. Amos Dorsey, d. 1793, m. May 8, 1784 Polly (Mary) Dorsey, d. 1831 (*A.A. Co. Wills T.T.S. No. 1,* f. 95)
4. Elizabeth Dorsey, m. Oct. 3, 1777 Richard Ridgely, d. 1830 (*Ibid.,* f. 95)
5. Eleanor Dorsey, m. Feb. 17, 1779 Daniel Dorsey

12. MARY^4 DORSEY (Caleb,^{3} John,^{2} Edward^1)

b. May 18, 1725; d. 1786 Baltimore County

m. John Ridgely, b. 1723; d. 1771 at Ridgely's Delight, Baltimore County

In 1762 John Ridgely son of Col. Charles Ridgely and Rachel, his wife, were on a committee to buy 2 acres of land for a Chapel of Ease in St. Paul's Parish, Baltimore County and to contract for workmen to build the Chapel. (*Arch. of Md.* LVIII, 201)

John Ridgely was a large landowner and held among other tracts, a part of White Wine and Claret, which his father had inherited from his grandfather Hon. John Dorsey. (See page 148)

The will of John Ridgely made March 19, 1771 and proved May 1, 1771 left:

To wife Mary, 250 pounds Sterling, negroes, all plate in my dwelling house, furniture, and during her life the use of my dwelling plantation with liberty to cut firewood from my tract of land called Pay My Debts. I give her annually 80 pounds current money to be paid in Spanish Dollars, first payment to be made at the end of twelve months after my death
To my son-in-law William Goodwin and to grandson William Goodwin, negroes
To my son Charles Ridgely and heirs, all my right and part of that tract called White Wine and Claret in Anne Arundel County, together with the following lands lying in Baltimore County, viz: all my part of land called Howard's Timber Neck, all that tract called Ridgely's Delight, all my part of lot 35 in Baltimore County on which my store and warehouses are built with all other improvements on the same, all my part of a tract of land called Oakhampton and also my half of the water mill and land resurveyed for the same given me by my father Charles Ridgely
To son Charles Ridgely, my gold watch
To son William Ridgely and heirs, all my part of Well's Mannor, and tracts, Nathaniel's Hope and Ayer's Desire in Baltimore County, with my half part of lot in 163 in Baltimore Town, the said part to be next to lot 164 by me conveyed to William Goodwin and to include the house I purchased from Wm Ponyaney together with that part of said lot by me also conveyed to Wm Goodwin
To son John Ridgely and heirs, my part of Taylor's Purchase, all that tract called Pay My Debts, and also the remaining half part of lot 163
To 4 daughters, Deborah, Rachel, Eleanor Ridgely, and Mary Nicholson and heirs, following tracts equally divided between them viz: part of Parish Range bought of Solomon Wooden, all that tract Bond's Meadows Enlarged which remains at present unsold, all that tract lately called Potaney's Desire and which is resurveyed and with necessary addition called Speculation, Ridgely's Ambition, Costly, Pierces Discovery, Stockdale's Neighbor, Benjamin's Addition, and Benjamin's Beginning, and in case either of my said daughters should die without issue, I give said part to her heirs
To daughters Rachel and Eleanor, negroes
Should son die without issue, land to be divided among my daughters
Whereas I am in partnership with my son Charles Ridgely in a store of goods in Baltimore Town, goods coming in to be sold for benefit of Partnership
To son Charles Ridgely and daughter Deborah Ridgely and Mary Nicholson my 1/3 part of the Northampton Furnace with stock in partnership of lands, slaves, servants, cattle, pay unto William Ridgely, John Ridgely, Rachel, Eleanor, William Goodwin my grandson, 500 pounds Sterling
Children to be brought up under direction of my wife
To son Charles, William, John, and son-in-law Benjamin Nicholson, daughters Deborah, Rachel, and Eleanor Ridgely, grandson William Goodwin, residue.
(*Wills 38*, f. 258)

The will of Mary Ridgely, widow of John, made February 19, 1786 and proved June 11, 1787 left:

To daughter Deborah, granddaughter Polly Sterret and Harriet Sterret and grandson Andrew Sterret, negroes
To son Edward Ridgely, under age negro
Executors to settle with my son Charles and executors of late husband
To son Edward Ridgely, all real estate I am entitled to under the will of my brother Edward Dorsey deceased, and 200 pounds Sterling
To daughters Polly Nicholson and Eleanor Lammy and children of my daughter Rachel, 1/3 to Polly, 1/3 to Eleanor, 1/3 to children of Rachel
Exr: John Ridgely (*Balt. Co. Wills 4*, f. 186)

Children of John and Mary (Dorsey) Ridgely:

(Named in parent's wills and in the will of Elizabeth Woodward)

1. Achsah^5 Ridgely, d. bef. 1770

2. Deborah Ridgely, d. 1817 (*A.A. Co. Wills J.G. No. 2*, f. 201) (See page 219)
   m. John Sterret, d. 1787 (*Balt. Co. Wills 4*, f. 194)
3. Mary Ridgely, d. 1804 (*Balt. Co. Wills 7*, f. 300), m. Benjamin Nicholson
4. Charles Ridgely, d. 1787 (*Balt. Co. Wills 4*, f. 184), m. Rebecca Lawson
5. William Ridgely, d. 1797 (*Balt. Co. Wills 5*, f. 511), m. Ann ——
6. John Ridgely, living in 1787
7. Rachel Ridgely, m. Thomas Nicholson
8. Eleanor Ridgely, m. Benjamin Lammy (*Balt. Co. Wills 5*, f. 68)
9. Edward Ridgely
10. —— Ridgely, m. William Goodwin

13. THOMAS BEALE^4 DORSEY (Caleb,^{3} John,^{2} Edward^1)
    b. Jan. 18, 1727; d. Nov. 1, 1771 (Bible Record) Anne Arundel County
    m. 1746 Ann Worthington, b. 1720; d. Nov. 23, 1771 (Bible Rec.)

In 1732 Thomas Beale Dorsey received by deed of gift from his father Caleb Dorsey, Howard's Discovery and Crouchfield containing in the whole 350 acres bought by the said Caleb of Benjamin Howard, and 150 acres part of Howard's Heirship, which was bought by John Dorsey Esq. deceased of Cornelius Howard and given by deed of gift to the said Caleb Dorsey, to be held in trust until he became of age. (A.A. Co. Deeds I.H.T.I, f. 420) In 1742 his father willed him Howard's Hills containing 200 acres and 60 acres more of Howard's Heirship to be his at the death of his mother, also 4 negroes, cattle, sheep, and hogs.

A tract of 48 acres of vacant land between Crouchfield and Howard's Discovery, called Last Discovery, was patented by Thomas Beale Dorsey, November 29, 1769.
(*Patents B.C.& G.S. No. 38*, f. 325)

In 1752 he served as churchwarden in St. Anne's Church and as vestryman from 1753 to 1756 and from 1769 until his death in 1771. (*St. Anne's Vestry Proc.*)

Ann Dorsey, wife of Thomas Beale Dorsey, was the daughter of John and Helen Worthington. She inherited from her father in 1766, his dwelling plantation called Wyatt's Harbor and Wyatt's Hills, negroes, household goods, and stock. (*Wills 34*, f. 30) (See pages 181 and 182)

Thomas Beale Dorsey in his will made October 28, 1771 and proved November 13, 1771 devised:

To eldest son Caleb Dorsey, dwelling plantation and lands thereon which are entailed to eldest son Caleb, also adjoining lands
To son John Worthington Dorsey, all lands at Elk Ridge, near Upton, commonly called Upper Quarter
To youngest son, Thomas Beale Dorsey, land on Elk Ridge called Lower Quarter
To daughter Sarah Merriweather, 1 negro and 10 pounds Sterling
Exrs: son Caleb Dorsey and son in law Reuben Merriweather
(*A.A. Co. Original Wills D*, Folder 54)
(*Wills 38*, f.378)

SIGNATURE AND SEAL FROM THE ORIGINAL WILL OF
THOMAS BEALE DORSEY
Filed in the Hall of Records, Annapolis, Maryland

DORSEY FAMILY

Children of Thomas Beale and Ann (Worthington) Dorsey:
(Records from Family Bible and Arcadia Cemetery, Howard Co.)

1. Sarah[5] Dorsey, b. Oct. 13, 1747 (*St. A.*)
   m. Reuben Merriweather, d. 1794 (*A.A. Co. Wills J.G. No. 1*, f. 437)
2. Caleb Dorsey, b. Mar. 13, 1749; d. Apr. 14, 1837 (Tombstone)(See page 212)
   (*A.A. Co. Wills TTS No. 1*, f. 292)
   m. Feb. 25, 1772 Elizabeth Worthington, b. Apr. 22, 1758; d. May 9, 1840
   (Tombstone) dau. of John and Susannah (Hood) Worthington (See page 182)
   Caleb Dorsey gave the land for St. John's Protestant Episcopal Church near Ellicott City, Howard County in 1850. (Diary of Reuben Dorsey by Robert C. Smith, *Md. Hist. Mag.* XL, f. 60)
3. John Worthington Dorsey, b. Oct. 8, 1751; d. May 13, 1823 (Tombstone)
   (*A.A. Co. Wills J.G.E.V. No. 1*, f. 168)
   m. Nov. 30, 1778 Comfort Worthington, b. 1759; d. July 23, 1837 (Tombstone)
   dau. of Samuel
4. Thomas Beale Dorsey Jr., b. Aug. 25, 1758; d. Sept. 6, 1828 (Tombstone)
   (*A.A. Co. Wills TTS No. 1*, f. 10)
   m. (1) Jan. 1, 1784 Achsah Dorsey
   m. (2) Oct. 28, 1806 Achsah Brown (Bible Rec.)

HOCKLEY IN THE HOLE
ANNE ARUNDEL COUNTY, MARYLAND
THE ORIGINAL TRACT OF LAND TAKEN UP BY EDWARD DORSEY,
THE IMMIGRANT

HOCKLEY IN THE HOLE, HOME OF THE DARCY-
DORSEYS OF ANNE ARUNDEL COUNTY

FROM SIDE-LIGHTS ON MARYLAND HISTORY
by
HESTER DORSEY RICHARDSON
Reproduced by Permission

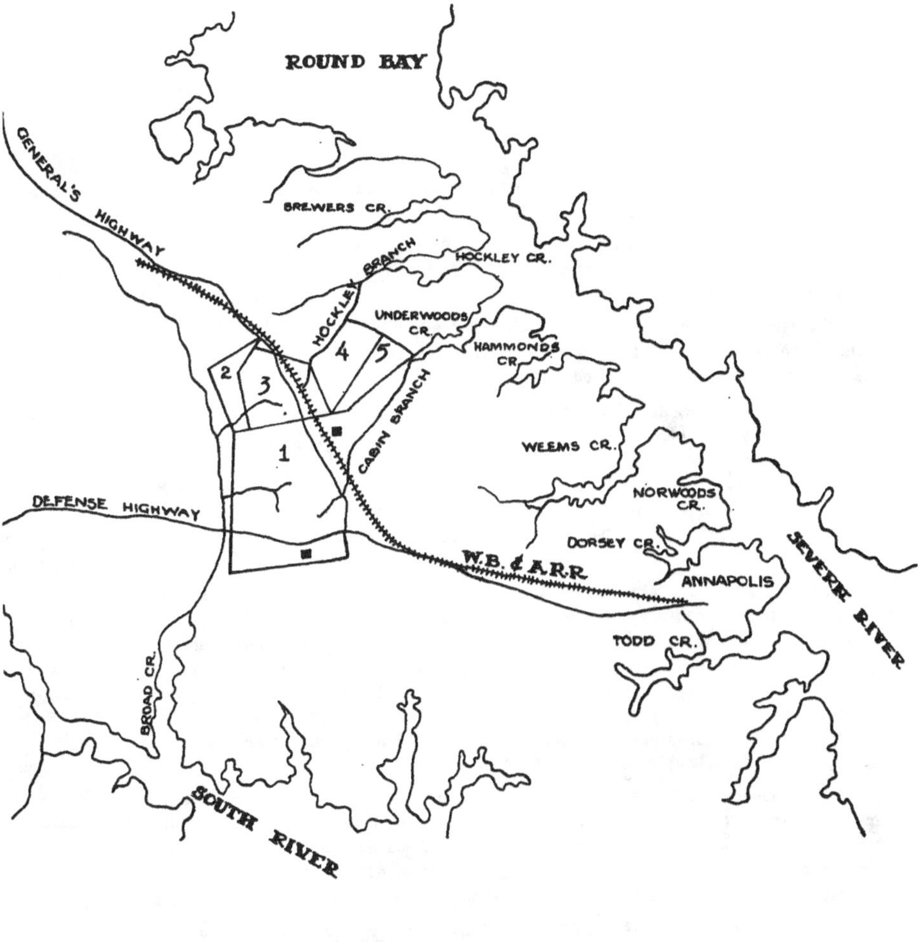

HOCKLEY IN THE HOLE ENLARGED

Map showing the location and bounds of Hockley in the Hole, Enlarged drawn from a plat made according to the resurvey for Richard Dorsey on March 17, 1794. The estate was composed of:

1. The original Hockley in the Hole.
2. Orphan's Addition.
3. Dorsey's Search—originally part of Howard's Heirship.
4. Howard's Heirship.
5. Howard's Hope.

The locations of the different Dorsey homes upon Hockley are indicated by squares, the first home being to the north, and the second and third upon the same site, just south of the Defense Highway. The third home is still standing on the plantation.

HOCKLEY IN THE HOLE

The original tract of land taken up by Edward Dorsey, the immigrant before 1659 in Anne Arundel County, Maryland, has passed from generation to generation of the Dorsey family.

On August 25, 1664, Edward Dorsey, Joshua Dorsey, and John Dorsey, the three sons of Edward Dorsey, took up and had patented their father's survey of 400 acres, calling it Hockley in the Hole. (*Patents 7, f.* 378) (See page 9)

On December 6, 1681, Edward and Joshua Dorsey sold their interest in Hockley in the Hole to their brother John, after which John asked for a resurvey of the tract, which increased its size to 842 acres. (*A.A. Co. Deeds I.H. No. 3,* folios 62, 65)

On August 6, 1702, John Dorsey gave to his son Caleb Dorsey, 442 acres of Hockley in the Hole, an adjoining tract of 85 acres called Orphan's Addition, originally patented by Lawrence and Robert Gudgeon, May 10, 1685, (*Patents N.S. No. B, f.* 150) and purchased by John Dorsey from William Griffith and Robert Gudgeon, March 10, 1697, (*A.A. Co. Deeds W.T. No. 1, f.* 236) and also 150 acres of Howard's Heirship, patented by Cornelius Howard August 4, 1664, (*Patents 7, f.* 249) and bought by John Dorsey of Cornelius and Elizabeth Howard, August 4, 1679. (*A.A. Co. Deeds W.T. No. 1, f.* 288)

On March 25, 1732, Caleb Dorsey gave to his son Richard Dorsey, 442 acres of Hockley in the Hole, and four adjoining tracts, Orphan's Addition of 85 acres, Howard's Heirship of 150 acres, originally part of Howard's Heirship patented by Cornelius Howard and purchased by Caleb Dorsey from Stephen Bently, November 13, 1709, (*A.A. Co. Deeds P.K, f.* 119) Howard's Hope of 100 acres, originally patented by Samuel Howard, August 4, 1664, (*Patents 7, f.* 251) and bought by Caleb Dorsey from Cornelius Brooksby, July 3, 1723, (*A.A. Co. Deeds R.C.W. No. 2, f.* 193) and 100 acres more of Howard's Heirship, also purchased from Cornelius Brooksby, July 3, 1723. (*A.A. Co. Deeds I.H.T.I. No. 1, f.* 419)

On September 2, 1760, Richard Dorsey died and his son Caleb Dorsey inherited his father's land. On March 17, 1766, Caleb Dorsey resurveyed and patented a portion of his inheritance previously known as Howard's Heirship. This tract was supposed to contain 150 acres, but the survey showed only 90 acres, to which Caleb Dorsey added 31 acres adjoining vacant land and patented same under the name of Dorsey's Search. (*Patents B.C.& G.S. No. 31, f.* 174)

In 1770 Caleb Dorsey died leaving only one child, Richard Dorsey, who came into possession of Hockley in the Hole and four adjoining tracts, Orphan's Addition, Dorsey's Search, Howard's Hope, and Howard's Heirship. (*Test. Proc. 43, f.* 617)

On March 17, 1794, Richard Dorsey had the estate resurveyed into one tract and patented same under the name of Hockley in the Hole Enlarged, November 3, 1795. (*Patents I.C. No. N, f.* 110) (See page 173)

In 1808 Richard Dorsey died, and in his will made July 28, 1808 he left his wife Ann and his mother Mary Watson a life interest in his property and at the death of his wife to be divided among his children - Caleb, Richard, Anne Elizabeth, Edward, and Mary Dorsey. (*A.A. Co. Wills J.G. No. 2, f.* 443)

By a decree of the Court of Chancery, March Term 1847, (*Chanc. Papers* 11243) the property was surveyed and divided into thirds among: Anne Elizabeth Dorsey, Essex Ridley Dorsey (husband of Anne Elizabeth) who had previously purchased the share of his wife's brother

Caleb. The remaining share or third went to the Sellman children, heirs of John S. Sellman and Mary (Dorsey) Sellman deceased. Before this time, Edward Dorsey of Richard sold his share of the estate to the other heirs, and also Richard, son of Richard, had previously died without issue, his share going in the same manner.

Anne Elizabeth Dorsey, daughter of Richard and wife of Essex Ridley Dorsey died September 10, 1862, and Essex Dorsey died November 19, 1884.

On March 9, 1886, by Deed of Partition, the estate was divided among the six children of Essex and Anne Elizabeth Dorsey, namely, Andrew J.M. Dorsey, Evelina (Dorsey) Sellman, Laura Mary Dorsey, Vachel Charles Dorsey, Richard Dorsey, and Anne Elizabeth Dorsey.

(*A.A. Co. Deeds S.H. No. 27,* f. 628)

Anne Elizabeth Dorsey, the last of the children, died January 24, 1914. Her share of the property was a part of the original tract of Hockley in the Hole. This land was inherited, and is now in the possession of Dr. Caleb Dorsey of Baltimore.

The original dwelling on Hockley in the Hole was located about a mile north of the present one near the old W.B. and A. railroad, which passed through the land. This house burned in the 1730's, and the first Richard Dorsey of Hockley in the Hole built further south. This second dwelling burned during the 1860's and the present house was rebuilt upon the same site. (See pages 172 and 173)

Note: The information concerning Hockley in the Hole and the map showing the location and bounds of Hockley in the Hole Enlarged was contributed by Dr. Caleb Dorsey of Baltimore.

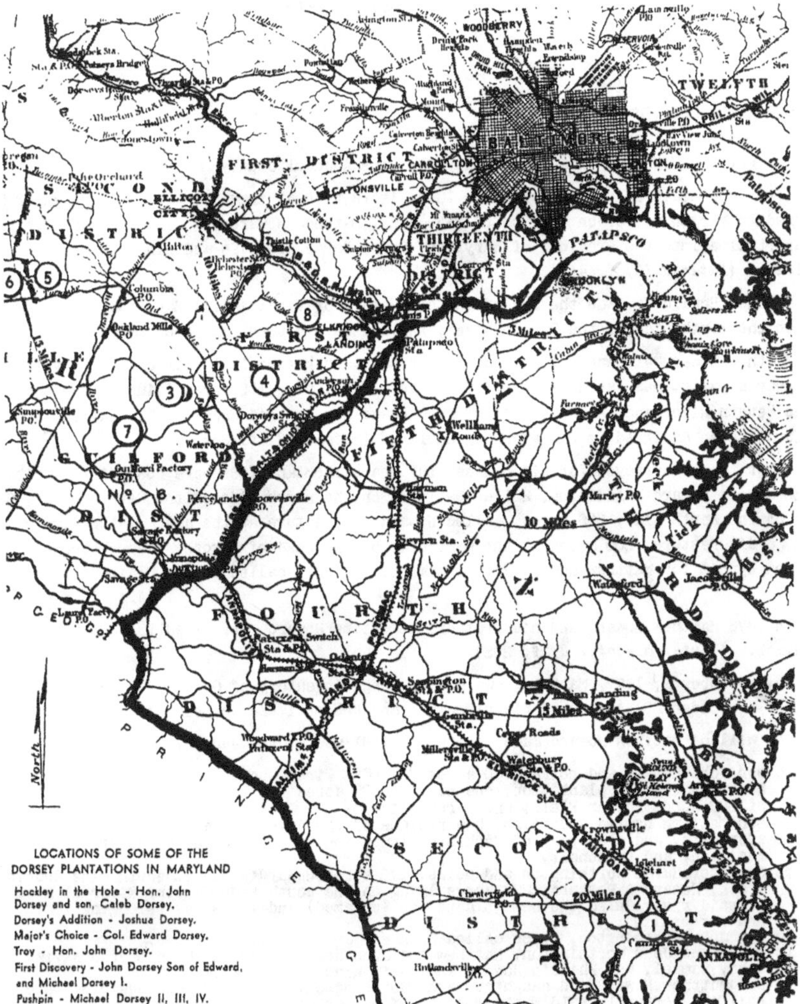

LOCATIONS OF SOME OF THE
DORSEY PLANTATIONS IN MARYLAND

Hockley in the Hole - Hon. John Dorsey and son, Caleb Dorsey.
Dorsey's Addition - Joshua Dorsey.
Major's Choice - Col. Edward Dorsey.
Troy - Hon. John Dorsey.
First Discovery - John Dorsey Son of Edward, and Michael Dorsey I.
Pushpin - Michael Dorsey II, III, IV.
Christ Church in Queen Caroline Parish.
Moore's Morning Choice - Caleb Dorsey Jr.

SARAH (DORSEY) HOWARD

IV. SARAH[2] DORSEY (Edward[1])

d. bef. 1691 Anne Arundel County

m. bef. 1667 Matthew Howard Jr., d. 1692 Anne Arundel County

After the death of Edward Dorsey in 1659, it is thought that his widow and daughter Sarah returned to Virginia, for on the 7th of May, 1667, Matthew Howard Jr. demanded land for the transportation into the Province of Maryland, Sarah Darcy his wife and nine other persons from Virginia. (*Patents 10*, f. 447)

Matthew Howard Jr. was the son of Matthew Howard of Virginia and Maryland, who took up land on the south side of the Severn River, Ann Arundell County, in 1650. (See pages 2,3 and 5)

Matthew Howard Jr. was in the Province of Maryland before 1661, for on February 15th of this year a patent was issued to him for a tract, containing 115 acres lying on the north side of the Severn River and the west side of Chesapeake Bay, called Hopkin's Plantation, which had previously been assigned to him by Henry Catlin. (*Patents 7*, f. 247)

Other tracts surveyed for him between the years 1663 and 1688 were Howard's Inheritance of 130 acres, Howard's Addition, 22½ acres lying on the north side of the Severn River, 60 acres on the south side, 500 acres, called Howard's Adventure at the head of the Severn River, and Howard's Pasture, 200 acres at the west side of the head of Magothy River. There was also surveyed by him for Matthew Howard Jr., the minor, a tract called Poplar Plain.

(*A.A. Co. Rent Rolls*)

In 1676 Matthew Howard and his brother, Cornelius Howard, appraised the estate of Nicholas Wyatt. (*Invts. & Accts. 2*, f. 263)

On September 1, 1677, Matthew Howard signed the inventory of George Norman. (*Test. Papers*, Box 4, Folder 22) A copy of his signature and the seal used appear on page 177.

The will of Matthew Howard made October 3, 1691 and proved January 12, 1692 left:

To son John Howard and heirs, 160 acres Howard's First Choice, commonly known as Howard's Quarter plantation, one-half of 500 acres The Adventure, and one-half of 500 acres Poplar Plain, and personalty
To son Matthew Howard and heirs, his residue of the Adventure and of Poplar Plain aforesaid, and also part of Hopkin's Plantation, and 22½ acres of Howard's Addition, and personalty.
To daughter Sarah Worthington and heirs, 176 acres Howard's Range, south side Bodkin Creek, Howard's Pasture, 200 acres lying on the south side Magothy River at head of said river, also the home plantation (unnamed) and 130 acres belonging to it, and personalty
To son John Worthington, horse called Prince
To grandsons John Worthington, Matthew and John Howard, and to three brothers viz, John, Samuel, and Phillip Howard and their wives, personalty
To son Matthew Howard and daughter Sarah Worthington, residuary legatees of estate real and personal, said Matthew to be of age at 21 years
Exrs: daughter Sarah Worthington and her husband John Worthington
Witness: Nicholas Greenberry
John Howard Sr. (*Wills 2*, f. 222)

Sarah Howard, not mentioned in the will of her husband, died prior to 1691

The estate of Matthew Howard Jr. was appraised by Morris Baker and Thomas Browne, July 15, 1692. The items listed and the legacies left to his children and grandchildren indicate

SIGNATURES OF MATTHEW HOWARD AND HIS DAUGHTER AND HUSBAND

From Testamentary Papers Filed in the Hall of Records
Annapolis, Marvland

that he was one of the substantial citizens of the Province.

(*Invts. & Accts. 11*, f. 30)

The account of John Worthington and Sarah his wife executrix of the last will of Matthew Howard Sr. of Anne Arundel County deceased was made in 1700/1.

Payments were made to John Howard for his two sons, Matthew and John, to Coll Edward Dorsey and William Taylor, to John Samuel, and Phillip Howard, to Sarah Worthington, to John Howard, to Matthew Howard, to John Worthington, to grandson John Worthington. All remaining money from the estate was divided between Matthew and Sarah Worthington, the executrix.

(*Invts. & Accts. 20*, f. 86)

On December 26, 1704, Sarah Brice executrix of the last will of Matthew Howard deceased, showed that the residue of his estate was divided between said accountant and her brother Matthew Howard, as the last account appears, and proved by the oath of Mrs. Susannah Crouch, lately called Susannah Howard, executrix of John Howard, who was the administrator of said Matthew Howard Jr., deceased, which estate was delivered him in full of his portion.

(*Invts. & Accts. 25*, f. 54)

Children and Matthew and Sarah (Dorsey) Howard:
(Named in father's will and in Joshua Dorsey's will)

1. John[3] Howard, d. 1702, m. Susannah Rockhould
2. Matthew Howard, d. 1701 unm.
3. Sarah Howard, d. 1726, m. (1) John Worthington, m. (2) John Brice
4. Samuel Howard, d. bef. 1691. Heir in uncle Joshua Dorsey's will of 1687. Not named in father's will.

JOHN HOWARD

1. JOHN[3] HOWARD (Sarah[2] (Dorsey) Howard, Edward[1])
   d. Nov. 6, 1702 Anne Arundel County
   m. Susannah Rockhould, d. Dec. 8, 1712 (*St. Mrgts.*)

John Howard was given a gray guilding in the will of his uncle Joshua Dorsey in 1687, and by the will of his father Matthew Howard Jr. in 1691 received 160 acres of Howard's First Choice, 250 acres of the Adventure, and 250 acres of Poplar Plain, and personalty.

In the year 1698, John and Susannah Howard conveyed Howard's First Choice to Lancelot Todd. (*A.A. Co. Deeds I.H. No. 1*, f. 114)

John Howard, as next of kin, was granted letters of administration on the estate of his brother Matthew Howard in 1701. John Howard died in 1702 before the estate of Matthew Howard was settled, and on April 12, 1703 the additional account of the estate of Matthew Howard deceased, was exhibited by Susannah Crouch als Howard, executrix of John Howard deceased, who was the administrator of Matthew Howard deceased. (*Invts. & Accts. 23*, f. 108)

Children of John and Susannah (Rockhould) Howard:
(Named in grandfather Matthew Howard's will)

1. Matthew[4] Howard, b. bef. 1692, living in 1713 (*A.A. Co. Deeds I.B. No. 2*, f. 53)
2. John Howard, b. bef. 1692; d. 1746
   m. Ruth Greniffe, widow of John (See page 141)
3. Abner Howard, b. Feb. 28, 1700 d.y. (*St. Mrgts.*)

Susannah Howard, widow of John, m. (2) Mar. 16, 1702 William Crouch (*St. Mrgts.*) d. 1709.

She was the daughter of John Rockhould and wife Mary Richardson, thought to be the daughter of Lawrence Richardson, and sister of Sarah Dorsey, wife of Joshua. (See page 202)

The will of William Crouch dated April 23, 1709 left his estate to his wife Susannah and his two children James and Hannah Crouch. (*Wills 12, Pt. 2, f.* 72)

Children of William and Susannah (Rockhould) Crouch:
(Births recorded in St. Margaret's Parish Register)

1. James Crouch, b. Mar. 31, 1704
2. Hannah Crouch, b. Nov. 5, 1706

Susannah Crouch, widow of William, m. (3) May 4, 1710 James Smith (*St. Mrgts.*), and as his wife administered the estate of William Crouch deceased. (*Test. Proc. 22, f.* 26)
No issue has been found

MATTHEW HOWARD

2. MATTHEW[3] HOWARD (Sarah[2] (Dorsey) Howard, Edward[1])
d. 1701 Anne Arundel County

Matthew Howard was given two hoghds of tobacco in the will of his uncle Joshua Dorsey in 1687. He was left by the will of his father in 1691, The Adventure, 250 acres, Poplar Plain, 250 acres, a portion of Hopkin's Plantation and 22½ acres of Howard's Addition, and personalty.

He died in 1701 intestate.
His brother John Howard, as next of kin, took out letters of administration on his estate in 1701. (*Test. Proc. 18b, f.* 27)
The account of John Howard of the goods and chattels of Matthew Howard deceased was presented September 8, 1701. (*Invts. & Accts. 20, f.* 246)
On April 12, 1703, the additional account of the estate of Matthew Howard deceased was exhibited by Susannah Crouch als Howard, executrix of John Howard deceased, who was the administrator of the estate of Matthew Howard deceased. This accountant charges the amount formerly exhibited by John Howard deceased, in his life time. Paid Mr. John Brice part due the estate of Capt. John Worthington. (*Invts. & Accts. 23, f.* 108)

SARAH HOWARD

3. SARAH[3] HOWARD (Sarah[2] (Dorsey) Howard, Edward[1])
d. Dec. 21, 1726 (*St. Mrgts.*) Anne Arundel County
m. (1) c 1686 Capt. John Worthington, b. 1650; d. Apr. 9, 1701

Sarah Worthington was devised by the will of her father in 1691, Howard's Range, Howard's Pasture, the home plantation and 130 acres belonging to it. She served as the executrix of the will of her father Matthew Howard and survived all three of her brothers.

Capt. John Worthington was associate Justice of Anne Arundel County in 1692 and in 1699 was a member of the legislative assembly. His tombstone has been moved to the churchyard of St. Anne's Church, Annapolis, and bears the inscription, Died April 9, 1701, Aged 51 yrs.

The will of John Worthington made April 4, 1699 and proved May 7, 1701 left:

To wife Sarah executrix, life interest in dwelling plantation and all personalty
To son John Worthington and heirs, 400 acres, dwelling plantation on Severn River
To son Thomas Worthington and heirs, 400 acres, Greenberry's Forest, and 350 acres Lewis' Addition, both near Magothy River
To son William Worthington and heirs, 130 acres Howard's Inheritance, and 200 acres where Richard Beard's mill now stands, and 270 acres near Bodkin Creek, Patapsco River, also a parcel of woodland ground, being a part of William Hopkins' as appears by will of Matthew Howard deceased
To daughter Sarah Worthington, personalty (*Wills 11, f.* 63)

Children of John and Sarah (Howard) Worthington:
(Births recorded in St. Margaret's Parish Register)

1. John[4] Worthington, b. Jan. 12, 1689, m. (1) Helen Hammond (2) Comfort ______

2. Thomas Worthington, b. Jan. 8, 1691, m. Elizabeth Ridgely
3. William Worthington, b. Apr. 16, 1694, m. Sarah Homewood
4. Sarah Worthington, b. Jan. 10, 1696, m. Nicholas Ridgely
5. Charles Worthington, d. inf.
6. Charles Worthington, b. Dec. 20, 1701, m. Sarah Chew

Sarah Worthington, widow of John, m. (2) Dec. 16, 1701 Capt. John Brice, d. Dec. 13, 1713 (St. Mrgts.) Anne Arundel County.

He is recorded as a gentleman, a merchant, and a planter, member of the House of Burgesses, Justice of Peace, and Capt. of the Severn Hundred. (*Arch. of Md.*) He was guardian for the Worthington heirs.

On July 14, 1713, John Brice, merchant, bought Hopkin's Plantation and Howards Addition from John Howard and Ruth, his wife, and Matthew Howard, sons of John Howard deceased.

(*A.A. Co. Deeds I.B. No. 2,* f. 53)

The will of John Brice made December 8, 1713 and proved December 22, 1713 left:

To daughter Ann Brice, 266½ acres Hopkin's Plantation and Howard's Addition bought of Matthew and John Howard
To daughter Rachel Brice, 200 acres Doderidge Forrest and residue of 250 acres Kendall's Delight
To brother Thomas Brice of London, sawmaker, personalty, to be paid him by my master, Benjamin Hattley
To John Butcher of London, eldest son of sister Eliza: Butcher of Goose Grave, Northhamptonshire, and to Thomas and Francis Butcher, sons of sister afsd, personalty
To cousin James Butcher and heirs, land bought of James Yiedhall
To cousin John Brice and heirs, 140 acres Merrikin's Purchase, and Point Look Out near long bridge saw mill
To sons-in-law and daughter-in-law, viz: John, Thomas, and William Worthington, and Sarah Ridgely, personalty
To son-in-law Charles Worthington and heirs, 900 acres, Brice's Share, on north side falls of Patapsco River and 50 pounds as per marriage bond
To children-in-law aforesaid, 10 pounds each, it being money which testator and brothers gave bond for, for Charles Worthington in county court office by error in supposing him to be the unborn child at date of drawing of the will of his father, Capt. John Worthington; however said child died and said Charles having nothing by will of his father aforesaid...
To Sarah Brice, executrix, plantation and 127 acres Baron's Neck, bought of Lord Baltimore, by escheat, and residue of lands in fee simple or by mortgage.

(See page 177) (*Wills 13,* f. 589)

On March 30, 1720, Sarah Brice bought from William Worthington and Nicholas Ridgely of Anne Arundel County and Sarah his wife, Howard's Inheritance.

(*A.A. Co. Deeds C.W. No. 1,* f. 150)

The will of Sarah Brice, widow, made April 13, 1725 and proved December 30, 1726 left:

To daughter Ann Denton, 130 acres, Howard's Inheritance, neither she nor son-in-law Vachel Denton to be charged for any salary for what was paid them on account of the said Ann's father's estate
To daughter Rachel Brice, 130 pounds and personalty
To son Charles Worthington, 130 pounds and personalty
To granddaughters Sarah, Rebecca, Ruth, Ann Ridgely, sons John, Thomas, and William Worthington and wives of said sons, sons-in-law, Nicholas Ridgely and Vachel Denton, cousins James Butcher and John Brice, personalty
To son John Brice and heirs, residue of real estate and personalty
To grandchildren viz. son John Worthington's children, son Thomas Worthington's children, daughter Sarah Ridgely's children, residue of personal estate
To son John Brice and daughter Rachel Brice, to be paid their portion of their father's estate according to balance remaining in the commissary's office.
In a codicil attached to the will, her son William Worthington and each son-in-law was to receive 30 pounds each, and two grandchildren born to sons John and William Worthington since making the will were also remembered.
Exrs: sons Thomas Worthington and John Brice (*Wills 19,* f. 264)
(See page 177)

Children of John and Sarah (Howard) Brice:
(Births recorded in St. Margaret's Parish Register)

1. John[4] Brice, b. Sept. 24, 1703, m. Sarah Frisby
2. Ann Brice, b. May 30, 1708, m. Vachel Denton
3. Rachel Brice, b. Apr. 13, 1711, m. Phillip Hammond

1. JOHN[4] WORTHINGTON (Sarah[3] (Howard) Worthington, Sarah[2] (Dorsey) Howard, Edward[1])
b. Jan. 12, 1689; d. 1766 Anne Arundel County
m. (1) Mar. 12, 1713 Helen Hammond (*St. Paul's*), d. bef. 1724
m. (2) bef. 1728 Comfort____, bur. Mar. 18, 1741 (*St. A.*)

John Worthington received by his father's will in 1701, the dwelling plantation of 400 acres on the Severn River.

Helen Worthington, first wife of John, was the daughter of Thomas Hammond, who died in 1724. He named his grandson William Worthington in his will, but since Helen is not mentioned, it is assumed that she had died before that date. (*Wills 18*, f. 350)

John Worthington m. (2) bef. 1728 Comfort____, maiden name unkhown.

The will of John Worthington made October 22, 1764 and proved June 12, 1766 left:

To daughter Ann Dorsey and heirs, my dwelling plantation, Wyatt's Harbor and Wyatt's Hills containing 160 acres, and all those negroes, stock, and household goods which the said Ann Dorsey and her husband Thomas Beale Dorsey are now in possession of
To son John Worthington and heirs, eleven tracts known by the names of Worthington's Beginning, Worthington's Fancy, part of Duvall's Delight, part of food Plenty, Chandler's Slaughter, Coples Fancy, no Name bought of Orlando Griffith, Boyd's Chance, Randals Purchase, part of Grays Increase and Randalls Fancy containing 2,620½ acres, also 363 acres of land in Frederick County, part of a tract called Whiskey Ridge, and also all those negroes, which he now has in his possession, and 100 pounds Sterling money
To son Charles Worthington and his heirs, five tracts in Anne Arundel County containing 905 acres known by names Hunting Ground, Ridgely's Range, part of Broken Ground, part of Howard's and Porter's Fancy and part of Abington, and also all those negroes which he now has in his possession, also two more negroes and 50 pounds Sterling
To son Samuel Worthington and heirs, 1,000 acres of land in Baltimore County where he now lives being part of a tract of 2,000 acres called Welsh's Cradle, also all those negroes which he now has in his possession, and one mulatto man now in possession of my son Thomas, also 100 pounds Sterling money
To son Thomas Worthington and heirs, all those three tracts on the north side of the Patapsco River in Baltimore County, near to Patapsco Falls known by names of Brice's Share, Stinchcombs Park and Wiltshire containing, 1,670 acres and also all the negroes which he now has in his psossession in Baltimore County, and also 10 negroes now in my possession and 5 pounds Sterling
To son Vachel Worthington, a negro woman, also 5 pounds Sterling
To daughter Elizabeth Dorsey, wife of Nicholas Dorsey and her heirs, two tracts of land in Anne Arundel County near Patapsco River known by name Todd's Risque and part of Andover containing 409 acres and also all the negroes which she and her husband has now in his possession
To grandsons John and William Worthington, sons of my son William Worthington, deceased and their heirs, part of a tract called Whiskey Ridge in Frederick County containing 700 acres to be equally divided between them
To grandson William Worthington, 4 negroes
To brother John Brice, 50 pounds Sterling money to be paid 12 months after my decease
To said sons John, Charles, and Samuel Worthington and my two daughters Ann Dorsey and Elizabeth Dorsey, all the remainder of my personal estate to be equally divided
Exrs: John and Charles Worthington, sons (*Wills 34*, f. 30)

Children of John and Helen (Hammond) Worthington:
(Named in father's will)

1. William[5] Worthington, b. bef. 1724; d. bef. 1766
m. June 30, 1734 Hannah (Rattenbury) Cromwell, widow of John (*St. Paul's*) dau. of John

2. Charles Worthington, m. Rachel Hood
3. Vachel Worthington, m. Priscilla Bond, dau. of William
4. Ann Worthington, m. Thomas Beal Dorsey (See page 169)
5. Elizabeth Worthington, m. Nicholas Dorsey (See page 44)
6. Thomas Worthington, m. Nov. 17, 1781 Elizabeth Hammond (*St. Thos.*)

Children of John and Comfort Worthington:

1. John[5] Worthington, b. 1728; d. 1790 (*A.A. Co. Wills J.G. No. 1*, f. 161)
   m. Susannah Hood, dau. of William
2. Samuel Worthington, b. 1734; d. 1815 (*Balt. Co. Wills 20*, f. 10)
   m. (1) June 17, 1759 Mary Tolley (*St. James*), b. 1740; d. 1777
   m. (2) Martha Garrettson, b. 1753; d. 1831

2. THOMAS[4] WORTHINGTON (Sarah[3] (Howard) Worthington, Sarah[2] (Dorsey) Howard, Edward[1])
b. Jan. 8, 1691/2 (*St. Mrgts.*); d. 1753 Anne Arundel County
m. July 23, 1711 Elizabeth Ridgely (*St. Mrgts.*); d. Dec. 8, 1734 (*St. A.*)

Thomas Worthington inherited 450 acres, Greenberry's Forest and 350 acres Lewis' Addition near Magothy River in 1701.

He was a vestryman and churchwarden of St. Anne's Church between 1726 and 1749, and member of the House of Burgesses in 1753.

The will of Thomas Worthington made January 9, 1752 and proved April 3, 1753 left:

To second son of my son-in-law Basil Dorsey and my daughter Sarah his wife, 368½ acres part of Worthington's Range as laid out by Col. Henry Ridgely on which said Basil hath settled a plantation, which said land I give to the 2nd son of said Basil and Sarah Dorsey and the heirs of theirs. In default of such issue to descend to next son or daughter of said Basil
To my daughter Elizabeth Dorsey, 368 acres of Worthington's Range on which her husband has settled a plantation and at her decease to her son Thomas Dorsey. Said Elizabeth to have what she and her husband already have of mine
To daughter Rachel Howard, 369 acres of Worthington's Range on which her husband has a plantation and after her decease to son Thomas Cornelius Howard. To daughter Sarah what she and her husband already have of mine
To daughter Catherine Gassaway, 300 acres called Partnership on which her husband and she live
To daughter Thomasin Warfield, 400 acres out of a tract Partnership and the Addition to Snowden's Manner
To daughter Ariana Watkins and heirs, 300 acres of Alltogether on which her husband hath settled a plantation and 63 acres out of a tract called Worthington's Range, also to daughter Ariana what she and her husband already have of mine
To son Nicholas Worthington and heirs, lands of Wyat's Ridge, 226 acres, Adventure 50 acres, also tracts bought of Amos Garrett, namely, Ridgely Neck, Addition, Broken Land, Pettycoat Benefit, Pettycoate Addition, 12 in number- in all 1,700 acres
To son Brice Thomas Beal Worthington, my lands not herein given and what has already been given him. My eight children to share alike.
Exr: Brice Thomas Beal Worthington (*Wills 28*, f. 445)

The account of Brice Thomas Beal Worthington, executor of Thomas Worthington, late of Anne Arundel County deceased was filed June 12, 1754. Legacies were paid to Nicholas Worthington, to daughter Rachel Howard, to accountant, to Bazil Dorsey for wife's share, to Nicholas Gassaway for wife's share, to Henry Dorsey for wife's share, to Cornelius Howard for wife's share, to Thomasin Warfield for her share paid to Francis Simpson, now husband said Thomasin Warfield, and to Nicholas Watkins for his wife's share. (*Accts. 36*, f. 268)

Elizabeth Worthington, wife of Thomas, was the daughter of Henry and Catherine (Greenberry) Ridgely. She was left 150 acres of land at the head of Morgan's Creek in her father's will of 1700. (*Wills 6*, f. 371)

Children of Thomas and Elizabeth (Ridgely) Worthington:
(Births recorded in St. Anne's Parish Register)

1. Sarah[5] Worthington, b. Feb. 2, 1715, m. Basil Dorsey (See page 157)
2. Elizabeth Worthington, b. Oct. 6, 1717, m. Henry Dorsey (See page 39)
3. Catherine Worthington, b. June 10, 1720; d. 1788 (*A.A. Co. Wills J.G. No. 1, f.* 19), m. Nicholas Gassaway
4. Rachel Worthington, b. Aug. 28, 1722, m. Cornelius Howard
5. Thomasin Worthington, b. June 9, 1724, m. (1) Alexander Warfield m. (2) Francis Simpson (*Accts. 36, f.* 268)
6. Brice Thomas Beal Worthington, b. Nov. 2, 1727; d. 1794 (*A.A. Co. Wills J.G. No. 1, f.* 419), m. Ann Ridgely
7. Ariana Worthington, b. Dec. 25, 1729, m. (1) Nicholas Watkins
   (2) John Ijams
8. Thomas Worthington, b. Jan. 6, 1731
9. Nicholas Worthington, b. Feb. 29, 1734, m. Catherine Griffith

3. WILLIAM[4] WORTHINGTON (Sarah[3] (Howard) Worthington, Sarah[2] (Dorsey) Howard, Edward[1])
b. Apr. 16, 1694; d. 1770 Anne Arundel County
m. Nov. 5, 1717 Sarah Homewood (*A.H.*)

William Worthington inherited from his father in 1701, Howard's Inheritance, 130 acres, 200 acres where Richard Beard's mill now stands, 270 acres near Bodkin Creek, Patapsco River, also parcel of woodland ground, part of William Hopkins.

The will of William Worthington made September 25, 1770 and proved November 22, 1770 devised:

To daughter Ruth, tract called the Plains, 200 acres, part of a tract called Dawson's Plains to be delivered one month after my decease. If daughter dies without heirs, land to descend to grandaughter Ruth Davis and heirs
To daughter Ruth Shaw, 1 negro, 100 pounds current money
To grandson William Worthington Davis, Homeward's Range, 300 acres north side Magothy River at age 21 years, silver tankard, silver can and six silver teaspoons, negroes, 100 pounds at 21 years
To granddaughter Sarah Davis, 4 tracts on south side of Magothy River, Homeward's Chance, 300 acres, Blay's Neck, 200 acres, Young Richard, 133 acres, and 40 acres more at age of 16 years. In case of death or no heirs land to go to granddaughter Ruth Davis, also to Sarah Davis granddaughter, negro named Hannah that lives with her father John Davis, also other negroes, 100 pounds current money at age 16 years
To granddaughter Ruth Davis and heirs, tract called Dorrels Luck north side Magothy River and part of Livingston, 260 acres at 16 years. In case of death or no heirs tract to go to granddaughter Mary Ann Davis, also negro, and 100 pounds
To granddaughter Mary Ann Davis and heirs, tracts south side Magothy River, Dawson's Chance, 64 acres, part of tract called Foothold, 67½ acres and Brushy Neck Bottom, 119 acres, negroes and 100 pounds current money. In case of death or no heirs above land to grandson William Worthington Davis
To grandson William Worthington Shaw, 1 negro boy
To grandson William Worthington, the remaining part of my lands lying in Maryland, negroes, silver tankard, one dozen silver tablespoons, and a silver watch, to be paid directly after my decease.
Remaining estate divided in 3 parts, one-third to daughter Ruth Shaw, the other two parts to be equally divided between five of my grandchildren, Sarah Davis, Ruth Davis, Mary Ann Davis to have parts at age 16, and William Worthington Davis, and William Worthington Shaw at age 21 years.
Exr: son-in-law John Davis (*Wills 38, f.* 73)

Sarah Worthington, wife of William, was the daughter of James and Mary (Peasley) Homewood. She was left lands and personalty in the will of her grandfather John Peasley in 1708.
(*Wills 12, f.* 32)

Children of William and Sarah (Homewood) Worthington:
(Births recorded in St. Margaret's Parish Register)

1. Wornel Worthington, b. July 27, 1719; d. 1749 (*Accts. 27, f.* 188)
   m. Dec. 10, 1745 Anna Hammond
2. Mary Ann Worthington, b. Aug. 10, 1722; d. bef. 1770
3. Sarah Worthington, b. Feb. 14, 1725; d. Dec. 15, 1744
4. Rachel Worthington, b. Mar. 30, 1728; d. bef. 1770
5. William Worthington, b. Sept. 18, 1734; d. Apr. 25, 1746
6. Arryanna Worthington, b. Oct. 26, 1736, m. John Davis of Richard
7. Ruth Worthington, b. July 5, 1742; d. 1786, m. Dr. John Shaw

4. SARAH[4] WORTHINGTON (Sarah[3] (Howard) Worthington, Sarah[2] (Dorsey) Howard, Edward[1])
b. Jan. 10, 1696; d. Mar. 16, 1721 Anne Arundel County
m. Sept. 26, 1711 (St. Mrgts.) Nicholas Ridgely, b. Feb. 2, 1694; d. Feb. 16, 1755, Dover, Delaware. (*Record of Tombstones in Kent County, Delaware*, Vol. 87)

Sarah Ridgely was left personalty in the will of her father in 1701, and Nicholas Ridgely received personalty in the will of his mother-in-law Sarah Brice, 1726.

Nicholas Ridgely, who was the son of Henry and Katherine (Greenberry) Ridgely was given in his father's will of 1699, to be his at 18 years of age, 275 acres of land called My Quarter Plantation and 272 acres called Ridgely's Lot, on the northeast side of the great branch of the Patuxent River. (*Wills 6, f.* 371)

On March 30, 1720, Nicholas Ridgely and William Worthington sold to Sarah Brice, Howard's Inheritance. Sarah, wife of Nicholas, signed. (*A.A. Co. Deeds C.W. No. 1, f.* 150)

Children of Nicholas and Sarah (Worthington) Ridgely:
(Named in grandmother's will in 1726)

1. Sarah[5] Ridgely
2. Rebecca Ridgely, m. Benjamin Warfield, son of John
3. Ruth Ridgely
4. Ann Ridgely

Nicholas Ridgely m. (2) Ann, widow of James Gordon, d. 1722 (*Wills 18, f.* 3) dau. of Robert and Mary French, New Castle, Delaware. She died soon after they moved to Delaware.

Nicholas Ridgely m. (3) Mary (Middleton) Vining, widow of Benjamin. She died Dec. 11, 1761. They had one son, Charles Greenberry Ridgely, b. 1740.

Nicholas Ridgely held the offices of Clerk of the Peace and Register Court of Chancery, and in 1746, he was made Judge of Supreme Court of New Castle, Kent, and Sussex Counties in Delaware.

6. CHARLES[4] WORTHINGTON (Sarah[3] (Howard) Worthington, Sarah[2] (Dorsey) Howard, Edward[1])
b. Dec. 20, 1701; d. 1774 Harford County
m. (1) Nov. 12, 1728 Hamutel Hammond, dau. of Charles and Hannah (*St. A.*)
m. (2) Oct. 5, 1732 Sarah Chew, dau. of John (*St. A.*)

The will of Charles Worthington Sr. made November 22, 1773 and proved March 24, 1774 devised:

To son John Worthington, dwelling plantation, Worthington's Dividend, 354 acres
To son Charles Worthington, 2 tracts bought from Henry Coles and Thomas Johnson, Phillips Purchase, 200 acres
To son Samuel Worthington, tract bought of Thomas Wells, called Well's Lott, part of Phillip's Purchase, 300 acres
To son John Worthington, two negroes
To son Charles Worthington, 2 negroes
To son Samuel Worthington, negroes, furniture, cows, tobacco

To daughter Sarah Worthington, negroes
To daughter Mary Worthington, negro
Son Samuel to be of age at 19 years
Remainder of estate to be divided between my five children John, Charles, Samuel, Sarah, and Mary
Exrs: sons John and Charles Worthington (*Wills 39*, f. 711)

Children of Charles and Sarah (Chew) Worthington:
(Births recorded in St. John's and St. George's Parish Register)

1. John[5] Worthington, b. Aug. 3, 1735; d. 1803 Harford County m. Nov. 7, 1769 Priscilla Wilson
2. Charles Worthington, b. July 6, 1736
3. Ann Worthington, b. June 10, 1738
4. Sarah Worthington
5. Mary Worthington, d. unm.
6. Samuel Worthington, d. 1777 unm.

1. JOHN[4] BRICE (Sarah[3] (Howard) Brice, Sarah[2] (Dorsey) Howard, Edward[1])
b. Sept. 24, 1703; d. Sept. 24, 1766 (*St. A.*) Anne Arundel County
m. Sept. 9, 1730 Sarah Frisby (*St. A.*); d. Apr. 8, 1782 (*St. A.*)

John Brice was left real estate and personalty in the will of his mother, 1726.

He was churchwarden and vestryman of St. Anne's Church in 1758 and 1759, and held the office of County Clerk.

John Brice, City of Annapolis, Esquire, made a will June 17, 1766, which was proved October 27, 1766. He left:

To wife Sarah Brice, the lot of land I now live on with the dwelling house and houses (Except the house where I formerly kept store) and which my son John Brice now uses for an office during her natural life provided she continue a widow after my decease, but in case she shall marry again then she and her husband shall have only 1/3 for her dower. Also to my wife during her widowhood 1/3 part of my lands on north side of Severn River known by names Sarah's Care, John Turner's Purchase, Barron Neck, Campbell's Purchase and Ferry Creek Branch, also sole profit of a grist mill on the main branch of Ferry Creek together with the land on which same stands for her maintenance and for support and education of my children during their minority and in case she marry again shall have only her dower.
To said wife, all my wearing apparel and that of my sister Ann Denton deceased and that of my sister Ariana Margaretta Harris deceased
To son John Brice, my heir at law, Pictures of Benja Hatley and Family, saddle horse, books belonging to me (except my law books which I reserve for my son James) and such others as he brought from England with him, also 500 pounds of Sterling in full as his part of my personal estate having been in considerable expense in his education in England and procured for him the office of county clerk of Anne Arundel County, which I resigned in his favor also, and several tracts of land named Sarah's Care for John, Turner's Purchase, Barren Neck, Lusby, Ferry Creek Branch the Landing, Middle Neck, Mutual Consent, Under Woods Addition and Cockey's Addition
To son James Brice and heirs, land in Cecil County known by names Frisby's Prime Choice, Frisby's Forest, part of Mill Pond, Brice's Triangle, and Hargraves Choice, In case James die before 21 years lands to go to son Benedict and Edmund Brice and heirs
To son Benedict and heirs, land on north side of Severn River, Jones Survey Triangle and 2 other tracts, also a lot in Annapolis and numbered by Stoddard's Survey of the city, 101, and land in Cecil County. If he die before age of 21 years, land to go to Edmund Brice
To Edmund Brice, all lands in Frederick County, and also lands north of Magothy River called Cuckholds Point, Cockey's Addition and Brice Security, and Bond's Forrest on Patapsco River. If Edmund die before 21 years lands to go to son Benedict Brice
To son James Brice, lots 94 and 103 in Annapolis and bricks stones and planks ready for building a dwelling house, also 500 pounds current money in lieu of land in Frederick County formerly devised to him and which was sold
To daughter Arianna Ross, 20 pounds currency together with what may be due from her husband for a tract called Nichols Hunting Quarter
To daughter Sarah Henderson, 20 pounds currency together with what may be due from her husband for a tract called Nichols Hunting Quarter

To daughters Ann Brice, Margaretta Brice, and Elizabeth Brice, a negro girl, 600 pounds Sterling and 200 pounds current money, each
Should my executrix marry again, appoint my son John Brice, sons-in-law David Ross and Richard Henderson to be guardians and trustees for my children and their estates
To sons James, Benedict, and Edmund Brice, all residue of personal estate
Exrx: wife Ann Brice (*Wills 34, f.* 243)

Sarah Brice, widow of John, was the daughter of James and Arianna Frisby. Her birth was recorded in St. Anne's Parish Register, and she was remembered in the will of her step-father, Edmond Jennings, in 1756. (*Wills 30, f.* 85)

Children of John and Sarah (Frisby) Brice:
(Births recorded in St. Anne's Parish Register)

1. Arianna[5] Brice, b. Jan. 19, 1731, m. Sept. 5, 1750 David Ross
2. Sarah Brice, b. June 3, 1735, m. Richard Henderson
3. John Brice, b. Mar. 7, 1736/7; d. Mar. 10th
4. John Brice, b. Sept. 22, 1738, m. Oct. 30, 1766 Mary Maccubbin, dau. of Nich.
5. Ann Brice, b. Apr. 4, 1744
6. James Brice, b. Aug. 26, 1746, m. May 24, 1781 Juliana Jennings
7. Benedict Brice, b. Apr. 1, 1749
8. Charles Brice, b. June 26, 1750; d. 14 mos. after
9. Edmund Brice, b. Nov. 24, 1751
10. Denton Brice, b. Aug. 20, 1753; d. bef. 1766
11. Margaretta Augustine Brice, b. Jan. 10, 1755
12. Elizabeth Brice, b. June 4, 1757

2. ANN[4] BRICE (Sarah[3] (Howard) Brice, Sarah[2] (Dorsey) Howard, Edward[1])
b. May 30, 1708; d. July 14, 1765 (Md. Gazette) Anne Arundel County
m. Nov. 23, 1721 Vachel Denton (*St. Mrgts.*) b. 1697; d. 1753

Ann Denton was devised 266½ acres of Hopkin's Plantation and Howard's Addition in the will of her father John Brice in 1713, and her mother Sarah Brice left her 130 acres of Howard's Inheritance.

Vachel Denton occupied pew No. 4 in St. Anne's Church and served as vestryman between 1725 and 1735.

Vachel Denton died in 1753 intestate. The account of Ann Denton, executrix of Vachel Denton Esq., late of Anne Arundel County deceased was filed July 27, 1753. (*Accts. 34, f.* 215)
His administration account was filed by John Brice, Beale Bordley, and Thomas Johnson Jr., July 8, 1765. (*Test. Proc. 41, f.* 160)

Ann Denton, widow of Vachel, made her will March 24, 1760 which was proved July 16, 1765. She named her brother John Brice. Witnesses were Benjamin Beall, A.M. Harris, James Harris and Wm Lynch. (*Wills 33, f.* 266)

3. RACHEL[4] BRICE (Sarah[3] (Howard) Brice, Sarah[2] (Dorsey) Howard, Edward[1])
b. Apr. 13, 1711; d. Apr. 11, 1786 Anne Arundel County
m. 1727/8 Col. Phillip Hammond, b. 1697, d. May 10, 1760

Rachel Brice inherited 200 acres of Doderidge Forest and residue of 250 acres of Kendall's Delight from her father in 1713. Her mother Sarah Brice, left her 130 pounds and personalty.

The will of Col. Phillip Hammond made June 6, 1753 and proved May 24, 1760 left:

To wife Rachel Hammond, dwelling house and tract called Howard's Adventure, Sheperd's Grove, the Intervention, Green Spring, Poplar Angle

To son John Hammond, 500 pounds Sterling
To son Charles Hammond, 2 tracts Hanover, Iron Mill. Also all cargo and goods in the store at Newton, with all outstanding money, he to take care of all my estate, not only of the goods now in this country but also those which shall arrive, agreeable to my former directions or invoice sent to England before this time, which said goods I direct to be sold in the best manner for the benefit of my estate
I desire that my brother John Hammond shall be employed as assistant to my son Charles, and he shall have an allowance of 50 pounds Sterling annually
To my daughter Ann Hammond, 1,000 pounds Sterling
To wife 1/6 part. balance to six sons, Charles, John, Phillip, Denton, Resin, Matthias Hammond
Daughters and sons, except John and Charles, to be maintained at expense of whole estate
Exr: son Charles Hammond

Wills 31, Pt. 1, f. 92

The will of Rachel Hammond made September 9, 1781 and proved April 25, 1786 left:

To son Denton Hammond and his heirs, 7 negroes and their increase
To son Rezin Hammond, negroes
To son Matthias Hammond, land called Hazard & Addition to Hazard, and Second Addition to Hazard. My dwelling plantation, 10 negroes, silver coffee pot with the Family Coat of Arms, silver tea pot, silver stand, silver waiter, silver Tankard, dozen silver tea spoons, silver tongs, furniture, and crops on the several plantations I occupy etc..
To granddaughter Rachel Hopkins, negroes, silver Can, 6 silver Table spoons
To granddaughter Margaret Hopkins, negroes, silver candlesticks, silver table spoons
To Rachel and Margaret, land in Anne Arundel County
To sons Denton and Mathias, rest of lands
Codicil - September 29, 1781, Denton Hammond dead.

(*A.A. Co. Wills T.G. No. 1, f.* 331)

Children of Phillip and Rachel (Brice) Hammond:
(Named in parent's wills)

1. Charles[5] Hammond, b. June 4, 1729 (*St. A.*); d. 1777, (*A.A. Co. Wills E.V. No. 1, f.* 25) m. Rebecca Wright
2. John Hammond, b. 1730; d. 1784, m. Henrietta Dorsey
3. Phillip Hammond, b. 1739/40; d. Apr. 2, 1783 unm.
4. Denton Hammond, b. 1743; d. 1781 unm.
5. Rezin Hammond, b. Sept. 26, 1744; d. 1809 unm.
6. Matthias Hammond, b. May 5, 1748; d. 1786 unm.
7. Ann Hammond, m. ________ Hopkins

ALLIED FAMILIES

WYATT, TODD, ELDER, HOWARD, ROCKHOULD, NORWOOD

NICHOLAS WYATT

NICHOLAS WYATT
1. 1673 Anne Arundel County
m. Damaris ______ widow, before 1653, probably in Virginia

Nicholas Wyatt had come to the Colony of Virginia and was living at the home of William Julian in 1646, when William Howell deposed that he heard Wm Julian's man Nicholas Wyatt say that after Henry Marriott was free, he had three years to serve.

(*Minute Bk. B*, f. 14, Lower Norfolk Co., Portsmouth, Va.)

He apparently left the colony, for on June 18, 1650 a certificate was granted to Wm Shipp and Sarah his wife for 800 acres of land for transporting ffran: and Matthew Shipp his 2 sonnes.... and Nicholas Wyatt into Virginia. (*New Eng. Hist. Gen. Reg.* Vol. 47, f. 66)

On October 22, 1651, Nicholas Wyatt was in Anne Arundel County, Maryland, where a tract of 90 acres called Wyatt was surveyed for him on the south side of the Severn River upon a creek running betwixt Underwood's Neck and Mountainy Neck on the south bound of Matthew Howard's land. (*Patents A.B.& H.* f. 265) (See page 5)

As attorney for John Hawkins, May 2, 1653, Nicholas Wyatt renewed the rights on land for John which he had lost. Nicholas Wyatt signed with his mark. (*Ibid.*, f. 316)

Being a Quaker, he refused to take the oath of Plantation, therefore had no right to sell land as was shown at a court held in 1659, when he was ordered to refund 510 pounds of tobacco, which he had received for the sale of ten acres of land, lying on the south side of the Severn River between the land belonging to Edward Dorcy and John Norwood, to Thomas Miles. (*Prov. Ct. Rec. S*, f. 289) (*Arch. of Md.* XLI, 320) (See page 5)

On October 10, 1662, Nicholas Wyatt was one of the Quakers brought before the court. (*Besse's Sufferings*, Vol. 2, f. 381) He also refused to take the oath in 1668, when he was summoned as one of the Grand Jury. (*Prov. Ct. Rec. F.F*, f. 654)

On April 15, 1663, Robert Clark assigned to Nicholas Wyatt all the said Robert's interest in the rights of two servants, for which a warrant of 100 acres had been granted to the said Robert. (*Patents 5*, f. 531)

The same year, 1663, Thomas Bradley assigned to Nicholas Wyatt 300 acres of land, and Nicholas assigned to Thomas Bradley all said Nicholas' right and title in land due to him for service done in the province by thirteen persons between the years 1653 and 1663.

(*Ibid.*, f. 513)

Wyatt's Hills, a tract of 60 acres on the south side of the Severn River, and Bear Ridge containing 175 acres were surveyed for him on October 16, 1663, and on the 20th of March, 1667, Wyatt's Harbour of 100 acres. (*Patents 7*, folios 345, 354) (*Patents 10*, f. 589)

On June 29, 1667, Nicholas Wyatt planter of Anne Arundel County, sold to John Annis and Francis Smith of London, 225 acres of Wyatt's Ridge lying on the north side of the South River on Broad Creek. This land had been surveyed for him on December 16, 1662. (*A.A. Co. Deeds I.H. No. 1*, f. 110) (*Patents 7*, f. 256)

He sold, on March 1, 1668, as Nicholas Wyatt of the Severn River, Anne Arundel County, to Richard Warfield and Edward Gardner a tract called Wayfield granted to him on August 11, 1664, containing 100 acres and lying on the south side of the Severn River. (*A.A. Co. Deeds I.H. No. 2*, f. 181) (*Patents 7*, f. 353)

In 1671 Nicholas Wyatt became ill and his wife Damaris, becoming alarmed, sent for Cornelius Howard to make a will for her husband. Although Nicholas Wyatt was very weak and sick and in no condition to make a will, he said he would give unto his son Samuel Wyatt his plantation and unto his daughter Sarah, 100 pounds, but when his wife interposed and asked if he did not remember that she was to be given the Lower plantation, Nicholas answered that he had forgot that. When his friends asked if he intended to leave his only son a bare plantation with neither a cow to give him milk nor a servant to wait on him, Nicholas seemed indifferent and answered that his son was as much his wife's son as his. As a result, the greater part of the estate was left to Damaris.

The will of Nicholas Wyatt written by Cornelius Howard on December 10, 1671 left:

To son Samuel Wyatt at 18 years of age, The Quarter. In event of death of Samuel without heirs, next of kin to inherit same
To daughter Sarah, Lower plantation where the widow Gibbons lives
To wife Damaris Executrix and residuary legatee
Test: Cor. Howard, Robert Gugen (*Wills 1*, f. 596)

Nicholas Wyatt, afterwards recovering from his illness, was urged by his friends who thought his will unfair to his children, to destroy it and make another one. When the subject came up while he was riding in the woods with his friend Cornelius Howard, Nicholas Wyatt at last appreciating the situation, turned to his friend and said, "Do you think I am in my right senses to leave my only son a bare plantation?" Cornelius Howard suggested he take his will and burn it, but he did not follow his advice. Later on much trouble arose in court, when Edward Dorsey and his wife, Sarah brought suit against Damaris, and her then husband, Thomas Bland, causing the will to be thrown out of court. (*Test. Proc. 4B*, folios 1-4) (*Test. Papers*, Box 3, Folder 30) (See page 13)

The inventory of the estate of Nicholas Wyatt was taken September 25, 1676 by Cornelius Howard and Matthew Howard.

It included articles in the Hall, Parlour, Hall Chamber, Porch Chamber, Parlour Chamber, Stair-case, Kitchen, the Quarter, Milk House, Seller, Store, Kitchen Buttery, Kitchen Chamber, Kitchen Loft, and at the Quarter.

Items of interest were tables, turky work charyes, leather chayres, Chest of drawers, side cupboards, bedsteads, ruggs, Curtains and valences, couches, trundle beds, brass andirons, tongs etc., looking glasses, 20 framed pictures, silver tankard, cups and spoons, books, nest of Houre glasses, linens, seal skin trunks, 20 pewter dishes, 14 porringers, pewter and brass candlesticks, cups etc. (*Invts. & Accts. 2*, f. 263)

Children of Nicholas and Damaris Wyatt:
(Named in father's will)

1. Samuel[2] Wyatt, under age of 18 years in 1671; d. bef. 1673
2. Sarah Wyatt, m. bef. 1670 Edward Dorsey (See page 10)

Damaris Wyatt, widow of Nicholas, m. (3) Thomas Bland

THOMAS TODD

THOMAS TODD

b. 1610; d. 1671 Anne Arundel County

m. before 1637 Elizabeth ______

On August 16, 1637, a tract of 250 acres lying on the south side of the easterne branch of Elizabeth River, New Norfolk County, Virginia, was surveyed for Thomas Todd for "transporting himself, his wife Elizabeth and 3 other persons into Virginia. This land he sold in 1649 to Alexander Hall and Abraham Paternot. (*Patents 1*, f. 437 State of Va.) (*Minute Bk. B*, f. 133a, Lower Norfolk Co., Portsmouth, Va.) Later he took up and disposed of other tracts of land. (See Nugent's, *Cavaliers and Pioneers*)

He was a churchwarden for the Parish of Lindhaven in 1640 and later served as vestryman. (*Va. Hist. Mag.* XL, 134)

At a court held at the house of Wm Shipp December 15, 1645, Thomas Todd was ordered to pay Edward Darcy and Thomas Hall 40 pounds of tobacco apiece for two days attendance at court, they having been subp[nd] at his request. (*Minute Bk. A*, f. 299, Lower Norfolk Co., Portsmouth, Va.)

In 1646 Thomas Todd, ship carpenter, gave his age as 36 years. (*Deeds B*, f. 34, Lower Norfolk Co., Va.) Thomas Todd, shipwright of Ann Arundell County, Maryland, so closely associated with Edward Dorsey and Thomas Hall, is thought to be the ship carpenter of Lower Norfolk County, Virginia.

On July 8, 1651, a 100-acre tract called Todd was laid out for Thomas Todd of Ann Arundell County, Shipwright, on the west side of Chesapeake Bay upon the Severn River, on the south side of the river, beginning at a marked white oak standing upon Oyster Shells Point running up the river to Deep Cove (later called Dorsey's Creek) bounded on the north with said creek, and on the west and south by Richard Acton's and Thomas Hall's lands and on the east with said river and Todd's Creek. (*Patents A.B.& H*, f. 258) (See page 5)

On October 27, 1651, there was laid out for Thomas Todd of Ann Arundell County, planter, 200 acres on the west side of Chesapeake Bay, adjoining the land of Leonard Guinns and bounded on the east by said bay. (*Ibid.*, f. 259)

He received a warrant for 1,040 acres of land the 23rd of July, 1658, for having transported a number of persons into the province, (*Patents Q*, f. 73) and in 1662 Todd's Range containing 120 acres was surveyed for him. (*Patents 13*, f. 40)

Thomas Todd was appointed Commissioner and Justice of Ann Arundell County in 1658. He was a commissioner and one of the Quorum in 1661, and on November 11th, as a commissioner, was present at the court. (*Arch. of Md.* XLI, 89; III, 424, 425)

Thomas Todd died intestate before 1671, at which time his son John was a minor under the guardianship of his brother Lancelot Todd and Cornelius Howard.

Children of Thomas and Elizabeth Todd:

1. Thomas[2] Todd, d. 1677, m. Sarah ______ (See page 193)
2. John Todd, d. 1677 unm. (*Test. Proc. 9*, f. 457)
3. Lancelot Todd, d. 1691
   m. bef. 1683 Sarah Phelps, dau. of Thomas

   The will of Lancelot Todd made February 30, 1690 and proved November 10, 1691 left:

   To kinsman Lancelot Todd, at 18 years of age, personalty
   To wife Sarah exrx, dwelling plantation
   To son John Todd and heirs, said land at death of wife, also ½ of Philk's Rest (Phelps Rest)
   To daughter Mary Todd, residue of Philk's Rest
   To daughter Elizabeth Todd, said land in event of death of daughter Mary without issue to pass in turn to daughters Sarah and Elinor
   To daughter Mary, afsd, personalty left her by aunt Elizabeth Howard
   Overseers: Jno. Hammond, Andrew Norwood
   Test: Jno. Dorsey, Hugh Bawden, Jno. Leary (*Wills 2*, f. 219)

Children of Lancelot and Sarah (Phelps) Todd:

1. John[3] Todd, d. July 11, 1733 (*St. Mrgts.*), m. 1710 Katherine Smith
2. Mary Todd
3. Elizabeth Todd
4. Sarah Todd, m. Apr. 10, 1705 Patrick Dare (*St. A.*)
5. Elinor Todd

THOMAS TODD

1. THOMAS[2] TODD (Thomas[1])
   d. 1677 Anne Arundel County
   m. Sarah ______

On October 16, 1670, a tract of 120 acres was surveyed for Thomas Todd on the west side of Chesapeake Bay on the south side of the Severn River, running down Todd's Creek. This land was called Todd's Harbour, now part of the Town of Annapolis. (*Patents 14*, f. 191)

Todd's Pasture was surveyed for Thomas Todd on November 16, 1674. This land lay in Todd's Neck, now Annapolis. (*Patents 19*, f. 122)

Thomas Todd died intestate. On April 18, 1677, Sarah Todd was granted administration on the estate of her husband Thomas Todd late of Ann Arundell County deceased.
(*Test. Proc. 9*, f. 54)

Sarah Todd, widow of Thomas, m. (2) William Stafford, who on September 24, 1678 was accused of wasting the orphan's estate. (*Test. Proc. 10*, f. 282)

An inquisition about the lands of Thomas Hall in 1679, which adjoined the tract called Todd, is of interest here.

Thomas Hall died in 1655 and was seized with 20 acres of land, lying near Anne Arundel River in Todd's Neck. This Thomas Hall left but one son Christopher, who appointed his mother Elizabeth Hall his sole heir. After the said Hall's death, Benjamin Record lived on the land 11 years, after which it was possessed and occupied by Thomas Todd, who procured a patent for said land in his own name, and since his death, by William Stafford, who doth receive the issues and profits therof and paid the rent for said land to his Lordships High Sheriffs, for the time being of Ann Arundel County. The court orders William Stafford to show at next provincial court why the grant should not be made void. As grants annulled and made void, returned to his Lordship, no chance was lost to procure them. Therefore, the court did not hesitate to claim one taken up dishonestly. The above record charges Thomas Todd as obtaining the patent surreptitiously. (*Arch. of Md.* LI. f. 267)

In 1679 William Stafford was living in Ann Arundell County. It is thought that Honor Stafford, who married John Dorsey of Edward, was related to this family of Staffords.

Children of Thomas and Sarah Todd:

1. Lancelot[3] Todd, b. 1674; d. 1735, m. Elizabeth Rockhould (See page 194)
2. Richard Todd, b. 1676; d. 1718, m. Margaret ______

   The will of Richard Todd, made October 10, 1718 and proved March 10, 1718 left:

   To eldest son Richard Todd, 50 acres of Whealler's Chance and 75 acres, a part of young Richard, being two tracts bought of Tytus Penniton. He dying without issue to go to son Lance
   To son Lance Todd, dwelling plantation at decease of wife. Should said son die without issue, to pass to nearest of blood
   To daughter Elizabeth Todd, silver porringer and 20 pounds
   To daughter Mary Todd, 12 pounds
   Residue of personal estate to two sons Richard and Lance and youngest daughter Anne.
   Exrx: wife Margaret Todd (*Wills 15*, f. 4)

Children of Richard and Margaret Todd:
(Births recorded in St. Margaret's Parish Register)

1. Elizabeth^4 Todd, b. Jan. 30, 1694
2. Mary Todd, b. Nov. 9, 1695, m. John Nickelson (*Accts. 2* f. 104)
3. Richard Todd, b. May 9, 1699, m. Mar. 3, 1727 Mary Stinchcomb
4. Lancelot Todd, b. Oct. 15, 1701; d. 1742 (*Wills 22,* f. 517)
   m. Oct. 11, 1727 Anna Burle
5. Anne Todd, b. Sept. 25, 1703

CAPTAIN LANCELOT TODD

1. CAPT. LANCELOT^3 Todd (Thomas,^{2} Thomas^1)
   b. 1674; d. 1735 Anne Arundel County
   m. Elizabeth Rockhould, d. 1741

In 1695 Lancelot Todd was paid 600 pounds of tobacco for building or repairing the Court House fence at Annapolis, and he was provincial grand juror in 1698.
(*Arch. of Md.* XIX, 201; XXIII, 530; XXV 9)

Lancelot Todd witnessed the will of his father-in-law, 1698, and he was executor of the will of Mary Rockhould, wife of John. (See page 202)

On April 12, 1698, Lancelot Todd conveyed to Samuel Norwood, 100 acres of Todd's Range on south side of Severn River. (*A.A. Co. Deeds W.H. No. 4,* f. 42) Soon after this he moved to Baltimore County, where in 1712 he was appointed overseer of highways.
(*Balt. Co. Ct. Rec. I.S.B,* f. 332)

On March 13, 1713, Lance Todd of Baltimore County conveyed to Thomas Bordly and Thomas 4
Larkin of Ann Arundell County, Todd's Pasture, 29 acres, Todd's Harbour, 120 acres, Todd's Range, 120 acres (except 100 acres sold to Samuel Norwood) and 100 acres surveyed July 8, 1651 for Thomas Todd on south side of Severn River. (*A.A. Co. Deeds I.B. No. 2,* f. 171)

Lance Todd of Baltimore County bought 300 acres out of a tract called Alltogether from Henry Ridgely of Ann Arundell County on March 15, 1720. (*A.A. Co. Deeds C.W. No. 1,* f. 268)

In 1724 Lancelot Todd was one of the Justices of Baltimore County. (*Balt, Ct. Minutes,* 1719-26) He returned to Ann Arundell County, where he was Justice from 1727 to 1732. He was appointed Captain in 1723 and as Capt. Lancelot Todd witnessed the will of John Gale, Ann Arundell County, in 1730.

On October 22, 1733, Lancelot Todd gave to his daughters Sarah, wife of Edward Dorsey, and Ruth, wife of Michael Dorsey, a tract of land called Alltogether, containing 300 acres, which he had purchased from Henry Ridgely in 1720. (*A.A. Co. Deeds R.D. No. 2,* f. 8)

The will of Lancelot Dorsey made May 6, 1735 and proved June 16, 1735 left:

To wife Elizabeth, dwelling plantation, Hope's Plain during her life, at her decease to son Thomas Todd during his life, at his decease to grandson Lance, and so to pass without being bought or sold
To said son Thomas Todd and heirs, Hunt's Range and personalty
To two sons Lance and John Todd and their heirs, Rebecker's Lott, having lately bought young Richard Colegate's right thereto of Daniel Dulany, and personalty
To son Nathan and heirs, Todd's Riske and personalty
To daughter Sarah Dorsey, a negro woman and her increase to be divided among said daughter Sarah's children, her daughter Elizabeth only excepted
To daughter Ruth Dorsey, personalty
To wife Elizabeth, certain personalty, including 49 pounds in hand of Edward Dorsey
To granddaughter Elizabeth Dorsey, personalty now in possession of Edward Dorsey, her father. Residue of estate to wife afsd and 3 sons, Lance, John, and Nathan, to be equally divided by Capt. Benjamin Howard and Edward Dorsey, son Nathan's portion to be in hands of mother until he arrives at age of 18 years. Land conveyed to children by two deeds of gift to stand as conveyed. (*Wills 21,* f. 368)

Elizabeth Todd, wife of Lancelot, was the daughter of John Rockhould and his wife Mary. Her will made June 19, 1741 and proved August 13, 1741 left her entire estate to daughters Sarah and Ruth Dorsey, sister Sabra Frizell, sons Lancelot, Nathan, John, and Thomas. Exrs: sons Thomas and Lancelot, John and Nathan, Edward and Michael Dorsey. (*Wills 22*, f. 373)

Children of Lancelot and Elizabeth (Rockhould) Todd: (See page 202)
(Named in parent's wills)

1. Thomas^4 Todd, m. Sophia ———
   Children: (Births records in St. Margaret's Parish Register)
   1. Elizabeth^5 Todd, b. Oct. 21, 1731
   2. Lancelot Todd, b. May 28, 1734
   3. Rachel Todd, b. June 2, 1736
   4. Ruth Todd, b. Sept. 25, 1739
   5. Thomas Todd, b. Mar. 17, 1741
   6. Peggy Todd, b. Mar. 1, 1746

2. Lancelot Todd, b. 1716 (*Chanc. Rec. W.K. No. 1*, f. 830); d. 1775
   m. Apr. 10, 1744 Eleanor Ford (*St. Mrgts*)
   Children: (St. Margaret's Parish Register)
   1. Mary Todd, b. Mar. 15, 1744/5
   2. Sarah Todd, b. July 10, 1746
   3. John Todd, b. Apr. 28, 1750
   4. Lancelot Todd, b. Nov. 2, 1754
3. John Todd, m. June 10, 1756 Elizabeth Linstead
4. Nathan Todd, d. 1770 (*Wills 38 Pt. 1*, f. 80), m. Apr. 10, 1766 Rebecca Boone
5. Sarah Todd, m. Edward Dorsey (See pages 144 and 145)
6. Ruth Todd, m. Michael Dorsey (See pages 80 and 81)

SIGNATURES OF LANCELOT TODD, SON OF THOMAS THE IMMIGRANT
AND LANCE AND NATHAN TODD, SONS OF CAPTAIN LANCELOT TODD
From Testamentary Papers Filed in the Hall of Records, Annapolis, Maryland

JOHN ELDER

JOHN ELDER

d. 1740 Anne Arundel County

m. by church bans October 19, 1708, Mary Morris, whom he had married by common law before that date. (*St. A.*); d. bef. 1740

On December 1, 1704, William Lazwell of Talbot County got a warrant for a fork of land in the Patuxent River in Anne Arundel County of 57 acres, but before getting the patent, he died, and it was given to his son John Lazwell. In 1707, he assigned the land to John Elder, who got a certificate of survey on it April 10, 1707, and patented it as Laxford.

(*Patents P.L. No. 6, f.* 628)

On March 13, 1717, John Elder, planter, bought 100 acres of Duvall's Delight, which was formerly surveyed by John Duvall. (*A.A. Co. Deeds I.B. No. 2, f.* 485)

In 1736, Addition to Huntington Quarter, a tract of 334 acres, surveyed June 18, 1736 for Joshua Dorsey and Henry Ridgely, was assigned to John Elder and patented to him.

(*Patents E.I. No. 1, f.* 506)

John Elder Sr. of Anne Arundel County conveyed to his son John Elder Jr., on the 15th of November, 1739, two tracts of land, Addition to Huntington Quarter and Laxford, in all 150 acres. (*A.A. Co. Deeds R.D. No. 3, f.* 205) (See page 57)

John Elder was a member of St. Anne's Church. He was a churchwarden in 1729 and in 1737, and with his son John occupied pew No. 25.

The will of John Elder made December 29, 1740 and proved March 11, 1740 left:

To son Alexander Elder, 100 acres of Addition to Huntington Quarter
To son James Elder, 100 acres dwelling plantation Duvall's Delight, 41 acres Laxford
To son Charles Elder, 100 acres Addition to Huntington Quarter
To Sarah Green, an orphan, personalty
To children, Alexander, James, Charles, and Mary, residue of estate
Exrs: sons Alexander and James Elder
Test: Richard Davis, Orlando Griffith, Edward Penn, Catherine Scott

(*Wills 22, f.* 391)

Children of John and Mary (Morris) Elder:
(Named in father's will and in deed of 1739)

1. John[2] Elder, bapt. Oct. 14, 1708 (*St. A.*), m. Jemima Dorsey (See page 56)
2. Alexander Elder, b. Nov. 29, 1711 (*St. A.*); d. Apr. 8, 1762 unm.
   Barbarously killed by his negro man Pompey (*Md. Gaz.*)
   His inventory taken May 16, 1762 gives John Elder and James Elder as kindred
   (*Invts. 80, f.* 331)
3. Charles Elder, bapt. Sept. 2, 1716, (*St. A.*); d. bef. 1752 (*Invts. 48, f.* 241)
   m. Ruth ——
4. James Elder, d. 1767/8, m. Rachel ——; d. 1772
   The inventory of James Elder was appraised by Nicholas Dorsey and Greenberry Griffith, March 25, 1768, Kindred, Rachel Elder and son James Elder Jr.
   (*Invts. 99, f.* 145)
   An account of November 15, 1769 shows representative Rachel Elder, the widow, and eight children. (*Bal. Bk.* 15) The will of Rachel Elder proved in 1772 mentions children Charles, Mary, Penn, Owen, and John. (*Wills 38, Pt. 2, f.* 772)
5. Mary Elder

MATTHEW HOWARD

MATTHEW HAYWARD - HOWARD

d. about or after 1650 probably in Maryland

m. Ann ______

Matthew Hayward was granted 150 acres of land in Lower County of New Norfolk, Virginia, May 26, 1638, on the west branch of Elizabeth River and north upon the broad creek running out of said branch, due for transporting his wife Ann and two other persons.

(*Patents 1, Pt. 2,* f. 561, State of Va.)

On February 8, 1637, Robert Taylor was granted 100 acres of land in New Norfolk County being two necks of land on the west branch of the Elizabeth River, bounded on the west side with Matthew Howard's land. (*Ibid.,* f. 516)

At a Court held at William Shipps the 6th of July, 1640, it appeareth to the Court, that Eady Hanking hath spoken reproachful words against the wife of Matthew Haward, which she cannot prove; It is therefore ordered that the said Eady Hankin shall ask the said Haward's wife forgiveness both at the house of Mr. William Julian on Friday next and also at the Parish Church the Sunday following, and defray the charges of the Court. (*Va. Hist. Mag.* XL, 41)

Simon Peeter age 28 years deposeth that he heard Eady Hanking say that Matthew Hayward's wife did live as brave a life as any woman in Virginia for she could lie abed every morning until her husband went a milking and came back again and washed the dishes and skimmed the milk, and then Mr. Edward Floide would come in and say, "Come neighbor, will you walk?" and so they went abroad and left the children crying. That her husband was fain to come and leave his work to quiet the children and further this deponant sayeth not. (*Ibid.,* f. 43)

On the 6th of November 1646, Matthew Howard and Robert Bowers asked for the administration on the estate of Robert Jones, who died intestate. It was granted them by William Berkley. (*Lower Norfolk Co. Ct. Rec.* 1636-46, f. 24)

On June 10, 1649, the will of Edward Hodge was witnessed by Matthew His M H Mark Howard

(*Norfolk Co. Va. Wills B,* f. 119)

The will of Richard Hall dated August 1, 1648 and proved November 16, 1649 left:

To Matthew Howard the elder, 1 yearling calf
To Ann Howard, a cow calf and a barrow shote
Elizabeth Howard, 2 cows and all their increase and a sow
Matthew Howard the younger, a sow shote
Cornelius Howard, a sow and my hat
John Howard, my wig and new clothes
Samuel Howard, my money and tobacco
Old Matthew, my best payr of breeches
Thomas Pill, my boulsters etc.
Exr: Matthew Howard ye elder
Wit: Cornelius Lloyd, Thomas Pill (*Norfolk Co. Va. Wills B,* f. 96)

In 1650 Matthew Howard received of Wm Seba 15 pounds of tobacco. (*Deeds B,* f. 163 Lower Norfolk Co., Portsmouth, Va.)

On July 3, 1650, he was in Maryland, where a tract of 350 acres called Howard was laid out for Matthew Howard of Ann Arundell County, planter, lying on the south side of the River Severn near a creek called Marshes Creek, beginning at a Hollow in the said creek and extending south of the creek and a swamp called Howard's Swamp. There was also laid out for him 45 acres adjoining the above tract on the east, and 255 acres south of Howard's Swamp lying on the west, all containing 650 acres. (*Patents A.B.& H,* f. 258) (See page 5)

Matthew Howard died before this tract was patented and it was later absorbed in other tracts.

Not all of the children of Matthew Howard were named in the will of Richard Hall and there is no assurance that they were all by his wife Ann, who was brought into Virginia by Matthew in 1638. However, it is known there were children in 1640 when Eady Hanking defamed the character of Matthew Hayward's wife.

Children of Matthew Howard:
(First six named in will of Richard Hall)

1. Matthew[2] Howard, d. 1692 (*Wills 2, f.* 222) (See page 177)
   m. Sarah Darcy (See page 176)

   Children:

   1. John[3] Howard, d. 1702, m. Susannah Rockhould
   2. Matthew Howard, d. 1701 unm.
   3. Sarah Howard, d. 1726, m. (1) John Worthington, m. (2) John Brice
   4. Samuel Howard, d. bef. 1691

2. Capt. Cornelius Howard, d. 1680 (*Wills 2, f.* 207) (See page 199A)
   m. Elizabeth ______

   Children named in father's will:

   1. Joseph Howard, m. Hannah Dorsey (See page 33)
   2. Cornelius Howard, d. 1716 (*Wills 14, f.* 275)
      m. Mary Hammond, dau. of Maj. Genl John
   3. Sarah Howard
   4. Mary Howard, d. unm.
   5. Elizabeth Howard, m. (1) Andrew Norwood (See page 205)
      m. (2) Andrew Wellplay m. (3) Charles Kilbourne

3. John Howard, d. 1696 (*Wills 7, f.* 164) (See page 199A)
   m. (1) Susannah Stevens, widow of Charles, d. 1658
   John Howard on May 30, 1666 demanded 600 acres of land due Charles Stevens for having brought 12 persons into the Province of Maryland, himself, Susannah, their children, Elizabeth, Susan, Sarah, and Charles and six others. John Howard demanded this land in the right of his wife Susannah Howard, the relict of Charles Stevens. (*Patents 9, f.* 448)
   Child named in father's will:
   John Howard, d. 1703 (*Wills 11, f.* 420)
   m. (1) Mary Warfield, dau. of Richard and Eleanor
   m. (2) Catherine (Greenberry) Ridgely, widow of Henry, d. 1700 (*Wills 11, f.* 371)
   m. (2) Eleanor Maccubbin, widow of John, d. 1711 (*Test. Proc. 15A, f.* 5)

4. Samuel Howard, d. 1703 (*Wills 11, f.* 396) (See page 199A)
   m. Catherine ______

   Children named in father's will:

   1. Phillip Howard, d. 1705 intestate
   2. Susan Howard
   3. Ruth Howard

5. Ann Howard
   m. James Greniffe, d. 1694 (*Wills 11*, f. 115)

   Children named in father's will:

   1. John Greniffe, d. 1708/9 (*Wills 12*, f. 323)
      m. Ruth Dorsey, widow of Edward, d. 1700/1 (See page 140)
   2. James Greniffe
   3. Samuel Greniffe, d. 1703 unm. (*Wills 11*, f. 340)
   4. Hannah Greniffe

6. Elizabeth Howard, d. bef. 1669
   m. Henry Ridgely, d. 1710 (*Wills 13*, f. 89) (*Warrants 7*, f. 461)
   He m. (2) Sarah ____ (Bible of Nicholas Ridgely)
   m. (3) Mary (Stanton) Duvall, widow of Mareen
   (*Prov. Ct. Judg. T.L. No. 1*, f. 727) No issue.

   Children named in father's will:

   1. Charles Ridgely
   2. Sarah Ridgely, m. Thomas Odall
   3. Henry Ridgely, b. 1669, son of Sarah (Bible of Nicholas Ridgely)

7. Phillip Howard, d. 1701 (*Wills 11*, f. 153)
   m. Ruth Baldwin, dau. of John (*Wills 4*, f. 43)

   Child named in father's will:

   Hannah Howard, m. (1) Charles Hammond
   m. (2) Aug. 15, 1714 Edward Benson (*St. A.*)

8. Mary Howard, d. 1721 (*Wills 16*, f. 366)
   m. Maj. Genl John Hammond, d. 1707 (*Wills 12*, f. 184)

   Children named in father's will:

   1. Charles Hammond, d. 1713 (*Wills 13, f. 608*), m. Hannah Howard
   2. Thomas Hammond, d. 1724 (*Wills 18*, f. 350)
      m. (1) Rebecca (Larkin) Lightfoot, widow of Thomas
      m. (2) Mary Heath
   3. John Hammond, d. 1742 (*Wills 23*, f. 7)
      m. Anne Greenberry, dau. of Col. Nicholas
   4. William Hammond, d. intestate 1711
      m. Elizabeth Cockey, d. 1731 (*Wills 20*, f. 286)
      who m. (2) July 15, 1713 James Govane (*St. Mrgts.*)
   5. Mary Hammond, m. Cornelius Howard
      Sons were named in Mary Howard's will

9. Henry Howard, d. 1684 (*Wills 4*, f. 25) (See page 199A)
   Near relative, probably a son

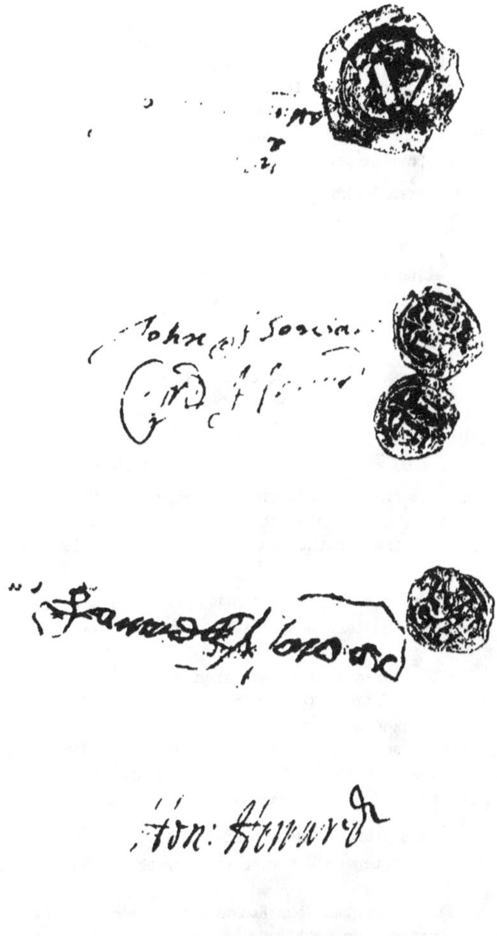

SIGNATURES OF SONS OF MATTHEW HOWARD, THE IMMIGRANT
From Testamentary Papers Filed in the Hall of Records
Annapolis, Maryland

ROBERT ROCKHOULD

ROBERT ROCKHOULD

d. bef. July 30, 1666 Anne Arundel County

m. Sarah ______

Robert Rockhould was seated upon 250 acres of land in Nansemond County, Virginia, before the 3rd of November, 1647. He came to Maryland about 1649.

(Nugent, *Cavaliers & Pioneers*, folios 134,203,268)

On August 26, 1651, Robert Rockhould and John Scotcher were granted 400 acres of land in Calvert County, Maryland, on top of the Cliffs, the former having transported himself, his wife Sarah, and his two sons, Robert and Thomas, into the province to inhabit. This land was laid out for Robert Rockhould, gunsmith, and John Scotcher, cooper. They are also named as being of Ann Arundell County October 23, 1651. (*Patents 4*, f. 94) (*Patents 5*, f. 53)

Children of Robert and Sarah Rockhould:

1. Robert[2] Rockhould, d. after 1672
2. Thomas Rockhould
3. John Rockhould, called an orphan in 1666, m. Mary Richardson
4. Ann Rockhould, m. (1) Stephen White, d. 1676
   m. (2) William Hawkins

JOHN ROCKHOULD

JOHN[2] ROCKHOULD - ROCKHOLD (ROBERT[1])

b. bef. 1638; d. 1704

m. Mary Richardson, d. 1704

On September 7, 1659, the tract, Rockhould, formerly surveyed for Robert Rockhould and John Scotcher in Calvert County was granted to John Rockhould and his brother Robert Rockhould. In 1672 it was resurveyed for them as the boundary trees had fallen down.

(*Patents 16*, f. 608)

On July 30, 1666, a tract of 90 acres on Scotcher's Creek was laid out for John Rockhould of Ann Arundell County, orphan, the land upon which he was then living, called Rich Neck.

(*Patents 10*, f. 235)

In 1667 a warrant for 100 acres of land was granted John Rockhould, which in 1669, he made over to William Hopkins. (*Patents 12*, f. 358)

On July 10, 1676, John Rockhould bought Richardson's Levell containing 207 acres on Salt-peter Creek from Thomas Richardson, son of Lawrence, (*Balt. Co. Rent Rolls*) and also 200 acres of Richardson's Folly surveyed June 19, 1661 for Lawrence Richardson on the South River, Later he bought Burntwood Common. (*A.A. Co. Rent Rolls*)

In 1684 Henry Hemslay, Ann Arundell County assigned to John Rockhould, gent, Rockhould's Range on the north side of the Patapsco River on Rich Creek. (*Patents 22*, f. 9)

A warrant of 583 acres was granted John Rockhould in 1695, out of which 243 acres were surveyed into Rockhould's Purchase on Curtis Creek on July 10, 1676, and 180 acres into Rockhould's Search on the south side of the Patapsco River. (*Balt. Co. Rent Rolls*)

In 1679 he was a witness for Edward Dorsey in his suit against Thomas Bland, and he and his son John Rockhould Jr. witnessed the will of Joshua Dorsey in 1687. Their signatures are reproduced

The will of John Rockhould proved February 17, 1698 left:

To son Thomas Rockhould and heirs, Rockhould's Purchase on Curtis Creek, Baltimore County
To son Charles Rockhould and heirs, 207 acres of Richardson's Levell on Salt Peter Creek, Baltimore County
To son Jacob Rockhould and heirs, 180 acres of Rockhould's Search on south side of Patapsco River
To wife Mary, executrix, dwelling plantation and Burntwood Common, during her life, to revert to her son Jacob at her decease
To two cousins (nephews) Stephen White and William Hawkins Jr., personalty
Sons desired not to sell land until reaching age of 30 years
Test: Lancelot Todd, Nathan Dorton and Thomas Ward. (*Wills 6, f.* 202)

Mary Rockhould, after her husband's death, wrote to Edward Batson, Depty Comm., on January 25, 1698.

"Mr. Batson,
Sir
These are to request you are not to give letters of administration to any one for Nat Dotton's estate until I have seen you or sent you a ring.
All in trouble from your friend to command
Mary Rockhould"
(*Test. Proc. 17, f.* 267)

Mary Rockhould was the daughter of Lawrence and Elizabeth Richardson, and sister of Sarah Richardson, who married (1) Joshua Dorsey, and (2) Thomas Blackwell. She was named in her father's will in 1666, (*Wills 1, f.* 276) and she was left 15 pounds Sterling in the will of her brother-in-law Thomas Blackwell in 1700. (*Wills 11, f.* 13) (See page 123)

The will of Mary Rockhould made March 2, 1703 and proved May 15, 1704 left:

To daughter Mary Rockhould, ten pounds
To son Charles and Jacob Rockhould, each ten pounds
To daughters Susan Crouch and Elizabeth Todd, 5 pounds each
To daughter Sebrah Rockhould, a feather bed and furniture
To son Thomas Rockhould, all my sheep
I give to Lance Tod my spaid Mare toads paying my debts
To my son Lance Todd, my tobacco made on my plantation last year and all that is on board the ship, with the rent of the said land that John Young owes me and all other tobacco debts, said Lance to pay my debts withall, and all the rent that shall be due in the next four years. Two sons Charles and Jacob to live with my son Lance Todd until they arrive at the age of 18 years.
Exr: Lance Todd (*Wills 3, f.* 248)

Children of John and Mary (Richardson) Rockhould:
(Named in parent's wills)

1. John[3] Rockhould, Jr. old enough to witness will of Joshua Dorsey, 1687; d. bef. 1698
2. Thomas Rockhould, living in 1704
3. Charles Rockhould, m. Elizabeth Wright, dau. of Henry
4. Jacob Rockhould
5. Susanna Rockhould, m. (1) John Howard, (2) William Crouch, (3) James Smith (See page 178) Her signature appears below.
6. Elizabeth Rockhould, d. 1741, m. Lancelot Todd (See pages 194 and 195)
7. Sebra Rockhould, m. Abraham Frizzell
8. Sarah Rockhould, m. 1704 John Garner (*St. A.*)
   She was named in the will of Samuel Greniff (son of James and Ann Howard)August 14, 1703. (*Wills 11, f.* 340) (See page 199)

CAPTAIN JOHN NORWOOD

CAPTAIN JOHN NORWOOD

d. 1672 Anne Arundel County

m. Ann ____; d. 1674

John Norwood arrived in Lower Norfolk County, Virginia, some time before August 15, 1645, for on this date a certificate of land was granted Mr. Math: Phillips on the behalf of Henry Seawell an Orphant for the transportation of twenty persons, among them John Norwood. (*New Eng. Hist. Gen. Reg.* Vol. 47, f. 64)

He was a member of the Elizabeth River Church, and on the 10th of August, 1648, was ordered to render an account of the Glebe lands since Parson Harrison had deserted his ministerial office and refused to administer the sacraments with the church of England. So much dissatisfaction had arisen within the church that many members refused to attend, among them John Norwood, Richard Owings, Thomas Marsh, who were presented to the board by the Sheriff. It was partly for freedom of worship that these men left Virginia for the newly-established county of Ann Arundell, Maryland.

In 1650 John Norwood transported his two sons John and Andrew into the Province of Maryland, and in 1756 he brought in his servant Elizabeth Fletcher. For their transportation, he received 230 acres of land called Norwood, lying on the west side of Chesapeake Bay, on the south side of the Severn River on Norwood's Cove, November 3, 1658. (*Patents Q*, f. 396)

A warrant for 400 acres was granted John Norwood and Edward Dorsey of Ann Arundell County in 1651, (*Patents 11*, f. 98) and that same year on the 27th of October, a 200-acre tract called Norwood was surveyed for John Norwood in Calvert County adjoining the land of Thomas Mears, its southernmost boundary extending to the tract later known as Theobush Manning owned by Edward Dorsey and Thomas Manning. This land, which was due John Norwood for transporting himself and wife into the province, was patented August 3, 1658. (*Patents Q*, f. 78) Thus it is seen that these two men had adjoining tracts in both Ann Arundell and Calvert Counties. (See page 1)

In 1659 John Norwood demanded land for bringing in 4 persons, and 20 acres of land due for the transportation of his servant Elizabeth Fletcher in 1657, and a few weeks later Norwood's Fancy containing 400 acres, lying on the south side of the Severn River on the west side of Round Bay, and 100 acres called The Intacke, on the south side of the Severn River and the west side of Darcys Creek, were surveyed for him. (*Patents 4*, folios 258, 257)(See page 5

On February 15, 1661, he entered rights for transporting 6 persons into the province. (*Patents 5*, f. 90)

John Norwood was appointed Sheriff of Ann Arundell County in 1655, which office he held for a number of years. In 1661 a commission was granted to Capt. John Norwood to command all the forces from the head of Ann Arundell River on the north side thereof to the south side of the Patapsco River. In 1662 he was Justice of Ann Arundell County. (*Arch. of Md.* III, 318, 348, 444, 449)

He died intestate in 1672.

The administration of the estate of Capt. John Norwood was granted to Ann Norwood his widow on June 19, 1672. (*Test. Proc. 5*, f. 290) His estate was appraised by Thomas Marsh and John Bennet on November 20, 1672. The inventory included articles in the Inner Room, Mrs. Norwood's Room, Outer Room, Kitchen, the Outer Room containing Capt. Norwood's wearing apparel. (*Invts. & Accts. 5*, f. 383)

Ann Norwood, widow of Capt. John, m. (2) 1672/3 James Boyd.

In 1673 Andrew Norwood son and heir to John Norwood late of Ann Arundell County, deceased, petitions this court, that whereas his father was in his life time possessed of considerable land, and his father had left behind him seaven children, the said Andrew being the eldest, that the said Andrew's mother Ann Norwood took letters of Administration and afterwards married James Boyd a young man, and the said Boyd and said Ann took over the administration and did order you petitioner out of doors,

The petitioner being loath to go to law with his own mother and thereupon to convey further trouble, he therefore prayes that his mother be given her third by the high sheriff, and your petitioner be given the share that belongs to him. (*Prov. Ct. Rec. M.M.* f. 129)

Ann Boyd, wife of James, died in 1674 intestate.

On November 28, 1674, James Boyd submitted the inventory of Capt. John Norwood, and on the same day the inventory of his wife, Ann, was taken by William Jones and John Benson. It included a debt of 130 pounds of tobacco owed by John Dorsey.

(*Invts. & Accts.* folios 142, 145)

The account of James Boyd of Ann Arundell County, administrator of John Norwood late of said county deceased intestate, administered by Ann Boyd the relict of said Norwood, was filed December 20, 1674. (*Invts. & Accts. 1,* f. 159)

In 1674 James Boyd of Ann Arundell County, administrator of the goods and chattels of Ann Boyd his wife, late widow and administratrix of John Norwood deceased, came into Court and showed that of the 21,751 pounds of tobacco from Capt. John Norwood's estate, Ann's portion of one-third was 7,250 pounds and the two-thirds to which the children were entitled was 14,501 pounds. (*Test. Proc. 7,* f. 58)

In 1675 Andrew Norwood on behalf of himself and the other orphans of Capt. John Norwood again petitioned the court. Andrew contended that the said James Boyd made it appear when he presented the 21,751 pounds of tobacco to the court that he had finished the administration of the estate of John Norwood, when it should have included cattle and other things and 9,000 pounds of tobacco obtained in a Judgment against Dr. Neal. Andrew asked for that amount and the cattle and other things, and that he be appointed to make the division.

The judge upon search of the records found that Ann Norwood took administration of the goods and chattels of her husband June 17, 1672,and that the commission was issued to Robert Burle to take bond for 50,000 pounds of tobacco, and that the said Ann the 13th of November following, when the administration of the goods and chattels of Jacob Neal by Thomas Marsh showed the said Norwood's account against Neal was 8,933 pounds of tobacco due the said John Norwood's estate, failed to include this in her inventory on November 20, 1672, and therefore the said Boyd cannot be charged with the bond of Ann Norwood. (*Test. Proc. 7,* f. 123)

Children of John and Ann Norwood:
(Known children)

1. Andrew[2] Norwood, d. Mar. 1, 1701, m. Elizabeth Howard
2. John Norwood, d. 1673, m. Elizabeth ______
3. Phillip Norwood, d. Jan. 1724, m. Hannah ______
4. Samuel Norwood, d. 1709, m. Sarah ______

Other children thought to be theirs)

5. Joseph Norwood, d. 1684
6. Edward Norwood, d. 1699

ANDREW NORWOOD

1. ANDREW[2] NORWOOD (Capt. John[1])

b. c 1634; d. Mar. 1, 1701 (*St. A.*) Anne Arundel County

m. Elizabeth Howard

Andrew Norwood was over 16 years of age when brought into Maryland by his father in 1650, for 100 acres of land was granted for his transportation.

As the eldest son of his father, who died intestate, he came into possession of 230 acres of Norwood, surveyed for his father November 3, 1658, and also the tract called The Intacke. These lands were later held by Andrew Wellplay for Norwood's Orphans. (*A.A. Co. Rent Rolls*)

On June 22, 1683, a tract of 103 acres called Norwood's Angles was surveyed for Andrew Norwood, lying on the branch of Todd's Creek, and on June 6, 1686, Norwood's Recovery of 104 acres. (*A.A. Co. Rent Rolls*) Later he purchased Proctor's Chance, a tract of 30 acres from Robert Proctor. (*A.A. Co. Deeds I.H. No. 1*, f. 222)

A warrant was granted him in 1683 for land that had been previously granted to George Yates and Robert Jones. (*Warrants W.G. No. 4*, f. 393)

Andrew Norwood's name appears as overseer and witness on a number of wills executed in Ann Arundell County. The following signature is found on the administration bond of Michael Cusick, 1687.

The will of Andrew Norwood made December 23, 1701 and proved March 7, 1701/2 left:

To brothers Samuel and Phillip Norwood, personalty
To son Andrew Norwood at 17 years of age, dwelling plantation
Exrs: wife unnamed and brother Samuel
Desires Strawberry Plain to be sold
Test: Cornelius Howard, Phillip Howard Jr., Geo. Sleicom (*Wills 11*, f. 174)

The will of Andrew Norwood did not name his daughters. That this was not intentional is indicated by the testimony of John Beale, his son-in-law in 1711.

> "In 1701 Andrew Norwood lay upon his death bed sick and languishing with a lingering illness. He wanted his estate divided equally between his children, his son and four daughters, his wife to have her part. His real estate was to be sold and the money divided. He loved his children with a great tenderness, and was never guilty of so much fondness for his wife as to suffer her to exclude his children."
> (*Chanc. Rec. C.D*, f. 825)

There was much litigation over the settlement of his estate.

On June 22, 1734, Elizabeth Beale, Ann Norwood and Hannah Norwood coheirs of Andrew Norwood, for divers causes and 5 sh in hand paid by Wm Yeadhall grandson and heir at law of Wm Yeadhall and Jane his wife, Eldest daughter of John Sisson of said county granted a quit claim deed unto said Wm Yeadhall grandson and to his heirs from all the estate, right claim in land called Norwood's Fancy, which our brother Andrew Norwood did not confer unto Wm Yeadhall of said county, aforesaid, the father of the first Wm Yeadhall, which land was formerly possessed by John Sisson.
Wit: Vachel Denton, Thos. Worthington (*A.A. Co. Deeds R.D. No. 2*, f. 204)

Elizabeth Norwood, widow of Andrew, was the daughter of Cornelius and Elizabeth Howard. She was named in the will of her father in 1680 and also in the will of her uncle Samuel Howard. (*Wills 11*, f. 396) (See page 198)

Children of Andrew and Elizabeth (Howard) Norwood:
(Named in father's will and in other records)

1. Andrew[3] Norwood, d. bef. 1734 without issue
In 1701 he inherited his father's dwelling plantation, and in 1708 a tract of 500 acres from his step-father. In 1718 he bought Blackwell's Search from John Dorsey. (*Balt. Co. Deeds T.R. No. A*, f. 504)

2. Elizabeth Norwood, d. Nov. 7, 1753 (*Md. Gaz.*)
m. Aug. 19, 1708 John Beale (*St. A.*); d. 1734 (*Wills 21*, f. 114)

Children:

1. Elizabeth[4] Beale, b. June 8, 1711 (*St. A.*); d. 1776
m. (1) May 22, 1729 William Nicholson, d. 1731 (*Wills 20*, f. 306)
m. (2) Richard Dorsey of Caleb (See page 164)
2. Thomas Beale, b. Mar. 3, 1714; bur. Sept. 3, 1717 (*St. A.*)
3. Ann Beale, b. Apr. 16, 1716; d. 1776 (*Wills 40*, f. 697)
m. Thomas Rutland, d. 1773 (*Wills 39*, f. 454)

3. Hannah Norwood, living in 1776. Mentioned as aunt in Ann Rutland's will, 1776, and as kinswoman in the will of William Nicholson, 1731
4. Ann Norwood, unm. in 1734, left personalty by William Nicholson, 1731

Elizabeth Norwood, widow of Andrew, m. (2) Andrew Wellplay, for whom on April 2, 1706, a tract of 500 acres called St. Albens was surveyed, which land was patented to Ann and Hannah Norwood. (*A.A. Co. Rent Rolls*)

The will of Andrew Wellplay proved July 14, 1708 left:

To Andrew Norwood, 500 acres at head of Bush River
To daughter-in-law Elizabeth Norwood, personalty
Exrs: wife Elizabeth, residuary legatee
Test: Cornelius Howard, Joseph Howard, Sam[1] Dorsey, Sam[1] Leatherwood
(*Wills 11*, f. 397)

The property of Andrew Wellplay went to Elizabeth Beale, Ann and Hannah Norwood, after the death of their brother Andrew. (*Chanc. Rec. P.L. No. 5*, f. 558)

Elizabeth Wellplay, widow of Andrew, m. (3) Charles Kilbourne (*Chanc. Rec. C.D. No. 2*, f. 825)

JOHN NORWOOD

2. JOHN[2] NORWOOD (Capt. John[1])
b. c 1638; d. 1673 Calvert County
m. Elizabeth ______

John Norwood was under 16 years of age when brought into Maryland by his father in 1650. He was one of those who took the oath as a juror December 11, 1671 in Calvert County, when an inquisition into the lands of Peter Johnson was held. Those taking the oath with him were Samuel Taylor, brother of Robert, and Michael Higgins. (*Arch. of Md.* LI, 68)

John Norwood's nuncupative will proved February 6, 1763 left:

To son (unnamed) all real estate
To wife Elizabeth, all personaly property
Test: Wm Singleton (*Wills 1*, f. 578)

On February 6, 1673, Elizabeth Norwood of Calvert County, administratrix of John Norwood late of Calvert County deceased, stated that her husband had made a nuncupative will, which she presents to the court and desires the same to be proved by witnesses.

Wm Singleton sayd that John Norwood desired him to make the will. He asked said John to whom he wanted to leave his land and he announced to his son and heir. When asked to whom he wanted to leave the rest of his estate, he immediately said to my wife.

Michael Higgins deposed that on the last day of June he was with the said John Norwood and reminded him to put his will in writing and he answered another time, saying that he would leave his lands to his child and the rest of his estate to his wife.

Letters of administration were granted to his wife Elizabeth Norwood.

(*Test. Proc. 6, f.* 80)

The inventory was taken April 6, 1674 by Michael Higgins and Wm Singleton.

(*Invts. & Accts. 6, f.* 202)

Children of John and Elizabeth Norwood:

1. John[3] Norwood, d. c 1700, m. Sarah Dorsey (See page 27)
2. Mary Norwood, b. after death of her father

Robert Taylor of Calvert County, in his will of 1681, named his wife Mary, and left to his cousin Mary Sidberry, personalty, and to John and Mary Norwood, a cow and yearling apiece, which were to runne on his plantation, Taylor's Rest. These cattle were to go to John and Mary at his death, and they were to have the increase of the cattle. If either John or Mary died before coming of age, the cattle were to go to the survivor. (*Wills 4, f.* 73)

From the will of Robert Taylor and the land records, it seems probable that Elizabeth Norwood, widow of John, m. (2) c 1673 Robert Taylor.

Elizabeth died before 1677, at which date Robert Taylor married Mary Allen, widow of Jasper, who died 1676.

PHILLIP NORWOOD

3. PHILLIP[2] NORWOOD (Capt. John[1])
Buried Jan. 6, 1724 (*St. A.*)
m. June 2, 1704 Hannah ______ (*St. A.*)

Howard's Rest containing 80 acres, which had been surveyed February 20, 1665 for John Howard on the south side of the Severn River, was possessed by Phillip Norwood.

(*A.A. Co. Rent Rolls*)

On November 11, 1698, Phillip and Samuel Norwood complained that the Lord Baltimore agents had turned their tenant out of a certain tract of land and kept the same against him pretending the same is escheated although no offense found. (*Arch. of Md.* XXV, 27)

Phillip and Hannah Norwood were testators of the will of Francis Wasely of Anne Arundel County in 1722

SAMUEL NORWOOD

4. SAMUEL[2] NORWOOD (Capt. John[1])
d. 1709 Anne Arundel County
m. Sarah ______

Samuel owned 100 acres called Acton, surveyed November 15, 1651 for Richard Acton near the Severn River, and also 400 acres of a tract called Woodyard, surveyed October 15, 1663 for John Howard and Charles Stephens. (*A.A. Co. Rent Rolls*)

On April 12, 1698, Samuel Norwood purchased from Lancelot Todd a tract called Todd's Range containing 100 acres, (*A.A. Co. Deeds W.H. No. 4, f.* 42) and the 15th of March, 1705/6, he bought 200 acres of Major's Choice from Samuel Dorsey. (*Prov. Ct. Rec. T.L. No. 2, f.* 901) He also possessed 20 acres of the Town of Annapolis.

Samuel Norwood was appointed overseer of highways in the Lower part of Middle Neck Hundred in 1702. (*A.A. Co. Judg. G, f.* 40) In 1705 he was a vestryman of St. Anne's Church, and the 15th of April, 1707, he petitioned the court on behalf of John Acton, an orphan boy.

(*Arch. of Md.* XXVII, 44)

The will of Samuel Norwood made November 21, 1706 and proved June 12, 1709 left:

To daughter Anne and heirs, personalty including that given her by her uncle Phillip Norwood at 16 years of age or marriage
To unborn child at 18 years, personalty and brother Phillip's personalty including that bequeathed testator by brother Andrew Norwood
To cousin Andrew Norwood, personalty
Land and dwelling plantation Tod's Range to be sold for benefit of wife and child or children
To unborn child, if son, tract Major's Choice, Baltimore County, lately bought from Samuel Dorsey, if a daughter, land to be disposed of for benefit of estate
Exrx: wife Sarah Norwood
Test: Geo. Valentine, John Beal, Ed. Benson, (*Wills 12, Pt. 2, f.* 68)

Children of Samuel and Sarah Norwood:
(Births recorded in St. Anne's Parish Register)

1. Anne[3] Norwood, b. Jan. 30, 1702
2. Sarah Norwood, b. Dec. 9, 1706; d. 1717 (*St. A.*)
3. Samuel Norwood, b. Nov. 26, 1705; bur. Apr. 2, 1706 (*St. A.*)
4. Samuel Norwood, bapt. Jan. 22, 1708

Sarah Norwood, widow of Samuel, was mentioned in the will of Amos Garrett on February 12, 1714.

Sarah Norwood, gentlewoman, Ann Arundel County, m. (2) March 4, 1714 George Mansell, gentleman, Anne Arundel County. (*St. John's* Piscattaway, Pr. Geo. Co.) (*Vestry Proc. St. Anne's Church, Md. Hist. Mag.* VI, 337)

JOSEPH NORWOOD

5. JOSEPH[2] NORWOOD (Capt. John[1])
d. 1684 Kent County, Maryland

There is nothing to show the land on which Joseph Norwood lived in Ann Arundel County, though he received a warrant for 50 acres in 1683. (*Warrants W.C. No. 4, f.* 383)

On September 10, 1681, Joseph Norwood petitioned the court for a better allowance to be made him being Master of the Generals Sloop Six weeks at the Eastern Shore for which they had allowed him only 400 pounds of tobacco, which petition was endorsed. That same year he was paid 400 pounds of tobacco, then 600 pounds. He was also paid 70 pounds of tobacco due him, while Andrew Norwood was paid 60 pounds. (*Arch. of Md.* VII, 163,213,209,252)

In 1682, as dorrkeeper of the Upper House, he was paid 800 pounds of tobacco. The same year he was paid 120 pounds tobacco, and 800 pounds.

On October 2, 1685, he was admitted as Dorrkeeper of the Lower House.
(*Ibid.*, 327,444,523)

Joseph Norwood of Anne Arundel County, on May 11, 1682, petitioned the court stating that being an inhabitant of Severn River and having several conveniences there to keep a Ferry and the consent and approbation of most of the inhabitants there, he had ferryed over several of the inhabitants of said county. A commission was issued. (*Arch. of Md.* XVII, 123)

Joseph Norwood died in 1684 intestate.

His inventory was taken in 1684. (*Invts. & Accts. 6, f.* 157)

EDWARD NORWOOD

6. EDWARD[2] NORWOOD (Capt. John[1])
d. bef. 1699 Baltimore County

His name is listed among those indebted to Thomas Hedge, merchant Patapsco Hundred of Baltimore County in 1699, and is recorded as "dead, no effects". He is assumed to be the son of Capt. John Norwood. (*Balt. Co. Adm. Accts. 1, f.* 49)

From this Edward Norwood is thought to descend Edward Norwood of the Patapsco River. (See page 208)

EDWARD[3] NORWOOD (Edward,[2] Capt. John[1])

d. bef. 1729 Baltimore County

m. Ruth Owings

In 1717 Edward Norwood of the Patapsco River, Baltimore County was attorney for Joseph Wheeler of Bristol. (*Balt. Co. Deeds I.S. No. G,* f. 22) With John Israel he appraised the estate of Nicholas Dorsey in 1719.

Norwood's Discovery of 100 acres was surveyed for him in 1720, and on July 6, 1722, Ruth's Lot containing 100 acres was surveyed for Edward Norwood of Baltimore County on the north side of the Patapsco River. (*Balt. Co. Rent Rolls*)

In 1719 he registered his mark for his cattle. (*Balt. Co. Deeds T.R. No. DS,* f. 94)
He became indebted to Thomas Worthington and on February 20, 1724, Edward Norwood, of Baltimore County, planter, sold to Thomas Worthington of Anne Arundel County, merchant, two tracts of land originally surveyed for Edward Norwood, 100 acres of Norwood's Discovery and 100 acres of Ruth's Lot. Ruth, wife of Edwara, gave her consent.

(*Balt. Co. Deeds I.S. No. G,* f. 411)

On November 1, 1729, Richard Owings made over to his sister, Ruth Norwood, widow, Owings Addition, during her life, and on the 14th of April, 1730, he gave to Ruth Norwood, widow of Edward Norwood, deceased, Owing's Addition and Owing's Adventure, during her natural life.

(*Balt. Co. Deeds I.S. No. K,* folios 113, 237)

Children of Edward and Ruth (Owings) Norwood:

1. Edward[4] Norwood, d. 1772 (*Wills 38,* f. 699)
   m. Mary ______

   Children: Named in father's will:
   1. Nicholas Norwood
   2. Edward Norwood
   3. Samuel Norwood
   4. Elizabeth Norwood
   5. Ruth Norwood
   6. Nancy Norwood
   7. John Norwood
2. Samuel Norwood, d. 1773 (*Wills 39,* f. 406)
   m. Sarah Bankson
   Children
   1. Ruth Norwood, m. Charles Ridgely
3. Rachel Norwood, m. ______ Gott
4. Ruth Norwood. m. June 8, 1739 (*St. Thos.*) John Hurd

ANCESTRAL LINES AND LINES OF DESCENT OF SOME OF THE DESCENDANTS OF EDWARD DARCY-DORSEY, THE IMMIGRANT

ANCESTRAL LINES OF
MAXWELL J. DORSEY AND JOHN MUIR DORSEY, URBANA, ILLINOIS

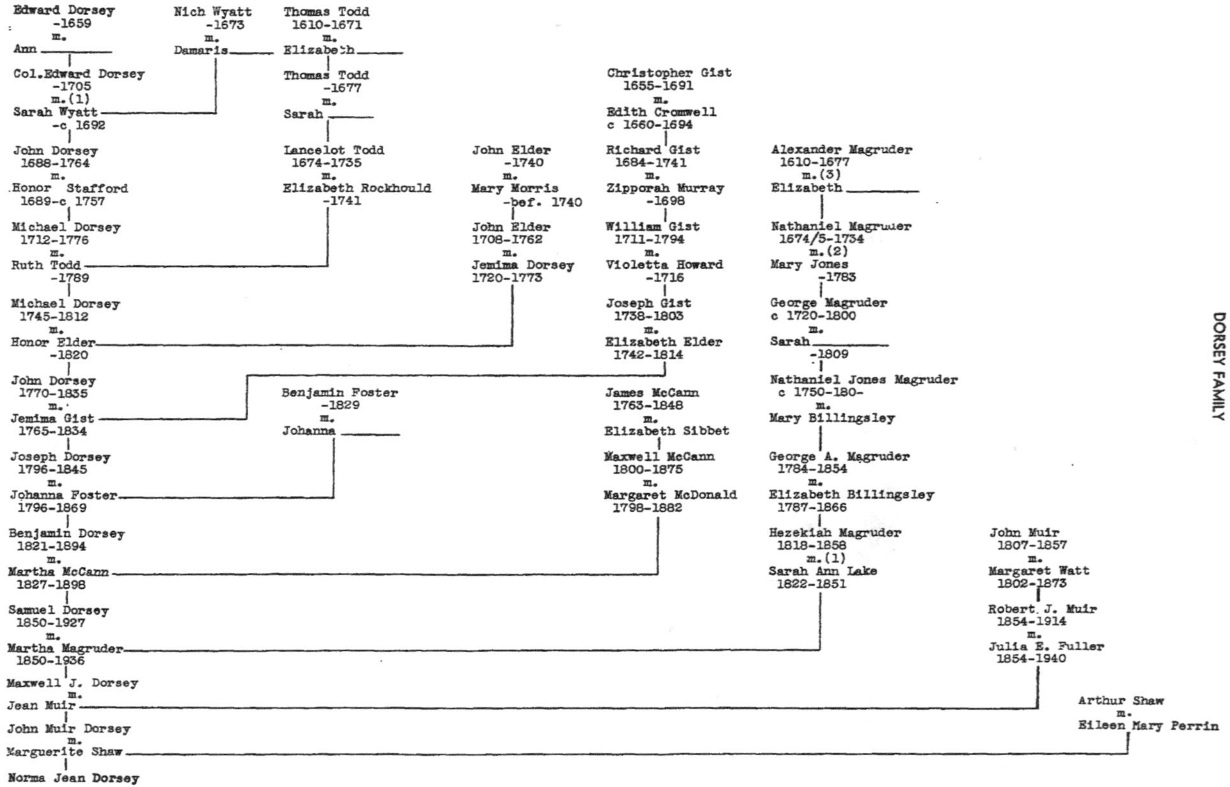
Edward Dorsey
-1659
m.
Ann
Col. Edward Dorsey
-1705
m. (1)
Sarah Wyatt
-c 1692
John Dorsey
1688-1764
m.
Honor Stafford
1689-c 1757
Michael Dorsey
1712-1776
m.
Ruth Todd
-1789
Michael Dorsey
1745-1812
m.
Honor Elder
-1820
John Dorsey
1770-1835
m.
Jemima Gist
1765-1834
Joseph Dorsey
1796-1845
m.
Johanna Foster
1796-1869
Benjamin Dorsey
1821-1894
m.
Martha McCann
1827-1898
Samuel Dorsey
1850-1927
m.
Martha Magruder
1850-1936
Maxwell J. Dorsey
m.
Jean Muir
John Muir Dorsey
m.
Marguerite Shaw
Norma Jean Dorsey
Nich Wyatt
-1673
m.
Damaris
Thomas Todd
1610-1671
m.
Elizabeth
Thomas Todd
-1677
m.
Sarah
Lancelot Todd
1674-1735
m.
Elizabeth Rockhould
-1741
Benjamin Foster
-1829
m.
Johanna
John Elder
-1740
m.
Mary Morris
-bef. 1740
John Elder
1708-1762
m.
Jemima Dorsey
1720-1773
Christopher Gist
1655-1691
m.
Edith Cromwell
c 1660-1694
Richard Gist
1684-1741
m.
Zipporah Murray
-1698
William Gist
1711-1794
m.
Violetta Howard
-1716
Joseph Gist
1738-1803
m.
Elizabeth Elder
1742-1814
James McCann
1763-1848
m.
Elizabeth Sibbet
Maxwell McCann
1800-1875
m.
Margaret McDonald
1798-1882
Alexander Magruder
1610-1677
m. (3)
Elizabeth
Nathaniel Magruder
1674/5-1734
m. (2)
Mary Jones
-1783
George Magruder
c 1720-1800
m.
Sarah
-1809
Nathaniel Jones Magruder
c 1750-180-
m.
Mary Billingsley
George A. Magruder
1784-1854
m.
Elizabeth Billingsley
1787-1866
Hezekiah Magruder
1818-1858
m. (1)
Sarah Ann Lake
1822-1851
John Muir
1807-1857
m.
Margaret Watt
1802-1873
Robert J. Muir
1854-1914
m.
Julia E. Fuller
1854-1940
Arthur Shaw
m.
Eileen Mary Perrin

ANCESTRAL LINES OF
MRS. NANNIE (BALL) NIMMO AND MRS. CALDER KIRK, BALTIMORE, MARYLAND

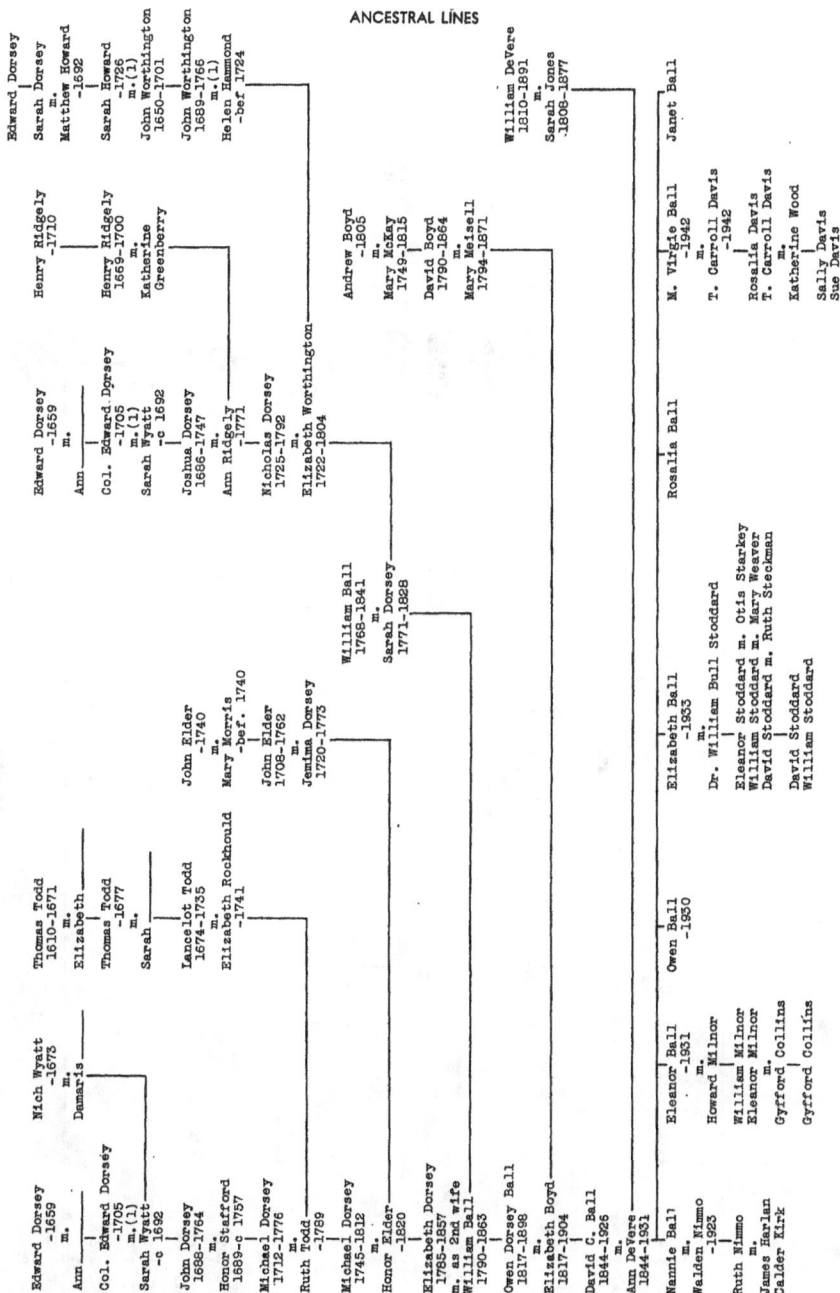

Edward Dorsey
-1659
m.
Ann

Col. Edward Dorsey
-1705
m.(1)
Sarah Wyatt
-c 1692

John Dorsey
1688-1764
m.
Honor Stafford
1689-c 1757

Michael Dorsey
1712-1776
m.
Ruth Todd
-1789

Michael Dorsey
1745-1812
m.
Honor Elder
-1820

Elizabeth Dorsey
1785-1857
m. as 2nd wife
William Ball
1790-1863

Owen Dorsey Ball
1817-1898
m.
Elizabeth Boyd
1817-1904

David C. Ball
1844-1926
m.
Ann DeVere
1844-1931

Nich Wyatt
-1673
m.
Damaris

Thomas Todd
1610-1671
m.
Elizabeth

Thomas Todd
-1677
m.
Sarah

Lancelot Todd
1674-1735
m.
Elizabeth Rockhould
-1741

John Elder
-1740
m.
Mary Morris
-bef. 1740

John Elder
1708-1762
m.
Jemima Dorsey
1720-1773

William Ball
1768-1841
m.
Sarah Dorsey
1771-1828

Edward Dorsey
-1659
m.
Ann

Col. Edward Dorsey
-1705
m.(1)
Sarah Wyatt
-c 1692

Joshua Dorsey
1686-1747
m.
Ann Ridgely
-1771

Nicholas Dorsey
1725-1792
m.
Elizabeth Worthington
1722-1804

Henry Ridgely
-1710

Henry Ridgely
1669-1700
m.
Katherine
Greenberry

Andrew Boyd
-1805
m.
Mary McKay
1749-1815

David Boyd
1790-1864
m.
Mary Meisell
1794-1871

Edward Dorsey

Sarah Dorsey
m.
Matthew Howard
-1692

Sarah Howard
-1726
m.(1)
John Worthington
1650-1701

John Worthington
1689-1766
m.(1)
Helen Hammond
-bef 1724

William DeVere
1810-1891
m.
Sarah Jones
1808-1877

Children of David C. Ball and Ann DeVere:

Nannie Ball
m.
Walden Nimmo
-1923

Ruth Nimmo
m.
James Harlan
Calder Kirk

Eleanor Ball
-1931
m.
Howard Milnor

William Milnor
Eleanor Milnor
m.
Gyfford Collins

Gyfford Collins

Owen Ball
-1930

Elizabeth Ball
-1933
m.
Dr. William Bull Stoddard

Eleanor Stoddard m. Otis Starkey
William Stoddard m. Mary Weaver
David Stoddard m. Ruth Steckman

David Stoddard
William Stoddard

Rosalia Ball

M. Virgie Ball
-1942
m.
T. Carroll Davis
-1942

Rosalia Davis
T. Carroll Davis
m.
Katherine Wood

Sally Davis
Sue Davis

Janet Ball

ANCESTRAL LINES OF
DR. CALEB DORSEY, BALTIMORE, MARYLAND

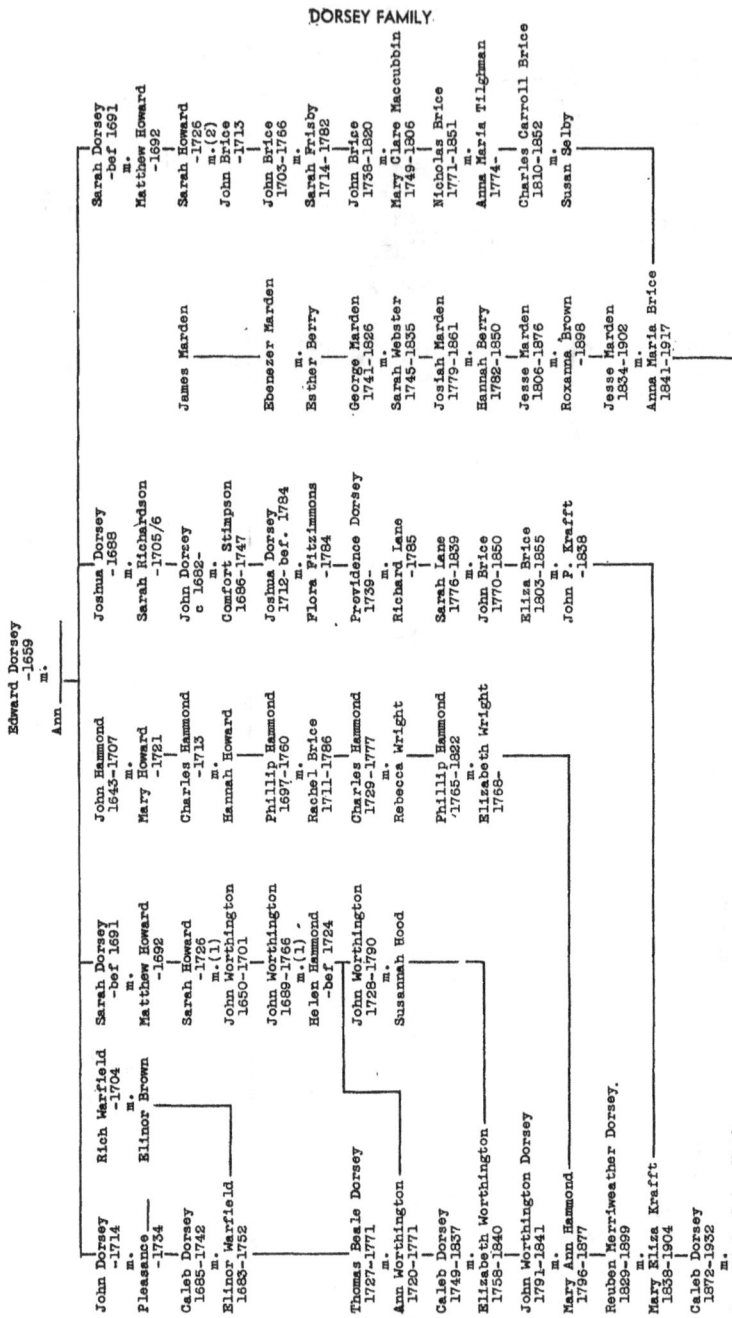

Edward Dorsey
-1659
m.
Ann

John Dorsey
-1714
m.
Pleasance
-1734

Caleb Dorsey
1685-1742
m.
Elinor Warfield
1683-1752

Thomas Beale Dorsey
1727-1771
m.
Ann Worthington
1720-1771

Caleb Dorsey
1749-1837
m.
Elizabeth Worthington
1758-1840

John Worthington Dorsey
1791-1841
m.
Mary Ann Hammond
1796-1877

Reuben Merriweather Dorsey.
1829-1899
m.
Mary Eliza Krafft
1838-1904

Caleb Dorsey
1872-1932
m.
Anna Marie Brice Marden
1876-1935

Caleb Dorsey
1904-
m.
Ruth Biemiller Barnes

Rich Warfield
-1704
m.
Elinor Brown

Sarah Dorsey
-bef 1691
m.
Matthew Howard
-1692

Sarah Howard
-1726
m.(1)
John Worthington
1650-1701

John Worthington
1689-1766
m.(1)
Helen Hammond
-bef 1724

John Worthington
1728-1790
m.
Susannah Hood

John Hammond
1643-1707
m.
Mary Howard
-1721

Charles Hammond
-1713
m.
Hannah Howard

Phillip Hammond
1697-1760
m.
Rachel Brice
1711-1786

Charles Hammond
1729-1777
m.
Rebecca Wright

Phillip Hammond
1765-1822
m.
Elizabeth Wright
1768-

Joshua Dorsey
-1688
m.
Sarah Richardson
-1705/6

John Dorsey
c 1682-
m.
Comfort Stimpson
1686-1747

Joshua Dorsey
1712- bef. 1784
m.
Flora Fitzimmons
-1784

Providence Dorsey
1739-
m.
Richard Lane
-1785

Sarah Lane
1776-1839
m.
John Brice
1770-1850

Eliza Brice
1803-1855
m.
John P. Krafft
-1838

James Marden

Ebenezer Marden
m.
Esther Berry

George Marden
1741-1826
m.
Sarah Webster
1745-1835

Josiah Marden
1779-1861
m.
Hannah Berry
1782-1850

Jesse Marden
1806-1876
m.
Roxanna Brown
-1898

Jesse Marden
1834-1902
m.
Anna Maria Brice
1841-1917

Sarah Dorsey
-bef 1691
m.
Matthew Howard
-1692

Sarah Howard
-1726
m.(2)
John Brice
-1713

John Brice
1703-1766
m.
Sarah Frisby
1714-1782

John Brice
1738-1820
m.
Mary Clare Maccubbin
1749-1806

Nicholas Brice
1771-1851
m.
Anna Maria Tilghman
1774-

Charles Carroll Brice
1810-1852
m.
Susan Selby

ANCESTRAL LINES OF
MRS. CALEB DORSEY, BALTIMORE, MARYLAND

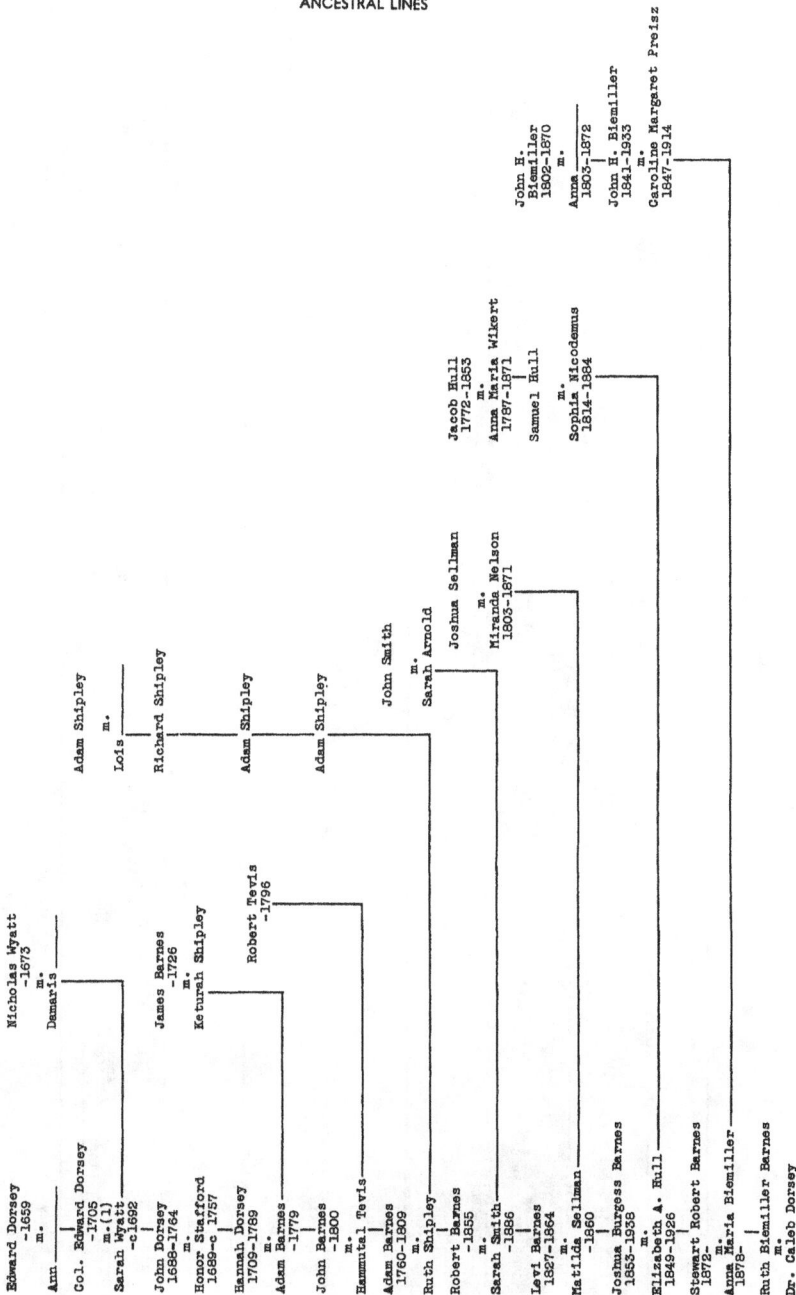

Edward Dorsey
-1659
m.
Ann

Col. Edward Dorsey
-1705
m.(1)
Sarah Wyatt
-c1692

John Dorsey
1688-1764
m.
Honor Stafford
1689-c 1757

Hannah Dorsey
1709-1789
m.
Adam Barnes
-1779

John Barnes
-1800
m.
Hammutal Tevis

Adam Barnes
1760-1809
m.
Ruth Shipley

Robert Barnes
-1855
m.
Sarah Smith
-1886

Levi Barnes
1827-1864
m.
Matilda Sellman
-1860

Joshua Burgess Barnes
1853-1938
m.
Elizabeth A. Hull
1849-1926

Stewart Robert Barnes
1872-
m.
Anna Maria Biemiller
1878-

Ruth Biemiller Barnes
m.
Dr. Caleb Dorsey

Nicholas Wyatt
-1673
m.
Damaris

James Barnes
-1726
m.
Keturah Shipley

Robert Tevis
-1796

Adam Shipley
m.
Lois

Richard Shipley

Adam Shipley

Adam Shipley

John Smith
m.
Sarah Arnold

Joshua Sellman
m.
Miranda Nelson
1803-1871

Jacob Hull
1772-1853
m.
Anna Maria Wikert
1787-1871

Samuel Hull
m.
Sophia Nicodemus
1814-1884

John H.
Biemiller
1802-1870
m.
Anna
1803-1872

John H. Biemiller
1841-1933
m.
Caroline Margaret Preisz
1847-1914

ANCESTRAL LINES OF
ANNA (DORSEY) COOKE, TOWSON, MARYLAND

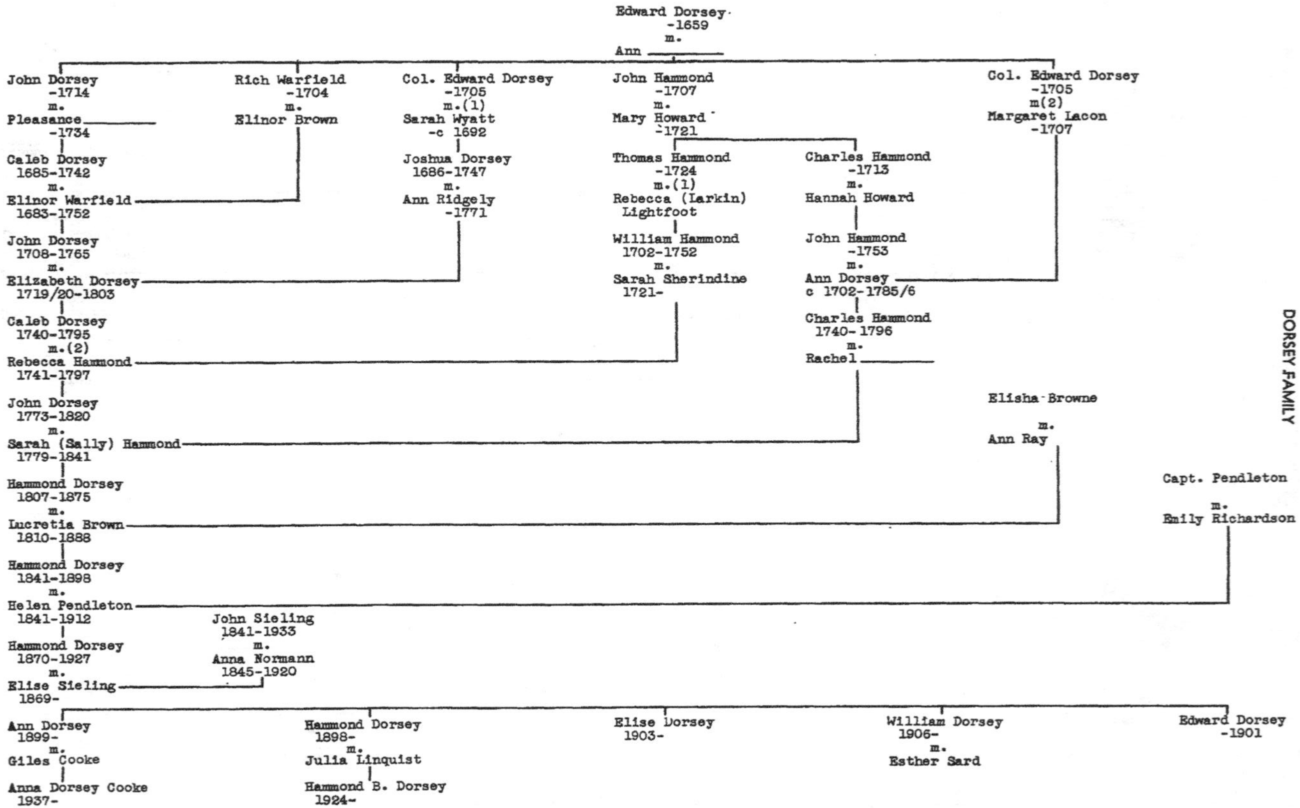
Edward Dorsey -1659 m. Ann
John Dorsey -1714 m. Pleasance -1734
Rich Warfield -1704 m. Elinor Brown
Col. Edward Dorsey -1705 m.(1) Sarah Wyatt -c 1692
John Hammond -1707 m. Mary Howard -1721
Col. Edward Dorsey -1705 m(2) Margaret Lacon -1707
Caleb Dorsey 1685-1742 m. Elinor Warfield 1683-1752
Joshua Dorsey 1686-1747 m. Ann Ridgely -1771
Thomas Hammond -1724 m.(1) Rebecca (Larkin) Lightfoot
Charles Hammond -1713 m. Hannah Howard
John Dorsey 1708-1765 m. Elizabeth Dorsey 1719/20-1803
William Hammond 1702-1752 m. Sarah Sherindine 1721-
John Hammond -1753 m. Ann Dorsey c 1702-1785/6
Caleb Dorsey 1740-1795 m.(2) Rebecca Hammond 1741-1797
Charles Hammond 1740-1796 m. Rachel
John Dorsey 1773-1820 m. Sarah (Sally) Hammond 1779-1841
Elisha Browne m. Ann Ray
Hammond Dorsey 1807-1875 m. Lucretia Brown 1810-1888
Capt. Pendleton m. Emily Richardson
Hammond Dorsey 1841-1898 m. Helen Pendleton 1841-1912
John Sieling 1841-1933 m. Anna Normann 1845-1920
Hammond Dorsey 1870-1927 m. Elise Sieling 1869-
Ann Dorsey 1899- m. Giles Cooke
Anna Dorsey Cooke 1937-
Hammond Dorsey 1898- m. Julia Linquist
Hammond B. Dorsey 1924-
Elise Dorsey 1903-
William Dorsey 1906- m. Esther Sard
Edward Dorsey -1901

LINE OF DESCENT OF HERBERT GROVE DORSEY, WASHINGTON, D.C.

Edward Dorsey
-1659
m.
Ann
|
Col. Edward Dorsey
-1705
m.(1)
Sarah Wyatt
-c 1692
|
John Dorsey
1688-1764
m.
Honor Stafford
1689-c 1757
|
Michael Dorsey
1712-1776
m.
Ruth Todd
-1789
|
Michael Dorsey
1745-1812
m.
Honor Elder
-1820
|
John Dorsey
1770-1835
m.
Jemima Gist
1765-1834
|
John Dorsey
1809-1877
m.
Prudence Means
1810-1878
|
Edward Jackson Dorsey
1835-1928 Newark, O.
m.
Mary Elma Grove
1847-1932
|
Herbert Grove Dorsey
m.
Virginia Rowlett
|

Herbert Grove Dorsey Jr.
m.
Elizabeth Copley Ballantine
|
Herbert Grove Dorsey, 1939-
William Ballantine Dorsey, 1942-
Diana Dorsey, 1943-

William Rowlett Dorsey
m.
Eleanor Poor Jones

LINE OF DESCENT OF NOAH ERNEST DORSEY, ANNAPOLIS JUNCTION, MARYLAND

Edward Dorsey
-1659
m.
Ann
|
Col. Edward Dorsey
-1705
m.(1)
Sarah Wyatt
c 1692
|
Joshua Dorsey
1686-1747
m.
Ann Ridgely
-1771
|
Nicholas Dorsey
1725-1792
m.
Elizabeth Worthington
1722-1804
|
Lloyd Dorsey
1762-1812
m.
Catherine Thompson
1762-1809
|
Noah Egbert Dorsey
1799-1871
m.
Sarah Hammond Dorsey
1803-1871
|
Lloyd Egbert Dorsey
1840-1918
m.
Laura Worthington
1848-1934
|
Noah Ernest Dorsey
1873-
m.
Mary Tasker Bowie
1878-1913

LINE OF DESCENT OF MRS. VIRGINIA (DORSEY) LIGHTFOOT TAKOMA PARK, MARYLAND

Edward Dorsey
-1659
m.
Ann
|
Col. Edward Dorsey
-1705
m.(1)
Sarah Wyatt
c 1692
|
Nicholas Dorsey
c 1690-1717
m.
Frances Hughes
1692-
|
Benjamin Dorsey
c 1713-1747
m.
Sophia
-1788
|
Elisha Dorsey
c 1743-1801/2
m.
Mary Slade
-1782
|
Nicholas Slade Dorsey
1782-1867
m.
Mary Anderson
1790-
|
Thomas Anderson Dorsey
1810-1852
m.
Maria Sweetser Hance
1826-1899
|
Rev. James Owen Dorsey
1848-1895
m.
Clara Virginia Wynkoop
1851-1926
|
Virginia Dorsey
m.
James Herndon Lightfoot
-1942
|
Virginia Lightfoot — Georgiana Lightfoot
m.
Fitzhugh Maclean
|
Anne Fitzhugh Maclean

LINE OF DESCENT OF ELLA LORRAINE DORSEY WASHINGTON D.C.

Edward Dorsey
-1659
m.
Ann
|
Col. Edward Dorsey
-1705
m.(1)
Sarah Wyatt
-c 1692
|
John Dorsey
1688-1764
m.
Honor Stafford
1689-c 1757
|
Michael Dorsey
1712-1776
m.
Ruth Todd
-1789
|
Michael Dorsey
1745-1812
m.
Honor Elder
-1820
|
Owen Dorsey
1771-1825
m.
Henrietta Dorsey
1776-
|
Lorenzo Dorsey
1808-
m.
Anna Hanson McKenney
|
Ella Lorraine Dorsey
d. unm.

LINE OF DESCENT OF
ALBERT BOGGESS, WASHINGTON, D.C.

Edward Dorsey
-1705
m.
Ann

Col. Edward Dorsey
-1705
m.(1)
Sarah Wyatt
-c 1692

Joshua Dorsey
1686-1747
m.
Ann Ridgely
-1771

Elizabeth Dorsey
1719/20-1803

m.

John Dorsey
-1714
m.
Pleasance
-1734

Caleb Dorsey
1685-1742
m.
Elinor Warfield
1683-1752

John Dorsey
1708-1765

Elizabeth Dorsey
1753-1824 Harrison Co., W. Va.
m.
Samuel Boggess
1742-1825

Alburtus Boggess
1791-1861
m.(2)
Anne Wood
1798-1877

Albert Boggess
1839-1891
m.
Nannie E. Shivers
1853-1945

Albert Boggess
1880-
m.
Alice Gray
Herring
1885-

Albert Boggess Jr.
1906-
m.
Mina Montgomery
1904-

Albert Boggess III
1929-

Ruth G. Boggess
1908-

Annie Lou Boggess
1828-
m.
Justin Kimball
Dallas, Texas

Offa Shivers Boggess
1884-
m.
Nina Belle Higginbotham
Dallas, Texas

John Wood Boggess
1887-1945
m.
Blanche Smith
West Texas, Texas

Robert W. Boggess
1891-
m.
Geraldine
Gegenworth
Dallas, Texas

LINE OF DESCENT OF
MRS. RALPH O. GRICE, FRANCIS TILTON GRICE, AND MRS. JOHN J. BRUFF
TAKOMA PARK, MARYLAND

Edward Dorsey
-1659
m.
Ann ______

John Dorsey
-1714
m.
Pleasance______
-1734

Deborah Dorsey
--bef. 1752
m.(2)
Richard Clagett
-1752

Samuel Clagett
c 1701-1756
m.(1)
Elizabeth Gantt

Priscilla Clagett
m.
Samuel Chew
1737-1790

John Hamilton Chew
1771-1830
m.
Priscilla Elizabeth Clagett
1778-1843

Mary Chew
1803-
m.
LaFayette Gibson
1805-

John Chew Gibson
1827-1896
m.
Henrietta Stevenson Carroll
1827-1896

Francis Tilton Gibson
1859-1937
m.
Ellen Althea Dorsey
1871-

Elizabeth Carroll Gibson
m.
Ralph Odeen Grice

Francis Tilton Grice

Eleanor Dorsey Gibson
m.
John J. Bruff

LINE OF DESCENT OF
DR. WILLIAM DANA HOYT JR., BALTIMORE MARYLAND

Edward Dorsey
-1659
m.
Ann
|
John Dorsey
-1714
m.
Pleasance
-1734
|
Caleb Dorsey
1685-1742
m.
Elinor Warfield
1683-1752
|
Caleb Dorsey
1710-1772
m.
Priscilla Hill
1718-1781
|
Priscilla Dorsey
1762-1814
m.
Genl Charles Carnan Ridgely
1762-1829
|
John Ridgely
1790-1867
m.
Eliza Eichelberger Ridgely
1802-1867
|
Capt. Charles Ridgely
1830-1872
m.
Margaretta Sophia Howard
1824-1904
|
Juliana Elizabeth Howard Ridgely
1862-
m.
John Southgate Yeaton
1850-1911
|
Margaret Howard Yeaton
1885-1943
m.
Dr. William Dana Hoyt
1880-1945
|
Dr. William Dana Hoyt Jr.
1911-

(Also from Genl Charles Carnan Ridgely:)
Sophia Gough Ridgely
1800-1828
m.
James Howard
1797-1870
| (parents of Margaretta Sophia Howard)

LINE OF DESCENT OF
WILLIAM BOSE MARYE, BALTIMORE MARYLAND

Edward Dorsey
-1659
m.
Ann
|
John Dorsey
-1714
m.
Pleasance
-1734
|
Deborah Dorsey
-bef. 1752
m.(1)
Charles Ridgely
-1705
|
Col. Charles Ridgely
c 1702-1772
m.
Rachel Howard
-1750
|
Capt. John Ridgely
1723-1771
m.
Mary Dorsey
1725-1786
|
Deborah Ridgely
1749-1817
m.
Capt. John Sterett
1750/1-1787
|
Mary Sterett
1772-1847
m.
Richard Gittings
1763-1830
|
David Sterett Gittings
1797-1887
m.(2)
Arabella Young
1816-1861
|
Elizabeth Mary Bose Gittings
1853-1928
m.
William Nelson Marye
1841-1929
|
William Bose Marye
1886-

(Also from John Dorsey and Pleasance:)
Caleb Dorsey
1685-1742
m.
Elinor Warfield
1683-1752
| (parents of Mary Dorsey)

LINE OF DESCENT OF HENRY RIDGELY EVANS, BALTIMORE, MARYLAND

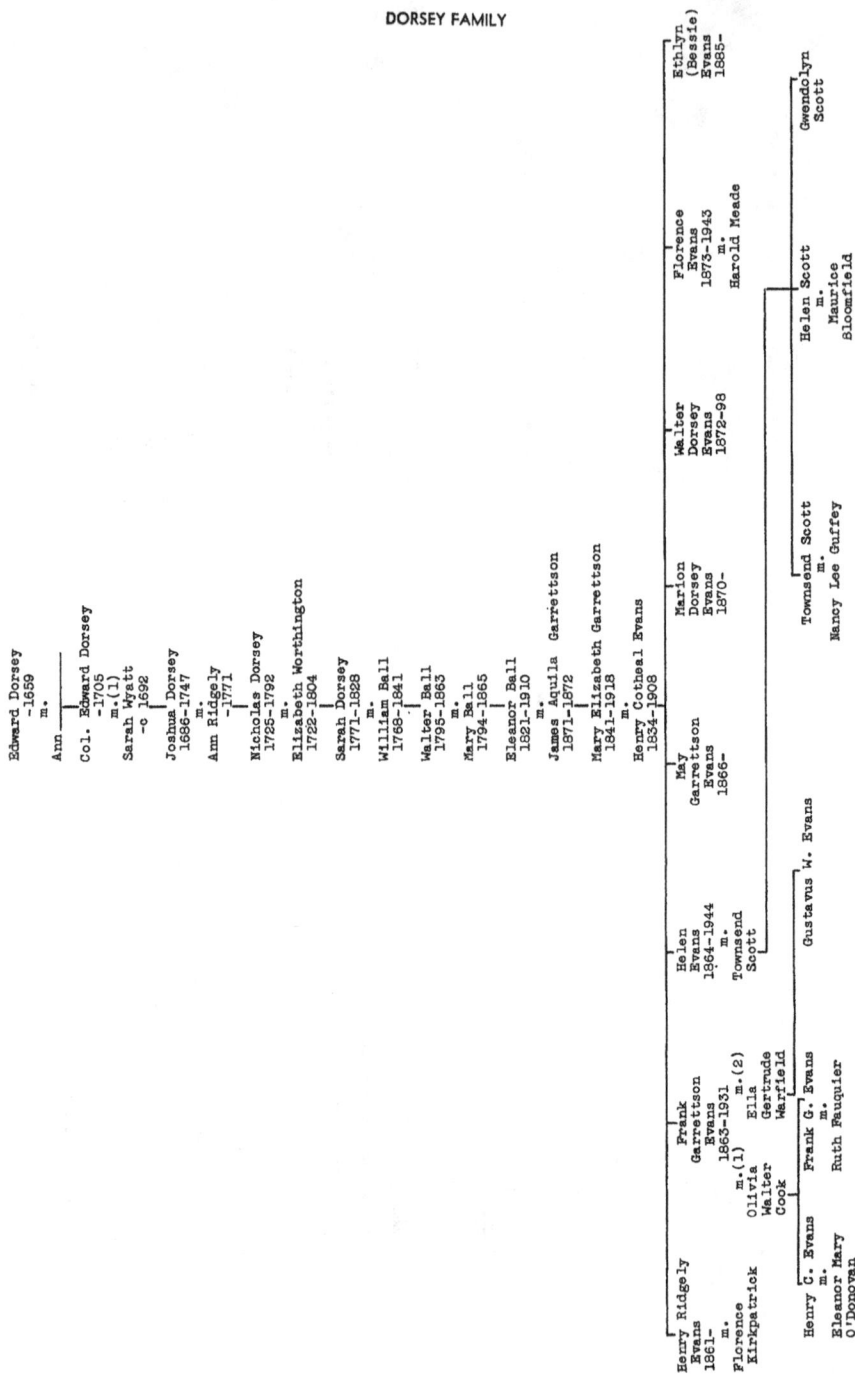

Edward Dorsey
-1659
m.
Ann

Col. Edward Dorsey
-1705
m.(1)
Sarah Wyatt
-c 1692

Joshua Dorsey
1686-1747
m.
Ann Ridgely
-1771

Nicholas Dorsey
1725-1792
m.
Elizabeth Worthington
1722-1804

Sarah Dorsey
1771-1828
m.
William Ball
1768-1841

Walter Ball
1795-1863
m.
Mary Ball
1794-1865

Eleanor Ball
1821-1910
m.
James Aquila Garrettson
1871-1872

Mary Elizabeth Garrettson
1841-1918
m.
Henry Cotheal Evans
1834-1908

Children:

- Henry Ridgely Evans, 1861-, m. Florence Kirkpatrick
- Frank Garrettson Evans, 1863-1931, m.(1) Olivia Walter Cook, m.(2) Ella Gertrude Warfield
  - Henry C. Evans m. Eleanor Mary O'Donovan
  - Frank G. Evans m. Ruth Fauquier
  - Gustavus W. Evans
- Helen Evans, 1864-1944, m. Townsend Scott
  - Townsend Scott m. Nancy Lee Guffey
  - Helen Scott m. Maurice Bloomfield
  - Gwendolyn Scott
- May Garrettson Evans, 1866-
- Marion Dorsey Evans, 1870-
- Walter Dorsey Evans, 1872-98
- Florence Evans, 1873-1943, m. Harold Meade
- Ethlyn (Bessie) Evans, 1885-

LINES OF DESCENT OF
HENRY TOWNSEND DUER AND ANNE EUGENIA (LEVERING) DUER, BALTIMORE, MARYLAND

Edward Dorsey
-1659
m.
Ann
|
Col. Edward Dorsey
-1705
m.
Sarah Wyatt
-c 1692

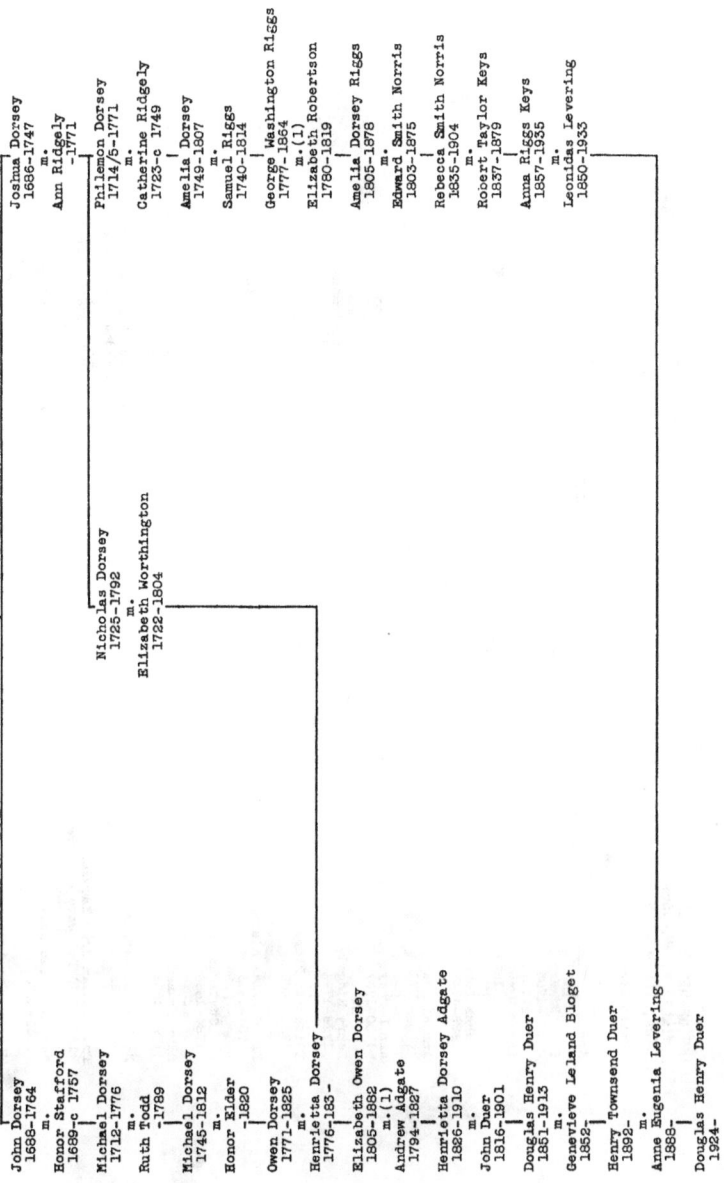

John Dorsey
1688-1764
m.
Honor Stafford
1689-c 1757
|
Michael Dorsey
1712-1776
m.
Ruth Todd
-1789
|
Michael Dorsey
1745-1812
m.
Honor Elder
-1820
|
Owen Dorsey
1771-1825
m.
Henrietta Dorsey
1776-183-
|
Elizabeth Owen Dorsey
1805-1882
m.(1)
Andrew Adgate
1794-1827
|
Henrietta Dorsey Adgate
1826-1910
m.
John Duer
1816-1901
|
Douglas Henry Duer
1851-1913
m.
Genevieve Leland Bloget
1852-
|
Henry Townsend Duer
1892-
m.
Anne Eugenia Levering
1888-
|
Douglas Henry Duer
1924-

Nicholas Dorsey
1725-1792
m.
Elizabeth Worthington
1722-1804

Joshua Dorsey
1686-1747
m.
Ann Ridgely
-1771
|
Philemon Dorsey
1714/5-1771
m.
Catherine Ridgely
1723-c 1749
|
Amelia Dorsey
1749-1807
m.
Samuel Riggs
1740-1814
|
George Washington Riggs
1777-1864
m.(1)
Elizabeth Robertson
1780-1819
|
Amelia Dorsey Riggs
1805-1878
m.
Edward Smith Norris
1803-1875
|
Rebecca Smith Norris
1835-1904
m.
Robert Taylor Keys
1837-1879
|
Anna Riggs Keys
1857-1935
m.
Leonidas Levering
1850-1933

LINE OF DESCENT OF
MRS. WILLIS K. GLAUSER
CHESTER, PENNSYLVANIA

Edward Dorsey
-1659
m.
Ann
|
Col. Edward Dorsey
-1705
m.(1)
Sarah Wyatt
-c 1692
|
Joshua Dorsey
1686-1747
m.
Ann Ridgely
-1771
|
Ann Dorsey
1730-1767
m.
Henry Ridgely
1728-1791
|
Elizabeth Ridgely
1752-1808
m.
Dr. Charles Alexander Warfield
1751-1813
|
Dr. Gustavus Warfield
1784-1866
m.
Mary Thomas
1793-1884
|
Martha Ann Warfield
1814-1898
m.
Dr. William Gray Knowles
1811-1890 Delaware Co., Pa.
|
Mary Warfield Knowles
1839-1876
m.
William Harrison Horner
1836-1902
|
Martha Thomas Horner
1865-1907
m.
Benjamin Frank Beatty
1850-1905
|
Anna Jemima Beatty
1899-
m.
Willis Klink Glauser
1890-1940

LINE OF DESCENT OF
MRS. ELIZABETH (JOHNSON) WRIGHT
NEWARK, DELAWARE

Edward Dorsey
-1659
m.
Ann
|
Joshua Dorsey
-1688
m.
Sarah Richardson
-1705/6
|
John Dorsey
c 1682-
m.
Comfort Stimpson
1686-1747
|
Joshua Dorsey
1712-
m.
Flora Fitzimmons
-1784
|
Joshua Dorsey
1745-1791
m.
Margaret Watkins
1767-
|
Nicholas Dorsey
1789-1812 Caroline Co., Md.
m.
Elizabeth Straughan (Straugon)
1788-1824
|
William Nicholas Watkins Dorsey
1811-1883 Milford, Del.
m.
Elizabeth Bradley Cropper
1815-1872
|
Elizabeth Ellen Dorsey
1840-1902
m. as 2nd wife
Alexander Johnson
1812-1896
|
Elizabeth Johnson
1881-
m.
John Pilling Wright
1881-

LINE OF DESCENT OF RALPH N. DORSEY, BERRYVILLE, VIRGINIA

Edward Dorsey
-1659
m.
Ann
|
Col. Edward Dorsey
-1705
m.(1)
Sarah Wyatt
-c 1692
|
John Dorsey
1688-1764
m.
Honor Stafford
1689-c 1757
|
Nathan Dorsey
1731-1773/4
m.
Sophia Owings
|
Vachel Dorsey
-c 1814
m.
Clementina Ireland
|
James Ireland Dorsey
m.
Susan Brooke
1788-1849
|
James Pembroke Dorsey
-1893 Clark Co., Va.
m.
Frances Phoebe LaRue
1847-1870
|
Edward Pembroke Dorsey
1869-1905
m.
Eliza Moore
1868-
|
Ralph N. Dorsey
1895-
m.
Sarah Elizabeth Meade
1896-
|

Lt. (j.g.) U.S.N.R. Ralph Meade Dorsey
1921-

Joseph Pembroke Dorsey
1926-
Cadet at West Point

LINE OF DESCENT OF ALBERT L. DORSEY, SPRINGFIELD, TENNESSEE

Edward Dorsey
-1659
m.
Ann
|
John Dorsey
-1714
m.
Pleasance
-1734
|
Edward Dorsey
-1700/1
m.
Ruth
-1747
|
John Dorsey
c 1699-1761
m.
Elizabeth
-1777
|
Basil Dorsey
-1799
m.(1)
Hannah Crockett
-bef. 1782
|
William Dorsey
-bef. 1799
m.
Rachel Hobbs
-1849
|
Corban Nicholas Dorsey
-c 1826 Jefferson Co., Ky.
m.
Martha Daniels
|
Richard Merriweather Dorsey
- Shelby Co., Ky.
m.
Martha (Patsy) Glass
|
Andrew Walker Dorsey
m.
Winnie Cathern Burrow
|
Albert L. Dorsey
m.
Lennie Sue Sprouse

LINES OF DESCENT OF

MRS. HILLIARD O. WOOD
NASHVILLE, TENNESSEE

MRS. WALLACE B. McFARLAND
STAUNTON, VIRGINIA

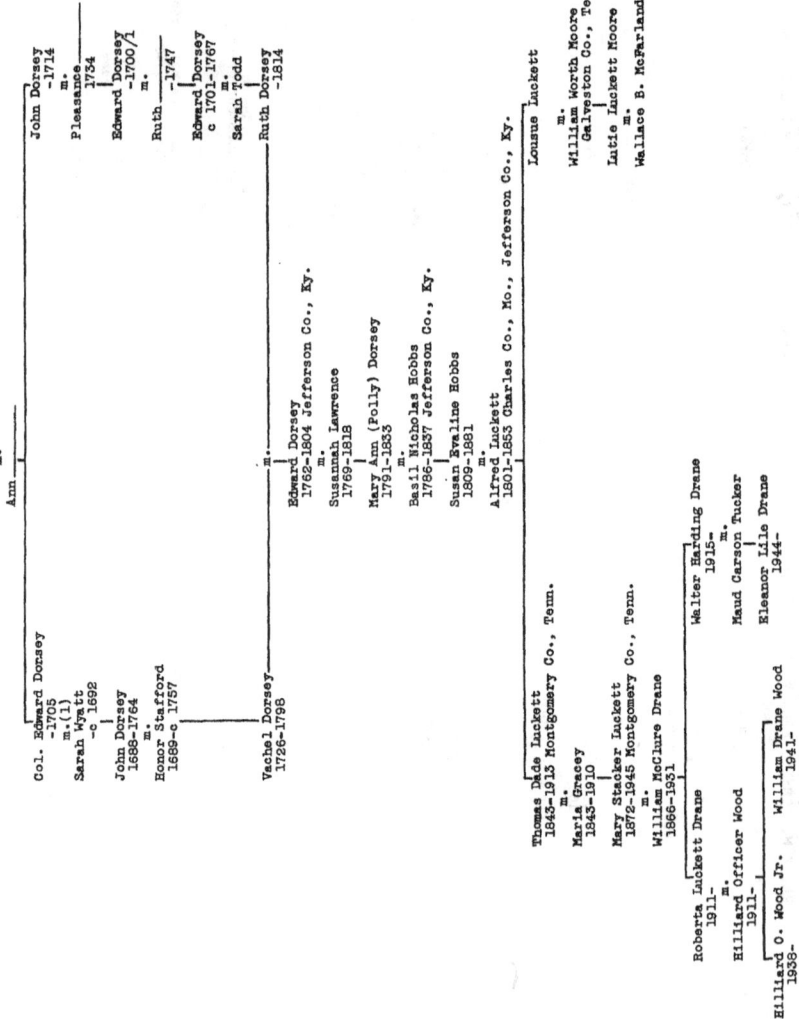

Edward Dorsey
-1659
m.
Ann

Col. Edward Dorsey
-1705
m.(1)
Sarah Wyatt
-c 1692

John Dorsey
1688-1764
m.
Honor Stafford
1689-c 1757

Vachel Dorsey
1726-1798

John Dorsey
-1714
m.
Pleasance
1734

Edward Dorsey
-1700/1
m.
Ruth
-1747

Edward Dorsey
c 1701-1767
m.
Sarah Todd

Ruth Dorsey
-1814

Vachel Dorsey m. Ruth Dorsey

Edward Dorsey
1762-1804 Jefferson Co., Ky.
m.
Susannah Lawrence
1769-1818

Mary Ann (Polly) Dorsey
1791-1833
m.
Basil Nicholas Hobbs
1786-1837 Jefferson Co., Ky.

Susan Evaline Hobbs
1809-1881
m.
Alfred Luckett
1801-1853 Charles Co., Mo., Jefferson Co., Ky.

Thomas Dade Luckett
1843-1913 Montgomery Co., Tenn.
m.
Maria Gracey
1843-1910

Mary Stacker Luckett
1872-1945 Montgomery Co., Tenn.
m.
William McClure Drane
1866-1931

Roberta Luckett Drane
1911-
m.
Hilliard Officer Wood
1911-

Hilliard O. Wood Jr.
1938-

William Drane Wood
1941-

Walter Harding Drane
1915-
m.
Maud Carson Tucker

Eleanor Lile Drane
1944-

Lousue Luckett
m.
William Worth Moore
Galveston Co., Texas

Lutie Luckett Moore
m.
Wallace B. McFarland

LINE OF DESCENT OF
HUGH MANSON DORSEY AND CAMMELIUS DAWSON DORSEY, ATLANTA, GEORGIA

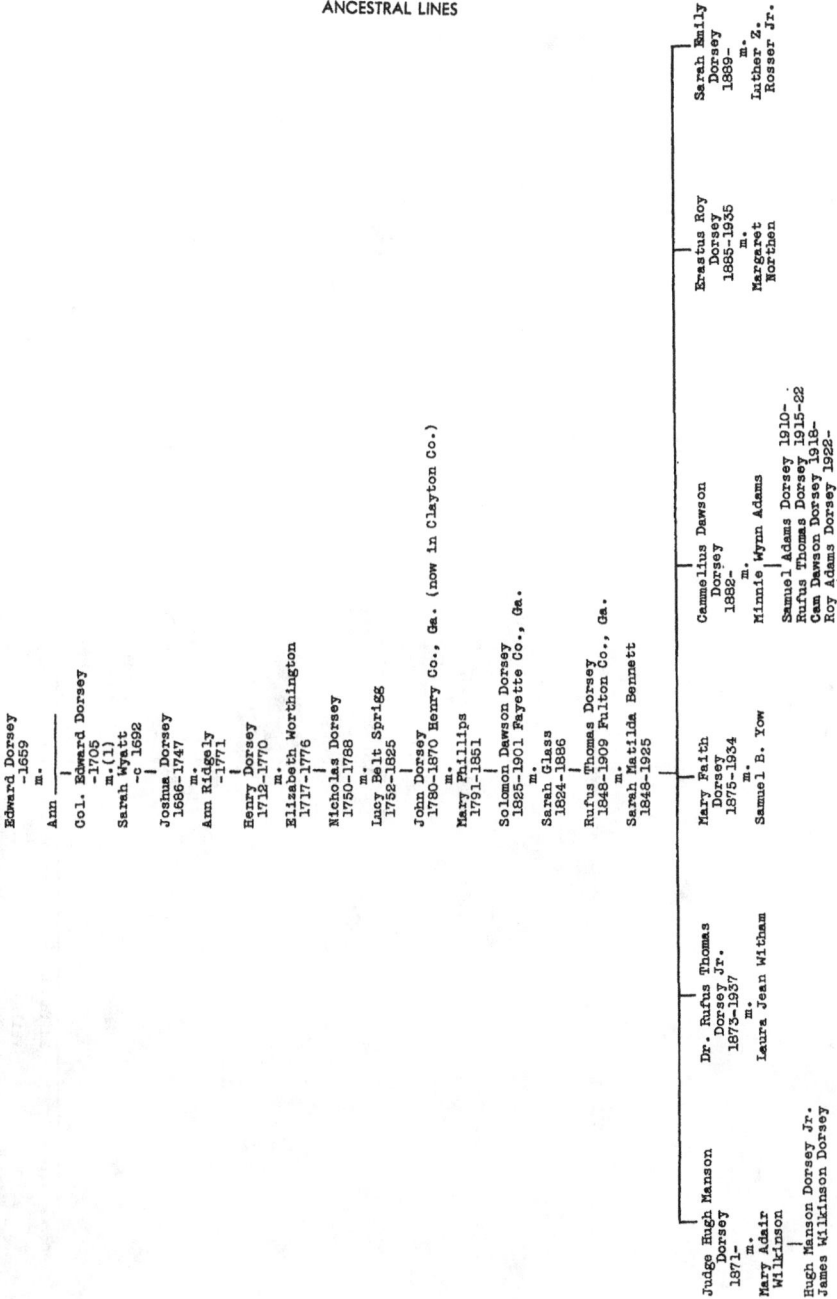

Edward Dorsey
-1659
m.
Ann

Col. Edward Dorsey
-1705
m.(1)
Sarah Wyatt
-c 1692

Joshua Dorsey
1686-1747
m.
Ann Ridgely
-1771

Henry Dorsey
1712-1770
m.
Elizabeth Worthington
1717-1776

Nicholas Dorsey
1750-1788
m.
Lucy Belt Sprigg
1752-1825

John Dorsey
1780-1870 Henry Co., Ga. (now in Clayton Co.)
m.
Mary Phillips
1791-1851

Solomon Dawson Dorsey
1825-1901 Fayette Co., Ga.
m.
Sarah Glass
1824-1886

Rufus Thomas Dorsey
1848-1909 Fulton Co., Ga.
m.
Sarah Matilda Bennett
1848-1925

Judge Hugh Manson Dorsey
1871-
m.
Mary Adair Wilkinson

Hugh Manson Dorsey Jr.
James Wilkinson Dorsey

Dr. Rufus Thomas Dorsey Jr.
1873-1937
m.
Laura Jean Witham

Mary Faith Dorsey
1875-1934
m.
Samuel B. Yow

Cammelius Dawson Dorsey
1882-
m.
Minnie Wynn Adams

Samuel Adams Dorsey 1910-
Rufus Thomas Dorsey 1915-22
Cam Dawson Dorsey 1918-
Roy Adams Dorsey 1922-

Erastus Roy Dorsey
1885-1935
m.
Margaret Northen

Sarah Emily Dorsey
1889-
m.
Luther Z. Rosser Jr.

LINE OF DESCENT OF
MRS. PHILIP A. BEATTY, BRANDENTON, FLORIDA

Edward Dorsey
-1659
m.
Ann ______
|
John Dorsey
-1714
m.
Pleasance ______
-1734
|
Edward Dorsey
-1700/1
m.
Ruth ______
-1747
|
John Dorsey
c 1699-1761
m.
Elizabeth ______
-1777
|
Samuel Dorsey
1740-1779
m.
Eleanor Woodward
1745-bef. 1779
|
Henry Woodward Dorsey
1767-1840 Montgomery Co., Md.
m. (1)
Mary MacCubbin
1769-1803
|
Achsah Dorsey
1789-1855
m.
Nathaniel Magruder Waters
1786-1863
|
Harry Woodward Dorsey Waters
1813-1880 Frederick Co., Md.
m.
Prudence Jane Griffith
1816-1853
|
Susanna Magruder Waters
1845-1933 Baltimore Co., Md.
m.
William Nevins Worley
1834-1912

Children of Susanna Magruder Waters and William Nevins Worley:

- Dorsey Waters Worley m. Inez Biggs Hinton
  - Dorsey W. Worley II
  - Capt. William Nevins Worley m. Marianne Treo
    - William Nevins Worley III
- Edith Worley m. Philip Asfordby Beatty
- John William Worley m. Laura Higgins
- Helen James Worley -1945
- N. Maynard Worley m. Corinna Moorman
  - Wilbur Moorman Worley m. Martha Higgins
    - Curtis Worley
  - Marion Worley m. Nat. Mantiply
    - Mary Corinna Mantiply
  - Virginia Worley
- Edgar Brewer Worley
- Sue Waters Worley

LINE OF DESCENT OF
MRS. EDYTH CLEMENTS (SHIPLEY) BRITTON, CLEARWATER, FLORIDA

Edward Dorsey
-1659
m.
Ann ______

Col. Edward Dorsey
-1705
m.(1)
Sarah Wyatt
-c 1692

Joshua Dorsey
1686-1747
m.
Ann Ridgely
-1771

Henry Dorsey
1712-1770
m.
Elizabeth Worthington
1717-1776

Thomas Dorsey
1737/8-
m.
Mary Warfield

Benedict Dorsey
1768-1814
m.
Margaret Watkins

Elizabeth Ann Dorsey
1793-1881
m.
George Wilmer Ford
1795-1887

Miliscent C. Ford
1815-1871
m.
Daniel Elliot Shipley
1810-1885

Robert C. Shipley
1850-1891
m.
Ida L. Clements
1856-

Edyth Clements Shipley
1880-
m.
Winchester Britton III
1879-

Winchester Britton IV. 1904- m. Dorothy Hyde Benzing	Miliscent Howard Britton 1909- m. Edmund Francis Heyn	Floyd Tyler Britton 1914- m. John Carbery Lay
Winchester Britton V. 1934- Robert Hyde Britton 1935-	Sarah Warfield Heyn 1938- Miliscent Ford Heyn 1940-	Britton Lay 1942- Richard Carbery Lay 1943- Elizabeth Clements Lay 1945-

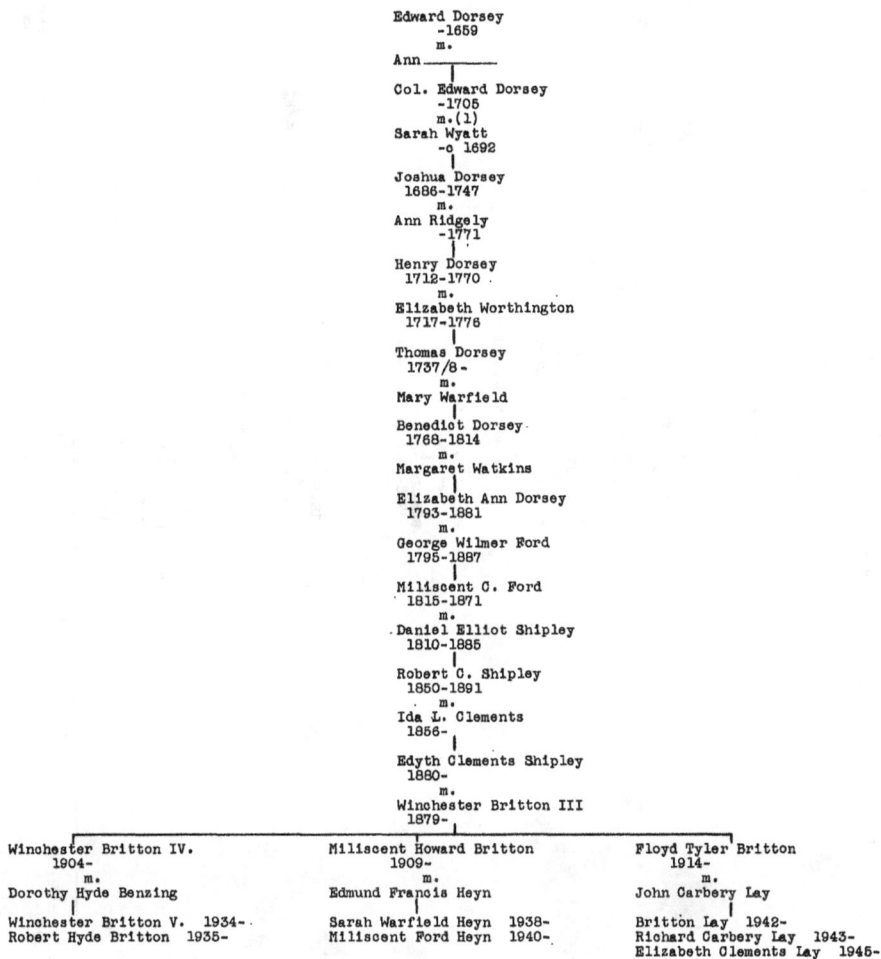

LINE OF DESCENT OF
JOHN LLOYD DORSEY JR., HENDERSON, KENTUCKY

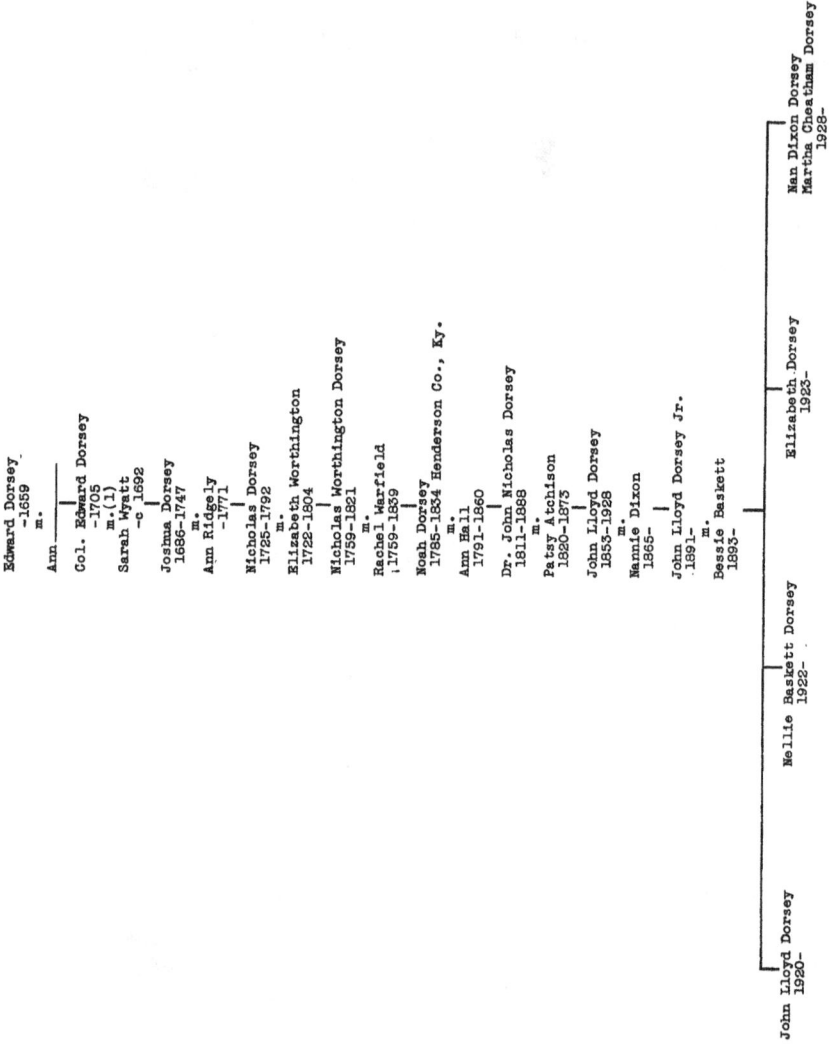

Edward Dorsey
-1659
m.
Ann ________

Col. Edward Dorsey
-1705
m.(1)
Sarah Wyatt
-c 1692

Joshua Dorsey
1686-1747
m.
Ann Ridgely
-1771

Nicholas Dorsey
1725-1792
m.
Elizabeth Worthington
1722-1804

Nicholas Worthington Dorsey
1759-1821
m.
Rachel Warfield
1759-1839

Noah Dorsey
1785-1834 Henderson Co., Ky.
m.
Ann Hall
1791-1860

Dr. John Nicholas Dorsey
1811-1888
m.
Patsy Atchison
1820-1873

John Lloyd Dorsey
1853-1928
m.
Nannie Dixon
1865-

John Lloyd Dorsey Jr.
1891-
m.
Bessie Baskett
1893-

John Lloyd Dorsey	Nellie Baskett Dorsey	Elizabeth Dorsey	Nan Dixon Dorsey Martha Cheatham Dorsey
1920-	1922-	1923-	1928-

LINE OF DESCENT OF FLORENCE DORSEY WELCH, NEW YORK CITY

Edward Dorsey
-1659
m.
Ann

Col. Edward Dorsey
-1705
m.(1)
Sarah Wyatt
-c 1692

John Dorsey
1688-1764
m.
Honor Stafford
1689-c 1757

Vachel Dorsey
1726-1798

John Dorsey
-1714
m.
Pleasance
-1734

Edward Dorsey
-1700/1
m.
Ruth
-1747

Edward Dorsey
c 1701-1767
m.
Sarah Todd

Ruth Dorsey
-1814

Vachel Dorsey m. Ruth Dorsey

Edward Dorsey
1762-1804 Jefferson Co., Ky.
m.
Susannah Lawrence
1769-1818

Elias Dorsey
1796-1871 Jefferson Co., Ky.
m.
Martha Booker
1796-1836

Benjamin Lawrence Dorsey
1820-1895 Macoupin Co., Ill.
m.(1)
Amelia Clarissa Blair
1818-1862

Henry Shreve Dorsey
1844-1921 Madison Co., Ill.
m.(1)
Harriet Jane Shirley
-1900

Robert Walker Dorsey
-1898

Mary Amelia Dorsey
-1876

Harriet Frances Dorsey
m.
John Russell Caudry

- John Shreve Caudry
  m.
  Bonnie Kirk Jones
- Harriet Prudence Caudry
  m.
  Richard Henry DeMotte
  - Harriet Anne DeMotte
  - Richard Keith DeMotte

Lydia Carmelite Dorsey
-1890

Florence Louise Dorsey
m.
Austin Hubbard Welch

Henry Shreve Dorsey Jr.
-1944
m.
Myrtle Jackson

Henry Shreve DorseyIII
m.
Loma Fouke

Harriet Edith Dorsey
m.
Alfred A. Tennison

Alfred Tennison Jr.

LINE OF DESCENT OF MACHIR J. DORSEY, EVANSTON, ILLINOIS

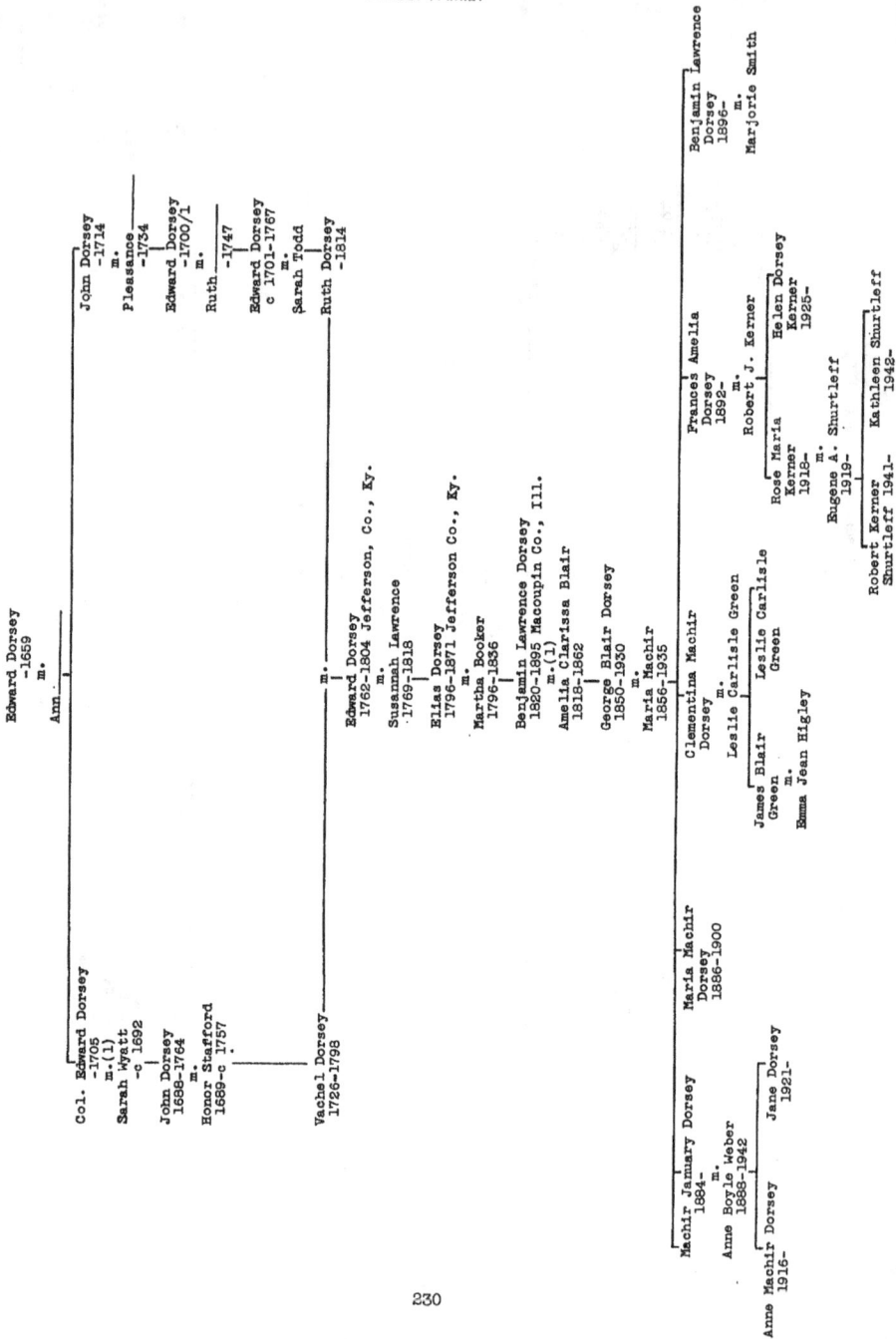

Edward Dorsey
-1659
m.
Ann

Col. Edward Dorsey
-1705
m.(1)
Sarah Wyatt
-c 1692

John Dorsey
1688-1764
m.
Honor Stafford
1689-c 1757

Vachel Dorsey
1726-1798

John Dorsey
-1714
m.
Pleasance
-1734

Edward Dorsey
-1700/1
m.
Ruth
-1747

Edward Dorsey
c 1701-1767
m.
Sarah Todd

Ruth Dorsey
-1814

Vachel Dorsey m. Ruth Dorsey

Edward Dorsey
1762-1804 Jefferson, Co., Ky.
m.
Susannah Lawrence
1769-1818

Elias Dorsey
1796-1871 Jefferson Co., Ky.
m.
Martha Booker
1796-1836

Benjamin Lawrence Dorsey
1820-1895 Macoupin Co., Ill.
m.(1)
Amelia Clarissa Blair
1818-1862

George Blair Dorsey
1850-1930
m.
Maria Machir
1856-1935

Machir January Dorsey
1884-
m.
Anne Boyle Weber
1888-1942

Anne Machir Dorsey
1916-

Jane Dorsey
1921-

Maria Machir
Dorsey
1886-1900

Clementina Machir
Dorsey
m.
Leslie Carlisle Green

James Blair
Green
m.
Emma Jean Higley

Leslie Carlisle
Green

Frances Amelia
Dorsey
1892-
m.
Robert J. Kerner

Rose Maria
Kerner
1918-
m.
Eugene A. Shurtleff
1919-

Robert Kerner
Shurtleff 1941-

Kathleen Shurtleff
1942-

Helen Dorsey
Kerner
1925-

Benjamin Lawrence
Dorsey
1896-
m.
Marjorie Smith

LINE OF DESCENT OF
LEROY H. DORSEY, CHICAGO, ILLINOIS

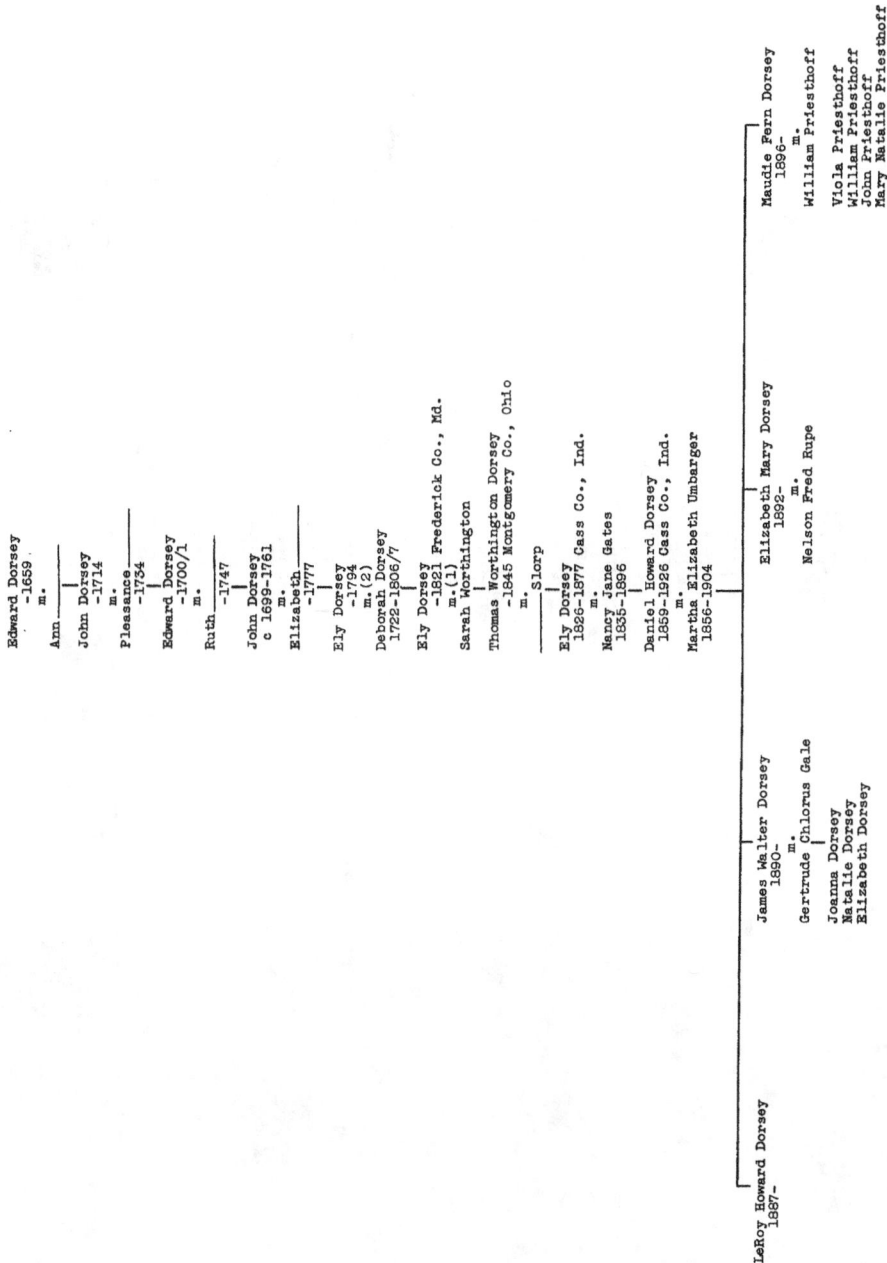

Edward Dorsey
-1659
m.
Ann

John Dorsey
-1714
m.
Pleasance
-1734

Edward Dorsey
-1700/1
m.
Ruth
-1747

John Dorsey
c 1699-1761
m.
Elizabeth
-1777

Ely Dorsey
-1794
m.(2)
Deborah Dorsey
1722-1806/7

Ely Dorsey
-1821 Frederick Co., Md.
m.(1)
Sarah Worthington

Thomas Worthington Dorsey
-1845 Montgomery Co., Ohio
m.
______ Slorp

Ely Dorsey
1826-1877 Cass Co., Ind.
m.
Nancy Jane Gates
1835-1896

Daniel Howard Dorsey
1859-1926 Cass Co., Ind.
m.
Martha Elizabeth Umbarger
1856-1904

LeRoy Howard Dorsey
1887-

James Walter Dorsey
1890-
m.
Gertrude Chlorus Gale

Joanna Dorsey
Natalie Dorsey
Elizabeth Dorsey

Elizabeth Mary Dorsey
1892-
m.
Nelson Fred Rupe

Maudie Fern Dorsey
1896-
m.
William Priesthoff

Viola Priesthoff
William Priesthoff
John Priesthoff
Mary Natalie Priesthoff

LINE OF DESCENT OF
MISS GRACE E. MAHIN, CHICAGO, ILLINOIS

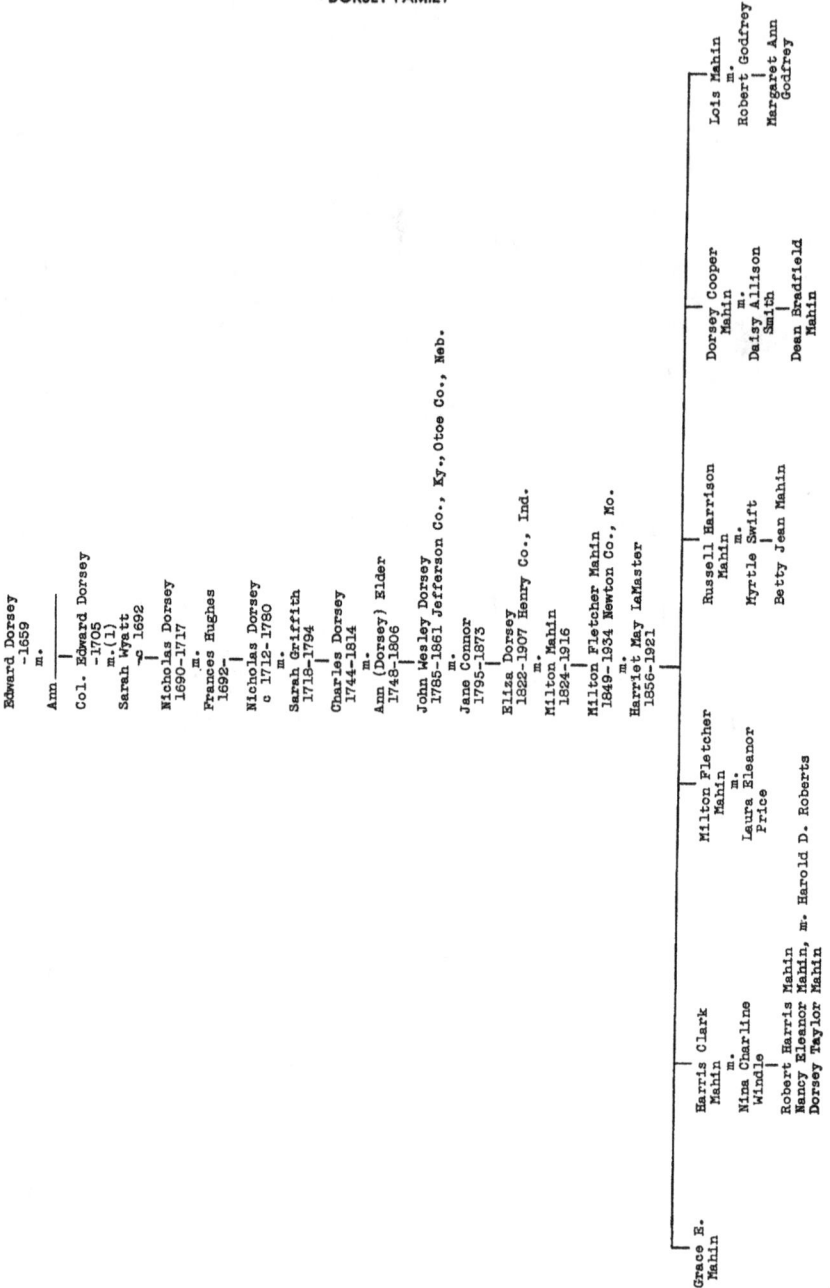

Edward Dorsey
-1659
m.
Ann ______
|
Col. Edward Dorsey
-1705
m.(1)
Sarah Wyatt
-c 1692
|
Nicholas Dorsey
1690-1717
m.
Frances Hughes
1692-
|
Nicholas Dorsey
c 1712-1780
m.
Sarah Griffith
1718-1794
|
Charles Dorsey
1744-1814
m.
Ann (Dorsey) Elder
1748-1806
|
John Wesley Dorsey
1785-1861 Jefferson Co., Ky., Otoe Co., Neb.
m.
Jane Connor
1795-1873
|
Eliza Dorsey
1822-1907 Henry Co., Ind.
m.
Milton Mahin
1824-1916
|
Milton Fletcher Mahin
1849-1934 Newton Co., Mo.
m.
Harriet May LaMaster
1856-1921
|

- Grace E. Mahin
- Harris Clark Mahin
  m.
  Nina Charline Windle
  |
  Robert Harris Mahin
  Nancy Eleanor Mahin, m. Harold D. Roberts
  Dorsey Taylor Mahin
- Milton Fletcher Mahin
  m.
  Laura Eleanor Price
- Russell Harrison Mahin
  m.
  Myrtle Swift
  |
  Betty Jean Mahin
- Dorsey Cooper Mahin
  m.
  Daisy Allison Smith
  |
  Dean Bradfield Mahin
- Lois Mahin
  m.
  Robert Godfrey
  |
  Margaret Ann Godfrey

LINE OF DESCENT OF
HARVEY EDWARD DORSEY, MORO, ILLINOIS

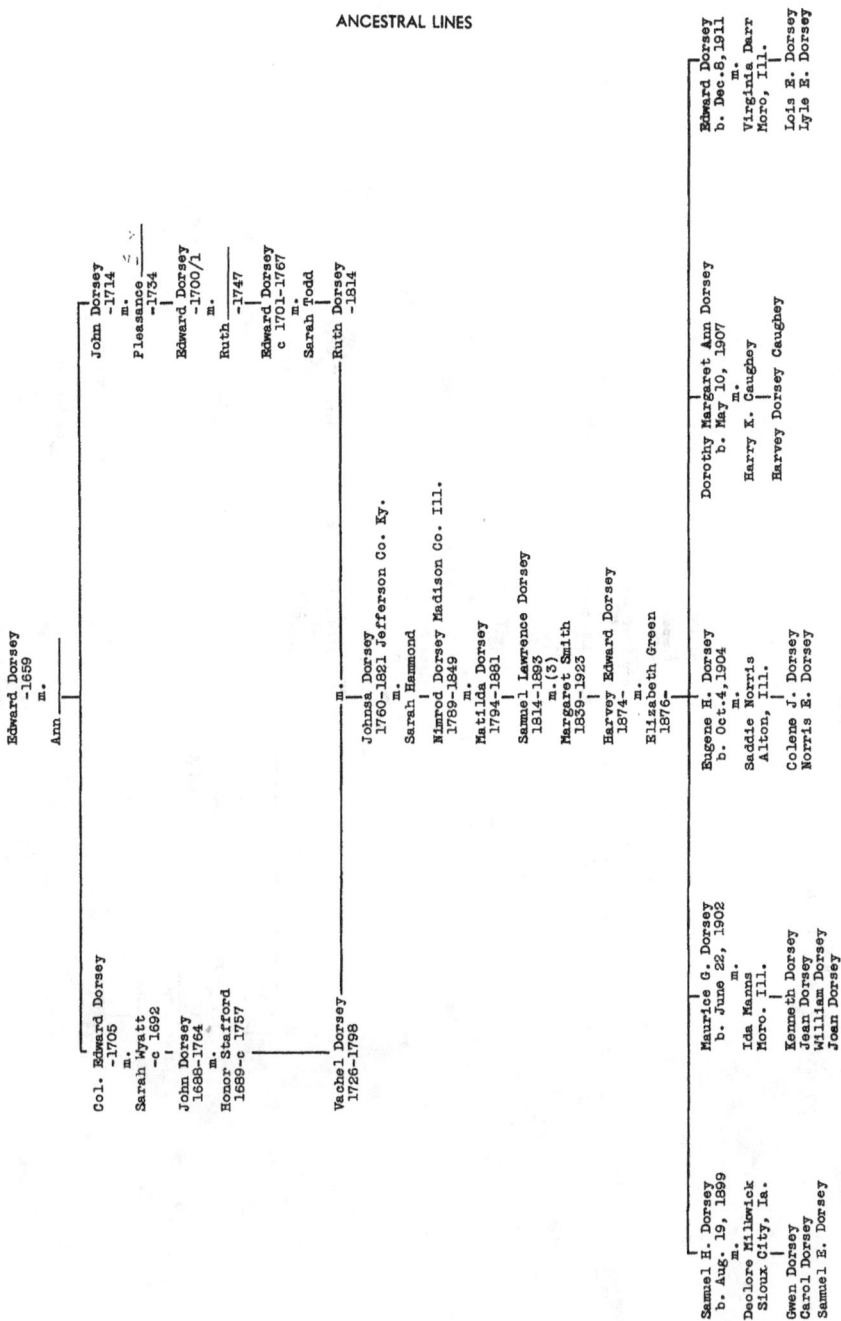

Edward Dorsey
-1659
m.
Ann ______

Line of Col. Edward Dorsey:

Col. Edward Dorsey
-1705
m.
Sarah Wyatt
-c 1692

John Dorsey
1688-1764
m.
Honor Stafford
1689-c 1757

Vachel Dorsey
1726-1798

Line of John Dorsey:

John Dorsey
-1714
m.
Pleasance ______
-1734

Edward Dorsey
-1700/1
m.
Ruth ______
-1747

Edward Dorsey
c 1701-1767
m.
Sarah Todd

Ruth Dorsey
-1814

Vachel Dorsey m. Ruth Dorsey

Johnsa Dorsey
1760-1821 Jefferson Co. Ky.
m.
Sarah Hammond

Nimrod Dorsey Madison Co. Ill.
1789-1849
m.
Matilda Dorsey
1794-1881

Samuel Lawrence Dorsey
1814-1893
m.(3)
Margaret Smith
1839-1923

Harvey Edward Dorsey
1874-
m.
Elizabeth Green
1876-

Children:

Samuel H. Dorsey
b. Aug. 19, 1899
m.
Deolore Milkwick
Sioux City, Ia.
- Gwen Dorsey
- Carol Dorsey
- Samuel E. Dorsey

Maurice G. Dorsey
b. June 22, 1902
m.
Ida Manns
Moro. Ill.
- Kenneth Dorsey
- Jean Dorsey
- William Dorsey
- Joan Dorsey

Eugene H. Dorsey
b. Oct.4,1904
m.
Saddie Norris
Alton, Ill.
- Colene J. Dorsey
- Norris E. Dorsey

Dorothy Margaret Ann Dorsey
b. May 10, 1907
m.
Harry K. Caughey
- Harvey Dorsey Caughey

Edward Dorsey
b. Dec.8,1911
m.
Virginia Darr
Moro, Ill.
- Lois E. Dorsey
- Lyle E. Dorsey

LINES OF DESCENT OF

PEARL DORSEY
MOUNDSVILLE, WEST VIRGINIA

THOMAS DORSEY
PEORIA, ILLINOIS

Edward Dorsey
-1659
m.
Ann

Col. Edward Dorsey
-1705
m.(1)
Sarah Wyatt
-c 1692

John Dorsey
1688-1764
m.
Honor Stafford
1689-c 1757

Michael Dorsey
1712-1776
m.
Ruth Todd
-1789

Ann (Nancy) Dorsey
1748-1806
m.(1)
Owen Elder
-1774

Terisha Elder
1767-1843 Brooke Co., W. Va., Washington Co., Pa.
m.
Dennis Dorsey
1769-1815

Samuel Dorsey
1789-1886 Marshall Co., W. Va.; Marshall Co., Ill.
m.(2)
Isabelle Richey
-1866

Rebecca Dorsey
1821-1906
m.
Thomas Dorsey
1814-1868

Samuel Dorsey
1846-1872
m.
Sarah Ellen Pierce

Pearl Dorsey
1874-

Samuel Dorsey Jr.
1831-1895 Washington Co., Neb.
m.
Joanna Holiday
1828-1916

William Dorsey
1853-1908 Wright Co., Ia.
m.
Maggie Scott
1857-1883

Orton Scott Dorsey
1882- Clinton Co., Ia.
m.
May Mc Farland
1883-

Thomas Dorsey
1911-
m.
Isla Sorensen 1912-

LINES OF DESCENT OF

RUPERT M. DORSEY
GRAND JUNCTION, COLORADO

LAWRENCE FOSTER KING
PITTSBURG, PENNSYLVANIA

Edward Dorsey
-1659
m.
Ann
|
Col. Edward Dorsey
-1705
m.(1)
Sarah Wyatt
-c 1692
|
John Dorsey
1688-1764
m.
Honor Stafford
1689-c 1757
|
Michael Dorsey
1712-1776
m.
Ruth Todd
-1789
|
Ann (Nancy) Dorsey
1748-1806
m.(1)
Owen Elder
-1774
|
Terrisha Elder
1767-1843 Brooke Co., W. Va., Washington Co., Pa.
m.
Dennis Dorsey
1769-1815
|
Dennis Basil Dorsey
1799-1860 Marion Co., W. Va.
m.
Frances Purdue
1806-1854

Samuel Jennings Dorsey
1828-1904 Lackawanna Co., Pa.
m.(1)
Louisa
-1860
|
John Dennis Dorsey
1854-1937 Fayette Co., Ill.
m.
Philomene St. Pierre
-1939
|
Rupert M. Dorsey
m.
Mattie Forester, Cairo, Ga.

Margaret May Dorsey
1854-1929 Pittsburg, Pa.
m.
Joseph V. King
1864-1918
|
Lawrence Foster King
1881-
m.
Verda Dorsey Carroll
1877-
|
Harry Dorsey Carroll King
1897-
m.
Gladys Oakley
|
June Oakley Carroll King
1920-
m.
Robert Lee Sughrue

LINE OF DESCENT OF MRS. MARY (MILLER) SMISER, WARRENSBURG, MISSOURI

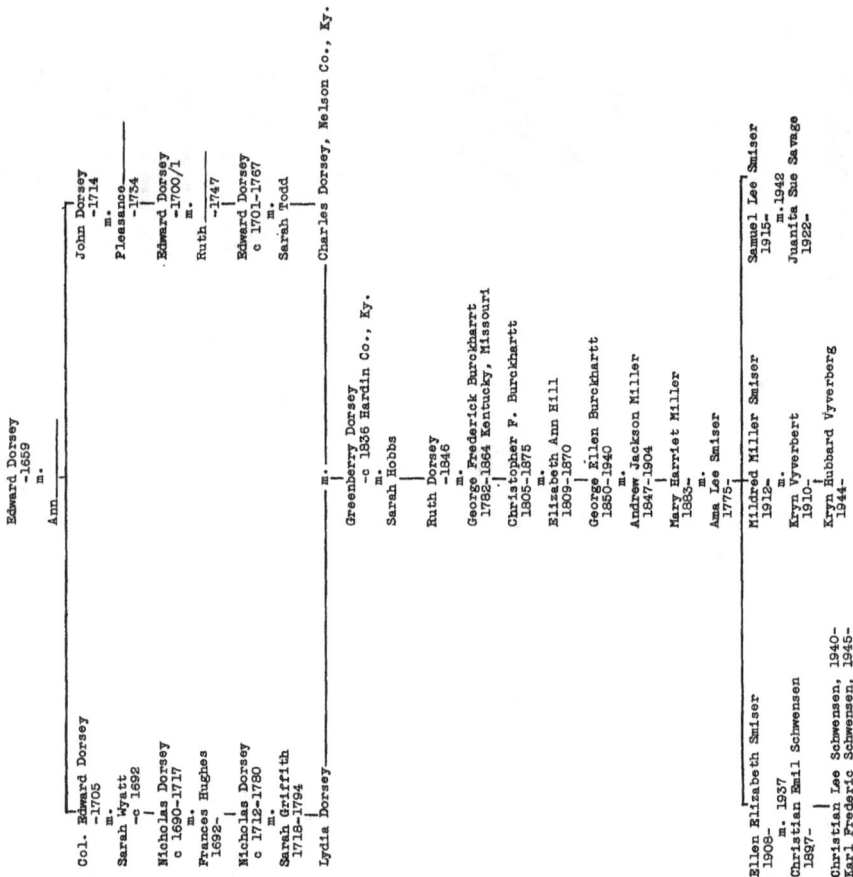

Edward Dorsey
-1659
m.
Ann

Col. Edward Dorsey
-1705
m.
Sarah Wyatt
-c 1692

Nicholas Dorsey
c 1690-1717
m.
Frances Hughes
1692-

Nicholas Dorsey
c 1712-1780
m.
Sarah Griffith
1718-1794

Lydia Dorsey

John Dorsey
-1714
m.
Pleasance
-1734

Edward Dorsey
-1700/1
m.
Ruth
-1747

Edward Dorsey
c 1701-1767
m.
Sarah Todd

Charles Dorsey, Nelson Co., Ky.

Lydia Dorsey m. Charles Dorsey, Nelson Co., Ky.

Greenberry Dorsey
-c 1836 Hardin Co., Ky.
m.
Sarah Hobbs

Ruth Dorsey
-1846
m.
George Frederick Burckharrt
1782-1864 Kentucky, Missouri

Christopher F. Burckhartt
1805-1875
m.
Elizabeth Ann Hill
1809-1870

George Ellen Burckhartt
1850-1940
m.
Andrew Jackson Miller
1847-1904

Mary Harriet Miller
1883-
m.
Ama Lee Smiser
1775-

Ellen Elizabeth Smiser
1908-
m. 1937
Christian Emil Schwensen
1897-

Christian Lee Schwensen, 1940-
Karl Frederic Schwensen, 1945-

Mildred Miller Smiser
1912-
m.
Kryn Vyverbert
1910-

Kryn Hubbard Vyverberg
1944-

Samuel Lee Smiser
1915-
m. 1942
Juanita Sue Savage
1922-

LINES OF DESCENT OF

MRS. EUGENE MARSH
WEBSTER GROVES, MISSOURI

MRS. MARIA LOUISE BURCKHARTT PATTON
ST. LOUIS, MISSOURI

Edward Dorsey
-1659
m.
Ann

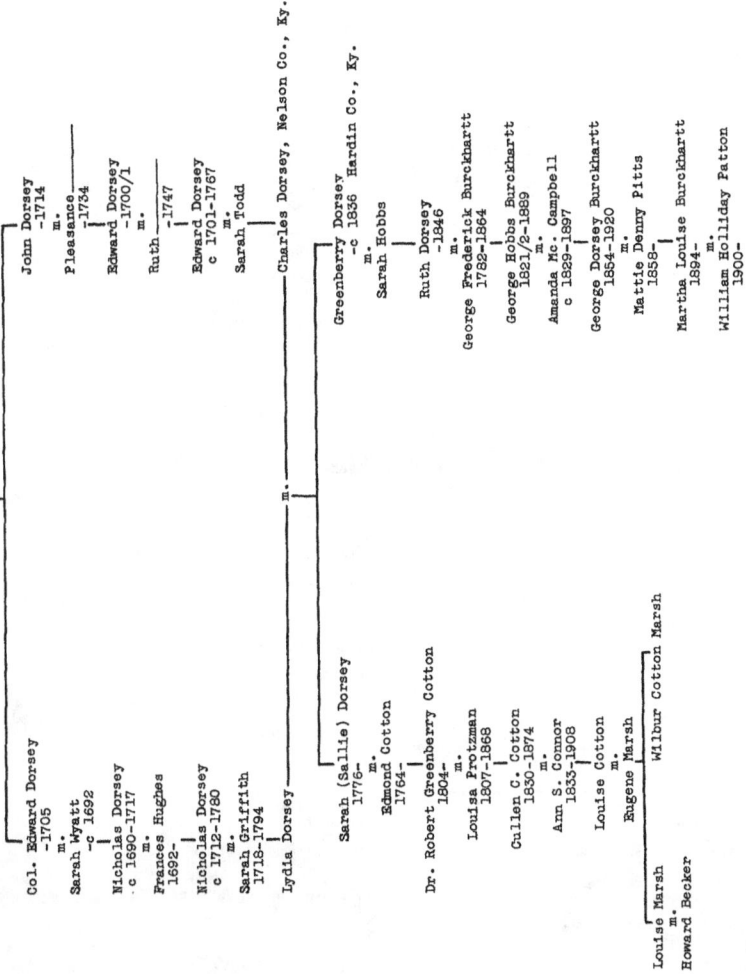

Col. Edward Dorsey
-1705
m.
Sarah Wyatt
-c 1692

Nicholas Dorsey
c 1690-1717
m.
Frances Hughes
1692-

Nicholas Dorsey
c 1712-1780
m.
Sarah Griffith
1718-1794

Lydia Dorsey

John Dorsey
-1714
m.
Pleasance
-1734

Edward Dorsey
-1700/1
m.
Ruth
-1747

Edward Dorsey
c 1701-1767
m.
Sarah Todd

Charles Dorsey, Nelson Co., Ky.

Lydia Dorsey m. Charles Dorsey

Sarah (Sallie) Dorsey
1776-
m.
Edmond Cotton
1764-

Dr. Robert Greenberry Cotton
1804-
m.
Louisa Protzman
1807-1868

Cullen C. Cotton
1830-1874
m.
Ann S. Connor
1833-1908

Louise Cotton
m.
Eugene Marsh

Louise Marsh
m.
Howard Becker

Wilbur Cotton Marsh

Greenberry Dorsey
-c 1836 Hardin Co., Ky.
m.
Sarah Hobbs

Ruth Dorsey
-1846
m.
George Frederick Burckhartt
1782-1864

George Hobbs Burckhartt
1821/2-1889
m.
Amanda Mc. Campbell
c 1829-1897

George Dorsey Burckhartt
1854-1920
m.
Mattie Denny Pitts
1858-

Martha Louise Burckhartt
1894-
m.
William Holliday Patton
1900-

DORSEY FAMILY

LINE OF DESCENT OF
MRS. FRANK ROLLINS, COLUMBIA, MISSOURI

Edward Dorsey
-1659
m.
Ann ______
|
John Dorsey
-1714
m.
Pleasance ______
-1734
|
Caleb Dorsey
1685-1742
m.
Elinor Warfield
1693-1752
|
Basil Dorsey
1705-1763
m.
Sarah Worthington
-1774
|
Thomas Dorsey
-1790
m.
Elizabeth Ridgely
1745-1815
|
Elizabeth Ridgely Dorsey
1763-1837
m.
Benjamin Berry
1763-1815
|
Daniel Dorsey Berry
1805-1862 Greene Co., Mo.
m.
Olivia Marbury Polk
1811-1850 Maury Co., Tenn., Greene Co., Mo.
|
Elizabeth Dodd Berry
1835-1885 Hardeman Co., Tenn., Greene Co., Mo.
m.(1)
Leonidas Caldwell Campbell
1827-1863 Hardeman Co., Tenn.
|
Laura Juliette Campbell
1861-1899 Boone Co., Mo.
m.
Charles Brightberry Bowling
1860-1944

Charles Campbell Bowling 1884- m. Abigail Morrill Poor | Laura Gail Bowling 1910- m. William Jackson Young 1907- | William Charles Young 1936-	Laura Juliette Bowling 1895- m. Frank Bingham Rollins 1884-1934 | Juliette Bowling Rollins 1924-	William Campbell Bowling 1888-

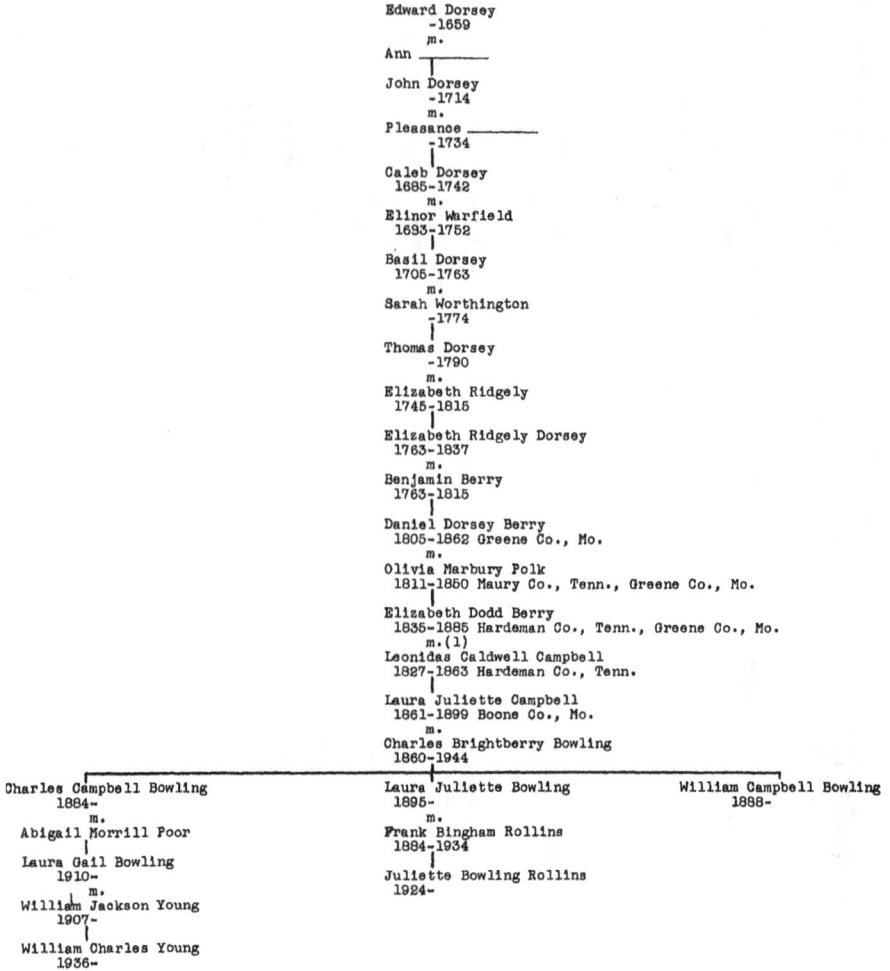

LINE OF DESCENT OF
MRS. WARREN W. FUQUA, COLUMBIA, MISSOURI

Edward Dorsey
-1659
m.
Ann ________
|
Col. Edward Dorsey
-1705
m.(2)
Margaret Lacon
-1707
|
Edward Dorsey
c 1700-1753
m.
Phebe ______
|
Joshua Dorsey
-1777 Frederick Co., Va.
m.
Rachel ______
|
Lacon (Leakin) Dorsey
1744-1822 Fleming Co., Ky.
m.
Elizabeth Ingram
1748-after 1847
|
John Dorsey
1783-1847 Nicholas Co., Ky.
m.
Nancy Spiers
1794-1872
|
Jeremiah Spiers Dorsey
1834-1908 Nicholas Co., Ky., Boone Co., Mo.
m.
Margaret Collier Williams
1838-1915
|
William Stockton Dorsey
1867-1934
m.
Susan Duncan Harris
1871-1892

Margaret Williams Dorsey 1893- m. Warren Watson Fuqua 1891- | Dorothy Anne Fuqua 1916- m. Frank Roark Goad 1914- | Margaret Dorsey Goad 1941-	James Harris Dorsey 1899- m. Lottie Swift	Dorothy Dorsey 1901-	Anne Dorsey 1904-

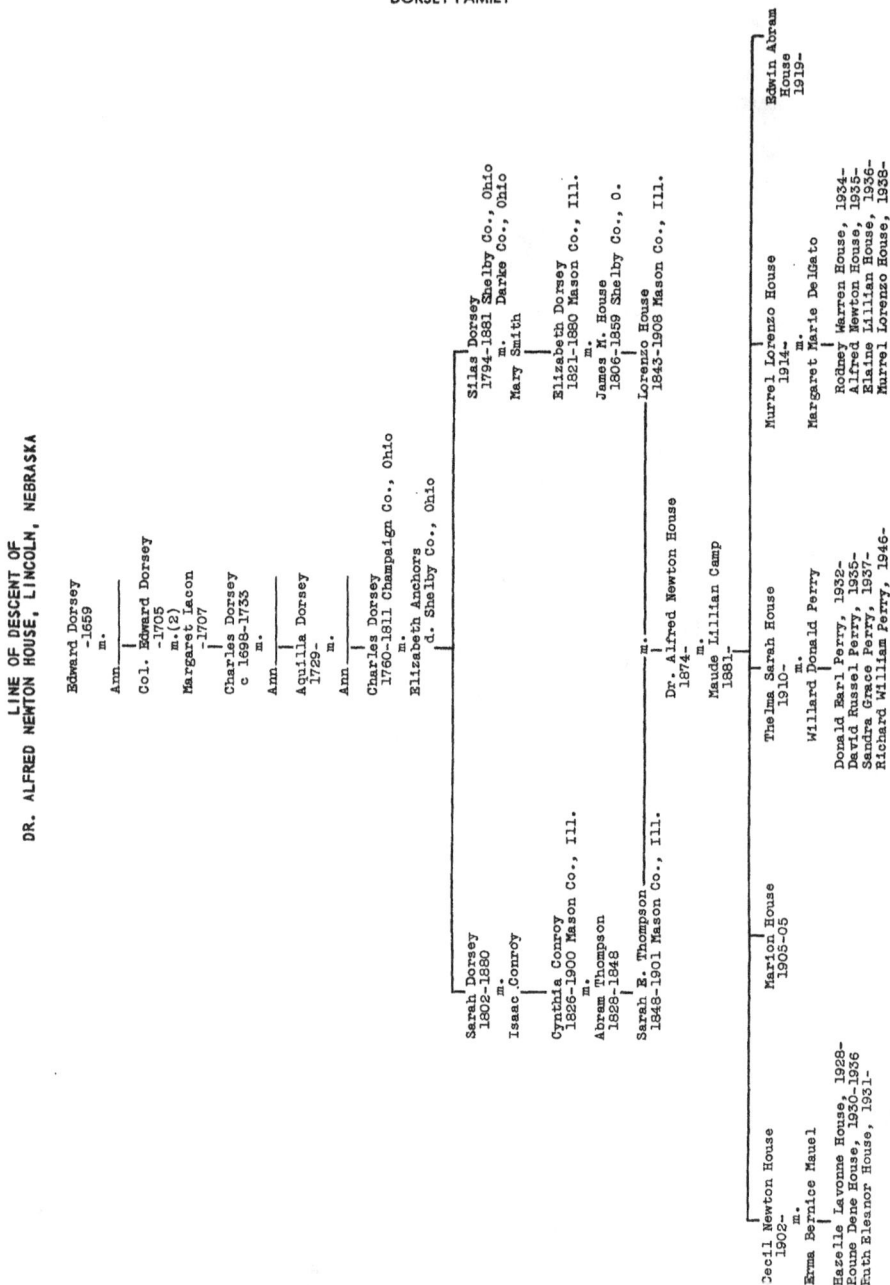

LINE OF DESCENT OF
DR. ALFRED NEWTON HOUSE, LINCOLN, NEBRASKA

Edward Dorsey
-1659
m.
Ann

Col. Edward Dorsey
-1705
m.(2)
Margaret Lacon
-1707

Charles Dorsey
c 1698-1733
m.
Ann

Aquilla Dorsey
1729-
m.
Ann

Charles Dorsey
1760-1811 Champaign Co., Ohio
m.
Elizabeth Anchors
d. Shelby Co., Ohio

Sarah Dorsey
1802-1880
m.
Isaac Conroy

Cynthia Conroy
1826-1900 Mason Co., Ill.
m.
Abram Thompson
1828-1848

Sarah E. Thompson
1848-1901 Mason Co., Ill.

Silas Dorsey
1794-1881 Shelby Co., Ohio
m. Darke Co., Ohio
Mary Smith

Elizabeth Dorsey
1821-1880 Mason Co., Ill.
m.
James M. House
1806-1859 Shelby Co., O.

Lorenzo House
1843-1908 Mason Co., Ill.

Sarah E. Thompson m. Lorenzo House

Dr. Alfred Newton House
1874-
m.
Maude Lillian Camp
1881-

Cecil Newton House
1902-
m.
Erma Bernice Mauel

Hazelle Lavonne House, 1928-
Roune Dene House, 1930-1936
Ruth Eleanor House, 1931-

Marion House
1905-05

Thelma Sarah House
1910-
m.
Willard Donald Perry

Donald Earl Perry, 1932-
David Russel Perry, 1935-
Sandra Grace Perry, 1937-
Richard William Perry, 1946-

Murrel Lorenzo House
1914-
m.
Margaret Marie DelGato

Rodney Warren House, 1934-
Alfred Newton House, 1935-
Elaine Lillian House, 1936-
Murrel Lorenzo House, 1938-

Edwin Abram
House
1919-

LINE OF DESCENT OF
MARY A. (GUSSIE) SAWYER, SALT LAKE CITY, UTAH

Edward Dorsey
-1659
m.
Ann

John Dorsey
-1714
m.
Pleasance
-1734

Caleb Dorsey
1685-1742
m.
Elinor Warfield
1683-1752

John Dorsey
1708-1765

Col. Edward Dorsey
-1705
m.(1)
Sarah Wyatt
-c 1692

Joshua Dorsey
1686-1747
m.
Ann Ridgely
-1771

Elizabeth Dorsey
1719/29-1803

John Dorsey — m. — Elizabeth Dorsey

Caleb Dorsey
1740-1795
m.(2)
Rebecca Hammond
1741-1797

John Dorsey
1773-1820
m.
Sarah (Sally) Hammond
1779-1841

Mary Dorsey
1811-1858 Pekin, Illinois
m.
Samuel Painter Baily
1804-1869

Rebecca Augusta Baily
1844-1930 Salt Lake City, Utah
m.
Abial B. Sawyer
1838-1907

Harriet B. Sawyer d.y.

Abial B. Sawyer

Mary A. (Gussie) Sawyer

Almira L. Sawyer

Josiah Griegg Sawyer

Susan Dorsey Sawyer
m.
Carl Grover Brown

Almira L. Sawyer m.(2) Norma G. Dickert, who also m.(2) Josiah Griegg Sawyer, who m.(2) Adeline Brinckerhoff

Norma G. Dickert's children:

Josiah D. Sawyer
m.
Sarah R. Christiansen

Robert Greigg Sawyer

Ferdinand F. Sawyer

Susan Dorsey Sawyer and Carl Grover Brown's children:

Dorothy B. Brown
m.
Kenneth C. Berry

Suzanne H. Berry
Kenneth G. Berry
Carl G. Berry

Carl G. Brown
m.
Helen Runnels

Thomas R. Brown

LINES OF DESCENT OF
MABEL L. DORSEY, LOS ANGELES, CALIFORNIA
FRANCES DORSEY, HOLLYWOOD, CALIFORNIA
AGNES DORSEY, CHICAGO, ILLINOIS

Edward Dorsey
-1659
m.
Ann ______

Col. Edward Dorsey
-1705
m.(1)
Sarah Wyatt
-c 1692

John Dorsey
1688-1764
m.
Honor Stafford
1689-c 1757

Michael Dorsey
1712-1776
m.
Ruth Todd
-1789

Ruth Dorsey
1743-1805

John Dorsey
-1714
m.
Pleasance ______
-1734

Edward Dorsey
-1700/1
m.
Ruth ______
-1747

Edward Dorsey
c 1701-1767
m.
Sarah Todd

Ely Dorsey
-1803

Ruth Dorsey m. Ely Dorsey

Edward Dorsey
1769-1848 Loudon Co., Va.
m.
Mary Klein
-1844

Hamilton Dorsey
1814-1879 Dodge Co., Neb., Taylor Co., W. Va.
m.
Sarah Catherine Polten
1821-1907 Santa Clara Co., Cal.

Frank M. Dorsey
1861-1934
m.
Laura Bonnybel Strong
1861-

Frances Dorsey
1893-

Howard Hamilton Dorsey
1857-1931 Los Angeles
m.
Maria Louise Benton
1854-1928

Agnes Dorsey
1883-

Alfred Dorsey
1810-1884
m.
Eleanor Moon
1807-1882 Buffalo Co., Neb.

Daniel Allen Dorsey
1838-1913
m.
Annie Catherine Miller
1840-1908 Buffalo Co., Neb.

Mabel L. Dorsey
1879-

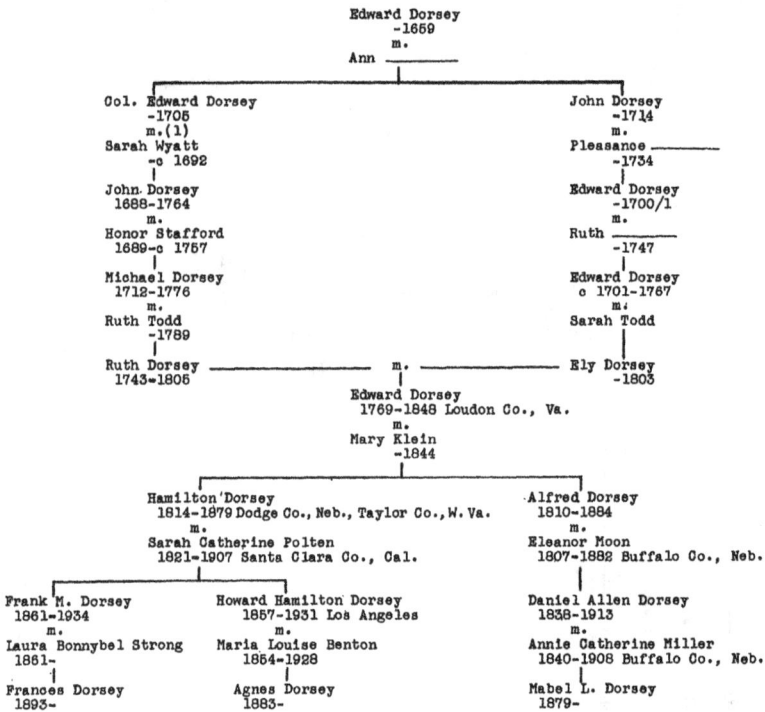

LINES OF DESCENT OF

JOHN TUCKER DORSEY
MARIETTA, GEORGIA

MRS. LUNA DORSEY DAVIS
FORGAN, OKLAHOMA

Edward Dorsey
m.
Ann ________
|
Col. Edward Dorsey
-1705
m. (2)
Margaret Lacon
-1707
|
Francis Dorsey
c 1696-1749
m.
Elizabeth Baker
-bef. 1749
|
Francis Dorsey
1741-1769
m.
Ann ________
|
Basil John Dorsey
1759-1807 Lincoln Co., N. Car., Franklin Co., Ga.
m.
Mary Robinson
-1806
|
John Dorsey
1800-1888 Lincoln Co., N. Car., Hall Co., Ga.
m.
Elizabeth McMillan Brice
1805-1886

Left line:

Jasper Newton Dorsey
1825-1883 Hall Co., Ga.
m.
Junius Cornelia Tucker
|
John Tucker Dorsey
1876-
m.
Annie Robertson Coryell
|
Jasper Newton Dorsey III
1913-
m.
Callender Hull Weltner
|
Sally Hull Dorsey, 1942-
John Tucker Dorsey II, 1944-

Right line:

John Fletcher Dorsey
1841-1899 Hall Co., Ga.
m. Wilbarger Co., Texas
Mary Isabelle Brown
|
Luna Dorsey
1879-
m.
Noah Benton Davis
|
Dorsey Kendall Davis, b and d. 1907
(Miss) Moita Dorsey Davis, 1908-

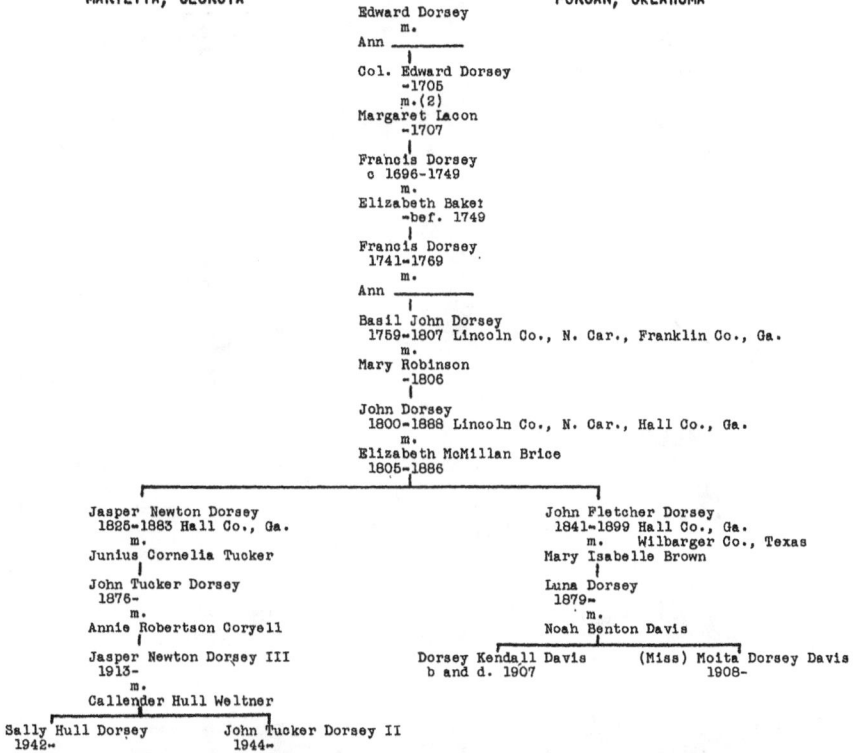

DORSEY FAMILY

LINE OF DESCENT OF MRS. WILLIAM HOEFLER AND ELEANOR V. HOEFLER

Edward Dorsey
-1659
m.
Ann ________
|
John Dorsey
-1714
m.
Pleasance ______
-1734
|
Caleb Dorsey
1685-1742
m.
Elinor Warfield
1683-1752
|
Basil Dorsey
1705-1763-
m.
Sarah Worthington
-1774
|
Thomas Dorsey
-1790
m.(1)
Elizabeth Ridgely
-1763
|
Daniel Dorsey
1757-1823 Wayne Co., N.Y.
m.
Eleanor Dorsey
1761-1834
|
Upton Dorsey
1788-1856 Ontario Co., N.Y.
m.
Ann Starrett
1797-1890
|
Mary Ann Dorsey
1827-1910
m.
Thomas Rice
1817-1891 Ontario Co., N.Y.
|
Lena Rice
1872-
m.
William C. Hoefler
1871-
|
Eleanor V. Hoefler
1898-

LINE OF DESCENT OF ALLEA BETTS, ATHENS, GEORGIA

Edward Dorsey
-1659
m.
Ann ________
|
Col. Edward Dorsey
-1705
m.(2)
Margaret Lacon
-1707
|
Francis Dorsey
c 1696-1749
m.
Elizabeth Baker
-bef. 1749
|
Francis Dorsey
1741-1769
m.
Ann ________
|
Basil John Dorsey
1759-1807 Lincoln Co., N. Car., Franklin Co., Ga.
m.
Mary Robinson
-1806
|
Andrew Dorsey
1790-1864 Lincoln Co., N. Car., White Co., Ga.
m.
Nancy Smith
1786-1874
|
William Harrison Dorsey
1810-1867
m.
Catherine Saphronia Erwin
1818-1883
|
Joseph Harwell Dorsey
1855-1928
m.(2)
Mary Allen Hargrove
1866-1921
|
Sally Asenath Dorsey
1886-
m.
Walter Frank Betts
1886-
|
Mary Allea Betts

LINE OF DESCENT OF MARY ELLEN DORSEY WASHINGTON D.C.

Edward Dorsey
-1759 1659.
m.
Ann ______
|
John Dorsey
-1715
m.
Pleasance ______
-1734
|
Edward Dorsey
-1700/1
m.
Ruth ______
-1747
|
John Dorsey
c 1699-1761
m.
Elizabeth ______
-1777
|
Samuel Dorsey
1740-1779
m.
Eleanor Woodward
1745-bef. 1779
|
Henry Woodward Dorsey
1767-1840 Montgomery Co., Md.
m.(2)
Rachel (Magruder) Cooke
|
Harry Woodward Dorsey
m.
Sarah Ann Waters
|
Harry Woodward Dorsey

m.(1) Ann Pottinger Waters

m.(2) Helen James

Children:

Sarah Dorsey
m.
Tanjore Griffith
- Dorsey J. Griffith m. Hilda Bowen
  - Mary E. Griffith
  - Elizabeth Griffith
- Howard T. Griffith m. Cecelia Hedgeman
- Mary Griffith m. Joseph Stansfield
  - Sarah Dorsey Stansfield

Mary Ellen Dorsey

Nicholas Worthington Dorsey
m.
Maude A. Keeps
- Elizabeth Dorsey m. Donald Rumsey Holt
  - Donald R. Holt Jr.
  - Dorsey Woodward Holt
  - William Arthur Holt
  - James W. Holt, d. inf.

William Waters Dorsey
d. inf.

Harry Woodward Dorsey
m.
Susie May Naylor
- Charlotte Dorsey m. Joseph Emmerick
  - Joseph Emmerick Jr.

LINE OF DESCENT OF
STEPHEN PALMER DORSEY, WASHINGTON D.C.

Edward Dorsey
-1659
m.
Ann

Col. Edward Dorsey
-1705
m.(1)
Sarah Wyatt
-c 1692

Nicholas Dorsey
c 1690-1717
m.
Frances Hughes
1692-

Nicholas Dorsey
c 1712-1777
m.
Sarah Griffith
1718-1794

Charles Dorsey
1744-1814
m.
Ann (Dorsey) Elder
1748-1806

John Dorsey
1688-1764
m.
Honor Stafford
1689-c 1757

Michael Dorsey
1712-1776
m.
Ruth Todd
-1789

John Wesley Dorsey
1785-1861 Jefferson Co., Ky., Franklin Co., Ind.
m. Otoe Co., Neb.
Jane Connor
1795-1873

William Dorsey
1815-1888 Franklin Co., Ind., Otoe Co., Neb.
m. Nance Co., Neb.
Lois Wymond
1817-1884

George Denton Dorsey
1854-1939 Marion Co., Ind. Otoe Co., Neb.,
m. Lancaster Co., Neb.
Carrie Amanda Palmer
1853-1908

Guy Palmer Dorsey
1879- Vigo Co., Ind., Douglas Co., Neb.
m.
Julia Augusta Geisthardt
1876-1942

Stephen Palmer Dorsey
1913-
m.
Carolyn DuBois Cosby
1913-

Carolyn Augusta Dorsey
1943-

ANCESTRAL LINES

LINE OF DESCENT OF
MRS. JULIAN C. CRANE
DAVIS, CALIFORNIA

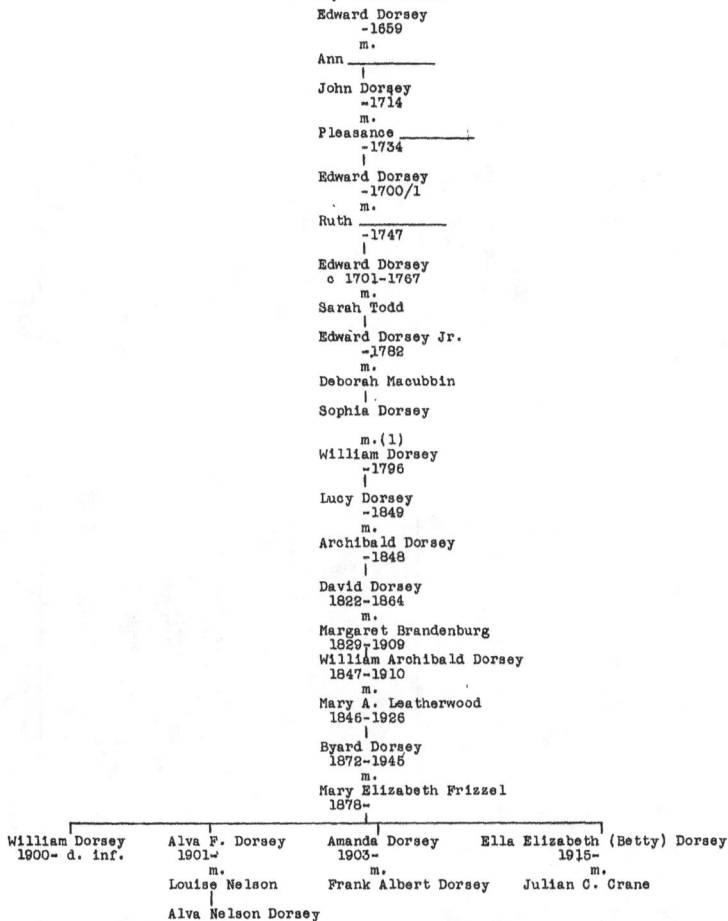

Edward Dorsey
-1659
m.
Ann
|
John Dorsey
-1714
m.
Pleasance
-1734
|
Edward Dorsey
-1700/1
m.
Ruth
-1747
|
Edward Dorsey
c 1701-1767
m.
Sarah Todd
|
Edward Dorsey Jr.
-1782
m.
Deborah Macubbin
|
Sophia Dorsey

m.(1)
William Dorsey
-1796
|
Lucy Dorsey
-1849
m.
Archibald Dorsey
-1848
|
David Dorsey
1822-1864
m.
Margaret Brandenburg
1829-1909
William Archibald Dorsey
1847-1910
m.
Mary A. Leatherwood
1846-1926
|
Byard Dorsey
1872-1945
m.
Mary Elizabeth Frizzel
1878-
|

William Dorsey	Alva F. Dorsey	Amanda Dorsey	Ella Elizabeth (Betty) Dorsey
1900- d. inf.	1901-	1903-	1915-
	m.	m.	m.
	Louise Nelson	Frank Albert Dorsey	Julian C. Crane
	|		
	Alva Nelson Dorsey		

LINE OF DESCENT OF
LAWRENCE LOOMIS DORSEY, LAND O'LAKES, WISCONSIN

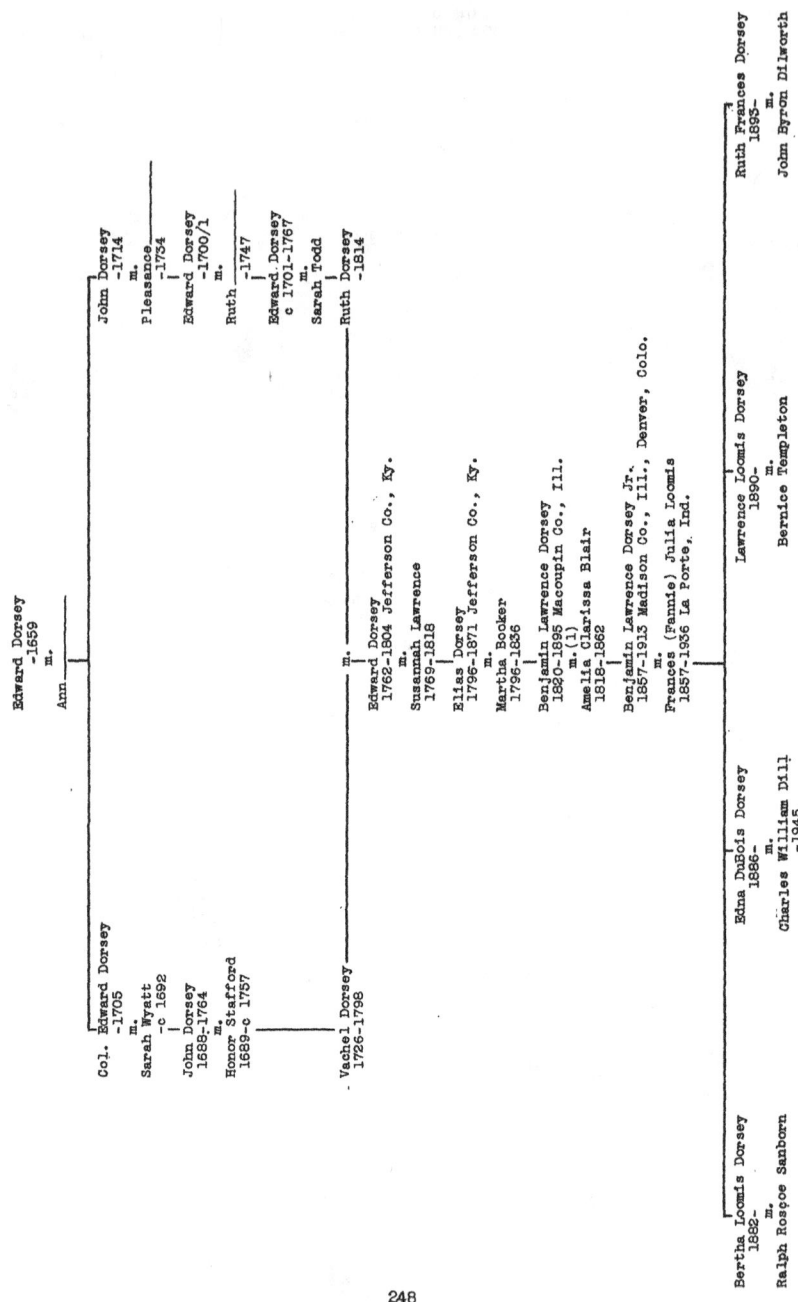

Edward Dorsey
-1659
m.
Ann

Col. Edward Dorsey
-1705
m.
Sarah Wyatt
-c 1692

John Dorsey
1688-1764
m.
Honor Stafford
1689-c 1757

Vachel Dorsey
1726-1798

John Dorsey
-1714
m.
Pleasance
-1734

Edward Dorsey
-1700/1
m.
Ruth
-1747

Edward Dorsey
c 1701-1767
m.
Sarah Todd

Ruth Dorsey
-1814

Vachel Dorsey m. Ruth Dorsey

Edward Dorsey
1762-1804 Jefferson Co., Ky.
m.
Susannah Lawrence
1769-1818

Elias Dorsey
1796-1871 Jefferson Co., Ky.
m.
Martha Booker
1796-1836

Benjamin Lawrence Dorsey
1820-1895 Macoupin Co., Ill.
m. (1)
Amelia Clarissa Blair
1818-1862

Benjamin Lawrence Dorsey Jr.
1857-1913 Madison Co., Ill., Denver, Colo.
m.
Frances (Fannie) Julia Loomis
1857-1936 La Porte, Ind.

Bertha Loomis Dorsey
1882-
m.
Ralph Roscoe Sanborn

Edna DuBois Dorsey
1886-
m.
Charles William Dill
-1945

Lawrence Loomis Dorsey
1890-
m.
Bernice Templeton

Ruth Frances Dorsey
1893-
m.
John Byron Dilworth

INDEX

INDEX

INDEX

INDEX

INDEX

INDEX

INDEX

INDEX

INDEX

INDEX

INDEX

INDEX

INDEX

INDEX

INDEX

INDEX

INDEX

INDEX

www.ingramcontent.com/pod-product-compliance
Lightning Source LLC
Chambersburg PA
CBHW050408280326
41932CB00013BA/1783
* 9 7 8 0 8 0 6 3 4 7 4 9 3 *